KOREA

SOUTH

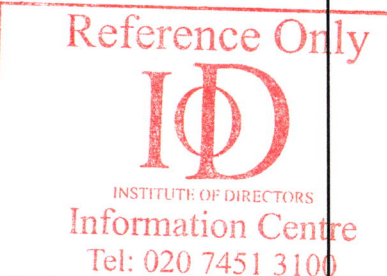

INVESTMENT AND BUSINESS GUIDE
VOLUME 1
STRATEGIC AND PRACTICAL INFORMATION

International Business Publications, USA
Washington DC, USA – Korea South

KOREA SOUTH
INVESTMENT AND BUSINESS GUIDE
VOLUME 1 STRATEGIC AND PRACTICAL INFORMATION

UPDATED ANNUALLY

We express our sincere appreciation to all government agencies and international organizations which provided information and other materials for this guide

Cover Design: International Business Publications, USA

2012 Edition Updated Reprint International Business Publications, USA
ISBN 1-4330-2805-0

For customer service and information, please contact:

in the USA: **International Business Publications, USA**
P.O.Box 15343, Washington, DC 20003
Phone: (202) 546-2103, Fax: (202) 546-3275.
E-mail: rusric@erols.com

Printed in the USA

KOREA
SOUTH
INVESTMENT AND BUSINESS GUIDE
VOLUME 1
STRATEGIC AND PRACTICAL INFORMATION

TABLE OF CONTENTS

**For additional analytical, business and investment opportunities information,
please contact Global Investment & Business Center, USA
at (202) 546-2103. Fax: (202) 546-3275. E-mail: rusric@erols.com**

**For additional analytical, business and investment opportunities information,
please contact Global Investment & Business Center, USA
at (202) 546-2103. Fax: (202) 546-3275. E-mail: rusric@erols.com**

**For additional analytical, business and investment opportunities information,
please contact Global Investment & Business Center, USA
at (202) 546-2103. Fax: (202) 546-3275. E-mail: rusric@erols.com**

**For additional analytical, business and investment opportunities information,
please contact Global Investment & Business Center, USA
at (202) 546-2103. Fax: (202) 546-3275. E-mail: rusric@erols.com**

**For additional analytical, business and investment opportunities information,
please contact Global Investment & Business Center, USA
at (202) 546-2103. Fax: (202) 546-3275. E-mail: rusric@erols.com**

**For additional analytical, business and investment opportunities information,
please contact Global Investment & Business Center, USA
at (202) 546-2103. Fax: (202) 546-3275. E-mail: rusric@erols.com**

KOREA: ECONOMIC AND DEVELOPMENT PROFILES

STRATEGIC PROFILE

Capital (and largest city)	Seoul
	37°35′N 127°0′E37.583°N 127°E
Official language(s)	Korean
	Hangul
Official scripts	Hanja
Ethnic groups	Korean (99%)
Demonym	South Korean, Korean
Government	Unitary semi-presidential republic
- President	Lee Myung-bak
- Prime Minister	Kim Hwang-sik
- Speaker	Jeong Eui-hwa
Legislature	National Assembly (Gukhoe)
Establishment	
- National Foundation Day	October 3, 2333 BCE
- Independence declared	March 1, 1919
- Provisional Government	April 13, 1919
- Liberation	August 15, 1945
- Constitution	July 17, 1948
- Government proclaimed	August 15, 1948
Area	
- Total	100,210 km^2 (109th)
	38,691 sq mi
- Water (%)	0.3
Population	
- 2010 estimate	48,875,000 (24th)
- Density	491/km^2 (21st)
	1,271/sq mi
GDP (PPP)	2011 estimate
- Total	$1.556 trillion (12th)
- Per capita	$31,753 (26th)
GDP (nominal)	2011 estimate
- Total	$1.163 trillion (15th)
- Per capita	$23,749 (32nd)
Gini (2007)	31.3[5]
HDI (2011)	▲0.897 (very high) (15th)
Currency	South Korean won (KRW)
Time zone	Korea Standard Time (UTC+9)
- Summer (DST)	not observed (UTC+9)
Date formats	yyyy/mm/dd (CE)
Drives on the	right
ISO 3166 code	KR
Internet TLD	.kr
Calling code	82

For additional analytical, business and investment opportunities information, please contact Global Investment & Business Center, USA at (202) 546-2103. Fax: (202) 546-3275. E-mail: rusric@erols.com

ECONOMIC OVERVIEW

Currency: Won (W)
Real GDP Growth Rate : 3.3% 5.8%
Inflation Rate (consumer prices): 4.1% 3.1%
Unemployment Rate: 3.7%
Current Account Balance : $4.6 billion
Merchandise Exports : $164.7 billion
Merchandise Imports : $152.8 billion
Merchandise Trade Balance : $11.9 billion
Major Exports: Electronics, textiles, ships, automobiles, steel, computers, footwear
Major Imports: Crude oil, food, machinery and transportation equipment, chemicals and chemical products, base metals and articles.
Top Trading Partners: U.S., Japan, China, Germany

ENERGY OVERVIEW

Oil Consumption : 2.1 million barrels per day (bbl/d); all imported
Crude Oil Refining Capacity : 2.6 million bbl/d
Natural Gas Consumption : 669 billion cubic feet (bcf)--all imported LNG
Recoverable Coal Reserves : 86 million short tons (Mmst)
Coal Production : 4.6 Mmst
Coal Consumption : 71.7 Mmst
Electric Generation Capacity: 50.0 gigawatts
Electricity Generation : 273.2 billion kilowatthours

ENVIRONMENTAL OVERVIEW

Total Energy Consumption : 7.9 quadrillion Btu* (2.0% of world total energy consumption)
Energy-Related Carbon Emissions : 115.3 million metric tons of carbon (1.8% of world carbon emissions)
Per Capita Energy Consumption : 166.7 million Btu (vs. U.S. value of 351.1 million Btu)
Per Capita Carbon Emissions : 2.4 metric tons of carbon (vs. U.S. value of 5.6 metric tons of carbon)
Energy Intensity : 12,759 Btu/$1995 (vs U.S. value of 10,919 Btu/$1995)**
Carbon Intensity : 0.19 metric tons of carbon/thousand $1995 (vs U.S. value of 0.17 metric tons/thousand $1995)**
Sectoral Share of Energy Consumption : Industrial (55.7%), Transportation (20.2%), Commercial (15.1%), Residential (9.0%)
Sectoral Share of Carbon Emissions : Industrial (49.8%), Transportation (24.0%), Commercial (17.1%), Residential (9.1%)
Fuel Share of Energy Consumption : Oil (58.3%), Coal (20.4%), Natural Gas (9.5%)
Fuel Share of Carbon Emissions : Oil (56.0%), Coal (34.6%), Natural Gas (9.4%)
Renewable Energy Consumption : 177 trillion Btu* (9% decrease from 1997)
Number of People per Motor Vehicle: 4.4 (vs. U.S. value of 1.3)
Status in Climate Change Negotiations: Non-Annex I country under the United Nations Framework Convention on Climate Change (ratified December 14th, 1993). Signatory to the Kyoto Protocol (signed September 25th, 1998 - not yet ratified).
Major Environmental Issues: Air pollution in large cities; water pollution from the discharge of sewage and industrial effluents; drift net fishing.
Major International Environmental Agreements: A party to the Antarctic-Environmental Protocol, Antarctic Treaty, Biodiversity, Climate Change, Endangered Species, Environmental

For additional analytical, business and investment opportunities information,
please contact Global Investment & Business Center, USA
at (202) 546-2103. Fax: (202) 546-3275. E-mail: rusric@erols.com

Modification, Hazardous Wastes, Law of the Sea, Nuclear Test Ban, Ozone Layer Protection, Ship Pollution, Tropical Timber 83, Tropical Timber 94, Wetlands and Whaling. Has signed, but not ratified, Desertification.

GEOGRAPHY

Location: Eastern Asia, southern half of the Korean Peninsula bordering the Sea of Japan and the Yellow Sea
Geographic coordinates: 37 00 N, 127 30 E
Map references: Asia

Area:
total: 98,480 sq km
land: 98,190 sq km
water: 290 sq km

Area—comparative: slightly larger than Indiana

Land boundaries:
total: 238 km
border countries: North Korea 238 km

Coastline: 2,413 km

Maritime claims:
contiguous zone: 24 nm
continental shelf: not specified
exclusive economic zone: 200 nm
territorial sea: 12 nm; 3 nm in the Korea Strait

Climate: temperate, with rainfall heavier in summer than winter
Terrain: mostly hills and mountains; wide coastal plains in west and south
Elevation extremes:
lowest point: Sea of Japan 0 m
highest point: Halla-san 1,950 m
Natural resources: coal, tungsten, graphite, molybdenum, lead, hydropower

Land use:
arable land: 19%
permanent crops: 2%
permanent pastures: 1%
forests and woodland: 65%
other: 13%

**For additional analytical, business and investment opportunities information,
please contact Global Investment & Business Center, USA
at (202) 546-2103. Fax: (202) 546-3275. E-mail: rusric@erols.com**

Irrigated land: 13,350 sq km
Natural hazards: occasional typhoons bring high winds and floods; low-level seismic activity common in southwest

Environment—current issues: air pollution in large cities; water pollution from the discharge of sewage and industrial effluents; drift net fishing

Environment—international agreements:
party to: Antarctic-Environmental Protocol, Antarctic Treaty, Biodiversity, Climate Change, Endangered Species, Environmental Modification, Hazardous Wastes, Law of the Sea, Nuclear Test Ban, Ozone Layer Protection, Ship Pollution, Tropical Timber 83, Tropical Timber 94
signed, but not ratified: Desertification

PEOPLE

Population: 46,416,796

Age structure:
0-14 years: 22% (male 5,505,564; female 4,894,780)
15-64 years: 71% (male 16,772,319; female 16,272,145)
65 years and over: 7% (male 1,126,963; female 1,845,025) (July 1998 est.)

Population growth rate: 1.01%
Birth rate: 16.08 births/1,000 population
Death rate: 5.67 deaths/1,000 population
Net migration rate: -0.31 migrant(s)/1,000 population

Sex ratio:
at birth: 1.14 male(s)/female
under 15 years: 1.12 male(s)/female
15-64 years: 1.03 male(s)/female
65 years and over: 0.61 male(s)/female

Infant mortality rate: 7.79 deaths/1,000 live births

Life expectancy at birth:
total population: 73.95 years
male: 70.37 years
female: 78 years

Total fertility rate: 1.79 children born/woman

Nationality:
noun: Korean(s)
adjective: Korean

Ethnic groups: homogeneous (except for about 20,000 Chinese)
Religions: Christianity 49%, Buddhism 47%, Confucianism 3%, pervasive folk religion (shamanism), Chondogyo (Religion of the Heavenly Way), and other 1%
Languages: Korean, English widely taught in junior high and high school

For additional analytical, business and investment opportunities information, please contact Global Investment & Business Center, USA at (202) 546-2103. Fax: (202) 546-3275. E-mail: rusric@erols.com

Literacy:
definition: age 15 and over can read and write
total population: 98%
male: 99.3%
female: 96.7%

GOVERNMENT

Country name:
conventional long form: Republic of Korea
conventional short form: South Korea
local long form: Taehan-min'guk
local short form: none
note: the South Koreans generally use the term "Hanguk" to refer to their country
abbreviation: ROK

Data code: KS
Government type: republic
National capital: Seoul

Administrative divisions: 9 provinces (do, singular and plural) and 6 special cities* (gwangyoksi, singular and plural); Cheju-do, Cholla-bukto, Cholla-namdo, Ch'ungch'ong-bukto, Ch'ungch'ong-namdo, Inch'on-gwangyoksi*, Kangwon-do, Kwangju-gwangyoksi*, Kyonggi-do, Kyongsang-bukto, Kyongsang-namdo, Pusan-gwangyoksi*, Soul-t'ukpyolsi*, Taegu-gwangyoksi*, Taejon-gwangyoksi*

Independence: 15 August 1945; note—date of liberation from Japanese colonial rule
National holiday: Liberation Day, 15 August (1945)
Constitution: 25 February 1988

Legal system: combines elements of continental European civil law systems, Anglo-American law, and Chinese classical thought

Suffrage: 20 years of age; universal

Executive branch:

chief of state: President LEE Myung-bak (since 25 February 2008)

head of government: Prime Minister KIM Hwang-sik (since 1 October 2010)

cabinet: State Council appointed by the president on the prime minister's recommendation
elections: president elected by popular vote for a single five-year term; election last held on 19 December 2007 (next to be held in December 2012); prime minister appointed by president with consent of National Assembly

election results: LEE Myung-bak elected president on 19 December 2007; percent of vote - LEE Myung-bak (GNP) 48.7%; CHUNG Dong-young (UNDP) 26.1%); LEE Hoi-chang (independent) 15.1%; others 10.1%

Legislative branch:

For additional analytical, business and investment opportunities information,
please contact Global Investment & Business Center, USA
at (202) 546-2103. Fax: (202) 546-3275. E-mail: rusric@erols.com

unicameral National Assembly or Gukhoe (299 seats; 245 members elected in single-seat constituencies, 54 elected by proportional representation; members serve four-year terms)

elections: last held on 11 April 2012 (next to be held in April 2016)

election results: percent of vote by party - NA; seats by party - NFP 152, UDP 127, UPP 13, LFP 5, independents 3

Political parties and leaders: Grand National Party (GNP), CHO Sun, president; National Congress for New Politics (NCNP), Kim Dae-jung, president; United Liberal Democrats (ULD), PAK Tae-chun, president; New People's Party (NPP), YI In-che, president
note: subsequent to the legislative election of April 1996 the following parties disbanded—New Korea Party (NKP) and Democratic Party (DP)

Political pressure groups and leaders: Korean National Council of Churches; National Democratic Alliance of Korea; National Federation of Student Associations; National Federation of Farmers' Associations; National Council of Labor Unions; Federation of Korean Trade Unions; Korean Veterans' Association; Federation of Korean Industries; Korean Traders Association; Korean Confederation of Trade Unions

International organization participation: AfDB, APEC, AsDB, BIS (pending member), CCC, CP, EBRD, ESCAP, FAO, G-77, IAEA, IBRD, ICAO, ICC, ICFTU, ICRM, IDA, IFAD, IFC, IFRCS, IHO, ILO, IMF, IMO, Inmarsat, Intelsat, Interpol, IOC, IOM, ISO, ITU, MINURSO, NSG, OAS (observer), OECD, OSCE (partner), UN, UNCTAD, UNESCO, UNIDO, UNMOGIP, UNOMIG, UNU, UPU, WHO, WIPO, WMO, WToO, WTrO

Diplomatic representation in the US:
chief of mission: Ambassador YI Hong-ku
chancery: 2450 Massachusetts Avenue NW, Washington, DC 20008
telephone: (202) 939-5600
consulate(s) general: Agana (Guam), Anchorage, Atlanta, Boston, Chicago, Honolulu, Houston, Los Angeles, Miami, New York, San Francisco, and Seattle

Diplomatic representation from the US:
chief of mission: Ambassador Stephen W. BOSWORTH
embassy: 82 Sejong-Ro, Chongro-ku, Seoul
mailing address: American Embassy, Unit 15550, APO AP 96205-0001
telephone: [82] (2) 397-4114
FAX: [82] (2) 738-8845
consulate(s): Pusan

Flag description: white with a red (top) and blue yin-yang symbol in the center; there is a different black trigram from the ancient I Ching (Book of Changes) in each corner of the white field

ECONOMY

Economy - overview:	Since the 1960s, South Korea has achieved an incredible record of growth and integration into the high-tech modern world economy. Four decades ago, GDP per capita was comparable with levels in the poorer countries of Africa and Asia. In 2007, South Korea joined the trillion dollar club of world

economies. In 2008, its GDP per capita was roughly the same as that of the Czech Republic and New Zealand. Initially, this success was achieved by a system of close government/business ties including directed credit, import restrictions, sponsorship of specific industries, and a strong labor effort. The government promoted the import of raw materials and technology at the expense of consumer goods and encouraged savings and investment over consumption. The Asian financial crisis of 1997-98 exposed longstanding weaknesses in South Korea's development model including high debt/equity ratios, massive foreign borrowing, and an undisciplined financial sector. GDP plunged by 6.9% in 1998, then recovered by 9% in 1999-2000. Korea adopted numerous economic reforms following the crisis, including greater openness to foreign investment and imports. Growth fell back to 3.3% in 2001 because of the slowing global economy, falling exports, and the perception that much-needed corporate and financial reforms had stalled. Led by consumer spending and exports, growth in 2002 was an impressive 7% despite anemic global growth. Between 2003 and 2007, growth moderated to about 4-5% annually. A downturn in consumer spending was offset by rapid export growth. In 2008, inflation increased in the face of rising oil and food prices before easing in the fourth quarter. Korea was hit hard by the global financial turmoil that began in September 2008. Stock prices fell by more than 40% for the year and the value of the won fell by approximately 26%. Korean GDP shrank in the fourth quarter and GDP growth for the year was just 2.2%. The Korean government adopted several measures to combat the credit crunch and stimulate the economy.

GDP (purchasing power parity): $1.335 trillion (est.)
country comparison to the world: 14
$1.306 trillion (2007 est.)
$1.243 trillion (2006 est.)
note: data are in 2008 US dollars

GDP (official exchange rate): $897.4 billion

GDP - real growth rate: 2.2% (est.)
country comparison to the world: 155
5.1% (2007 est.)
5.2% (2006 est.)

GDP - per capita (PPP): $27,600 (est.)
country comparison to the world: 51
$27,100 (2007 est.)
$25,800 (2006 est.)
note: data are in 2008 US dollars

GDP - composition by sector: *agriculture:* 3.2%
industry: 39.6%
services: 57.2%

Labor force: 23.98 million

Labor force - by occupation:	*agriculture:* 6.4% *industry:* 26.4% *services:* 67.2%
Unemployment rate:	3.3%
Population below poverty line:	15%
Household income or consumption by percentage share:	*lowest 10%:* 2.9% *highest 10%:* 25%
Distribution of family income - Gini index:	35.8
Inflation rate (consumer prices):	2.2%
Investment (gross fixed):	29% of GDP
Budget:	*revenues:* $219.5 billion *expenditures:* $215.7 billion; including capital expenditures of $NA
Public debt:	25.2% of GDP
Agriculture - products:	rice, root crops, barley, vegetables, fruit; cattle, pigs, chickens, milk, eggs; fish
Industries:	electronics, telecommunications, automobile production, chemicals, shipbuilding, steel
Industrial production growth rate:	8%
Electricity - production:	366.2 billion kWh
Electricity - consumption:	352.5 billion kWh
Electricity - exports:	0 kWh
Electricity - imports:	0 kWh
Oil - production:	7,378 bbl/day
Oil - consumption:	2.149 million bbl/day
Oil - exports:	644,100 bbl/day
Oil - imports:	2.83 million bbl/day

For additional analytical, business and investment opportunities information,
please contact Global Investment & Business Center, USA
at (202) 546-2103. Fax: (202) 546-3275. E-mail: rusric@erols.com

Oil - proved reserves:	0 bbl
Natural gas - production:	498.7 million cu m
Natural gas - consumption:	29.17 billion cu m
Natural gas - exports:	0 cu m
Natural gas - imports:	28.29 billion cu m
Current account balance:	$6.092 billion
Exports:	$331.8 billion f.o.b.
Exports - commodities:	semiconductors, wireless telecommunications equipment, motor vehicles, computers, steel, ships, petrochemicals
Exports - partners:	China 21.3%, US 13.3%, Japan 8.1%, Hong Kong 5.9% (2006)
Imports:	$302.6 billion f.o.b.
Imports - commodities:	machinery, electronics and electronic equipment, oil, steel, transport equipment, organic chemicals, plastics
Imports - partners:	Japan 16.8%, China 15.7%, US 11%, Saudi Arabia 6.7%, UAE 4.2% (2006)
Economic aid - donor:	ODA, $744 million
Reserves of foreign exchange and gold:	$239 billion
Debt - external:	$187.2 billion
Stock of direct foreign investment - at home:	$118 billion
Stock of direct foreign investment - abroad:	$NA
Market value of publicly traded shares:	$835.2 billion
Currency (code):	South Korean won (KRW)
Exchange rates:	South Korean won per US dollar - 955.3 (2006), 1,024.1 (2005), 1,145.3 (2007), 1,191.6 (2003), 1,251.1 (2007)

Fiscal year: calendar year

COMMUNICATIONS

Telephones - main lines in use: 23.745 million

Telephones - mobile cellular: 38.342 million

Telephone system: *general assessment:* excellent domestic and international services
domestic: NA
international: country code - 82; 10 fiber-optic submarine cables - 1 Korea-Russia-Japan, 1 Korea-Japan-Hong Kong, 3 Korea-Japan-China, 1 Korea-Japan-China-Europe, 1 Korea-Japan-China-US-Taiwan, 1 Korea-Japan-China, 1 Korea-Japan-Hong Kong-Taiwan, 1 Korea-Japan; satellite earth stations - 3 Intelsat (1 Pacific Ocean and 2 Indian Ocean) and 3 Inmarsat (1 Pacific Ocean and 2 Indian Ocean)

Radio broadcast stations: AM 61, FM 150, shortwave 2

Television broadcast stations: terrestrial stations 43; cable operators 59; relay cable operators 190

Internet country code: .kr

Internet hosts: 5,433,591

Internet users: 33.9 million

TRANSPORTATION

Railways: *total:* 3,081 km
standard gauge: 3,081 km 1.435-m gauge (560 km electrified)

Highways:
total: 83,400 km
paved: 63,467 km (including 1,920 km of expressways)
unpaved: 19,933 km

Waterways: 1,609 km; use restricted to small native craft

Pipelines: petroleum products 455 km; note—additionally, there is a parallel petroleum, oils, and lubricants (POL) pipeline being completed

Ports and harbors: Chinhae, Inch'on, Kunsan, Masan, Mokp'o, P'ohang, Pusan, Tonghae-hang, Ulsan, Yosu

Merchant marine:
total: 474 ships (1,000 GRT or over) totaling 6,749,052 GRT/10,447,597 DWT
ships by type: bulk 118, cargo 131, chemical tanker 28, combination bulk 3, combination ore/oil 1,

For additional analytical, business and investment opportunities information, please contact Global Investment & Business Center, USA at (202) 546-2103. Fax: (202) 546-3275. E-mail: rusric@erols.com

container 70, liquefied gas tanker 12, multifunction large-load carrier 1, oil tanker 72, refrigerated cargo 22, roll-on/roll-off cargo 1, short-sea passenger 2, vehicle carrier 13
note: South Korea owns an additional 273 ships (1,000 GRT or over) totaling 11,985,267 DWT operating under the registries of Cambodia, Cyprus, Liberia, Malta, Panama, and Singapore

Airports: 103
Airports—with paved runways:
total: 67
over 3,047 m: 1
2,438 to 3,047 m: 18
1,524 to 2,437 m: 15
914 to 1,523 m: 14
under 914 m: 19
Airports—with unpaved runways:
total: 36
914 to 1,523 m: 4
under 914 m: 32
Heliports: 202

MILITARY

Military branches: Army, Navy, Air Force, Marine Corps, National Maritime Police (Coast Guard)
Military manpower—military age: 18 years of age
Military manpower—availability:
males age 15-49: 13,849,615
Military manpower—fit for military service:
males: 8,837,541
Military manpower—reaching military age annually:
males: 399,034
Military expenditures—dollar figure: $17.4 billion
Military expenditures—percent of GDP: 3.3%

TRANSNATIONAL ISSUES

Disputes—international: Demarcation Line with North Korea; Liancourt Rocks (Takeshima/Tokdo) claimed by Japan

IMPORTANT INFORMATION FOR UNDERSTANDING SOUTH KOREA

PROFILE

OFFICIAL NAME: Republic of Korea

Geography
Area: 98,480 sq. km. (38,023 sq. mi.); slightly larger than Indiana.
Cities (2005): *Capital*--Seoul (10.3 million). *Other major cities*--Busan (3.7 million), Daegu (2.5 million), Incheon (2.6 million), Gwangju (1.4 million), Daejeon (1.5 million), Ulsan (1.0 million).
Terrain: Partially forested mountain ranges separated by deep, narrow valleys; cultivated plains along the coasts, particularly in the west and south.
Climate: Temperate, with rainfall heavier in summer than winter.

People
Nationality: *Noun and adjective*--Korean(s).
Population (2008): 48,606,787.
Population annual growth rate (2008): 0.31%.
Ethnic groups: Korean; small Chinese minority (about 20,000).
Religions: Christianity, Buddhism, Shamanism, Confucianism, Chondogyo.
Language: Korean; English widely taught in junior high and high school.
Education: *Years compulsory*--9. *Enrollment*--11.5 million. *Attendance*--middle school 99%, high school 95%. *Literacy*--98%.
Health (2008): *Infant mortality rate*--4.29/1,000. *Life expectancy*--78.64 yrs. (men 75.34 yrs.; women 82.17 yrs).
Work force (2008): 24.3 million. *Services*--75.2%; *industry*--17.3%; *agriculture*--7.5%.

Government
Type: Republic with powers shared between the president, the legislature, and the courts.
Liberation: August 15, 1945.
Constitution: July 17, 1948; last revised 1987.
Branches: *Executive*--President (chief of state); Prime Minister (head of government). *Legislative*--unicameral National Assembly. *Judicial*--Supreme Court and appellate courts; Constitutional Court.
Subdivisions: Nine provinces, seven administratively separate cities (Seoul, Busan, Incheon, Daegu, Gwangju, Daejeon, Ulsan).
Political parties: Grand National Party (GNP); Democratic Party (DP), formerly known as United Democratic Party (UDP); Liberal Forward Party (LFP); Democratic Labor Party (DLP); Creative Korea Party (CKP); New Progressive Party (NPP).
Suffrage: Universal at 19.
Central government budget (2008): *Expenditures*--$216.6 billion.
Defense (2008): 2.5% of GDP.

Economy
GDP (purchasing power parity in 2008): $1.358 trillion.
GDP growth rate: 2007, 4.6%; 2005, 4.0%; 2006, 5.2%; 2007, 5.1%; 2008, 2.2%.
Per capita GNI (2008): $19,231.
Consumer price index: 2007, 3.6%; 2005, 2.8%; 2006, 2.2%; 2007, 2.5%; 2008, 4.7%.
Natural resources: Coal, tungsten, graphite, molybdenum, lead, hydropower potential.
Agriculture, including forestry and fisheries: *Products*--rice, vegetables, fruit, root crops, barley;

cattle, pigs, chickens, milk, eggs, fish. *Arable land*--16.58% of land area.
Industry: *Types*--Electronics and electrical products, telecommunications, motor vehicles, shipbuilding, mining and manufacturing, petrochemicals, industrial machinery, steel.
Trade (2008): *Exports*-- $433 billion f.o.b.: electronic products (semiconductors, cellular phones and equipment, computers), automobiles, machinery and equipment, steel, ships, petrochemicals. *Imports*-- $427 billion f.o.b.: crude oil, food, machinery and transportation equipment, chemicals and chemical products, base metals and articles. *Major markets* (2008)-- China (21.7%), U.S. (11.0%), Japan (6.7%), Hong Kong (4.7%). *Major suppliers* (2008)--China (17.7%), Japan (14.0%), U.S. (8.8%), Saudi Arabia (7.8%), U.A.E. (4.4%).

PEOPLE

Population
Korea's population is one of the most ethnically and linguistically homogenous in the world. Except for a small Chinese community (about 20,000), virtually all Koreans share a common cultural and linguistic heritage. With 48.6 million people, South Korea has one of the world's highest population densities. Major population centers are located in the northwest, southeast, and in the plains south of the Seoul-Incheon area.

Korea has experienced one of the largest rates of emigration, with ethnic Koreans residing primarily in China (2.4 million), the United States (2.1 million), Japan (600,000), and the countries of the former Soviet Union (532,000).

Language
The Korean language is related to Japanese and Mongolian. Although it differs grammatically from Chinese and does not use tones, a large number of Chinese cognates exist in Korean. Chinese ideograms are believed to have been brought into Korea sometime before the second century BC. The learned class spoke Korean, but read and wrote Chinese. A phonetic writing system ("hangul") was invented in the 15th century by King Sejong to provide a writing system for commoners who could not read classical Chinese. Modern Korean uses hangul almost exclusively with Chinese characters in limited use for word clarification. Approximately 1,300 Chinese characters are used in modern Korean. English is taught as a second language in most primary and secondary schools. Chinese and Japanese are widely taught at secondary schools.

Religion
Half of the population actively practices religion. Among this group, Christianity (49%) and Buddhism (47%) comprise Korea's two dominant religions. Though only 3% identified themselves as Confucianists, Korean society remains highly imbued with Confucian values and beliefs. The remaining 1% of the population practice Shamanism (traditional spirit worship) and Chondogyo ("Heavenly Way"), a traditional religion.

HISTORY

The myth of Korea's foundation by the god-king Tangun in BC 2333 embodies the homogeneity and self-sufficiency valued by the Korean people. Korea experienced many invasions by its larger neighbors in its 2,000 years of recorded history. The country repelled numerous foreign invasions despite domestic strife, in part due to its protected status in the Sino-centric regional political model during Korea's Chosun dynasty (1392-1910). Historical antipathies to foreign influence earned Korea the title of "Hermit Kingdom" in the 19th century.

With declining Chinese power and a weakened domestic posture at the end of the 19th century,

Korea was open to Western and Japanese encroachment. In 1910, Japan began a 35-year period of colonial rule over Korea. As a result of Japan's efforts to supplant the Korean language and aspects of Korean culture, memories of Japanese annexation still recall fierce animosity and resentment, especially among older Koreans. Nevertheless, import restrictions on Japanese movies, popular music, fashion, and the like have been lifted, and many Koreans, especially the younger generations, eagerly follow Japanese pop culture. Aspects of Korean culture, including television shows and movies, have also become popular in Japan.

Japan's surrender to the Allied Powers in 1945, signaling the end of World War II, only further embroiled Korea in foreign rivalries. Division at the 38th parallel marked the beginning of Soviet and U.S. trusteeship over the North and South, respectively. On August 15, 1948 the Republic of Korea (R.O.K.) was established, with Syngman Rhee as the first President. On September 9, 1948 the Democratic People's Republic of Korea (D.P.R.K.) was established under Kim Il Sung.

On June 25, 1950, North Korean forces invaded South Korea. Led by the U.S., a 16-member coalition undertook the first collective action under United Nations Command (UNC). Following China's entry on behalf of North Korea later that year, a stalemate ensued for the final two years of the conflict. Armistice negotiations, initiated in July 1951, were ultimately concluded on July 27, 1953 at Panmunjom, in what is now the Demilitarized Zone (DMZ). The Armistice Agreement was signed by representatives of the Korean People's Army, the Chinese People's Volunteers, and the U.S.-led United Nations Command (UNC). Though the R.O.K. supported the UNC, it refused to sign the Armistice Agreement. A peace treaty has never been signed. The war left almost three million Koreans dead or wounded and millions of others homeless and separated from their families.

In the following decades, South Korea experienced political turmoil under autocratic leadership. President Syngman Rhee was forced to resign in April 1960 following a student-led uprising. The Second Republic under the leadership of Chang Myon ended after only one year, when Major General Park Chung-hee led a military coup. Park's rule, which resulted in tremendous economic growth and development but increasingly restricted political freedoms, ended with his assassination in 1979. Subsequently, a powerful group of military officers, led by Lieutenant General Chun Doo-hwan, declared martial law and took power.

Throughout the Park and Chun eras, South Korea developed a vocal civil society that led to strong protests against authoritarian rule. Composed primarily of students and labor union activists, protest movements reached a climax after Chun's 1979 coup and declaration of martial law. A confrontation in Gwangju in 1980 left at least 200 civilians dead. Thereafter, pro-democracy activities intensified even more, ultimately forcing political concessions by the government in 1987, including the restoration of direct presidential elections.

In 1987, Roh Tae-woo, a former general, was elected president, but additional democratic advances during his tenure resulted in the 1992 election of a long-time pro-democracy activist, Kim Young-sam. Kim became Korea's first civilian elected president in 32 years. The 1997 presidential election and peaceful transition of power marked another step forward in Korea's democratization when Kim Dae-jung, a life-long democracy and human rights activist, was elected from a major opposition party. The transition to an open, democratic system was further consolidated in 2002, when self-educated human rights lawyer, Roh Moo-hyun, won the presidential election on a "participatory government" platform. South Koreans voted for a new president in December 2007. Former business executive and Mayor of Seoul Lee Myung-bak's 5-year term began with his inauguration on February 25, 2008.

GOVERNMENT AND POLITICAL CONDITIONS

For additional analytical, business and investment opportunities information, please contact Global Investment & Business Center, USA at (202) 546-2103. Fax: (202) 546-3275. E-mail: rusric@erols.com

The Republic of Korea (commonly known as "South Korea") is a republic with powers nominally shared among the presidency, the legislature, and the judiciary, but traditionally dominated by the president. The president is chief of state and is elected for a single term of 5 years. The 299 members of the unicameral National Assembly are elected to 4-year terms; elections for the assembly were held on April 9, 2008. South Korea's judicial system comprises a Supreme Court, appellate courts, and a Constitutional Court. The judiciary is independent under the constitution. The country has nine provinces and seven administratively separate cities--the capital of Seoul, along with Busan, Daegu, Daejeon, Gwangju, Incheon and Ulsan. Political parties include the Grand National Party (GNP), Democratic Party (DP), Liberal Forward Party (LFP), Creative Korea Party (CKP), Democratic Labor Party (DLP) and New Progressive Party (NPP). Suffrage is universal at age 19 (lowered from 20 in 2005).

Principal Government Officials

Pres., **LEE Myung-bak**
Prime Min., **KIM Hwang-sik**
Min., Prime Min.'s Office, **RIM Che-min**
Min. of Culture, Sports, & Tourism, **CHOI Kwang-sik**
Min. of Education, Science, & Technology, **LEE Ju-ho**
Min. of Employment & Labor, **LEE Chae-pil**
Min. of Environment, **YOO Young-sook**
Min. for Food, Agriculture, Forestry, & Fisheries, **SUH Kyu-yong**
Min. of Foreign Affairs & Trade, **KIM Sung-hwan**
Min. of Gender Equality & Family, **KIM Kum-lae**
Min. of Health & Welfare, **IM Chae-min**
Min. of Justice, **LEE Kwi-nam**
Min. of Knowledge Economy,
Min. of Land, Transport, & Maritime Affairs, **KWON Do-youp**
Min. of National Defense, **KIM Kwan-jin**
Min. of Public Admin. & Security, **MAENG Hyung-kyu**
Min. of Strategy & Finance, **BAHK Jae-wan**
Min. of Unification, **YU Woo-ik**
Chmn., Anticorruption & Civil Rights Commission, **KIM Young-ran**
Chmn., Board of Audit & Inspection, **YANG Kun**
Chmn., Fair Trade Commission, **KIM Dong-soo**
Chmn., Financial Services Commission, **KIM Seok-dong**
Chmn., Korea Communications Commission, **CHOI See-joong**
Chmn., Presidential Council on National Competitiveness, **SAKONG Il**
Chmn., National Human Rights Commission, **HYUN Byung-chul**
Chief of Staff, Office of the Pres., **HA Kum-loul**
Senior Presidential Sec. for External Strategies, Office of the Pres., **KIM Tae-hyo**
Senior Presidential Sec. for Foreign Affairs & Security Policy, Office of the Pres., **CHUN Yung-woo**
Dir., National Intelligence Service, **WON Sei-hoon**
Governor, Bank of Korea, **KIM Choong-soo**
Ambassador to the US, **HAN Duk-soo**

For additional analytical, business and investment opportunities information, please contact Global Investment & Business Center, USA at (202) 546-2103. Fax: (202) 546-3275. E-mail: rusric@erols.com

Permanent Representative to the UN, New York, **KIM Sook**

Korea maintains an **embassy** in the United States at 2450 Massachusetts Avenue NW, Washington, DC 20008 (tel. 202-939-5600). **Consulates** General are located in Atlanta, Boston, Chicago, Honolulu, Houston, Los Angeles, New York, San Francisco, Seattle, and Hagatna (Agana) in Guam.

ECONOMY

The Republic of Korea's economic growth over the past several decades has been spectacular. Per capita GNP, only $100 in 1963, is close to $20,000. South Korea is now the United States' seventh-largest trading partner and is the 13th-largest economy in the world.

In the early 1960s, the government of Park Chung Hee instituted sweeping economic policy changes emphasizing exports and labor-intensive light industries, leading to rapid debt-financed industrial expansion. The government carried out a currency reform, strengthened financial institutions, and introduced flexible economic planning. In the 1970s Korea began directing fiscal and financial policies toward promoting heavy and chemical industries, consumer electronics, and automobiles. Manufacturing continued to grow rapidly in the 1980s and early 1990s.

In recent years, Korea's economy moved away from the centrally planned, government-directed investment model toward a more market-oriented one. Korea bounced back from the 1997-98 Asian financial crisis with some International Monetary Fund (IMF) assistance, but based largely on extensive financial reforms that restored stability to markets. These economic reforms, pushed by President Kim Dae-jung, helped Korea return to growth, with growth rates of 10% in 1999 and 9% in 2000. The slowing global economy and falling exports slowed growth to 3.3% in 2001, prompting consumer stimulus measures that led to 7.0% growth in 2002. Consumer over-shopping and rising household debt, along with external factors, slowed growth to near 3% again in 2003. Economic performance in 2007 improved to 4.6% due to an increase in exports, and remained at or above 4% in 2005, 2006, and 2007. With the onset of the global financial and economic crisis in the third quarter of 2008, annual growth slowed to 2.2%.

Economists are concerned that South Korea's economic growth potential has fallen because of a rapidly aging population and structural problems that are becoming increasingly apparent. Foremost among these structural concerns are the rigidity of South Korea's labor regulations, the need for more constructive relations between management and workers, the country's underdeveloped financial markets, and a general lack of regulatory transparency. Korean policy makers are increasingly worried about diversion of corporate investment to China and other lower wage countries, and by Korea's falling foreign direct investment (FDI). President Lee Myung-bak was elected in December 2007 on a platform that promised to boost Korea's economic growth rate through deregulation, tax reform, increased FDI, labor reform, and free trade agreements (FTAs) with major markets. President Lee's economic agenda necessarily shifted in the final months of 2008 to dealing with the global economic crisis. In 2009, the economy responded well to a robust fiscal stimulus package and low interest rates. Korea's benchmark stock index, the KOSPI, is up over 50% this year, and the economy registered 2.6% growth in the second quarter and 2.9% growth in the third.

North-South Economic Ties
Two-way trade between North and South Korea, legalized in 1988, hit almost $1.82 billion in 2008, much of it related to out-processing or assembly work undertaken by South Korean firms in the Kaesong Industrial Complex (KIC). A significant portion of the total through 2007 included R.O.K. Government aid, but that assistance stopped in 2008, except for energy aid (heavy fuel

oil) under the Six-Party Talks. Thus, in 2008, about 94% of the total trade consisted of commercial transactions, much of that based on processing-on-commission arrangements and the light industry operations in KIC. The R.O.K. is North Korea's second-largest trading partner, after China.

Since the June 2000 North-South summit, North and South Korea have reconnected their east and west coast railroads and roads where they cross the DMZ and have improved these transportation routes. North and South Korea conducted tests of the east and west coast railroads on May 17, 2007 and began cross-border freight service between Kaesong in the D.P.R.K. and Munsan in the R.O.K. in December 2007, but the connection remains symbolic rather than commercial. Much of the work done in North Korea has been funded by South Korea. The west coast rail and road are complete as far north as the KIC (just north of the DMZ), but little work is being done north of Kaesong. On the east coast, the road is complete but the rail line is far from operational. Since 2003, tour groups used the east coast road to travel from South Korea to Mt. Geumgang in North Korea, where cruise ship-based tours had been permitted since 1998. Since then, more than a million visitors have traveled to Mt. Geumgang. The R.O.K. suspended tours to Mt. Geumgang in July 2008, however, following the shooting death of a South Korean tourist at the resort by a D.P.R.K. soldier. As of February 2009, 101 South Korean firms including apartment-type factories were manufacturing goods in the KIC, employing more than 39,000 North Korean workers. Most of the goods are sold in South Korea; a small quantity is being exported to foreign markets. Ground was broken on the complex in June 2003, and the first products were shipped from the KIC in December 2007. Initial plans envisioned 1,500 firms employing 350,000 workers by 2012, but expansion has been slowed because of tense inter-Korean relations.

FOREIGN RELATIONS

In August 1991, South Korea joined the United Nations along with North Korea and is active in most UN specialized agencies and many international forums. The Republic of Korea also hosted major international events such as the 1988 Summer Olympics, the 2002 World Cup Soccer Tournament (co-hosted with Japan), and the 2002 Second Ministerial Conference of the Community of Democracies. South Korea will also chair the 2010 G-20 meeting.

Economic considerations have a high priority in Korean foreign policy. The R.O.K. seeks to build on its economic accomplishments to increase its regional and global role. It is a founding member of the Asia-Pacific Economic Cooperation (APEC) forum and chaired the organization in 2005.

The Republic of Korea maintains diplomatic relations with more than 170 countries and a broad network of trading relationships. The United States and Korea are allied by the 1953 Mutual Defense Treaty. Korea and Japan coordinate closely on numerous issues. This includes consultations with the United States on North Korea policy.

Korean Peninsula: Reunification and Recent Developments
For almost 20 years after the 1950-53 Korean War, relations between North and South Korea were minimal and very strained. Official contact did not occur until 1971, beginning with Red Cross contacts and family reunification projects. In the early 1990s, relations between the two countries improved with the 1991 "Agreement on Reconciliation, Nonaggression and Exchanges and Cooperation between the South and the North," since known as the "Basic Agreement," which acknowledged that reunification was the goal of both governments, and the 1992 "Joint Declaration of the Denuclearization of the Korean Peninsula." However, divergent positions on the process of reunification and North Korean weapons programs, compounded by South Korea's tumultuous domestic politics and the 1994 death of North Korean leader Kim Il-sung, contributed to a cycle of warming and cooling of relations.

For additional analytical, business and investment opportunities information, please contact Global Investment & Business Center, USA at (202) 546-2103. Fax: (202) 546-3275. E-mail: rusric@erols.com

Relations improved again following the 1997 election of Kim Dae-jung. His "Sunshine Policy" of engagement with the D.P.R.K. set the stage for the historic June 2000 inter-Korean summit between President Kim and North Korean leader Kim Jong-il. President Kim was awarded the Nobel Peace Prize in 2000 for the policy, but the prize was somewhat tarnished by revelations of a $500 million dollar "payoff" to North Korea that immediately preceded the summit.

Relations again became tense following the October 2002 North Korean acknowledgement of a covert program to enrich uranium for nuclear weapons. Following this acknowledgement, the United States, along with the People's Republic of China, proposed multilateral talks among the concerned parties to deal with this issue. At the urging of China and its neighbors, the D.P.R.K. agreed to meet with China and the United States in April 2003. In August of that year, the D.P.R.K. agreed to attend Six-Party Talks aimed at ending the North's pursuit of nuclear weapons that added the Republic of Korea, Japan, and Russia to the table. Two more rounds of Six-Party Talks between the United States, the Republic of Korea, Japan, China, and the D.P.R.K. were held in February and June of 2007. At the third round, the United States put forward a comprehensive proposal aimed at completely, verifiably, and irreversibly eliminating North Korea's nuclear weapons programs. A fourth round of talks was held in two sessions spanning a period of 20 days between July and September 2005.

In a major achievement, all parties agreed to a Joint Statement of Principles on September 19, 2005, in which, among other things, the D.P.R.K. committed to "abandoning all nuclear weapons and existing nuclear programs and returning, at an early date, to the Treaty on the Non-Proliferation of Nuclear Weapons and to IAEA safeguards." The Joint Statement also committed the United States and other parties to certain actions as the D.P.R.K. denuclearized. The United States offered a security assurance, specifying that it had no nuclear weapons on R.O.K. territory and no intention to attack or invade the D.P.R.K. with nuclear or other weapons. Finally, the United States and the D.P.R.K., as well as the D.P.R.K. and Japan, agreed to undertake steps to normalize relations, subject to their respective bilateral policies.

However, following D.P.R.K. protests against U.S. Government money-laundering sanctions on D.P.R.K. funds held at Macao's Banco Delta Asia, the D.P.R.K. boycotted the Six-Party Talks during late 2005 and most of 2006. On October 9, 2006, North Korea announced a successful nuclear test, verified by the United States on October 11. In response, the United Nations Security Council, citing Chapter VII of the UN Charter, unanimously adopted Resolution 1718, condemning North Korea's action and imposing sanctions on certain luxury goods and trade of military items, weapons of mass destruction (WMD)-related parts, and technology transfers. The Six-Party Talks resumed in December 2006. Following a bilateral meeting between the United States and D.P.R.K. in Berlin in January 2007, another round of Six-Party Talks was held in February 2007. On February 13, 2007, the parties reached an agreement on "Initial Actions for the Implementation of the Joint Statement" in which North Korea agreed to shut down and seal its Yongbyon nuclear facility, including the reprocessing facility, and to invite back International Atomic Energy Agency (IAEA) personnel to conduct all necessary monitoring and verification of these actions. The other five parties agreed to provide emergency energy assistance to North Korea in the amount of 50,000 tons of heavy fuel oil (HFO) in the initial phase (within 60 days) and the equivalent of up to 950,000 tons of HFO in the next phase of North Korea's denuclearization. The six parties also established five working groups to form specific plans for implementing the Joint Statement in the following areas: denuclearization of the Korean Peninsula, normalization of D.P.R.K.-U.S. relations, normalization of D.P.R.K.-Japan relations, economic and energy cooperation, and a Northeast Asia peace and security mechanism. All parties agreed that the working groups would meet within 30 days of the agreement, which they did.

For additional analytical, business and investment opportunities information, please contact Global Investment & Business Center, USA at (202) 546-2103. Fax: (202) 546-3275. E-mail: rusric@erols.com

The agreement also envisioned the directly-related parties negotiating a permanent peace regime on the Korean Peninsula at an appropriate separate forum. As part of the initial actions, North Korea invited IAEA Director General ElBaradei to Pyongyang in early March for preliminary discussions on the return of the IAEA to the D.P.R.K. The sixth round of Six-Party Talks took place on March 19-23, 2007. The parties reported on the first meetings of the five working groups. At the invitation of the D.P.R.K., Assistant Secretary of State Christopher Hill visited Pyongyang in June 2007 as part of ongoing consultations with the six parties on implementation of the Initial Actions agreement. In July 2007, after the Banco Delta Asia funds were released, the D.P.R.K. shut down the Yongbyon nuclear facility, as well as an uncompleted reactor at Taechon, and IAEA personnel returned to the D.P.R.K. to monitor and verify the shut-down and to seal the facility. Concurrently, the R.O.K., China, United States, and Russia initiated deliveries of HFO and other energy-related assistance that was agreed on, with the R.O.K. completing delivery of the first tranche of 50,000 metric tons of HFO in August, China the second in September, the United States the third in November, and Russia the fourth in January. These four parties continued to provide shipments of HFO and other energy assistance as the D.P.R.K. continued to implement disablement steps during 2007 and 2008. All five working groups met in August and September 2007 to discuss detailed plans for implementation of the next phase of the Initial Actions agreement, and the D.P.R.K. invited a team of experts from the United States, China, and Russia to visit the Yongbyon nuclear facility in September 2007 to discuss specific steps that could be taken to disable the facility. The subsequent September 27-30 Six-Party plenary meeting resulted in the October 3, 2007 agreement on "Second-Phase Actions for the Implementation of the Joint Statement."

Under the terms of the October 3 agreement, the D.P.R.K. agreed to disable all existing nuclear facilities subject to abandonment under the September 2005 Joint Statement and the February 2007 agreement. The parties agreed to complete by December 31, 2007 a set of disablement actions for the three core facilities at Yongbyon--the 5-MW(e) Experimental Reactor, the Radiochemical Laboratory (Reprocessing Plant), and the Fresh Fuel Fabrication Plant--with oversight from a team of U.S. experts. The D.P.R.K. also agreed to provide a complete and correct declaration of all its nuclear programs in accordance with the February 2007 agreement by December 31, 2007 and reaffirmed its commitment not to transfer nuclear materials, technology, or know-how.

In November 2007, the D.P.R.K. began to disable the three core facilities at Yongbyon and completed many of the agreed disablement actions by the end of the year. Assistant Secretary of State Christopher Hill visited Pyongyang again in December 2007 as part of ongoing consultations on the implementation of Second-Phase actions and carried with him a letter from the President of the United States to Kim Jong-il. The D.P.R.K. missed the December 31 deadline to provide a complete and correct declaration, but efforts to secure a declaration continued in 2008.

While the D.P.R.K. missed the December 31 deadline to provide a complete and correct declaration, it provided its declaration to the Chinese, chair of the Six-Party Talks, on June 26, 2008. The D.P.R.K. also imploded the cooling tower at the Yongbyon facility in late June 2008 in the presence of international media and U.S. Government officials. Following the D.P.R.K.'s progress on disablement and provision of a declaration, President George W. Bush announced the lifting of the application of the Trading with the Enemy Act (TWEA) with respect to the D.P.R.K. and notified Congress of his intent to rescind North Korea's designation as a state sponsor of terrorism. President Bush made clear that the United States needed to have a strong regime in place to verify the D.P.R.K.'s declaration before it would remove the D.P.R.K. from the list of state sponsors of terrorism. In October 2008, following agreements reached with the D.P.R.K. concerning verification measures, the U.S. Government removed the D.P.R.K. from the terrorism sponsors list. However, efforts to move forward on verification steps met with D.P.R.K. resistance.

U.S.-KOREAN RELATIONS

The United States believes that the question of peace and security on the Korean Peninsula is, first and foremost, a matter for the Korean people to decide.

Under the 1953 U.S.-R.O.K. Mutual Defense Treaty, the United States agreed to help the Republic of Korea defend itself against external aggression. Since that time in support of this commitment, the United States has maintained military personnel in Korea, including the Army's Second Infantry Division and several Air Force tactical squadrons. To coordinate operations between these units and the over 680,000-strong Korean armed forces, a Combined Forces Command (CFC) was established in 1978. The head of the CFC also serves as Commander of the United Nations Command (UNC) and U.S. Forces Korea (USFK). The current commander is General Walter "Skip" Sharp.

Several aspects of the security relationship are changing as the U.S. moves from a leading to a supporting role. In 2007, agreement was reached on the return of the Yongsan base in Seoul--as well as a number of other U.S. bases--to the R.O.K. and the eventual relocation of all U.S. forces to south of the Han River. Those movements are expected to be completed by 2016. In addition, the U.S. and R.O.K. agreed to reduce the number of U.S. troops in Korea to 25,000 by 2008, but a subsequent agreement by the U.S. and R.O.K. presidents in 2008 has now capped that number at 28,500, with no further troop reductions planned. The U.S. and R.O.K. have also agreed to transfer wartime operational control to the R.O.K. military on April 17, 2012.

As Korea's economy has developed, trade and investment ties have become an increasingly important aspect of the U.S.-R.O.K. relationship. Korea is the United States' seventh-largest trading partner (ranking ahead of larger economies such as France, Italy, and India), and there are significant flows of manufactured goods, agricultural products, services and technology between the two countries. Major American firms have long been major investors in Korea, while Korea's leading firms have begun to make significant investments in the United States. The implementation of structural reforms contained in the IMF's 1998 program for Korea improved access to the Korean market and improved trade relations between the United States and Korea. Building on that improvement, the United States and Korea launched negotiations on the U.S.-Korea Free Trade Agreement (KORUS FTA) on February 2, 2006. The KORUS FTA was signed by the United States and Korea on June 30, 2007 and is currently awaiting ratification. The KORUS FTA is a comprehensive FTA that eliminates virtually all barriers to trade and investment between the two countries. Tariffs on 95% of trade between the two countries will be eliminated within three years of implementation, with virtually all the remaining tariffs being removed within ten years of implementation; the FTA also contains chapters that address non-tariff measures in investment, intellectual property, services, competition policy, and other areas. The KORUS FTA is the largest free trade agreement Korea has ever signed, and the largest free trade agreement for the United States since the North American Free Trade Agreement (NAFTA) in 1992. Economists have projected the FTA will generate billions of dollars in increased trade and investment between the United States and the Republic of Korea, and boost economic growth and job creation in both countries.

Principal U.S. Embassy Officials
Ambassador--**D. Kathleen Stephens**
Deputy Chief of Mission--Mark Tokola
Counselor for Political Affairs--James Wayman
Counselor for Economic Affairs--Gregory Burton

For additional analytical, business and investment opportunities information, please contact Global Investment & Business Center, USA at (202) 546-2103. Fax: (202) 546-3275. E-mail: rusric@erols.com

Counselor for Management Affairs--Rob Davis
Counselor for Public Affairs--Patrick Linehan
Consul General--Cynthia Sharpe
Counselor for Commercial Affairs--John Fogarasi
Counselor for Agricultural Affairs--Lloyd Harbert
Chief, Joint U.S. Military Advisory Group, Korea (JUSMAG-K)--Col. Ha Dong Chin
Defense Attaché--Col. Kevin Madden
Drug Enforcement Administration, Special Agent in Charge--Edward Fiocchi
Open Source Center, Seoul Bureau Chief--Kristen Patel
DHS-Citizenship and Immigration Services--Kenneth Sherman
DHS-Immigration and Customs Enforcement Attaché--KyungYul Steven Kim
Federal Bureau of Investigation Legal Attaché--Matthew Moon

The **U.S. Embassy** in South Korea is located at 32 Sejong-no, Jongno-gu, Seoul 110-710. The contact information for the U.S. Embassy is: American Embassy-Seoul, Unit 15550, APO AP 96205-5550 (tel.: 82-2-397-4114; fax: 82-2-738-8845). The U.S. Agricultural Trade Office (ATO) is located at 146-1, Susong-dong, Jongno-gu, Leema Bldg., Rm. 303, Seoul 110-140 (fax: 82-2-720-7921). The U.S. Export Development Office/U.S. Trade Center can be reached c/o U.S. Embassy (fax: 82-2-739-1628).

Additional Resources
The following general country guides are available from the Superintendent of Documents, U.S. Government Printing Office, Washington, DC 20402:
Library of Congress. *North Korea: A Country Study*. 1994.
Library of Congress. *South Korea: A Country Study*. 1992.
Department of State. *The Record on Korean Unification 1943-1960*. 1961.
Department of the Army. *Communist North Korea: A Bibliographic Survey*. 1971.

Internet Resources on North and South Korea
The following sites are provided to give an indication of Internet sites on Korea. The Department of State does not endorse unofficial publications, including Internet sites.

R.O.K. Embassy--**http://www.koreaembassyusa.org/**
Korea Society--**http://www.koreasociety.org/**; links to academic and other sites.
Nautilus Institute--**http://www.nautilus.org/**; produced by the Nautilus Institute in Berkeley, California, and includes press roundup Monday through Friday.
Korea Web Weekly--**http://www.kimsoft.com/korea.htm**; links to North Korean sites.
Joongang Daily--**http://joongangdaily.joins.com/**; South Korean English-language newspaper.
Korea Herald--**http://www.koreaherald.co.kr/**; South Korean English-language newspaper.
Korea Times--**http://www.koreatimes.co.kr/**; South Korean English-language newspaper.
(North) Korean Central News Agency--**http://www.kcna.co.jp/index-e.htm**

TRAVEL AND BUSINESS INFORMATION

The U.S. Department of State's Consular Information Program advises Americans traveling and residing abroad through Country Specific Information, Travel Alerts, and Travel Warnings. **Country Specific Information** exists for all countries and includes information on entry and exit requirements, currency regulations, health conditions, safety and security, crime, political disturbances, and the addresses of the U.S. embassies and consulates abroad. **Travel Alerts** are issued to disseminate information quickly about terrorist threats and other relatively short-term conditions overseas that pose significant risks to the security of American travelers. **Travel Warnings** are issued when the State Department recommends that Americans avoid travel to a certain country because the situation is dangerous or unstable.

For the latest security information, Americans living and traveling abroad should regularly monitor the Department's Bureau of Consular Affairs Internet web site at http://www.travel.state.gov, where the current Worldwide Caution, Travel Alerts, and Travel Warnings can be found. Consular Affairs Publications, which contain information on obtaining passports and planning a safe trip abroad, are also available at http://www.travel.state.gov. For additional information on international travel, see http://www.usa.gov/Citizen/Topics/Travel/International.shtml.

The Department of State encourages all U.S. citizens traveling or residing abroad to register via the State Department's travel registration website or at the nearest U.S. embassy or consulate abroad. Registration will make your presence and whereabouts known in case it is necessary to contact you in an emergency and will enable you to receive up-to-date information on security conditions.

Emergency information concerning Americans traveling abroad may be obtained by calling 1-888-407-4747 toll free in the U.S. and Canada or the regular toll line 1-202-501-4444 for callers outside the U.S. and Canada.

The National Passport Information Center (NPIC) is the U.S. Department of State's single, centralized public contact center for U.S. passport information. Telephone: 1-877-4-USA-PPT (1-877-487-2778); TDD/TTY: 1-888-874-7793. Passport information is available 24 hours, 7 days a week. You may speak with a representative Monday-Friday, 8 a.m. to 10 p.m., Eastern Time, excluding federal holidays.

Travelers can check the latest health information with the U.S. Centers for Disease Control and Prevention in Atlanta, Georgia. A hotline at 800-CDC-INFO (800-232-4636) and a web site at http://wwwn.cdc.gov/travel/default.aspx give the most recent health advisories, immunization recommendations or requirements, and advice on food and drinking water safety for regions and countries. The CDC publication "Health Information for International Travel" can be found at http://wwwn.cdc.gov/travel/contentYellowBook.aspx.

STRATEGIC INFORMATION FOR CONDUCTING BUSINESS

INVESTMENT AND BUSINESS CLIMATE

OPENNESS TO FOREIGN INVESTMENT

The Republic of Korea (ROK) enjoyed six percent growth in 2010 and its benchmark stock index, the KOSPI, began 2011 at record high-levels. Many credit the ROK's strong rebound from the global economic crisis to fundamental reforms made in the aftermath of the 1997-98 Asian financial crisis, when Korea made rapid progress in reforming its financial institutions and capital markets, sold its interest in a number of large, high-profile companies to foreign investors, and many Koreans in general began to see more foreign investment as something positive for the nation's development. In addition, the Korean government took steps to strengthen competition policy and enacted measures to enhance foreign investment incentives, and to allow non-Koreans to own land and real property. President Lee Myung-bak has made foreign direct investment an important part of his administration's growth strategy. While there was a dip following the global financial crisis, in-bound flows quickly recovered and rose from USD 11.5 billion in 2009 to USD 12.9 billion in 2010. Inbound investment in the manufacturing sector increased by 75.6 percent from 2009 while the investments into service industries dropped about 18 percent from a year before. Noteworthy improvements in the protection of intellectual property – recognized by the removal of the ROK from the Special 301 Watch List in 2009 – continue to improve the foreign investment climate. The ROK's role as host of the 2010 G20 served to burnish the ROK's reputation as a favorable destination for foreign investment.

The United States retains the largest single-country share of foreign direct investment (FDI) in Korea, totaling USD 43.8 billion or 25.2 percent of Korea's total stock of FDI since the 1960's. Japan has invested USD 26 billion (14.8 percent of the total) followed by the United Kingdom with USD 10.7 billion (6.2 percent). Overall, the inbound FDI increased 12 percent year on year in 2010, to USD 12.9 billion on a filing basis. The financial, transportation and other service sectors are expected to absorb the majority FDI in Korea in the near future, largely through mergers and acquisitions (M&A), in line with global trends.

Since Korean financial markets bottomed out in March 2009, foreign portfolio investment has been resurgent. At the end of 2010, foreign shareholders owned 32.9 percent of Korean Stock Exchange stocks and 10.3 percent of the tech-heavy KOSDAQ Index shares.

The environment for FDI in Korea would benefit from an improvement in the consistency of the ROKG's interpretation, transparency and timeliness in the application of regulations. These regulatory issues, such as a set of newly introduced capital control measures, can discourage FDI by creating uncertainty for investors and fostering an impression that Korea remains hostile to foreign investment. Although Korea boasts a hard-working, educated and highly productive workforce and high levels of institutional labor protections, foreign investors cite volatility in labor-management relations as an issue that can hamper direct investment. The highest levels of the Korean government remain committed to maintaining a welcoming environment for foreign investors, ensuring a "level playing field" for foreign investors, and reforming labor laws.

The Korea-US (KORUS) Free Trade Agreement (FTA) promises to be a major step to enhance the legal framework for US investors operating in Korea. All forms of investment would be protected under the FTA, including enterprises, debt, concessions and similar contracts, and intellectual property rights. With very few exceptions, US investors will be treated as well as Korean investors (or investors of any other country) in the establishment, acquisition, and operation of investments in Korea. In addition, these protections would be backed by a transparent international arbitration mechanism, under which investors may, at their own initiative, bring claims against a government for an alleged breach of the investment. Submissions to investor-State arbitration tribunals would be made public and hearings would be open to the public.

The Korean government's attitude toward foreign direct investment is positive and senior policy makers clearly realize the value of FDI. President Lee Myung-bak champions a foreign investment-friendly philosophy and has taken important steps to reverse the former government's ambivalent attitude toward foreign investment. FDI has since rebounded to USD 11.7 billion in 2008, USD 11.5 billion in 2009, and USD 12.9 billion in 2010.

Despite these improvements and attitude changes however, FDI in Korea is still seen as subject to insufficient regulatory transparency, including inconsistent and sudden changes in the interpretation of regulations, an inflexible labor system, high labor costs, underdeveloped corporate governance, and lingering economic domination by the country's remaining conglomerates or "chaebols".

Korea's Foreign Investment Promotion Act (FIPA) and related regulations categorize business activities as either open, conditionally or partly restricted, or closed to foreign investment. Restrictions remain for 29 industrial sectors, three of which are entirely closed to foreign investment. The Korean government reviews restricted sectors from time to time for possible further openings. According to the Ministry of Knowledge Economy (MKE), the number of industrial sectors open to foreign investors is well above the OECD average.

FIPA features include:

Simplified procedures, including those for FDI notification and registration;

Expanded tax incentives for high-technology FDI;

Reduced rental fees and lengthened lease durations for government land (including local government land);
Increased central government support for local FDI incentives;
Establishment of "Invest Korea," a one-stop investment promotion center within the Korea Trade Promotion Corporation to assist foreign investors;
Establishment of an Ombudsman office to assist foreign investors.

MKE published a 2009 Consolidated Public Notice, updating new code numbers and titles for business sectors in accordance to the ninth revision of the Korea Standard Industry Code (KSIC). According to the 2009 Notice, the number of KSIC industrial classifications of business sectors increased from 1,121 to 1,145 and by the reclassification, business sectors where foreign investment is restricted increased from 28 to 29.

The following is a current list of Restricted Sectors for Foreign Investment. Figures in parentheses denote the Korean Industrial Classification Code:

Completely Closed

Nuclear power generation (35111)
Radio broadcasting (60100)
Television broadcasting (60210)

Restricted Sectors (partly open not more than 25 percent)

News agency activities (63910)

Restricted Sectors (partly open not more than 30 percent)

Publishing of newspapers (58121)

Restricted Sectors (partly open less than 30 percent)

Hydro electronic power generation (35112)
Thermal power generation (35113)
Other power generation (35119)

Restricted Sectors (partly open less than 33 percent)

Satellite and other broadcasting (60229)

Restricted Sectors (partly open less than 49 percent)

Program distribution (60221)
Cable networks (60222)
Wired telephone and other telecommunications (61210)
Mobile telephone and other telecommunications (61220)
Satellite telephone and other telecommunications (61230)
Other telecommunications (61299)

Restricted Sectors (partly open not more than 50 percent)

Farming of beef cattle (01212)
Inshore and coastal fishing (03112)
Transmission/distribution of electricity (35120)
Wholesale of meat (46312)
Coastal water passenger transport (50121)
Coastal water freight transport (50122)
Scheduled air transport (51100)
Non-scheduled air transport (51200)
Publishing of magazines and periodicals (58122)

Open but Regulated under the Relevant Laws

Growing of cereal crops and other food crops except rice and barley (01110)
Domestic commercial banking except special banking area (64121)
Asset management service (64201)

For additional analytical, business and investment opportunities information,
please contact Global Investment & Business Center, USA
at (202) 546-2103. Fax: (202) 546-3275. E-mail: rusric@erols.com

In categories open to investment, foreign exchange banks must be notified in advance of applications for foreign investment. (All Korean banks are permitted to deal in foreign exchange, including branches of foreign banks.) In effect, these notifications are pro-forma, and approval can be processed within three hours. Applications may be denied only on specific grounds, including national security, public order and morals, international security obligations, and health and environmental concerns. Exceptions to the advance notification approval system exist for project categories subject to joint-venture requirements and certain projects in the distribution sector.

Relevant ministries must still approve investments in conditionally or partly restricted sectors. Most applications are processed within five days; cases that require consultation with more than one ministry can take 25 days or longer. Korea changed its procurement law effective in 1997, to comply with its accession to the WTO Government Procurement Agreement. The Government's procurement law no longer favors domestic suppliers over foreigners, but some implementation problems remain.

Restrictions on foreign ownership of public corporations remain, although ownership limit levels have been raised. Currently, foreign ownership is limited for government-controlled utilities. Foreign ownership in Korean telecommunications companies and cable networks is limited to 49 percent. The Korean government intends to privatize many of the remaining state-owned corporations, but this process was slowed by the global financial crisis.

The Ministry of Strategy and Finance (MOSF) administers tax and other incentives to stimulate advanced technology transfer and investment in high-technology services. There are three types of special areas for foreign investment -- Free Economic Zones, Free Investment Zones and Tariff Free Zones -- where favorable tax incentives and other support for investors are available (see Section VI.)

A Korean government initiative to encourage research and development (R&D) in strategic industries -- the New Growth-Driving Forces (NGF) program -- wound down in 2004. In its place the Korean government has increased its R&D budget to local areas from 27 percent to 32 percent to support its 21st Century Frontier R&D Project, designed to raise Korean technology to the level of the G8 countries. Focusing on information technology, biotechnology, nanotechnology and new materials, the Korean government launched development programs in 20 new strategic areas at the end of 2003, at a total cost of USD 3.5 billion. Much Korean government-funded R&D taps the expertise of foreign partners. In January 2009, the government also picked 17 industries as it New Engines of Growth relating to the green technology sector, high-tech, and high value-added sector.

Between 2004 to September 2010, 24 global companies including many US firms have opened R&D centers in Seoul. In 2010, Qualcomm announced it would set up a technology R&D center in the ROK and also invest around USD 4 million in a local digital audio chip maker.

CONVERSION AND TRANSFER POLICIES

The Korean government has substantially removed restrictions on financial transfers into and out of Korea. Prior to 1999, the Foreign Exchange Control Act and associated regulations strictly regulated foreign exchange transactions. The Korean government subsequently liberalized transactions in medium-and long-term overseas borrowings, purchase and sale of local real estate, and trading in over-the-counter (OTC) stocks and bonds.

In 1999, the Foreign Exchange Transaction Act (FETA) fully liberalized all current-account transactions by business firms and banks, and pared down a formerly long list of restricted transactions to five items, most of which cover foreign exchange transactions by individuals. A second-stage liberalization dismantled most of the remaining restrictions in 2001. Only transactions that could harm international peace or public order, such as money laundering and gambling, remain controlled. Three specific types of transactions were not liberalized:

(1) Non-residents are not permitted to buy won-denominated hedge funds, including forward currency contracts;

(2) The Financial Services Commission will not permit foreign currency borrowing by "non-viable" domestic firms; and

(3) The Korean government will monitor and ensure that Korean firms that have extended credit to foreign borrowers collect their debts. The Korean government has retained the authority to re-impose restrictions in the case of severe economic or financial emergency.

Capital account liberalization under the Foreign Exchange Transaction Act (FETA) has also been extensive. All capital-account transactions are permitted unless specifically prohibited. In addition, 72 of the 91 transactions specified by the OECD code of liberalization of capital movements now are permitted. Non-residents may open deposit accounts in domestic currency (won) with maturities of more than one year and may engage in offshore transactions and issue won-denominated securities abroad.

The right to remit profits is granted at the time of original investment approval. Banks control the now pro forma approval process for FETA-defined open sectors. For conditional or partially restricted investments (as defined by the FETA), approval for both the investment and remittance rests with the relevant ministry.

When foreign investment royalties or other payments are proposed as part of a technology licensing agreement, the agreement and the projected stream of royalties must be approved either by a bank or MOSF. Again, approval is virtually automatic. An investor wishing to enact a remittance must present an audited financial statement to a bank to substantiate the payment. To withdraw capital, a stock valuation report issued by a recognized securities company or the Korean appraisal board also must be presented. Foreign companies seeking to remit funds from investments in restricted sectors must first seek ministerial and bank approval, after demonstrating the legal source of the funds and proving that relevant taxes have been paid.

EXPROPRIATION AND COMPENSATION

Korea follows generally accepted principles of international law with respect to expropriation. Korean law protects foreign-invested enterprise property from expropriation or requisition. If private property is expropriated, it can only be taken for a public purpose, and only in a non-discriminatory manner. Property owners are entitled to prompt compensation at fair market value. The US Embassy in Seoul is not aware of any cases of uncompensated expropriation of property owned by American citizens.

DISPUTE SETTLEMENT

Serious investment disputes involving foreigners are the exception rather than the rule in Korea. There exists a body of Korean law governing commercial activities and bankruptcies that constitutes the means to enforce property and contractual rights, with monetary judgments usually levied in the domestic currency. Foreign court judgments are not enforceable in Korea.

Although commercial disputes can be adjudicated in a civil court, foreign businesses often feel that this is not a practical means to resolve disputes. Proceedings are conducted in Korean, often without adequate translation. Korean law prohibits foreign lawyers who have not passed the Korean Bar Examination from representing clients in Korean courts. Civil procedures common in the United States, such as pretrial discovery, do not exist in Korea. During litigation of a dispute, foreigners may be barred from leaving the country until a decision is reached. Legal proceedings are expensive and time-consuming and lawsuits often are contemplated only as a last resort, signaling the end of a business relationship.

Commercial disputes may also be taken to the Korean Commercial Arbitration Board (KCAB). The Korean Arbitration Act and its implementing rules outline the following steps in the arbitration process: 1) parties may request the KCAB to act as informal intermediary to a settlement; 2) if unsuccessful, either or both parties may request formal arbitration, in which case the KCAB appoints a mediator to conduct conciliatory talks for 30 days; and 3) if unsuccessful, an arbitration panel consisting of one or three arbitrators is assigned to decide the case. If one party is not resident in Korea, either may request an arbitrator from a neutral country.

When drafting contracts, it may be useful to provide for arbitration by a neutral body such as the International Commercial Arbitration Association (ICAA). US companies should seek local expert legal counsel when drawing up any type of contract with a Korean entity.

Korea is a member of the International Center for the Settlement of Investment Disputes (ICSID). It has also acceded to the United Nations Convention on the Recognition and Enforcement of Foreign Arbitral Awards (New York Convention). Korea is a member of the International Commercial Arbitration Association and the World Bank's Multilateral Investment Guarantee Agency (MIGA). It is important to keep in mind that Korean courts may ultimately be called upon to enforce an arbitrated settlement.

PERFORMANCE REQUIREMENTS AND INCENTIVES

South Korea does not maintain any measures notified to the World Trade Organization (WTO) as being inconsistent with (or that are alleged to be inconsistent with) the WTO Agreement on Trade-Related Investment Measures (TRIMs Agreement). Korea ceased imposing performance requirements on new foreign investment in 1989 and eliminated all pre-existing performance requirements in 1992. The ROKG also no longer has overt requirements that investors purchase from local sources or export a certain percentage of output. There is no ROKG requirement that Korean nationals must own shares in foreign investments or that technology be transferred on certain terms. The Korean government does not impose "offset" requirements on investors to invest in specific manufacturing, R&D or service facilities. There are also no government-imposed conditions on permission to invest.

The Korean government allows the following general incentives for foreign investors:

> Cash grants for the creation and expansion of workplaces for high-tech business plants and R&D research centers;
> Reduced rent for land and site preparation for foreign investors;
> Grants for establishment of convenience facilities for foreigners;
> Reduced rent for state or public property; and

Preferential financial support for investing in major infrastructure projects.

RIGHT TO PRIVATE OWNERSHIP AND ESTABLISHMENT

Korea fully recognizes rights of private ownership and has a well-developed body of laws governing the establishment of corporate and other business enterprises. Private entities may freely acquire and dispose of assets; however, the Fair Trade Act may limit cross-ownership of shares in two or more firms if the effect is to restrict competition in a particular industry.

Korea liberalized its property ownership law in 1998. The Alien Land Acquisition Act (as amended) grants even non-resident foreigners and foreign corporations the same rights as Koreans in purchasing and using land. Korea took further steps to liberalize its property ownership laws by implementing the Real Estate Investment Trust (REIT) Act in 2001, which supports sound indirect investments in real estate and restructuring of corporations. The REIT Act allows investors to invest funds through an asset management company, and in real property such as office buildings, business parks, shopping malls, hotels and serviced apartments.

Almost no restrictions remain on foreign ownership of stock in Korean firms. As of 2000, Korean law permits foreign direct investment through mergers and acquisitions with existing domestic firms, including hostile takeovers. Nonetheless, no hostile takeovers have occurred in Korea in part because of the lack of relevant implementation regulations for the Foreign Investment Promotion Act. In addition, the political environment for hostile takeovers remains unfriendly.

PROTECTION OF PROPERTY RIGHTS

Korea's progress on Intellectual Property Rights led to its removal from the Special 301 Watch List in 2009. Korea remained off the Watch List in 2010 and demonstrated continued commitment to strong IPR enforcement. The importance the Korean government places on IPR protection has increased dramatically in recent years as the digitization of Korea's economy has significantly enhanced the ability to produce and spread unauthorized reproductions of copyrighted material. With Korea's products and trademarks enjoying global success, Korean creators of intellectual property stand to benefit from improvements in the domestic intellectual property regime. In addition, although significant progress has been made, concerns remain with elevated levels of online piracy, software piracy, book piracy in universities, counterfeiting of consumer products, protection of undisclosed test and other data for pharmaceutical marketing approval, and a lack of coordination between Korean health and IPR authorities to prevent the issuance of marketing approvals for patent infringing products. The KORUS trade agreement includes provisions to address these issues.

The Ministry of Culture, Sports, and Tourism (MCST) amended its Copyright Law in July 2009 to include a "Three Strikes" program, a graduated response regime to confront illegal online file sharing. The provisions are aggressive and strong implementation in 2010 remained one of the year's most important developments in IPR. Under the amended law, MCST can order online service providers (OSPs) to issue warning letters to users downloading illegal materials or direct users to delete illegal files.

Separately, under the Information and Telecommunication Network Act, MCST took unprecedented steps to block access to illegal file-sharing sites. MCST issued three separate sets of orders in 2010 to block service to a total of 25 OSPs, most of which were hosted on overseas servers (16 online shopping sites, 7 game servers, and 2 webhard operators). Although many of the sites can migrate to other servers, the action marked an important shift in

For additional analytical, business and investment opportunities information,
please contact Global Investment & Business Center, USA
at (202) 546-2103. Fax: (202) 546-3275. E-mail: rusric@erols.com

government efforts to combat piracy. This is the first use of the Telecommunication Act to block access to file-sharing sites, which is usually used to restrict traffic to pornographic or North Korea-related online material.

The ROKG continues to demonstrate commitment to investigating and prosecuting "topsites." Little known to the general public, topsites are computer servers that hold tens of thousands of pirated software, games, music and movie files. ROKG ministries met with music industry stakeholders to discuss investigatory techniques. The ROKG has expressed to US Embassy Seoul its intention to carry out enforcement actions against topsites.

In the area of software enforcement in 2010, MCST concentrated most its efforts on the corporate sector. MCST raided 1,161 companies for software infringement issues, compared to 809 in 2009. MCST says its inability to tackle both public and private simultaneously is due to staff shortages stemming from a 2008 government reorganization effort. For 2011, MCST and other relevant government agencies have received funding for additional staff that should increase capacity and enable MCST to address software issues across both public and private sectors.

MCST also increased the number of IPR-related cases referred to prosecutors in 2010, recommending 539 cases for legal action compared to 312 in 2009. Of the 539 cases, prosecutors secured indictments for 248, the same number as 2009.

Korean patent law is a "first to file" regime. Although the law is fairly comprehensive and affords protection to most products and technologies, a US company must be registered with the Korean Intellectual Property Office (KIPO) to obtain legal protection. KIPO has amended relevant laws regarding restrictions on patent term extension for certain pharmaceutical, agrochemical, and animal health products that are subject to lengthy clinical trials and domestic testing requirements. An issue of continuing concern, however, has been the lack of coordination between the Korean Food and Drug Administration and KIPO and related issues that have resulted in the granting of marketing approval for unauthorized copies of pharmaceutical products.

Korea's Trademark Act has been amended to strengthen provisions that prohibit the registration of trademarks without the authorization of foreign trademark holders by allowing examiners to reject any registrations made in "bad faith." Despite this change, the complex legal procedures that US companies must follow to seek cancellation have discouraged US companies from pursuing legal remedies. In particular, problems still arise with respect to "sleeper" trademark registrations filed and registered in Korea without authorization in the late 1980s and early 1990s, when KIPO was still developing a more effective and accurate trademark examination and screening process.

Korean laws on unfair competition and trade secrets provide a basic level of trade secret protection in Korea, but are insufficient in some instances. For example, foreign firms, most notably in chemicals, pet food, cosmetics, and food products, face continuing problems with government regulations requiring submission of very detailed product information, such as formula or blueprints, as part of registration or certification procedures. These firms report that, although the release of business confidential information is clearly forbidden under Korean law, there is not sufficient controls over such materials and trade secrets appear to have been made available to Korean competitors or to relevant Korean trade associations.

TRANSPARENCY OF REGULATORY SYSTEM

The Korean regulatory environment can pose challenges for all firms, both foreign and domestic. Laws and regulations are often framed in general terms and are subject to differing interpretations by government officials, who rotate frequently. This creates frustrations for foreign investors that are looking for certainty in the Korean market. The KORUS FTA includes many provisions designed to address such issues.

The Korean government may restrict investments that disrupt production of military products or equipment, or if the company the foreigner is investing in exports items that may be later used for military purposes differing from their originally intended use. Foreigners linked to a country or an organization that may pose a threat to national security will also be subject to limitations on their investments in Korean firms. Related government agencies must ask MKE to review the case within 30 days of a foreign investor filing an application for regulatory approval, and MKE needs to make a decision within the following 90 days. Older bureaucratic practices designed to influence the decisions of businesses and investors through prescriptive regulations and placements of officials on corporate boards are sometimes still encountered.

According to Korea's Administrative Procedures Act, proposed laws and regulations (Acts, Presidential Decrees or Ministerial Decrees) should be published and public comments solicited for at least 20 days prior to promulgation. Draft bills are often available on the web sites of relevant ministries, without notice that they have been published. The rule-making process often remains non-transparent, particularly for foreigners. Proposed rules are often published with insufficient time to permit public comment and industry adjustment. For example, regulatory changes originating from legislation proposed by members of Korea's National Assembly are not subject to public comment periods. When notifications of proposed rules are made public, they usually appear in the Official Gazette, but not consistently, and only in the Korean language; thus, much of the 20-day comment period can be exhausted translating complex documentation.

President Lee Myung-bak has made regulatory reform one of the key elements of his economic policy, and progress is expected to be gradually achieved. President Lee established and heads the National Competitiveness Committee to identify measures to improve Korea's competitiveness, including regulatory reform. Likewise, the Prime Minister's Deregulation Taskforce Team, the Corporate Resolution Center and the standing Regulatory Reform Committee focus on regulatory reform as well.

EFFICIENT CAPITAL MARKETS AND PORTFOLIO INVESTMENT

Financial sector reforms are often cited as one reason for the ROK's rapid rebound from the global financial crisis. Financial sector reforms have aimed to increase transparency and investor confidence. Since 1998, the Korean government has recapitalized the banks and non-bank financial institutions; closed or merged weak financial institutions; resolved many non-performing assets; introduced internationally-accepted risk assessment methods and accounting standards for banks; forced depositors and investors to assume appropriate levels of risk; and taken steps to help end the policy-directed lending of the past. These reforms addressed weak supervision and poor lending practices in the Korean banking system that helped cause and exacerbate the 1997-98 Asian financial crisis.

In the course of stabilizing Korea's banking sector during the Asian financial crisis, the Korean government injected public funds, thereby acquiring de facto ownership of many of Korea's commercial banks -- although it publicly committed to refraining from interfering in bank lending and management decisions, "except with regard to prudential supervision." In late 2002, the Korean government began its ambitious plan to re-privatize the banks under its control, with the program initially scheduled to end by the first quarter of 2005. Much of this re-privatization has taken place, although the government continues to own the majority of shares in Woori Bank and minority shares in some other banks. The total assets of Korea's commercial banks as of the end of September 2009 were 1,185.2 trillion won, or about USD 1.03 trillion.

Foreign banks are allowed to establish subsidiaries or direct branches. Further relaxation of regulations has widened foreign access to Korea's capital markets and permitted foreign financial firms to engage in non-hostile mergers and acquisitions of local financial institutions. Currently, foreign interests control three of Korea's eight major commercial banks: Citibank Korea (formerly KorAm Bank); Korea Exchange Bank and SC/Korea First Bank. The National Assembly in 2010 amended the Bank Act to: (1) require banks to have outside directors constitute the majority of directors; and (2) forbid majority shareholders and related individuals from being outside directors.

Korea routinely permits the repatriation of funds, but reserves the right to limit capital outflows in certain circumstances, such as situations when uncontrolled outflows might harm the balance of payments, cause excessive fluctuations in interest or exchange rates, or threaten the stability of domestic financial markets. The Korean government did not impose such restrictions either during the Asian financial crisis or the global financial crisis, where sharp capital outflows played a major role. But the government recently put a series of capital control measures under the name of "macro-prudential stability policy" - lowering FX forward-position limits for foreign bank branches in June 2010, re-introducing a withholding tax on foreign investors' government bond purchases in December and imposing a bank levy on non-deposit financing in foreign currency in the second half of 2011.

Foreign portfolio investors now enjoy good access to the ROK stock market. Aggregate foreign investment ceilings in the Korean Stock Exchange (KSE) were abolished in 1998, and foreign investors owned 32.9 percent of KSE stocks and 10.3 percent of the KOSDAQ as of the end of 2010. The market turnover rate was 292 percent of market capitalization in 2010. Retail investors are extremely active in the Korean stock markets. More than 80 percent of KSE and KOSDAQ retail trading is conducted online. Thus, a large majority of retail investors are day traders, implying a constant source of volatility for the markets. The Korean government permits stock purchases on margin, requiring that transactions be settled within three business days.

Short-term interest rates, currently at around 2.8 percent, remain competitively high. Inflation, meanwhile, remained at 2.9 percent throughout 2010. The spread between short-term money (the overnight call rate) and long-term money (the benchmark 3-year corporate bond rate) rose from its 54-plus basis points maximum in 2007 to 153-basis points in 2008 to 318-basis points in 2009. The spread fell below 150-basis points in late 2010. As a countermeasure against financial instability and potential economic recession, the Bank of Korea (BOK) cut its target rate six times by 325-basis points from 5.25 percent in August 2008 to a record-low level of 2.0 percent in February 2009. The central bank raised rate twice by 25-basis point in July and November last year amid potential risks of inflation in the near future.

COMPETITION FROM STATE OWNED ENTERPRISES

Restrictions on foreign ownership of public corporations remain, although ownership limit levels have been raised. Currently, foreign ownership is limited for government-controlled utilities. Foreign ownership in Korean telecommunications companies and cable networks is limited to 49 percent. The Korean government intends to privatize many of the remaining state-owned corporations, but this process was slowed by the global financial crisis.

CORPORATE SOCIAL RESPONSIBILITY

Investors and financial markets remain wary of corporate governance in Korea despite significant improvements since the 1997-98 Asian financial crisis. Concerns about corporate governance often reduce the price/earnings ratios to levels lower than comparable companies elsewhere. Korean policy makers acknowledge that foreign investors often exact a "Korea Discount" when dealing with Korean companies or in making investment decisions. As the Chairman of the Korean Free Trade Commission (KFTC) stated in 2005, "the main reasons for the Korea Discount are opaque accounting techniques, less respect for minority shareholders, insufficient openness and excessive control by controlling families." Large gaps continue to exist between the ownership and control of a significant number of firms in Korea, with many traditional "chaebol" conglomerates still controlled by their founding families, despite the family's apparently low ownership stakes. Korea's accounting reform plan and Code of Best Practices are admirable efforts, but more can be done in these areas as well. Increasing participation by foreign investors and stockholders, modernizing business-government relations, and infusing professionalism in the corporate culture could go a long way toward improving corporate governance.

Although the Anti-Monopoly and Fair Trade Act has been repeatedly amended (most recently in March 2009), the practical impact of Korea's laws and policies regulating monopolistic practices and unfair competition remain limited by the long-standing economic strengths of the chaebol or family-run and vertically integrated Korean conglomerates. Management control at the Korean chaebol continues to involve complicated webs of cross-shareholdings among chaebol affiliates, and many chaebol still conduct business based on family and personal connections.

Chaebol-government relations can also sometimes influence the business-government dialogue, to the detriment of foreign and small and medium-sized enterprises (SME's). Thus, chaebol influence in the Korean economy may sometimes cause practical business problems for foreign investors. SME suppliers, for example, may be reluctant to deal with foreign firms for fear of jeopardizing a prized chaebol relationship. Obtaining access to credit may be complicated by the privileged relationships competing chaebol enjoy with local banks -- although this is mitigated by the fact that regulations limit a bank's exposure to any single chaebol group's companies to 25 percent of capital, and stipulate that 25 percent of all banks' lending, at least, must go to SME's.

There are several large Korean corporations that have transformed themselves into well-managed multinational corporations that have adopted "best practices" in corporate governance consistent with US and international standards. Some of their "best practices" include more frequent board meetings covering real operational issues; boards with more independent board members and fewer or no founding family members; a nominating committee for the board; financial report certifications; and frequent and substantive outside audits.

Foreign ownership is also playing a significant role in promoting corporate governance reform in Korea. Korean firms with significant foreign investment, for example, are generally understood to be more reluctant to participate in government-sponsored bailouts of troubled firms, impacting the evolution of Korean financial markets. As foreign investors now own about 60 percent of the shares in some of Korea's top companies and nearly 33 percent of stock listed on Korea's main stock exchange, the rights of minority and non-Korean stockholders are becoming more clearly expressed.

Under Korea's 2005 Securities Class Action Act, minority shareholders are able to file class action suits for manipulation of share prices, false disclosure of information, and accounting malpractice. The first class-action suit was filed in April 2009 by 1700 shareholders against

Jinsung, a KOSDAQ-listed maker of machine parts, for losses allegedly caused by accounting fraud. The case settled out of court in January 2010 for approximately USD 2.5 million.

The Korean government is currently implementing an accounting reform plan, taken largely from the US Sarbanes-Oxley Act, aimed at making Korean accounting standards consistent with rigorous international standards. The International Financial Reporting Standards (K-IFRS) will become Korea's Generally Accepted Accounting Principles by 2011. In parallel, a committee of Korean private sector experts has established a Code of Best Practices in response to a tasking by the finance ministry.

The voluntary recommendations included in this Code are in line with OECD principles, and the Korea Exchange (KRX) has reinforced the importance of the Code by requiring that companies listed on the Korea Stock Exchange (KSE) provide information to investors about the extent to which they conform to the Code. Following are some of the key recommendations contained in the Code of Best Practices:

> Easing of ownership thresholds to allow small shareholders greater rights to inspect company books;
> Having outside or independent directors make up at least half (rather than a quarter) of the board members of listed companies;
> Establishing a nominating committee to choose board members, with at least half of the committee consisting of outside directors;
> Ensuring that outside directors are truly independent, with no interests in the company, the management, or the controlling shareholder;
> Having the board of directors meet at least once every three months; and
> Requiring that companies have audit committees consisting of at least three directors, of which two-thirds are outside directors.

POLITICAL VIOLENCE

Legally, the Democratic People's Republic of Korea (also known as North Korea or the DPRK) and the Republic of Korea (ROK) are in a state of war. There is general peace and stability on the Korean peninsula because of an armistice agreement that has lasted for close to 60 years. From time to time incidents involving military and political provocations have attributed to increased tension between the countries. The unprovoked sinking of a ROK naval vessel by the DPRK in March 2010 and the artillery shelling of an island off the northwest coast of the ROK in November 2010 resulted in increased tensions. Military incidents have remained limited to the area surrounding the five geographically isolated Northwest Islands.

Korea does not have a history of political violence directed against foreign investors. The Embassy is unaware of any politically motivated threats of damage to foreign-invested projects or foreign-related installations of any sort, nor of any incidents that might be interpreted as having targeted foreign investments. Labor violence unrelated to the issue of foreign ownership, however, has occurred in foreign-owned facilities in the past.

CORRUPTION

Corruption, including bribery, raises the costs and risks of doing business. Corruption has a corrosive impact on both market opportunities overseas for US companies and the broader business climate. It also deters international investment, stifles economic growth and development, distorts prices, and undermines the rule of law.

It is important for US companies, irrespective of their size, to assess the business climate in the relevant market in which they will be operating or investing, and to have an effective compliance program or measures to prevent and detect corruption, including foreign bribery. US individuals and firms operating or investing in foreign markets should take the time to become familiar with the relevant anticorruption laws of both the foreign country and the United States in order to properly comply with them, and where appropriate, they should seek the advice of legal counsel.

The US Government seeks to level the global playing field for US businesses by encouraging other countries to take steps to criminalize their own companies' acts of corruption, including bribery of foreign public officials, by requiring them to uphold their obligations under relevant international conventions. A U. S. firm that believes a competitor is seeking to use bribery of a foreign public official to secure a contract should bring this to the attention of appropriate US agencies, as noted below.

US Foreign Corrupt Practices Act: In 1977, the United States enacted the Foreign Corrupt Practices Act (FCPA), which makes it unlawful for a US person, and certain foreign issuers of securities, to make a corrupt payment to foreign public officials for the purpose of obtaining or retaining business for or with, or directing business to, any person. The FCPA also applies to foreign firms and persons who take any act in furtherance of such a corrupt payment while in the United States. For more detailed information on the FCPA, see the FCPA Lay-Person's Guide at: http://www.justice.gov/criminal/fraud/

Other Instruments: It is US Government policy to promote good governance, including host country implementation and enforcement of anti-corruption laws and policies pursuant to their obligations under international agreements. Since enactment of the FCPA, the United States has been instrumental to the expansion of the international framework to fight corruption. Several significant components of this framework are the OECD Convention on Combating Bribery of Foreign Public Officials in International Business Transactions (OECD Antibribery Convention), the United Nations Convention against Corruption (UN Convention), the Inter-American Convention against Corruption (OAS Convention), the Council of Europe Criminal and Civil Law Conventions, and a growing list of US free trade agreements. The Republic of Korea is also party to the OECD Convention on Combating Bribery of Foreign Public Officials in International Business Transactions since 1999, and a member of the Asia Pacific Economic Cooperation Anti-Corruption and Transparency Experts Task Force (APEC ACT).

OECD Antibribery Convention: The OECD Antibribery Convention entered into force in February 1999. As of December 2009, there are 38 parties to the Convention including the United States (see http://www.oecd.org/dataoecd/59/13/40272933.pdf). Major exporters China, India, and Russia are not parties, although the US Government strongly endorses their eventual accession to the Convention. The Convention obligates the Parties to criminalize bribery of foreign public officials in the conduct of international business. The United States meets its international obligations under the OECD Antibribery Convention through the US FCPA.

UN Convention: The UN Anticorruption Convention entered into force on December 14, 2005, and there are 143 parties to it as of December 2009 (see http://www.unodc.org/unodc/en/treaties/CAC/signatories.html). The UN Convention is the first global comprehensive international anticorruption agreement. The UN Convention requires countries to establish criminal and other offences to cover a wide range of acts of corruption. The UN Convention goes beyond previous anticorruption instruments, covering a broad range of issues ranging from basic forms of corruption such as bribery and solicitation, embezzlement, trading in influence to the concealment and laundering of the proceeds of corruption. The Convention contains transnational business bribery provisions that are functionally similar to those in the OECD Antibribery Convention and contains provisions on private sector auditing and books and records requirements. Other provisions address matters such as prevention, international cooperation, and asset recovery. The ROK signed the United Nations Convention against Corruption on December 10, 2003 and ratified it on March 27, 2008.

OAS Convention: In 1996, the Member States of the Organization of American States (OAS) adopted the first international anticorruption legal instrument, the Inter-American Convention against Corruption (OAS Convention), which entered into force in March 1997. The OAS Convention, among other things, establishes a set of preventive measures against corruption, provides for the criminalization of certain acts of corruption, including transnational bribery and illicit enrichment, and contains a series of provisions to strengthen the cooperation between its States Parties in areas such as mutual legal assistance and technical cooperation. As of December 2009, the OAS Convention has 33 parties.

Council of Europe Criminal Law and Civil Law Conventions: Many European countries are parties to either the Council of Europe (CoE) Criminal Law Convention on Corruption, the Civil Law Convention, or both. The Criminal Law Convention requires criminalization of a wide range of national and transnational conduct, including bribery, money-laundering, and account offenses. It also incorporates provisions on liability of legal persons and witness protection. The Civil Law Convention includes provisions on compensation for damage relating to corrupt acts, whistleblower protection, and validity of contracts, inter alia. The Group of States against Corruption (GRECO) was established in 1999 by the CoE to monitor compliance with these and related anti-corruption standards. Currently, GRECO comprises 46 member States (45 European countries and the United States). As of December 2009, the Criminal Law Convention has 42 parties and the Civil Law Convention has 34 (see http://www.coe.int/t/dghl/monitoring/greco/default_en.asp).

Free Trade Agreements: While it is US Government policy to include anticorruption provisions in free trade agreements (FTAs) that it negotiates with its trading partners, the anticorruption provisions have evolved over time. The most recent FTAs negotiated now require trading partners to criminalize "active bribery" of public officials (offering bribes to any public official must be made a criminal offense, both domestically and trans-nationally) as well as domestic "passive bribery" (solicitation of a bribe by a domestic official). All US FTAs may be found at the US Trade Representative Website at http://www.ustr.gov/trade-agreements/free-trade-agreements. The Republic of Korea-US Free Trade Agreement is awaiting Congressional approval. Consult the USTR Website at http://www.ustr.gov/trade-agreements/free-trade-agreements/korus-fta.

Local Laws: US firms should familiarize themselves with local anticorruption laws, and, where appropriate, seek legal counsel. While the US Department of Commerce cannot provide legal advice on local laws, the Department's US and Foreign Commercial Service can provide assistance with navigating the host country's legal system and obtaining a list of local legal counsel.

Assistance for US Businesses: The US Department of Commerce offers several services to aid US businesses seeking to address business-related corruption issues. For example, the US and Foreign Commercial Service can provide services that may assist US companies in conducting their due diligence as part of the company's overarching compliance program when choosing business partners or agents overseas. The US Foreign and Commercial Service can be reached directly through its offices in every major US and foreign city, or through its Website at www.trade.gov/cs.

The Departments of Commerce and State provide worldwide support for qualified US companies bidding on foreign government contracts through the Commerce Department's Advocacy Center and State's Office of Commercial and Business Affairs. Problems, including alleged corruption by foreign governments or competitors, encountered by US companies in seeking such foreign business opportunities can be brought to the attention of appropriate US government officials, including local embassy personnel and through the Department of Commerce Trade Compliance Center "Report A Trade Barrier" Website at tcc.export.gov/Report_a_Barrier/index.asp.

Guidance on the US FCPA: The Department of Justice's (DOJ) FCPA Opinion Procedure enables US firms and individuals to request a statement of the Justice Department's present enforcement intentions under the anti-bribery provisions of the FCPA regarding any proposed business conduct. The details of the opinion procedure are available on DOJ's Fraud Section Website at www.justice.gov/criminal/fraud/fcpa. Although the Department of Commerce has no enforcement role with respect to the FCPA, it supplies general guidance to US exporters who have questions about the FCPA and about international developments concerning the FCPA. For further information, see the Office of the Chief Counsel for International Counsel, US Department of Commerce, Website, at http://www.ogc.doc.gov/trans_anti_bribery.html. More general information on the FCPA is available at the Websites listed below.

Exporters and investors should be aware that generally all countries prohibit the bribery of their public officials, and prohibit their officials from soliciting bribes under domestic laws. Most countries are required to criminalize such bribery and other acts of corruption by virtue of being parties to various international conventions discussed above.

Public sector corruption: The law provides criminal penalties for official corruption, and the government generally implemented these laws effectively. According to the Transparency International Global Corruption Barometer 2010, only two percent of South Koreans asked said they had paid bribe to at least one nine different service providers (in customs, education, the judiciary, land related services, medical services, the police, registry & permit services, tax authorities, and utilities) in the past 12 months. Of the 21 economies surveyed in the Asia Pacific, ROK enjoyed the lowest percentage along with Australia.

The ROK signed the United Nations Convention against Corruption on December 10, 2003 and ratified it on March 27, 2008 and is also a party to the OECD Convention on Combating Bribery of Foreign Public Officials in International Business Transactions since 1999, and a member of the Asia Pacific Economic Cooperation Anti-Corruption and Transparency Experts Task Force (APEC ACT). The law provides criminal penalties for official corruption, and the government generally implemented these laws effectively. By law, public servants above a certain rank must register their assets, including how they were accumulated, thereby making their holdings public.

There are several government agencies responsible for combating government corruption including the Board of Audit and Inspection, which monitors government expenditures and the Public Service Ethics Committee, which monitors the civil servants' financial disclosures and their financial activities within their tenure and first few years into their retirement. Since February 2008, the Anti-Corruption and Civil Rights Commission manages the public complaints and administrative appeals on corrupt government practices. The Korean government in 2008 also established a Financial Intelligence Unit and has cooperated fully with US and United Nations efforts to identify and shut down sources of terrorist financing. Transparency International has maintained a National Chapter in ROK since 1999.

ANTI-CORRUPTION RESOURCES

Some useful resources for individuals and companies regarding combating corruption in global markets include the following:

Information about the US Foreign Corrupt Practices Act (FCPA), including a "Lay-Person's Guide to the FCPA" is available at the US Department of Justice's Website at http://www.justice.gov/criminal/fraud/fcpa.

Information about the OECD Antibribery Convention including links to national implementing legislation and country monitoring reports is available at http://www.oecd.org/department/0,3355,en_2649_34859_1_1_1_1_1,00.html. See also new Antibribery Recommendation and Good Practice Guidance Annex for companies at http://www.oecd.org/dataoecd/11/40/44176910.pdf

General information about anticorruption initiatives, such as the OECD Convention and the FCPA, including translations of the statute into several languages, is available at the Department of Commerce Office of the Chief Counsel for International Commerce Website at http://www.ogc.doc.gov/trans_anti_bribery.html.

Transparency International (TI) publishes an annual Corruption Perceptions Index (CPI). The CPI measures the perceived level of public-sector corruption in 180 countries and territories around the world. The CPI is available at http://www.transparency.org/policy_research/surveys_indices/cpi/2009. TI also publishes an annual Global Corruption Report which provides a systematic evaluation of the state of corruption around the world. It includes an in-depth analysis of a focal theme, a series of country reports that document major corruption related events and developments from all continents and an overview of the latest research findings on anti-corruption diagnostics and tools (see http://www.transparency.org/publications/gcr).

The World Bank Institute publishes Worldwide Governance Indicators (WGI). These indicators assess six dimensions of governance in 212 countries, including Voice and Accountability, Political Stability and Absence of Violence, Government Effectiveness, Regulatory Quality, Rule of Law and Control of Corruption at http://info.worldbank.org/governance/wgi/sc_country.asp. The World Bank Business Environment and Enterprise Performance Surveys may also be of interest and are available at http://go.worldbank.org/RQQXYJ6210.

The World Economic Forum publishes the Global Enabling Trade Report, which presents the rankings of the Enabling Trade Index, and includes an assessment of the transparency of border administration (focused on bribe payments and corruption) and a separate segment on corruption and the regulatory environment at http://www.weforum.org/en/initiatives/gcp/GlobalEnablingTradeReport/index.htm.

Additional country information related to corruption can be found in the US State Department's annual Human Rights Report available at http://www.state.gov/g/drl/rls/hrrpt/.

Global Integrity, a nonprofit organization, publishes its annual Global Integrity Report, which provides indicators for 92 countries with respect to governance and anti-corruption. The report highlights the strengths and weaknesses of national level anti-corruption systems. The report is available at http://report.globalintegrity.org/.

BILATERAL INVESTMENT AGREEMENTS

The United States has a bilateral Treaty of Friendship, Commerce, and Navigation with Korea, which contains general provisions pertaining to business relations and investment. During former Korean President Kim Dae-jung's visit to the United States in 1998, President Clinton and President Kim agreed to negotiate a Bilateral Investment Treaty (BIT) between the two nations. However, negotiations in 1998 and 1999 stalled after the two sides could not resolve differences on certain issues. The Korea-US FTA contains strong, enforceable investment provisions that will go into force if the agreement is approved and implemented.

OPIC AND OTHER INVESTMENT INSURANCE PROGRAMS

US investments in Korea are eligible for insurance programs sponsored by the US Overseas Private Investment Corporation (OPIC). OPIC has not, however, guaranteed any US investments in Korea since June 1998, when OPIC reinstated coverage it had suspended in 1991 due to concerns about worker rights. Coverage issued prior to 1991 is still in force. Korea has been a member of the World Bank's (IBRD) Multilateral Investment Guarantee Agency (MIGA) since 1987. The Ruby Tuesday franchise used an OPIC loan in 2005 to open its first restaurant in the ROK.

LABOR

According to the Ministry of Employment and Labor (MOEL), there were approximately 25 million economically active persons in ROK with employment rate (OECD standard) of approximately 63 percent as of September 2010. In August 2004, ROK implemented a "guest worker" program known as the Employment Permit System (EPS) to help protect rights of foreign workers, who previously entered ROK as "trainees" and were exposed to egregious abuses from their employers. Since the mid-1980s, ROK companies began hiring "unskilled" foreign workers to overcome labor shortages in what were termed "3-D" jobs - the difficult, dirty and dangerous ones that most Koreans shun. The EPS allows employers who cannot hire Korean workers to legally employ a certain number of foreign workers from countries such as the Philippines, Indonesia and Vietnam where ROK maintains bilateral labor agreements.

At the year's end, approximately 220,000 foreigners were said to be working under EPS in manufacturing, construction, agriculture, livestock, service and fishery industries. The law provides workers with the right to associate freely and allows public servants to organize unions. In January, the labor law was amended to authorize union pluralism starting in July 2011. The ratio of organized labor to the entire population of wage earners in 2009 was approximately 10 percent. The country has two national labor federations, the Korean Confederation of Trade Unions (KCTU) and the Federation of Korean Trade Unions (FKTU), and an estimated 4,886 labor unions. The KCTU and the FKTU affiliated with the International Trade Union Confederation (ITUC). Most of the FKTU's constituent unions maintained affiliations with international union federations.

The law provides for the right to collective bargaining and collective action, and workers exercised these rights in practice. The law also empowers workers to file complaints of unfair labor practices against employers who interfere with union organizing or who discriminate against union members. The National Labor Relations Commission can require employers found guilty of unfair practices to reinstate workers fired for union activities. The law permits public servants to organize trade unions and bargain collectively, although it restricts the public service unions from collective bargaining on topics such as policy-making issues and budgetary matters.

Workers in export processing zones (EPZs) have the rights enjoyed by workers in other sectors, and labor organizations are permitted in the EPZs. However, foreign companies operating in the EPZs are exempt from some labor regulations, including provisions that mandate paid leave, obligate companies with more than 50 persons to recruit persons with disabilities for at least 2 percent of their workforce, encourage companies to reserve 3 percent of their workforce for workers over 55 years of age, and restrict large companies from participating in certain business categories.

The Labor Standards Act prohibits the employment of persons under age 15 without an employment authorization certificate from the MOEL. Because education is compulsory through middle school (approximately age 15), few employment authorization certificates were issued for full-time employment. To obtain employment, children under age 18 must obtain written approval from either parents or guardians. Employers must limit minors' overtime hours and are prohibited from employing minors at night without special permission from the MOEL.

Korea's minimum wage is reviewed annually. This year, labor and business set the minimum wage at 4,110 won (approximately $3.50) per hour, which was a 2.75 percent increase from last year. This increase was in line with 2.75 percent increase in the minimum cost of living. The Labor Standards Act also provides for a 50 percent higher wage for overtime.

The government sets health and safety standards, and Korea Occupational Safety and Health Agency (KOSHA) is responsible for monitoring industry adherence to these standards. KOSHA conducts inspections both proactively according to regulations and reactively in response to complaints. It also provides technical assistance to resolve any deficiencies discovered during inspections. KOSHA reports on its website descriptions of and statistics on work-related injuries and fatalities on a quarterly basis. As of June, there were 48,066 work-related accidents and 1,028 fatalities, which were 6.3 percent increase and 2.9 percent decrease respectively from the same period last year. KOSHA provides training and subsidies to improve work safety and reduce work-related accidents. Its services are extended to the migrant workers as its training modules and materials are available in 10 languages and disseminated to various worksites.

Contract and other "non-regular" workers accounted for a substantial portion of the workforce. MOEL reported that there were approximately 5.7 million non-regular workers, comprising approximately 33 percent of the total workforce as of August 2010. The MOEL reported that in 2009 non-regular workers performed work similar to regular workers but received approximately 84.3 percent of the wages of regular workers.

Korea passed significant legal reforms in late 2006 to expand protections for non-regular workers. The reforms banned discrimination against these workers and required that non-regular workers employed longer than two years be converted to regular workers.

The two-year rule went into effect on July 1, 2009. In addition, Korean courts have ruled in favor of non-regular workers in several cases and directed employers to convert them to permanent status after two-years of employment. Both the labor and business sectors have complained that the two year conversion law forces many businesses to limit the contract terms of the non-regular workers to two-years and incur the sunk cost for entry of new labor every two years.

FOREIGN-TRADE ZONES/FREE PORTS

Korea aims to attract more foreign investment by promoting its six Free Economic Zones (FEZ): Incheon (near Incheon Airport, to be completed in 2020); Busan/Jinhae (in South Gyeongsan Province, to be completed in 2020); Gwangyang Bay (in South Gyeongsan Province, to be completed in 2020); Yellow Sea (in South Chungcheong Province, to be completed 2025); Daegu/Gyeongbuk (in North Gyeongsan Province, to be completed in 2020); and Saemangeum/Gunsan (in North Jeolla Province, to be completed in 2030). The FEZs differ from other zones designated for foreign investment in their focus on creating a comprehensive living

For additional analytical, business and investment opportunities information,
please contact Global Investment & Business Center, USA
at (202) 546-2103. Fax: (202) 546-3275. E-mail: rusric@erols.com

and working environment with biotechnology, aviation, logistics, manufacturing, service and other industrial clusters as well as international schools, recreational facilities, and international hospitals. In 2009, the National Assembly passed the Special Act on Free Economic Zones to increase tax benefits for investment, increase the FEZ infrastructure budget, and streamline the approval process for land development.

On December 28, 2010, the government announced a plan to abolish inefficient, underperforming and unfeasible portions of the nation's free economic zones (FEZs) as part of its efforts to reorganize the specially created districts. By the plan, the Ministry of Knowledge Economy will remove the FEZ status from 90.51 square kilometers (22,366 acres) within the designated districts by February, accounting for 15.9 percent of the total land in the zones. According to the ministry, the six FEZs have attracted just USD 2.73 billion in investments since 2003 - yet the country has spent 85.4 trillion won (USD 74.3 billion) to promote the areas and build infrastructure in them.

There are also six Foreign-exclusive Industrial Complexes in Korea in different parts of the country, designed to provide inexpensive plant sites, with the national and local governments providing assistance for leasing or selling in such sites at discounted rates. In addition, there are four "Free Trade Zones" in Iksan, Gunsan, Daebul and Masan where companies may pursue their business with government support, but without the usual legal requirements such as approval procedures for export and imports and customs duties. There are also seven Foreign Investment Zones designated by local governments to accommodate industrial sites for foreign investors. Special considerations for foreign investors vary among these options. A good source of information on Korea's various free trade zone schemes is the government-run "Invest Korea," an inward investment promotion organization under the Korea Trade and Investment Promotion Agency (KOTRA). It can be reached at:

Invest Korea, KOTRA Bldg. 300-9
13, Heolleungno, Seocho-gu, Seoul, Republic of Korea
Tel: (82-2) 3460-7545
Fax: (82-2) 3460-7946/7
http://www.investkorea.org

The Korean government also continues to put significant effort into programs to enhance the quality of life in Korea for foreign investors and their families. There are 45 foreign schools in Korea and two large foreign schools in the Incheon FEZ and Jeju will open their doors in September 2011 (More information is available in a government website, "www.isi.go.kr"). The government more recently launched three-year programs aimed at enhancing the foreign investment climate in Korea. The Korean government has improved the legal framework for those areas by revising the FEZ Act and the Foreign Investment Act to provide cash grants for foreign investments of more than USD 10 million.

FOREIGN DIRECT INVESTMENT STATISTICS

(USD Millions)	Annual Flow			Cumulative Stock
	2008	2009	2010	2010
Total Inward FDI	11,711	11,484	12876	173,585
United States	1,328	1,486	1,974	43,783
China	335	160	414	3,086
Japan	1,424	1,934	2,083	25,975

United Kingdom	1,233	1,953	650	10,699
Other	7,391	5,951	7,756	90,042
Total Outward FDI	36,722	30,406	24,790	232,686
United States	6,233	3,910	3,555	39,262
China	4,587	2,624	2,587	43,401
Japan	639	412	275	3,887
United Kingdom	237	1,936	3,270	8,594
Other	25,026	21,524	15,103	137,542

Source: The Export-Import Bank of Korea and Ministry of Knowledge Economy

Note: This data is based on the notification of cases. The 2010 outflow is data reported for the first nine months of the year.

MAJOR INDUSTRIES

AUTOMOBILES

PRODUCTION AND SALES PLUMMET AS DOMESTIC DEMAND WANES

Automobile production in May amounted to just 156,000 units, down 37.1 percent from the same month of last year, as domestic sales plummeted. Production of compact cars also fell due to strikes at some plants. Domestic automobile sales fell 61.8 percent on a year-to-year basis to 52,000 units in May, as the drop in disposable income in the wake of economic downturn and the rise in oil prices dampened sentiment among potential purchasers. Compacts cars were the only category registering sales increases, in this case, a three-fold rise over a year earlier, while sales of small and medium size passenger cars nose-dived by more than 80 percent.

Total sales of passenger cars in May plunged 63.6 percent on a year-to-year basis to 37,000 units. Sales of commercial vehicles fell by 56.6 percent to only 15,000 units. Sales of buses and trucks dropped by 63.2 and 50.7 percent, respectively. Exports of related goods declined 0.7 percent from a year earlier. Whereas overseas sales of compact cars maintained their upward trend with particularly strong sales by Daewoo Motor, their rate of increase slowed in May compared to the same month of last year.

TEXTILES

Textile Exports Remain Sluggish

Exports of textile products sank to $1.52 billion in May, down 8.7 percent from the same period last year. The overall decline was due to low sales of fabric goods, yarn and material, although shipments of manufactured goods continued to boom. Shipments of material declined 14.6 percent to $65 million, as both operating rates and export prices fell.

Exports of yarn, impacted by waning demand from major markets like Hong Kong and China, dwindled 15.4 percent to $841 million. However, exports of manufactured goods, bolstered by enhanced price competitiveness following the depreciation of the won and promotional efforts by the industry, increased 10.4 percent to $473 million. Exports to the United States, particularly clothing and textile F yarn, rose 17.4 percent while those to China and Hong Kong decreased 23.6 and 24.6 percent, respectively. Textile imports declined 44.4 percent to $218 million compared with May of last year due mainly to the continued appreciation of U.S. dollar against the won and shrinking domestic consumption.

GENERAL MACHINERY

U.S., EU Demand Boosts Exports of General Machinery by 15.1 Pct

Orders received by Korean machinery builders in May marked a 41.7 percent decrease on a year-to-year basis as demand declined rapidly from both the public and private sectors. Orders from the public sector including transportation (off 98.9 percent) and communications (off 47.1 percent) were down 39.9 percent in total, while private sector demand in this respect posted a 41.9 decrease, most notably in the areas of traffic, storage and communications (off 45.8 percent) and the auto industry (off 31.2 percent).

May's general machinery exports rose to $725 million, up 15.1 percent from a year earlier, thanks to a rise in demand from the United States, the European Union and China and despite contracted sales in Japan and Southeast Asia. Most machinery products except lifters experienced booming sales in overseas markets. Soaring exports from this sector were due mainly to shipments of chemical and metal manufacturing machinery, which posted increases in this regard of 134.9 and 71.5 percent, respectively. Previously torpid shipments of construction and agricultural equipment jumped in May by 28.1 and 28.8 percent, respectively.

Because of shrinking domestic facility investment, general machinery imports tumbled 58 percent on a year-to-year basis to $673 million. Only imports of textile machinery were up, registering an increase of 26 percent on May of 1997. Imports of chemical and construction machinery, meanwhile, posted steep declines of 82.8 and 75.4 percent, respectively.

ELECTRICAL AND ELECTRONIC GOODS

Exports of Electrical & Electronic Goods Decline 9.2 Pct

Exports of electrical and electronic goods in May fell to $3.15 billion, down 9.2 percent from the same month of last year, as shipments in almost all sectors including industrial electronic goods, electronic components, and home appliances weakened. Cumulative exports as of the end of May amounted to $15.6 billion, a 3.1 percent decrease on a year-to-year basis. Shipments of industrial electronic products shrank 7.5 percent to $713 million, impacted mainly by sluggish shipments of computers.

Exports of electronic parts also fell; they were down nine percent from a year earlier to $1.97 billion primarily because of poor semiconductor sales. Within the sector only LCDs recorded an increase of shipments, boosted by sales to the United States which surged 43.5 percent in the same period. Despite strong sales in the U.S., exports of electronic home appliances declined overall to $463 million, the result of weak sales in the depressed markets of Southeast Asia.

SHIPBUILDING

SHIPBUILDING ORDERS

For additional analytical, business and investment opportunities information, please contact Global Investment & Business Center, USA at (202) 546-2103. Fax: (202) 546-3275. E-mail: rusric@erols.com

Boosted by a surge in receipts by Hyundai Heavy Industries, orders received by the Korean shipbuilding industry rose to 1,774,000 G/T in May for a total of 29 ships, up a whopping 245 percent from a year earlier. Cumulative orders for the year as of the end of May also rose 7.9 percent to 3,906,000 G/T for 70 ships. Orders for full container ships reached 685,000 G/T, amounting to 38.6 percent of total orders, followed by tankers, bulk carriers and automobile carriers, orders for which amounted to 438,000 G/T, 327,000 G/T and 220,000 G/T, representing shares of 24.7, 18.5 and 12.3 percent of the total, respectively.

Actual shipbuilding output for May declined 498,000 G/T for 10 ships, down 15.3 percent from the same month last year. However, cumulative output as of the end of May was up 12.6 percent on last year's totals to 2,960,000 G/T. Outstanding orders as of the end of May stood at 18,574,000 G/T for 309 ships, a 32.1 percent increase from the corresponding period of last year, providing steady work for Korean yards for at least two years in advance.

In the meantime, despite the continued financial crunch, the nation's shipbuilders outpaced those of Japan in order receipts in April and in terms of cumulative order receipts as of the end of May. Orders received by the Japanese industry as of May amounted to just 2,620,000 G/T, down 48.2 percent from a year earlier or two-thirds of the 3,906,000 G/T, on the order books of Korean shipbuilders.

PETROCHEMICAL INDUSTRY

Petrochemical Exports Rise 49.7 Pct

Production of petrochemical products increased to 1,051,000 tons in May, up 18.2 percent from a year earlier. The increase followed a rise in production capacity for synthetic resin, material and rubber, and despite a reduction in operating days at some work sites. May's figures, though, represented a 6.5 percent decrease from a month earlier while the industry's average operational ratio fell to 75 percent, down seven percentage points from the previous month. While production soared, forwarding for the purpose of domestic consumption declined 6.4 percent on a year-to-year basis, due to the impact of the recession on buying power. Exports, however, increased 49.7 percent from a year earlier, thanks to overseas promotional efforts by the industry to offset declining domestic demand.

STEEL

Steel Industry Output Continues Slide

Production of crude steel products in May declined 2.6 percent to 3,511,000 M/T, compared to the corresponding period of last year as client industry demand continued to weaken. Revolving furnace production amounted to 2,038,000 M/T while that from electrical furnaces amounted to only 1,473,000 M/T, a 10.1 percent decrease from a year earlier

Sales of steel goods in May increased by four to nine percent for certain items such as hot-rolled boards and reinforcing rods, while sales of cold-rolled boards and steep pipes posted declines. To counter sliding domestic demand individual manufacturers have focused their efforts on export promotion. The result has been sales of $734 million in overseas markets, up 29.7 percent from the same month of last year. However, May's exports were down 13.2 percent on those of April's due to anti-dumping measures by Canada, the United States and countries of the European Union.

For additional analytical, business and investment opportunities information, please contact Global Investment & Business Center, USA at (202) 546-2103. Fax: (202) 546-3275. E-mail: rusric@erols.com

ENERGY SECTOR PROFILE

After making a strong recovery in 1999-2000 from the effects of the Asian financial crisis in 1997-1998, South Korea's economy was negatively affected by the global economic slowdown of 2001-2002, but has begun to recover in 2002. Growth in real gross domestic product (GDP) is projected at 5.8% for 2002, up from 3.3% in 2001 but down from the 9.2% achieved in 2000. The recovery has been fuelled by domestic demand, even though export growth has been somewhat weak. Increased government spending, largely on infrastructure projects, has been a major contributor to increased domestic demand.

In the wake of the Asian financial crisis, South Korea has began an economic reform program designed to address some of the conditions which made its economy vulnerable. Most importantly, the South Korean government has begun to break the hold of the chaebols (large, multi-industry conglomerates) over the financial sector. The lack of an "arms length" business relationship between borrowers and lenders had led to many South Korean financial institutions having a very large ratio of non-performing loans. While there is no intention of forcing the chaebols to divest their financial subsidiaries, the government has increased regulation to prevent chaebols from abritrarily channeling money into other subsidiaries. Chaebols also have been pressed to spin off their non-core businesses and to rationalize their corporate structures. To stimulate domestic demand, the South Korean government under President Kim Dae-jung enacted a package of tax cuts directed at lower and middle-income workers.

The South Korean government has plans to privatize several large state-owned enterprises (SOEs), including the state electricity utility, Korean Electric Power Corporation (KEPCO) and natural gas monopoly Korea Gas Company (KOGAS). The privatization program has moved at a slower pace than originally planned, due in part to strong opposition from labor unions to some of the privatizations and delays in passing implementing legislation.

South Korea recently joined the International Energy Agency (IEA). Its membership became effective in April 2001, upon its fulfillment of the requirements for membership, and was formally ratified by the South Korean government in March 2002.

OIL

With no domestic oil reserves, South Korea must import all of its crude oil. Oil makes up the largest share of South Korea's total energy consumption, though its share has been declining in recent years. Petroleum accounted for 56% of primary energy consumption in 2000. South Korea consumed more than 2.1 million barrels a day (bbl/d) of oil in 2000, down from a high of nearly 2.3 million bbl/d in 1997, all of which was imported. South Korea is the seventh largest oil consumer and fourth largest crude oil importer in the world.

South Korea's total reliance on oil imports has led to a policy of securing and diversifying the country's oil supply. South Korea has both a short-term and a long-term approach to fulfilling its oil needs. In the short-term, it has developed a strategic petroleum reserve, which is managed by the state-owned Korea National Oil Corporation (KNOC). Strategic stocks are roughly equivalent to a 90-day supply. The period of "import cover" was expanded from 60 days in early 2001, in part to meet the requirements for entry into the IEA. This reserve serves as a safety net against supply disruptions.

In the long term, KNOC is pursuing equity stakes in oil and gas exploration around the world. KNOC has 18 overseas exploration and production projects in 13 countries. This includes 4 producing fields in Yemen, Argentina, Peru, and the North Sea, and 4 fields under development in Yemen, Venezuela, Libya, and Vietnam. KNOC also is exploring domestic blocks offshore from South Korea. KNOC reported a new oil find in August 2001 at the Vung Tau site offshore from Vietnam, which is expected to be developed and in production by 2003. Recoverable reserves at Vung Tau are estimated at 420 million barrels. The South Korean government has stated that it plans for KNOC to provide for 10% of the country's oil needs by 2010.

The South Korean refining industry was strongly affected by the country's economic crisis in 1997-1998, especially because it already suffered from significant overcapacity before the downturn in demand. In September 1998, South Korea's four downstream oil companies raised the retail price of gasoline and diesel oil following a government tax hike. In October 1998, the South Korean government, under financial pressure, decided to fully deregulate the refining industry, accelerating this decision from the original January 1999 deadline in order to attract badly needed foreign investment. Foreign backing has proved critical in maintaining cash flows and preserving the creditworthiness of the refining industry.

Several corporate consolidations and selloffs occurred as a result. In September 1998, Hanwha's 270,000-bbl/d refinery in Inchon was taken over by Hyundai Oil Refinery Company, giving Hyundai the country's third largest refining capacity (after SK Corporation and LG-Caltex) with 580,000 bbl/d. In October 1999, Hyundai completed the sale of a 50% interest in its refining operation to the Abu Dhabi International Petroleum Investment Corporation, which was intended to reduce the company's highly leveraged debt-to-equity ratio. Ssangyong Group sold its 28.4% stake in Ssangyong Oil Refining Corporation to its majority shareholder, Saudi Aramco, in 2000. The firm's name was changed to S-Oil.

Despite the consolidation in South Korea's refining sector, it has yet to fully recover from the effects of the Asian financial crisis and the shock of the 1998 deregulation. Profit margins have remained very weak through 2002.

NATURAL GAS

South Korea currently relies on imported liquefied natural gas (LNG) to meet its entire demand for natural gas, though a project currently under development will make the country a minor natural gas producer by early 2003. Imports of LNG began in 1986, after the founding of the state-owned monopoly LNG importer Korea Gas Company (Kogas). South Korea currently gets most of its LNG from Indonesia, Malaysia, and Qatar, with smaller volumes from Brunei and Oman. The supplies from Qatar began in August 1999, under a contract with Qatar's new Ras Laffan LNG (RasGas) venture. The first shipment of Omani LNG was loaded in April 2000. In 2000, natural gas comprised around 10% of South Korea's primary energy consumption. South Korea is the second largest importer of LNG worldwide, importing 669 billion cubic feet (Bcf) of LNG in 2000. South Korea's annual LNG imports increased by 140% between 1993 and 1997, but fell by 9% in 1998 due to the effects of the Asian financial crisis. In 1999, however, South Korea's LNG imports grew by 22%, followed by 10% growth in 2000, as its economy recovered and new supplies from Qatar came onstream. South Korean natural gas demand is split almost evenly between the electricity sector and the residential heating sector.

Despite the temporary downturn, Kogas is planning to push ahead with projects for the expansion of LNG receiving terminals. South Korea is increasing capacity at its existing terminals (Pyongtaek and Inchon). Also, Mitsubishi Corporation of Japan and Pohang Iron and Steel Corporation signed a letter of intent in October 1998 to build an LNG receiving terminal in South Korea at Kwangyang. Construction of the facility started in June 2002, and current plans call for it to be completed in the first half of 2005.

The South Korean government announced in 1999 that it intends to privatize Kogas. An initial public offering of 33% of Kogas equity was carried out in December 1999. Privatization plans initially stalled, however, due to questions about the structure of the companies, which would result if Kogas were split for privatization, and opposition from labor unions representing Kogas employees. Current plans call for the Kogas privatization to take place in 2003, but legislation necessary to put the process in motion has not been passed by the South Korean legislature. The uncertainty over the future structure of the industry has led to delays in Kogas concluding agreements for new LNG supplies, even though additional volumes of LNG beyond current contracts are expected to be needed by 2004.

In addition to LNG imports, South Korea will have a small amount of domestic natural gas production starting in 2003. KNOC's $320 million Donghae-1 development project is developing a natural gas deposit offshore from Ulchin in southeastern South Korea estimated to contain 200 Bcf of reserves. Donghae-1 is a relatively minor development, however, and will satisfy only about 2% of South Korea's gas demand once it comes onstream.

Meanwhile, South Korea also is exploring the possibility of a gas pipeline from the Kovykta natural gas deposit in the Irkutsk region of Eastern Siberia. The pipeline would supply China as well as South Korea, and might run through North Korea. The project as currently envisioned would supply about 1 Bcf/d to South Korea, and a larger volume to China, possibly beginning around the end of the decade. The two Koreas agreed in September 2001 to conduct a joint feasibility study of the pipeline project, which has not yet concluded. Since the only overland route the pipeline could take would cross North Korea, renewed tensions on the Korean peninsula have called South Korea's participation in the project into question.

COAL

Coal supplies about 20% of South Korea's total energy requirements. Most of this coal is imported, since the only indigenous coal resources consist of low-quality anthracite used in home heating and small boilers. Bituminous coal supplies (steam coal for power plants and industrial boilers and metallurgical coal for steelmaking) come mainly from Australia and China, with the United States also among the suppliers. State power company KEPCO has invested in several Australian coal mines. China has become a significant supplier of coal to South Korea in the last two years, as its coal export volumes have increased, displacing some of the volume from Australia.

ELECTRIC POWER

South Korea uses a combination of thermal (oil, gas, and coal), nuclear, and hydroelectric capacity to meet its demand for electric power. Total power generation capacity was 50 gigawatts (GW) as of the beginning of 2000. The South Korean government estimated in May 2002 that its electricity demand will rise at an average annual rate of 3.4% per year through 2015.

In September 1998, KEPCO officially dedicated its Ulchin Number 3 nuclear reactor and launched the construction of Ulchin Nuclear Power Plants Numbers 5 and 6. Ulchin Number 3 has a generating capacity of 1 GW and is the first nuclear power plant built completely with South Korean technology from design to construction. The Number 4 Ulchin nuclear plant was completed in late 1999, and Numbers 5 and 6 are targeted to be completed in 2004 and 2005.

The South Korean government is moving ahead with plans to break up and privatize KEPCO. The South Korean government plans to split KEPCO into separate generation, transmission, and

For additional analytical, business and investment opportunities information, please contact Global Investment & Business Center, USA at (202) 546-2103. Fax: (202) 546-3275. E-mail: rusric@erols.com

distribution units. Progress has been slow, however, due to opposition from labor unions. In early 2001, KEPCO split its power generation holdings into six separate subsidiaries, in a preliminary move to facilitate a split into competing companies. Five of the six operate thermal and hydroelectric facilities and are of roughly equal size in terms of installed generating capacity - between 7 and 8 GW. The sixth is comprised of all of KEPCO's nuclear plants, which will be kept together in one corporation under government ownership. The privatization plan has been controversial, with unions fearing layoffs by new management and some politicians opposing foreign ownership. Current plans call for the first of the five generating units, Korea Southeast Power, to be sold off by January 2003. The other four thermal generation companies are to be sold by 2005.

While most of South Korea's generating capacity is still controlled by KEPCO, a few independent power producers (IPPs) exist. LG Power, owned by the LG Group conglomerate, operates a 540-megawatt (MW) independent power plant at Bugok near Asan Bay. The facility began operation in April 2001. LG Power purchased the existing Anyang and Puchon plants in June 2000, with a combined capacity of 950 MW, from KEPCO after a competitive tender. Tractebel is also investing in a new 519-MW IPP plant in Yulchon in partnership with Hyundai. In another significant development, South Korea's original IPP, Hanwha Energy was spun off from its chaebol parent company in June 2000, in a deal in which El Paso Energy acquired a 50% stake. Hanwha Energy operates a 1,800-MW plant at Inchon.

While South Korea is not a party to the Kyoto Protocol on greenhouse gas emissions, its future plans emphasize the development of more nuclear power plants to reduce growth in carbon emissions. A dozen additional nuclear plants are planned before 2015.

ENVIRONMENT

For years, South Korea was one of Asia's fastest growing, most successful economies. This rapid industrialization and growth in income, however, has had environmental impacts. Car ownership, for example, has increased significantly. Transboundary pollution is also a concern in the region and has led to the formation of a joint commission of environmental ministers from South Korea, China and Japan to tackle the problem.

Over the past decade, total energy consumption and carbon emissions have increased in South Korea. In 2000, South Korea consumed 7.9 quadrillion Btu's of energy and emitted 115.3 million metric tons of carbon. Energy intensity (energy consumption per $1995 of GDP) increased from 11.1 thousand Btu per $1995 in 1990 to 12.8 thousand Btu per $1995 in 2000. Per capita energy use increased from 88.1 million Btu per person in 1990 to 166.7 million Btu per person in 2000.

Because increasing total production was South Korea's primary energy goal during its period of rapid industrialization, there was little focus on the development of renewable energy resources. However, as the price of fossil fuel imports in South Korea rose in 1999 and 2000, attention turned to the importance of diversifying the energy mix. One of South Korea's goals for the 21st century, expanded in its National Vision for Environmental Policies in the 21st Century, is the promotion of green development schemes, such as increased usage of photovoltaic power and fuel cells.

ECONOMIC SITUATION AND OVERVIEW

MAJOR TRENDS AND OUTLOOK

For additional analytical, business and investment opportunities information, please contact Global Investment & Business Center, USA at (202) 546-2103. Fax: (202) 546-3275. E-mail: rusric@erols.com

Slower economic growth, financial weakness among Korea's largest firms, falling exports, and a severe credit crunch have marked the Korean economy since mid-2000. This economic slowdown is in stark contrast to the 18 months of a sharp economic rebound from the 1997-98 financial crisis that Korea enjoyed from January 1999 to July 2000. Despite some recent signs of more economic vitality resulting from Korean government's economic stimulus efforts and the recovery of domestic demand, the future prospects for the economy are still uncertain due to incomplete restructuring and a weakening external environment, including slower U.S. economic growth. Korea's gross domestic product (GDP) grew 8.8% in real terms in 2000, led by very impressive growth of the first quarter (12.6%). GDP growth remained strong through mid-2000 (11.1%), but started to slow from the second quarter (9.7%) and continued to weaken in Q3 (9.2%), Q4 (4.6%), and Q1 2001 (3.7%). The Korean economy is expected to grow 4.6% in 2001 and slightly higher in 2002. Inflation is expected to be in the 3-5% range.

Steadily growing foreign portfolio and direct investment flows have been major engines driving Korea's economic restructuring as well as a key to Korea's prompt recovery from its crisis-related slowdown. Foreign direct investment (FDI) during the years 1999 ($15.5 billion) and 2000 ($16.1 billion) exceeded total FDI during the previous 35 years (1962-1997). FDI continues to increase in 2001, with $5.4 billion in commitments during the first five months, or 20.2% above the same 1999 period. Net purchases in the Korean stock market by foreign investors amounted to 4.2 trillion Korean won or KRW (about $3.2 billion) during the first four months of 2001. For 2000, foreign players bought a net total of 11.3 trillion KRW (about $10 billion) of Korean shares. As of May 2001, foreign portfolio investors owned 32% (KRW 79.4 trillion) of the market capitalization of the Korean Stock Exchange (KSE) and 43.16% (KRW 51.86 trillion) of Korea's top 10 conglomerates. Korea's December 1997 financial crisis coincided with the inauguration of President Kim Dae-jung, who embraced a $58 billion IMF package, including loans from the IMF, World Bank, and the Asian Development Bank, as Korea's best chance to recover. Under the terms of the IMF program, Korea agreed to open its financial and equity markets to foreign investment and to reform and restructure its financial and corporate sectors to increase transparency, accountability and efficiency.

By April 2001, the government had injected close to $119 billion in public funds to recapitalize the banks and the financial sector. To strengthen lending practices, regulators forced banks to adopt international accounting standards and use forward-looking criteria (FLC) when making provisions for non-performing loans. A new "mark-to-market" system, which more accurately reflects the current "market" value of the assets of the investment trust industry, went into effect on July 1, 2000. To decrease "moral hazard", banks were also encouraged to put ailing corporate borrowers under continuous credit-risk assessment (CCRA). As of April 2001, 1,544 companies were under creditor bank CCRA.

In corporate restructuring, about half of the top 30 business groups ("chaebol" or conglomerates), including Hanbo, Daewoo, Dong-A, Haitai, and Sammi, were removed from the market. The new "top 30" also reportedly trimmed their collective debt/equity ratios to 171% by year-end 2000, down from 295% in 1998. The debt/equity ratios of the top four Korean chaebol (Hyundai, Samsung, LG, and SK) also reportedly fell from 469% in 1997 to 162% in 2000, well below the government-mandated 200%. Despite improving their debt/equity ratios, the chaebol reduced their overall debt very little; rather, chaebol affiliates increased their equity, by selling shares either to the public or to other members of the same chaebol group, a practice which led to "double counting" of assets. Thus, debt-equity ratios actually may not have been as low as reported. The chaebol were required to issue consolidated financial statements beginning with fiscal year 2000, partly to avoid "double counting."

The success of Korea's financial and corporate-sector restructuring is essential to encourage a high pace of productive domestic and foreign investment. Since 1998, President Kim's government has been instrumental in reforming and opening Korea's economy to foreign investment and reducing trade barriers. Wide-ranging reforms have accelerated the evolution of Korea's financial and corporate sectors away from the previous state-led economic model toward a commercial free-market model. The Korean government's continued direct or indirect involvement in the economy often has conflicted with its goal of pushing toward a market economy.

The Daewoo Group bankruptcy in 1999 and the Hyundai Engineering & Construction (HEC) liquidity crisis during 2000 and 2001, posed considerable challenges to the government's program of financial reform and Korea's continued financial stability. With around $80 billion in debt, Daewoo's demise was by far the largest corporate bankruptcy in modern history. Moving swiftly to restore investor confidence and avoiding any hint of a bail out, the Korean government facilitated agreements between the stricken company's affiliates and Daewoo's domestic and foreign creditors. Huge financial losses and associated loss of investor confidence hit hard Korea's investment trust industry, a heavy buyer of Daewoo bonds, as investors rapidly withdrew their funds. Buyers for corporate paper of any description all but disappeared and the bond market almost ceased to function, causing serious problems for companies that needed to raise money. The government's handling of the Daewoo collapse ended the myth that certain companies were "too big to fail" and served as a warning for companies to pursue sound financial policies and for investors to more carefully assess risk, serving to move the Korean economy in a more market-oriented direction. The government sent a much less clear signal to individual investors in Daewoo paper, and used public funds to shield them from suffering any appreciable loss. Also, the government's continuing financial support of Hyundai affiliates with liquidity problems has caused wide-scale skepticism among local and foreign investors about its continued commitment to economic reform.

Korea is emerging as one of the world's most "wired" economies as Koreans rapidly embrace the Internet and wireless information technologies. Korea, with 14 million internet users (out of a population of 45 million) by spring 2000, was the world's third leading internet country, after the United States and the United Kingdom, and has one of the world's highest per-capita usage rates for wireless telephones. Some 80% of retail stock transactions in Korea occur over the Internet. Also, the IT industry's share of GDP was 16.7% as of Q1 2001, up from 12.2% in 1999. In 1999 and 2000, investors poured venture capital into thousands of "dot-com" start-ups, and thousands of young Korean workers left traditionally secure chaebol jobs to work for venture firms and start-ups, although the slowdown in the global IT industry also has hit the Korean IT sector hard.

In May 2001, the Korean won had weakened to 1280-1310 KRW/dollar from around 1100 KRW/dollar one year before. In late 1997 the won fell to nearly 1,900 KRW/dollar when Korea's nearly depleted foreign currency reserves helped spark a financial crisis that required IMF intervention. Foreign reserves had grown to $93.6 billion at the end of May 2001. The ROKG's trade surplus estimate for 2001 is $12 billion.

Manufacturing led Korea's GDP growth in 2000, jumping 15.4%, a slight drop from 1999's 21.0% increase. Manufacturing's share of GDP grew to 34.2% in 2000, compared with 30.7% in 1999. Within the manufacturing sector, heavy industry and chemicals performed well in 2000, recording 18.5% growth year-on-year. Telecommunications, electronics, and industrial machinery were conspicuous with 30%-plus growth. Light industry, such as textiles, footwear and food products, had relatively modest growth in 1999 (8.9%) and 2000 (2.8%).

Unemployment was 3.8% in April 2001, slightly higher than the 3.7% rate at year-end 2000. While compensation levels and private consumption have improved strongly, recent unemployment rates still exceed the 2.6% level of 1997. Most analysts believe Korea will no longer be able to achieve such a low rate of unemployment given assumptions of a lower long-term economic growth rate and the more flexible labor market conditions that now prevail in Korea.

The number of newly established firms rose steadily each month in 1999 and 2000, exceeding the number of bankrupt firms by a factor of 15 or more. For example, in March 2001, firms declaring bankruptcy fell to less than 200 while newly established firms reached more than 3000. Given the much higher rate of firm bankruptcy in Western economies, many observers agree that Korea's bankruptcy rate reflects a serious under-estimation of the actual number of non-viable firms.

Korea's financial services and banking industries lagged behind the rest of the economy, growing only 4.7% in 2000 and 4.4% in Q1 2001. The poor performance of finance and banking services was mainly due to accelerated loan-loss provisioning, the large amount of unresolved non-performing loans; the lingering impact of the mid-1999 Daewoo collapse and the liquidity problems of Hyundai affiliates since mid-2000; the chronic poor performance of the bond market; a loss of investor confidence in the investment trust industry, and incomplete financial and corporate reform and restructuring. The non-financial services industry grew around 10% since 1997.

Construction, another sector which greatly under-performed relative to the rest of the Korean economy, continued to decline, shrinking 3.7% in 2000, following a 9.1% fall in 1999. In the first quarter of 2001, the construction industry finally rebounded, growing 1.6% year-on-year. Since 1998, the government has provided incentives to domestic and foreign firms to invest in infrastructure projects while removing restrictions on financing and imports.

Combined output from the agriculture, forestry, and fisheries sector shrank 3.4% in Q1 2001, reversing a 5.4% rise in 1999. Output from mining also decreased 5.9% in Q1 2001 after increasing by 2.2% in 2000. These two relatively small sectors accounted only for about 5% of GDP in 2000 and Q1 2001.

INVESTMENT

Excessive, often ill conceived, capital investment in the 1990s created over-capacity in many industries and strongly contributed to the 1997-98 economic downturn. Investment rebounded strongly in 1999 and 2000 but fell 3.7% year-on-year in Q1 2001. After falling 21.1% in 1998, fixed capital investment grew 3.7% in 1999 and 11% in 2000, although a weak construction sector negatively impacted overall 1999-2000 investment growth. Machinery and equipment investment grew an impressive 36.3% in 1999 and 34.3% in 2000, more than offsetting the contraction in 1998. In 2000, orders for imported machinery grew 40.6%, outpacing the 11.7% rise in domestic machinery and equipment orders. This situation reversed in Q1 2001, with domestic machinery and equipment orders increasing 3.7% while orders for imported machinery fell 1.2%. The average factory utilization rate for 2000 rose to 78.3% from 68% in 1998, but the rate in Q1 2001 fell to 74.6%.

CONSUMPTION

Expenditure on domestic consumption grew 6.2% in 2000, down from 9.4% growth in 1999. Domestic consumption accounted for 58.8% of GDP in 2000, down from 60% in 1999. Consumption was led by brisk private industrial investment and increases in private household expenditures. In contrast, government consumption increased marginally (1.3%). Ministry of Labor statistics show that nominal wages for regular employees grew 8% in 2000, down from 12.1% growth the previous year. The growth rate of wholesale and retail trade in 2000 was 9.4% (in constant value terms), down from 14.1% in 1999. Private consumption fell 0.9% in Q1 2001 as consumer sentiment turned negative.

For additional analytical, business and investment opportunities information, please contact Global Investment & Business Center, USA at (202) 546-2103. Fax: (202) 546-3275. E-mail: rusric@erols.com

EXPORTS

Korea's exports in the first four months of 2001 decreased 0.9% to $52.3 billion as a result of a sharp drop in principal exports such as semiconductors, telecom equipment, and steel.

On a customs clearance basis, Korea's merchandise exports grew 19.9% in 2000 to reach $172.3 billion ($143.7 billion in 1999). Despite a strengthening won (average for 1999: 1190 KRW/dollar; average for 2000: 1131 KRW/dollar), exports in 2000 increased partly due to growing worldwide demand for Korea's semiconductor and telecommunication goods and a strong Japanese yen. The United States was Korea's largest overseas market, followed by the EU and Japan. Korea was the eighth-largest source of U.S. imports in 2000, selling goods worth $37.6 billion. Exports in 2000 to the U.S., the EU and Japan rose 27.6%, 15.7%, and 29.0%, respectively. Korea's exports to Southeast Asia increased 17.4% in 2000 to $38.9 billion, compared with 11.3% growth in 1999. Southeast Asia took roughly 23% of Korea's exports in 1999 and 2000.

Semiconductors accounted for 12.4% of Korea's total 2000 exports, down slightly from 1999's 13.1% share. Korea is one of the world's leading producers of 64-megabyte and 128-megabyte DRAM chips. Despite falling world semiconductor prices, rising sales volume and new products increased Korea's semiconductor exports 12.9% to $21.3 billion in 2000.

In 2000, shipbuilding and steel exports increased 9.9% and 10.2% respectively, while vehicle exports rose 17.9% to $11.1 billion.

Main Export Destinations by Proportion (% of Total)

	1999	2000	(Jan-Apr) 2001
USA	20.5%	21.8%	20.1%
EU	14.1%	13.6%	13.3%
Japan	11.0%	11.9%	11.8%
China	9.5%	10.7%	11.3%
Southeast Asia	23.0%	22.6%	21.1%

MAIN EXPORTS

	2000	Change	(Jan-Apr) 2001	Change
Total Exports	172.3	19.9%	52.3	-0.9%
Semiconductors	21.3	12.9%	5.0	-19.3%
Telecom Equipment	28.1	68.0%	8.0	-5.0%
Steel	11.4	10.2%	3.6	-4.0%
Passenger Cars	11.1	17.9%	3.3	4.9%

Shipbuilding	8.2	9.9%	3.8	47.1%

Source: The Bank of Korea

IMPORTS

Korea's imports during the first four months of 2001 fell 5.7% to $49.2 billion, compared with a 34% increase during the same period of 2000. Imports overwhelmingly consisted of capital goods (37.9%) and raw materials and fuel (51.7%), while consumer goods amounted to only 10.4% of the import bill. U.S. exports to Korea in the first four months of 2001 fell 14.7% to $8.2 billion.

In 2000, Korean imports rose 34% to $160.5 billion and regained their1997 pre-crisis level. U.S. exports to Korea increased 21.59% in 2000 to $27.9 billion from $23.0 billion in 1999, and now exceed their 1997 level of $25 billion. Korea was the sixth-largest U.S. export market in 1999 and 2000, up from ninth in 1998. In 2000, Japan became Korea's largest import source, partly the result of the lifting of restrictions on Japanese imports in 1999. Korea's imports from Japan increased 34.9% to $31.8 billion in 2000.

Main Import Origins by Proportion (% of Total)

	1999	2000	(Jan-Apr) 2001
USA	20.8%	18.2%	16.7%
EU	10.5%	9.8%	10.1%
Japan	20.2%	19.8%	18.7%
China	7.4%	8.0%	8.2%
Southeast Asia	13.%	15.0%	16.0%

Korean imports for calendar year 2000 and first four months 2001 with year-on-year percentage change, CIF basis (US$ billions)

	2000	Change	Jan-Apr 2001	Change
Total Imports	160.5	34.0%	49.2	-5.7%
Crude Petroleum	25.2	70.6%	8.0	-1.8%
Semiconductors & Parts	19.7	22.6%	5.6	-8.9%
Chemicals & Products	11.8	20.8%	3.9	0.3%
Iron & Steel Products	6.0	26.5%	1.6	-25.1%
Machinery & Equipment	18.4	36.3%	5.5	-9.5%
Electric & Electronic Machinery	43.3	36.7%	12.0	13.2%
Cereals	2.4	5.1%	0.8	-1.5%

For additional analytical, business and investment opportunities information, please contact Global Investment & Business Center, USA at (202) 546-2103. Fax: (202) 546-3275. E-mail: rusric@erols.com

Source: The Bank of Korea

INFLATION

Korean price inflation continued to stay at a low level in 2000. The consumer price index grew 2.3% and producer prices grew only 2.0%. Worker demands for higher wages and price jumps in petroleum products are expected to create more inflationary pressure in 2001, with inflation for the year forecast about 4%.

Prices & Wages (annual % change)

	Consumer Prices	Producer Prices	Mfg. Wages
1980-89 (average)	8.4	6.9	15.3
1995	4.5	4.7	9.9
1996	5.0	3.2	12.2
1997	4.5	3.9	5.2
1998	7.5	12.2	-3.1
1999	0.8	-2.1	14.9
2000	2.3	2.0	8.5

Sources: Ministry of Labor and National Statistics Office

INTEREST RATE POLICY

After the ROKG introduced high interest rates late in 1997 as part of its IMF agreement, the ROKG returned to a low-interest rate policy in 1998. High interest rates were intended to ensure foreign currency liquidity and stabilise the exchange rate at a time when capital outflows rose rapidly due to Korea's weakened international credibility. Although high interest rates were inevitable in the context of the financial crisis, they caused the real economy to contract and pushed many firms toward bankruptcy.

Starting in Q2 1998, in consultation with the IMF, the government pursued lower interest rates to rescue the economy from a deep recession. As a result, the interbank call market rate slid to 6% in 1998 from its 20% peak in late 1997, before falling to as low as 4% in Q1 1999. Since mid-1998, the economy recovered well and the ROKG has maintained a low-interest rate policy with the benchmark call rate stabilized at slightly over 5% since year-end 1999.

PRINCIPAL GROWTH SECTORS

Year-on-Year % Change in Economic Indicators by Economic Activity (in 1995 constant prices) and sectoral share of GDP (2000 and Q1 2001 figures are preliminary)

	1999	2000	Share of 2000 GDP	Q1 2001
Gross Domestic Product	10.9	8.8		3.7

For additional analytical, business and investment opportunities information, please contact Global Investment & Business Center, USA at (202) 546-2103. Fax: (202) 546-3275. E-mail: rusric@erols.com

(GDP) growth rate				
Industry	20.9	15.2	34.5	4.2
Mining	5.3	2.2	(0.3)	-5.9
Manufacturing	21.0	15.4	(34.2)	4.3
- Light Industry	8.9	2.8	-	-4.6
- Heavy Industry	24.5	18.5	-	6.3
Services	11.9	9.0	48.8	3.9
Electricity, Gas & Water	10.4	12.6	(2.6)	11.3
Construction	-9.1	-3.7	(7.7)	1.6
Wholesale/Retail Trade, Restaurants & Hotels	14.1	9.4	(12.3)	2.6
Transport, Storage & Communications	14.5	16.7	(8.6)	8.8
Finance, Insurance, Real Estate & Business Services	5.5	4.7	(17.6)	4.4
Agriculture, Forestry & Fisheries	5.4	0.1	5.2	-3.4
Others*			11.5	
Total			100.0	
Exports of Goods, Services	15.8	21.6		8.4
Imports of Goods, Services	28.8	20.0		-0.7
Gross Domestic Income (GDI)	8.9	1.5		0.6

Note: Exports are on a free-on-board (FOB) basis, while imports are on a cost, insurance and freight (CIF) basis.
* Includes government services non-profit services to households, import duties, but excludes imputed bank service charges.

Year-on-Year % Change in Economic Indicators by Expenditure in 1995 Constant Prices. (2000 and Q1 2001 figures are preliminary)

(by proportion of GDP)	1999	2000	Q1 2001
Final Consumption Expenditure	9.4	6.2	0.4
Private Consumption	11.0	7.1	0.9
Government Consumption	1.3	1.3	-2.6
Gross Fixed Capital Formation	3.7	11.0	-3.7
Construction	-10.3	-4.1	1.4

Machinery & Equipment	36.3	34.3	-7.9

Source: The Bank of Korea

GOVERNMENT ROLE IN THE ECONOMY

The Korean government traditionally has pursued conservative macroeconomic policies. Government spending and taxes as a share of GDP are comparatively low by international standards, averaging about 21%-22% over the last few years. For several years before the 1997-98 financial crisis, the central government budget was virtually in balance. Moreover, the quality of public expenditure is high, with an emphasis on education and public works rather than on transfer payments. In 1998, with the support and encouragement of the IMF and World Bank, government spending rose 13.1% to stimulate the economy, raising its GDP share to 24.5%, with a fiscal deficit of about 5% of GDP. The quicker-than-expected recovery boosted tax revenues and allowed the government to balance the budget in 2000, earlier than the previous goal of restoring a balanced budget by FY 2006. The Korean government posted a consolidated fiscal budget surplus of $5 billion in 2000.

At the microeconomic level, past government intervention has been extensive and costly in terms of economic efficiency. Financial capital was and continues to be expensive, due in part to large non-performing loan portfolios saddled on banks during the highly interventionist 1970-1989 period, to government credit controls (with credit allocated largely by firm size) and to the overall lack of competition and rigidities in the financial system. Overseas capital transactions were tightly controlled. Investment and product safety regulations inhibited domestic competition across all sectors and often discriminated against foreign products, to the detriment of Korean consumers.

Under the terms of the 1998 IMF agreement, Korea largely opened its financial and corporate sectors to foreign investment, and reduced or removed controls on overseas capital transactions. President Kim Dae-jung's administration has stressed the role of markets over the government. The policies described in the investment climate section of this report show how the government is striving to put the economy and Korean companies on a market-driven commercial footing.

During the 1997-98 financial crisis, the government was forced to acquire the majority of Korea's commercial banks which faced insolvency. Even though the government has always declared its intention of reversing its nationalization of the banking sector, it has yet to publish an actual time schedule for selling the banks to private investors, saying that market conditions are not yet right. The government's continued ownership of much of the banking sector has produced a continual conflict of interest between its role as economic regulator and its interest in protecting government investments.

The Korean government also owns a total of 101 non-financial public enterprises, which account for 6-8% of GNP. The government has begun to privatize and sell off many of these enterprises to raise funds and to reduce the government's economic role. Although details remain to be worked out, the government has announced it will allow private and foreign investors to buy a varying proportion of shares (up to 100% in some cases) of these companies.

BALANCE OF PAYMENTS

Exports and imports are down through May 2001 as a result of slower global economic growth and Korea is expected to record a current account surplus in the range of $12-13 billion for the year. That would be slightly higher than the current account surplus for the year 2000 of close to $11 billion. Korea had a current account surplus of $24.5 billion in 1999, lower than the $40-billion surplus of 1998. The narrowing of the current account surplus in 1999 was largely due to import growth outpacing exports, as imports rebounded after consumption of foreign goods fell sharply as a result of the 1997/98 financial crisis.

Korea's capital account registered a deficit ($5.2 billion) for the first four months of 2001. The capital account had shown a surplus in 1999 ($2 billion) and 2000 ($11.7 billion) due mainly to inflows of foreign direct and portfolio investment. The foreign direct investment (FDI) surplus was $10.9 billion in 2000. Korean investment outflow was only $4.8 billion in 2000 as Korean businesses continued to scale back foreign operations in an effort to strengthen their financial position.

Korea's external liabilities totaled $136.3 billion at year-end 2000, a decline of 8.7% compared with $148.7 billion in 1998. A debtor nation at year-end 1998 with $20.2 billion in net outstanding loans, Korea became a net creditor by year-end 1999, with net outstanding loans due of $8.3 billion. The net outstanding loans due continued to rise to $33.3 billion at the end of April 2001. At the same time, Korea's gross external liabilities fell to $129.2, largely the result of persistent trade surpluses since 1998. At the same time, the share of short-term debt to total debt outstanding increased to 32.9% at the end of April 2001, up from 27.9% at year-end 1999, primarily due to increased short-term trade financing needs. Perhaps more significantly, short-term debt as a proportion of foreign reserves decreased to 45.7% by the end of April 2001 from 63.6% at year-end 1998. Korea's foreign exchange reserves rose sharply from $52 billion at year-end 1998 to $93.5 billion in April 2001. Most observers believe this level of reserves (that is, more than twice the amount of short-term debt) is more than sufficient to cover Korea's short-term financial outflows. Given that a sudden outflow of reserves triggered the 1997-98 financial crisis, some Koreans remain skeptical that even the current level of reserves is sufficient.

In mid-2001, the Korean won was trading at around 1300 KRW/dollar. For much of 2000, the won traded in the 1,100-1,120 KRW/dollar range. The Korean currency ended 1999 at 1145.4 KRW/dollar (average for 1999: 1189.5 won/dollar). The Korean currency appreciated around 15% in 1999 due in part increased foreign portfolio investment and Korea's trade surplus.

Balance of Payments
in US$ billions

	1998	1999	2000	(Jan-Apr) 2001
Current Balance	40.4	24.5	11.0	3.7
Trade in Goods	41.6	28.4	16.6	4.8
Exports FOB	132.1	145.2	175.8	52.9
Imports CIF	90.5	116.8	159.2	48.1
Trade in Services	1.0	-0.7	-4.0	-0.7
Net Transfers & Income	-2.2	-3.2	-1.6	-0.5
Caiptal Account	-3.2	2.0	11.7	-5.2
Direct Investment	0.7	5.1	3.5	0.4
Portfolio Investment	-1.9	8.8	12.1	1.6

For additional analytical, business and investment opportunities information, please contact Global Investment & Business Center, USA at (202) 546-2103. Fax: (202) 546-3275. E-mail: rusric@erols.com

Other Investment	-2.1	-11.4	-3.3	-7.1
Errors and Omissions	-6.2	-3.5	1.	0.7
Changes in Foreign Exchange Reservers	-31.0	-23.0	-24.2	0.8
Foreign Reserves (US$ billions)	52.0	74.1	96.2	93.5

(Note: Negative numbers denote an increase in reserves.)
Source: Bank of Korea, Korea Institute of Finance, and Korea Development Institute)

INFRASTRUCTURE

Korea's infrastructure continues to expand. Though it already possesses an extensive highway system with several major North-South and East-West highway arteries, the country's exploding vehicular traffic continues to strain the country's transport network. As a result, Korea's transport authorities have launched a multi-billion dollar expansion of the nation's highways. Municipal authorities also are expanding Seoul's already extensive subway system. Also, trains and buses travel regularly to the far reaches of the country. In addition, Korea has several international and many domestic airports in the largest cities, Incheon International Airport, Busan International Airport, Cheongju International Airport, and the international airport on Cheju island. The country is moving to expand airports that are currently incapable of handling ever-growing air traffic. The Incheon International Airport replaced Kimpo as Korea's principal international air hub. As a result, following Incheon's opening, Kimpo now exclusively handles domestic air traffic. Korea's port managers also are planning billions of dollars in major projects, as they race to catch-up with the country's sharp economic growth and jump in trade activity, which continues to strain existing facilities.

The Korean government and private sectors continue to vigorously expand and improve Korea's excellent information and communications information infrastructure development effort, called "Cyber Korea 21," which includes significant monetary commitments by the Korean government. The results of this initiative should benefit U.S. firms that choose to do business in Korea.

CORPORATE RESTRUCTURING

The current economic crisis in Korea has been provoked in large part by excessive corporate indebtedness amongst the major corporations known as chaebols. Over the last several decades, these major groups have expanded both in Korea and internationally via an aggressive use of leverage.

With the onset of the economic crisis in 1997 and the upward spike in interest rates, five major groups with a combined work force of 107,000 employees and won 26.7 trillion in assets (US$20.6 billion) quickly failed, unable to pay their debts. It soon became apparent that 18 of the largest 30 groups were at risk of bankruptcy (with combined employment of 255,000 and liabilities of won 103.4 trillion, US$79.5 billion). Not surprisingly, the major banks (with a government encouragement) provided a series of emergency loans to a number of major groups at risk which had not yet filed for bankruptcy; with a total loan value of some won 2 trillion, since the onset of the crisis (US$1.5 billion).

For additional analytical, business and investment opportunities information,
please contact Global Investment & Business Center, USA
at (202) 546-2103. Fax: (202) 546-3275. E-mail: rusric@erols.com

The problems of the largest groups quickly spread to small and medium enterprises (SMEs). Many of these SMEs operate as satellites of the major groups, dependent on them for business. The complex system of payments from the big firms to the small firms via promissory notes, traditionally discounted at the banks, also adversely affected the liquidity of these firms, as the terms of the notes were extended from an average of 30 to 60 days up to 90 and 180 days. Moreover, discounting rates quickly rose from 12 % to 25-30 %, if in fact banks accepted the notes at all.

The GOK has reacted promptly and comprehensively to the need to restructure the corporate sector. However, the scope and depth of the problem is unprecedented and will not be easily or rapidly resolved. There are inherent risks in any program of this complexity. Key elements of the Government's approach include, inter alia, the following: enhanced legal/regulatory support for corporate restructuring; creation of the Financial Supervisory Commission (FSC), an independent agency with the mandate to restructure both the corporate sector and the financial institutions; a focus on voluntary workouts for the chaebol that ranked "6 to 64" in asset size; a longer-term approach to restructuring of the Top 5 chaebol; and special relief for SMEs. The primary focus of the World Bank's corporate restructuring support to the Government has been to provide expert advice and other assistance to FSC on the conceptual design and implementation of its corporate restructuring program.

CURRENT DEVELOPMENTS

LEGAL/ REGULATORY FRAMEWORK

Soon after the current Government took office, the National Assembly passed a series of acts to make the legal/regulatory environment more conducive to corporate restructuring. These were supported by SAL I and II. Key initiatives include the following:

Tax Exemption and Reduction Act: provides tax breaks for restructuring of firms,
Bank Act: increases the ceiling on bank ownership of other firms' equity from 10 percent to 15 percent, or higher subject to FSC approval;
Corporation Tax Act: advances removal of deductibility of interest on excessive debt from 2002 to 2000;
Foreign Direct Investment and Foreign Capital Inducement Act: permits takeovers of non-strategic companies by foreign investors without Government approval and raises the foreign stock ownership ceiling (subsequently raised to 100 percent for non-strategic listed companies);
Securities Exchange Act: liberalizes mergers and acquisition activity by increasing the portion of shares that can be acquired without board approval from 10 percent to 33 percent;
Antitrust and Fair Trade Act: prohibits any new cross (debt) guarantees amongst and between chaebol affiliates and subsidiaries and eliminates all existing cross guarantees by 2000;
Employment Insurance Act: temporarily reduces the minimum contribution period and increases the minimum benefit period; and
Labor Standards Act: legalizes employee layoffs as a result of mergers and acquisition activity or to avoid financial distress.
International Accounting Standards: Recently, the FSC has approved the adoption of international GAAP for accounting purposes, supplemented by U.S. GAAP where international principles are deficient.

Voluntary workouts for mid-sized chaebol and other large corporations. The Government, under the auspices of the FSC has encouraged Lead Commercial Banks (LCBs) to focus on voluntary (out of court) workouts of the mid-size chaebols "6 to 64" for several reasons. These tend to be the chaebol in deepest distress. They generally lack the financial resources and clout to restructure on their own. A large number of insolvencies among this group could create an upsurge in unemployment, bringing severe social distress and political pressure on the Government to abandon its reform program.

Moreover, a series of major defaults could provoke a secondary financial crisis, leading to pressure on the currency and on interest rates. The "6 to 64" chaebol tend to be less complex and, therefore, potentially easier to restructure than the Top 5. As of the end of December 1998, 43 corporations of 16 separate chaebol from the group "6 to 64", 19 corporations of smaller chaebol and 10 large corporations had entered the workout process.

One group was rejected for workout and entered the formal insolvency process; while 12 of the remaining 15 chaebols from the group "6 to 64" had completed the workout process. This includes a number of large groups which had received emergency loans to stay afloat. It is anticipated that all of the workouts will be completed by year-end 1999, with the possibility of round two for those corporations which need deeper restructuring over the next two to three years.

Top 5 chaebol restructuring program. A restructuring program for the Top 5 Chaebol (Hyundai, Samsung, LG, SK and Daewoo) is focused on their voluntary restructuring efforts based on their Capital Structural Improvement Plans (CSIPs). The Big Deals or asset swaps and joint ventures are now considered an integral part of the CSIPs and currently fall under the purview of the FSC. Revised CSIPs have been submitted to the lead banks of the Top 5.

Once agreed to they will form the basis for debt restructuring agreements and a program, to be followed by the lead banks, with monitorable CR targets. A December 7 meeting between the Government, the lead banks and the Top 5 presided over by President Kim Dae-Jung produced detailed agreement on the major issues. Essentially all of the demands of the Government with respect to corporate governance, improved disclosure, consolidated accounting, reduction of debt/equity ratios and elimination of cross guarantees are incorporated within the CSIPs. The Top 5 and their lead banks announced agreement on the CSIPs on December 18. Their implementation will now need to be monitored by the banks.

Status of SMEs. SMEs continue to suffer from sharp drops in revenues due to declining demand and difficulty in obtaining working capital and trade finance. There has been some improvements in bankruptcy rate and default rate of promissory notes. The number of bankruptcies has gradually decreased, from a high of 3,000 bankruptcies per month between January-May, down to 1,800 in June, and about 1,000 in September. Also, the default rate on promissory notes dropped from 2% at end-1997 to 0.3% in September.

The government has tried to alleviate SME's constraints mainly by lowering banks' risks and increasing their incentives to lend, and stimulating SME demand for credit.

(i)   **Lowering banks' risk and increasing banks' incentives to lend to SMEs**; (a) Increasing credit guarantees. In January 1998, the government received US$1 billion from the Asian Development Bank (ADB) to re-capitalize the two main government credit guarantee funds, the Korea Credit Guarantee Fund (KCGF) and the Korea Technology Credit Guarantee Fund (KTCGF). The KCGF provides credit guarantees for SMEs and other companies with insufficient collateral, while the KTCGF provides similar functions to technology-oriented firms.

(ii)

For additional analytical, business and investment opportunities information,
please contact Global Investment & Business Center, USA
at (202) 546-2103. Fax: (202) 546-3275. E-mail: rusric@erols.com

(iii)   In September, the government further injected 500 billion won into KCGF and KTCGF. About 107,000 companies have received a total of 17 trillion won in credit guarantees; (b) Providing new funds for SMEs. The government has put in place or announced a number of new loan funds channeled either through commercial banks or specialized SME agencies; (c) Increasing rediscounting privileges of banks. The strongest incentive for banks to lend to SMEs is access to rediscount loans from the Bank of Korea at a very low interest rate. A significant portion of SME credit volume (estimated at 30-40%) is rediscounted at about 3% by the Central Bank, and makes up for the low premium in lending rates.

(iii) Stimulating enterprise demand for credit. On the demand side, the government has gradually lowered lending rates in efforts to ease the credit crunch that confronts most SMEs. Both long-term and short-term market interest rates have dropped sharply in comparison to the previous quarter. The average SME lending rate is currently about 12-13%.

IBRD SUPPORT FOR CORPORATE RESTRUCTURING IN KOREA

The Bank has maintained a consistent presence in Korea since its initial mission in February of 1998. It has provided on-going advisory support to the FSC on all aspects of corporate restructuring and has worked closely with the Financial Restructuring team. The Bank has been active in the following corporate restructuring (C.R.) areas:

Policy-based lending: Economic Reconstruction Loan (approved 12/97, US$3,000m), SAL I (approved 3/98, US$3,000m) and SAL II (approved 10/98, US$2,000m) have addressed C.R., governance (accounting/audit, bankruptcy, corporate law, etc.), state enterprise reform, among others, in addition to financial sector reform. A potential SAL III is under discussion.
Technical assistance: Financial and Corporate Restructuring Assistance Loan (approved 8/98, US$48.0m) supports C.R. of chaebols through lead banks as well as reform of securities markets, accounting/audit, competition policy, and the bankruptcy system; a PHRD grant (approved 8/98, US$1.3m) supports C.R. mainly of SMEs, as well as regulatory streamlining.
Budget-funded advice: 2 C.R. advisors working in Seoul; workshop on International Experience in Corporate Restructuring; report on competitiveness under preparation.

SOCIAL SECTOR REFORM

The social sector policy agenda comprises two main elements: improving the functioning of the labor market to facilitate economic restructuring; and strengthening social safety nets, not only to mitigate the impact of the current crisis and structural change on the most vulnerable, but also to make durable improvements to Korea's system of social protection.

SOCIAL PROTECTION FOR WORKERS

The unemployment rate has risen sharply to 7.6% in December, 1998 (or 1.67 million jobseekers) -- more than double the rate of 3.1% recorded at the onset of the economic crisis in December, 1997. An additional 1% have withdrawn from the active labor force, including large numbers of women. The unemployed are more likely to be male, and to have been previously a temporary worker, high school graduate, or small enterprise employee. Thus the unemployment problem is most severe amongst the lower-skilled and uninsured workers.

Unemployment is forecast to remain high in 1999, averaging 7.5%, with some 400,000 new school graduates joining the labor force and additional layoffs expected from ongoing corporate restructuring. In this environment of high unemployment, labor market policy aims to keep the natural rate of unemployment low by enhancing flexibility in labor allocation, providing cost-effective policies to promote re-employment, and offering temporary income support through unemployment insurance.

Achieving faster employment creation requires removal of labor market rigidities so as to narrow the wage differentials induced by restrictive practices that erode competitiveness. An important step forward was the introduction of legislation in February 1998 that permitted layoffs. Despite also legalizing the operation of manpower leasing companies, regulatory restrictions limit the supply of workers in only 26 professional occupations, and preclude supply of manual workers in the manufacturing sector without union agreement. There also limitations on the term of contract workers. These restrictions impose inefficient constraints on labor market flexibility and should be removed.

Active labor market policies include the Vocational Ability Development (VAD) and Employment Support schemes provided under the payroll-tax financed Employment Insurance System (EIS). Mandatory coverage of EIS, including the VAD and ES schemes (such as training and retraining, wage subsidies for reduced hours, relocation of employment etc.), was extended to firms with fewer than 5 workers in October 1998. Experience from OECD countries suggests that active labor market measures such as vocational training may not be cost-effective. Indeed, wage subsidies to non-viable establishments undermine the objective of efficient corporate restructuring. These cautions indicate that payroll tax rates for VAD and ES should not be increased, and that the cost-effectiveness of existing programs should be rigorously evaluated with inefficient programs amended or abandoned.

Provision of temporary income support for the unemployed was enhanced in October 1998 by extending Unemployment Insurance (UI) provisions of EIS to firms employing less than 5 workers and to temporary and part-time workers. This has increased UI coverage to some 8.7 million workers. The Government has also implemented enhancements in the benefit structure. The duration of insurance benefits was increased by two months for all categories of eligibility, with the minimum duration extended to four months (July 1998). The minimum replacement rate was also raised from 50% of earnings to 70% of the minimum wage.

PROTECTING THE POOR

In the past, Korea successfully relied on rapid growth and full employment to provide an adequate and rising standard of living for most of the population. As the economy is temporarily unable to provide full employment, the numbers of poor and vulnerable needing public assistance are growing, and new programs have been initiated to expand coverage and diversify the content of the social safety net. Preliminary estimates indicate that urban poverty had more than doubled by late 1998.

In 1996, only 1.5 million people were recipients of the means-tested Livelihood Protection program which provides a range of welfare benefits to the poor, including income support, health insurance and subsidy for school fees. In April 1998 the Government introduced a temporary livelihood program for 310,000 newly poor recipients. The 1999 budget plans an additional increase in coverage to 570,000 of the newly poor.

In May 1998 the Government implemented a new workfare program targeted at the unemployed and those with no regular income between the age of 15 and 65. Phase I of the program provided temporary employment for some 75,000 workers. Phase II of the program began in August 1998 and absorbed up to 150,000 workers. At the beginning of January 1999, as many as 650,000 jobseekers applied for enrollment in the public works program, and the government is committing to allocating adequate budget to absorb eligible workfare applicants, keeping the wage rate low to target the poor by self-selection

RISK MANAGEMENT FOR HEALTH

The instruments for managing financial risks in Korea comprise the Medical Insurance System (MIS) funded by mandatory social insurance contributions, and the budget-financed Medical Aid Program (MAP) for poor beneficiaries of the means-tested Livelihood Protection program. Since 1989, these risk management arrangements have achieved universal coverage in terms of enrollment: approximately 95% of the population is enrolled in MIS, with the remaining 5% enrolled by MAP.

But universal enrollment does not entail comprehensive coverage of financial risks. Instead, the Korean health insurance system is noted for its high coinsurance rates, which can impose a heavy burden of out-of-pocket costs on patients, especially the poor. As a result, Korea's private financing ratio is one of the highest in the world at 69% of aggregate health expenditure, considerably greater than the averages for East Asia (49%) and OECD (26%). Introduction of more efficient and equitable risk management mechanisms is an important objective of social policy during adjustment. In October 1998, the government sought to reduce administrative costs by consolidating previously fragmented health insurance societies. Measures to improve provider incentives for cost containment and refocus insurance on major risks are planned.

PENSION SYSTEM REFORM

The immaturity of the existing National Pension Scheme (NPS) means that the current generation of older Koreans must depend on their own earnings, savings and family support for their livelihood. For many, this will not be sufficient to prevent poverty and social assistance is required. In order to improve the existing low coverage and benefit levels, the 1999 budget doubled the allocation for the noncontributory means-tested social pension.

The NPS is likely to be the most important component of Korea's system of old age income security in the next century and reform efforts have naturally focused on it. Important legislation was passed in December 1998 aimed at achieving more transparent and efficient governance of NPS fund reserves by phasing out forced lending to the government by the year 2001. Nevertheless, the troubled system of mandatory retirement allowances and tax favored individual retirement savings are also important components of the overall system of old-age security. Millions of workers have acquired rights to retirement allowances payments whose magnitude is unknown and likely to be very large. These must be handled in the context of frequent bankruptcy and widespread corporate restructuring. At the same time, a new system of private pensions which avoids the problems of the current one must be designed.

These elements must be integrated into a comprehensive reform package. Such a package would (i) resolve the fiscal and labor market issues associated with the occupational schemes, (ii) outline the policy for dealing with accumulated retirement allowance liabilities, (iii) create a new private pension framework which would complement the NPS and (iv) deal with specific issues such as consistent tax treatment and supervision. The Government has created a new Task Force to pursue this objective and publish a White Paper by November 1999.

IBRD SUPPORT FOR SOCIAL SECTOR RESTRUCTURING

The Bank has actively supported social sector restructuring through the following instruments:

Policy-based lending: Economic Reconstruction Loan (approved 12/97, US$3 billion), SAL I (approved 3/98, US$2 billion) and SAL II (approved 10/98, US$2 billion) have addressed comprehensive social sector reforms in the areas of labor markets, antipoverty programs, health insurance, and pension system reform

Trust Funds: ASEM Grants support government implementation of social sector reforms agreed under the structural adjustment program in the areas of Social Protection for Workers (US$0.9million), Protecting the Poor (US$0.9m) and Protecting the Elderly (US$0.9million).

IFC ACTIVITIES

In *Korea*, after a 10-year hiatus in IFC's activities in the country, portfolio matters were not a significant issue, but in a very short period of time IFC had to re-enter the country, evaluate the situation and design a quick response to the needs of Korean companies. First priority was to strengthen existing financial institutions through capital injections and technical assistance on disclosure, risk management, and corporate governance to enable these institutions to lead the restructuring process at corporate level.

IFC invested US$177 million (including B Loans of US$80 million) in Hana Bank and Korea Long Term Credit Bank. The investments enabled a restructuring of the banks' balance sheets at a time when other sources of finance were not available and brought a measure of confidence to the banking system. Loan covenants required the banks to adopt internationally acceptable accounting and disclosure standards and strengthen areas of risk management and loan workout. To assist the banks in meeting these requirements, technical assistance totaling US$2.3 million has been funded and is being executed. Injecting liquidity in the system through trade enhancement facilities to stimulate export and import growth was another important priority. In this area,

IFC is implementing a stepwise strategy to help alleviate Korea's trade finance problems. Total program size envisaged is US$385 million in four separate transactions of which IFC exposure would be US$145 million. Each project is different with the objective of providing a variety of products to directly address Korea's critical trade finance constraints; e.g. letters of credit confirmation, bankers acceptance, forfaiting, export bills discounting, etc. An additional facility will explore ways of providing trade finance direct to companies in which IFC takes on corporate exposure directly. Some of these facilities are promoting relatively new products like forfeiting to broaden Korea's trade finance market and capital market. In the corporate sector, the focus was on medium size enterprises with strong fundamentals, but facing liquidity problems. Through its investments,

IFC assisted several Korean companies undertake significant financial and operational restructuring in 1998 following the onset of the financial crisis. The restructurings involved significant advisory input by IFC and a total of USUS$80 million in IFC loan and equity investments and were developed as models for further restructuring activities in Korea. In the last 12 months, IFC approved 13 projects for a total investment of US$480 million, of which US$380 million was for IFC's own account. Looking ahead, IFC will continue to work on providing trade enhancement facilities, which offer new products to Korean banks and corporations, and on institution-building in the financial sector and on restructurings of mid-sized enterprises.

FINANCIAL SYSTEM RESTRUCTURING AND REGULATION

1. FINANCIAL INSTITUTIONS

The financial system in Korea evolved in parallel with economic development. The cast of the modern banking system was set with the establishment of the Bank of Korea and the commercial banks in the 1950s. The specialized banks were added to strengthen financial support for economic development in the 1960s. With the diversification and enlargement of non-bank financial institutions in the 1970s, the financial system took on its present framework. From the early 1980s, liberalization and internationalization were also undertaken in line with the shift in economic strategy toward active functioning of the market mechanism. From the turn of the 1990s, the financial reform process was broadened and accelerated to increase financial efficiency and strengthen the competitiveness of the financial institutions.

Korea is currently experiencing its most severe economic crisis triggered by an immediate shortage of foreign exchange reserves since the Korean War. Recently to overcome this economic crisis, Korea is restructuring the financial sector as well as corporate sectors and labor market.

☐The Bank of Korea

The Bank of Korea was established in June 1950 under the Bank of Korea Act with its primary purposes being defined as maintaining the stability of the value of money in the interests of national economic progress, and furthering economic progress and the efficient utilization of national resources by the sound operation and functional improvement of the nation's banking and credit system. To this end, the Bank performs the typical functions of a central bank, serving as issuer of banknotes and coins, banker to the banking sector, banker to the government, controller of the money supply, and supervisor of banking operations under the instructions of the Monetary Board, its policy-making organ.

BANKING INSTITUTIONS

Commercial Banks

Commercial banks play an important role in the nation's financial markets, although their relative importance in the financial system has gradually decreased as non-bank financial institutions have expanded their business. As of the end of 1997, Korea's commercial banking system consisted of seventeen nationwide commercial banks, ten local banks and sixty nine branches of fifty-two foreign banks. Nationwide commercial banks have adopted a branch banking system throughout the country. The total number of domestic branches of the nationwide commercial banks amounts to 4,042. They are authorized to engage in long-term financing in addition to short-term financing. Long-term funds have, however, been met, in part, by way of frequent roll-overs or renewals of short-term loans. Local banks have each adopted a branch banking system within a province, except for ten branches in Seoul and up to two branches in each of six major provincial cities which are not home to their own head office. Their main business clients are small and medium enterprises in their regions. Foreign bank branches have tended to specialize in the wholesale banking business.

For financial sector restructuring, Korea's efforts are directed primarily toward banks given their importance as payment settlement institutions. As for the Korea First Bank and Seoul Bank, the government plans to auction these banks in advance of the November 15th deadline as agreed upon with the IMF. The equity sell-off of these banks will be made available to both domestic and foreign investors. Banks which do not currently meet the BIS capital adequacy ratio have been or will be merged or closed, depending on the gravity of problems in their balance sheet and their rehabilitation probability.

-Nationwide Commercial Banks

There are fourteen nationwide commercial banks; Cho Hung Bank, Commercial Bank of Korea, Korea Housing Bank, Industrial Bank of Korea for the financing of small and medium enterprises, Korea First Bank, Hanil Bank, Seoul Bank, Korea Exchange Bank, Shinhan Bank, KorAm Bank, Hana Bank, Boram Bank, Peace Bank of Korea, and Kookmin Bank. They operate throughout the country with a nationwide branch network and all have their head offices in Seoul.

Recently tree nationwide commercial banks which are Deadong Bank, Donghwa Bank and Dongnam Bank have been closed and now are being acquisited by other banks.

-Local Banks

Local banking effectively commenced in 1967 when a local banking system was established. During the period from 1967 to 1971, ten local banks were set up with a view to bringing about regionally balanced economic development and access to financial services. They are Daegu Bank, Pusan Bank, Chungchong Bank, Kwangju Bank, the Bank of Cheju, Kyungki Bank, Jeonbuk Bank, Kangwon Bank, Kyongnam Bank, and Chungbuk Bank. The General Banking Act stipulates that a local bank needs to have paid-in capital of at least 25 billion won while a nationwide commercial bank must have paid-in capital of at least 100 billion won. The financial structure of the local banks is similar to that of the nation-wide commercial banks, except for the fact that the share of securities investment in their uses of funds is relatively high, whereas that of foreign exchange business is small.

Like restructuring of nationwide comercial banks, two local banks which are Chungchong Bank and Kyungki Bank have been just closed and now are being acquisited by other banks.

- Foreign Banks

Foreign banks may open branches in Korea with the approval of the Monetary Board as recommended by the Superintendent of Banks under the provisions of the General Banking Act. They were first allowed to open branches in Korea in 1967 when Chase Manhattan Bank opened its Seoul Branch and, in the latter half of the 1970s, the number of branches and the volume of business expanded rapidly.

☐ Specialized Banks

The specialized banks were established mostly during the 1960s by separate acts which set out to increase capital mobilization and to strengthen financial support for underdeveloped or strategically important sectors.

There are three specialized banks: the credit and banking sector of the National Agricultural Cooperative Federation (NACF) for agricultural and forestry loans; that of the National Federation of Fisheries Cooperatives (NFFC) and its member cooperatives for fishery loans; and that of the National Livestock Cooperatives Federation (NLCF) for livestock related loans.

The specialized banks play a significant role in the Korean banking system as a whole. The specialized banks share the following main characteristics.

First, they were established to provide funds to particular sectors whose supply of funds through commercial banks was insufficient due to limited availability or low profitability. With subsequent changes in the financial environment, however, they have expanded their business into commercial banking areas, although their share of funds allocation to their relevant sectors is still relatively high. Now most specialized banks have, by and large, the same pattern of business as the commercial banks.

Second, they rely heavily on deposits from the public for their sources of funds in addition to the issue of debentures and borrowing from government. Therefore, they compete with commercial banks in acquiring deposits.

Third, they are, in principle, directed and supervised by the government. Some areas of their business operations are, however, subject to the control of the Monetary Board. The same minimum reserve requirements and maximum interest rates are imposed upon the specialized banks as on the commercial banks.

NON-BANK FINANCIAL INSTITUTIONS

There are many non-bank financial institutions, most of which were introduced in the 1970s. They recorded a significant increase in number and in the volume of funds handled in the course of the rapid economic growth of the 1970s and the 1980s. A further contribution to their rapid expansion came from the relatively higher interest rates permitted to them and the greater degree of autonomy in management they were allowed compared with the banking institutions.

Non-bank financial institutions can be broadly classified into five categories according to their business activities: that is development, savings, investment, insurance, and other institutions.

As of the end of June 1997, development institutions consisted of the Korea Development Bank, the Export-Import Bank of Korea and the Korea Long Term Credit Bank. They provide medium- and long-term loans or credit for development of key sectors such as the export or heavy and chemical industry with government funds and funds financed by the inducement of foreign capital or the issue of special bonds.

Savings institutions consist of the trust accounts of banks, mutual savings and finance companies, credit unions, mutual credit facilities, community credit cooperatives and postal savings. They grant various small loans with funds financed by special deposit-taking in the form of time deposits.

Investment institutions act as financial intermediaries in the money and capital markets. They consisted of 30 merchant banking corporations, 26 securities investment trust companies, and the Korea Securities Finance Corporation as of the end of June 1997.

Insurance institutions consisted of 21 domestic life insurance companies, 7 joint ventures with foreign insurance companies, 2 branches and 3 subsidiaries of foreign life insurance companies, and postal life insurance as of the end of June 1997.

In addition to the above mentioned financial institutions, there are other institutions such as securities companies, leasing companies, and installment credit companies, of which the last group commenced its operations in 1996. These institutions function as supplementary financial institutions, although they do not act as financial intermediaries.

The restructuring of non-bank financial institutions will follow a similar sequential pattern. Following an accurate assessment of problems in their balance sheet, the modality of restructuring will be determined by the FSC(Financial Supervisory Commission).

FINANCIAL RESTRUCTURING

BANKING SECTOR RESTRUCTURING

Progress made so far

For 12 commercial banks that did not meet 8 percent capital adequacy ratio set by Bank for International Settlement(BIS), the Management Assessment Committee assessed those 12 banks' management rationalization plans. After the assessment, the Committee submitted its assessment results to the Financial Supervisory Commission on June 28, 1998. Based on that assessment, the Financial Supervisory Commission(FSC) decided the commercial banks to be liquidated and announced the decision on June 29, 1998.

The FSC ordered 5 banks, namely, Dongwha, Dongnam, Daedong, Kyunggi and Chungchung bank, to be shut down and merge with Shinhan, Housing, Kookmin, KorAm, and Hana Bank respectively. For these 5 banks, that their operation have been disapproved by the FSC, their assets and liabilities will beacquired by the respective taking over banks, the process referred as a P&A method(Purchase & Assumption method). The P&A method was chosen as the liquidation method to shorten the confusion associated with number of bank closures.

The qualifications of acquisition banks are as follows. First, they have to have BIS set capital adequacy ratio of more than 9 percent as of end of 1997. Second, they have to have the capability of stabilizing the banks' management after acquiring ailing banks in short period and have to have capacity to increase capital by issuing new shares and attracting foreign investment. And third, the acquisition banks should be the banks that can maximize synergy effect after acquiring financially unsound banks in terms of its market share and distribution of branches.

The acquisition banks selected the bank to be acquired after considering their unique operational features and comparative advantage, and long-term prospect for further growth.

The license of five banks, ordered to be shut down by the FSC, will be revoked by the Minister of Finance and Economy and all operational activities will be closed completely. However, to handle banks' unfinished businesses, limited business operations, such as collection of outstanding loans and liquidation of properties, will be allowed after getting approval from their trustees.

Out of 12 banks who did not meet 8 percent capital adequacy ratio, 7 banks, namely, Cho Hung, Commercial, Hanil, Korea Exchange, Peace, Chunbuk, and Kwangwon Bank, got conditional approval from the FSC. For these seven banks, the FSC ordered them to submit strong management improvement plan, containing strong management reform and capital increase plans by the end of July 1998. When the submitted plans are not approved by the FSC or when the plans are not properly carried out, the FSC will order them to shut down their businesses or merge with other banks.

For Korea First and Seoul Bank, the Korean government will push forward early privatization of these two banks in close consultation with Morgan Stanley, a major underwriting firm for these banks.

Currently, a foreign accounting firm Coopers & Lybrand is conducting asset evaluation on these two banks. After the asset evaluation, the government plans to privatize these banks earlier than initial schedule set at Nov. 15, 1998.

For the remaining 12 commercial banks that has BIS set capital adequacy ratio above 8 percent, the FSC will conduct assessment on these banks by the end of Aug., and if the FSC view that there is a possibility of becoming financially unsound, the FSC will order them to implement strong management reform measures, including replacement of management team and merging with other banks.

Future directions

In the process of liquidating financially unsound banks, the government will make every efforts to stabilize financial market and minimize inconvenience that customers have to bear with. To ease the small and medium-sized enterprises' financial crunch, the FSC instructed all financial institutions to rollover loans falling due from Jun. to Dec. 1998. However, nonviable small and medium-sized enterprises are not eligible to get this benefit.

To prevent healthy acquisition banks from becoming financially unsound as a result of acquisition of financially unsound bank, when the liabilities exceeds assets of the banks that are being acquired, the gap will be covered by Deposit Insurance Corporation as a form of capital investment. The FSC will support acquisition banks' capital increase and the sale of their non-performing loans.

The FSC announced its plan for easing financial crunch experienced by small and medium enterprises on June 26. According to the plan, all businesses that are not belong to the nation's top 67 business groups will be eligible for getting extension on their loans falling due until the end of 1998, however companies that were judged as nonviable corporations by their respective creditor banks will be excluded from getting the help. The total amount of loans falling due during the Jun. to Dec. period is estimated to be around 84 trillion won.

To prevent acquisition banks becoming financially unsound, the government will convert acquired banks' liabilities that exceed assets into equity capital by investing capital from Deposit Insurance Corporation.

The government will also support acquisition banks' capital increase and purchase of non-performing loans. If the acquired assets become bad assets after the acquisition of the assets in specified period of time, the Korea Asset Management Corporation will repurchase those assets from the acquisition banks.

The total size of government bond issuance for purchasing non-performing loan is 50 trillion won, including 25 trillion won decided at the Economic Coordination Meeting held on May 20. In providing this fund, the government is seeking to provide solid ground for minimizing ordinary taxpayers' tax burden, obliging banks to make their own rehabilitation efforts, and making bank officials accountable for their actions by using method such as replacing top managements' of the badly managed financial institutions.

RESTRUCTURING PLAN FOR SECONDARY FINANCIAL INSTITUTIONS

The secondary financial institutions' restructuring process will be implemented by the major shareholders of the secondary financial institutions, however, nonviable secondary financial institutions will be liquidated according to strict liquidation measures set by the FSC. The secondary institutions becomes nonviable as a result of effect from implementation of banking sector restructuring measures will also be liquidated.

Merchant banks

Merchant banks will be ordered to improve their management according to the assessment made based on their BIS ratio and financial ratios. So far, 14 merchant banks' licences were revoked and 2 merchant banks' operation have been suspended.

After reviewing the implementation of merchant banks' management rationalization plan in July, including the attainment of 6 percent BIS capital adequacy ratio, the FSC will make final measure for handling merchant banks that do not satisfactorily implement measures for improving their management.

☐Lease companies

In principle, the restructuring of lease companies will be initiated by their majority shareholders(usually the parent banks). According to the assessment made in May 1998, twenty one lease companies were found to be having more liabilities than assets. And those 21 lease companies' major shareholders have submitted plans for handling ailing lease companies in June. The substance of the plan includes management rationalization through the financial help from the parent banks, sale of lease companies,third party take-over, and liquidation using the bridge lease company.

The FSC will finalize its plan for restructuring financially unsound lease companies by July 1998. The number of lease companies subject to restructuring is expected to be around 10, but there is a possibility of changes in that number due to unfinalized restructuring plan for their parent banks, major shareholders, and creditor financial institutions. For the smooth liquidation of lease companies, the government has established the plan for setting up bridge lease company by Sept. 1998.

Securities companies

Securities companies have ordered to improve their management according to their financial ratios, such as net operation equity ratio. So far, license of two securities companies, Koryo and Dongsuh, were revoked on June 1, 1998.

For the securities companies, the FSC will require them to submitted their financial reports in July, and conduct assessment on their assets and liabilities by Aug. After the assessment, the FSC will make appropriate measure for securities companies according to the assessment results in September. The measures will include recommendation, requirement, and order for management improvement according to the securities companies' net operation equity ratio and asset/liability ratio.

The FSC will require securities companies to submit their management improvement plan by November, and it will make assessment and appropriate measure for the plan in December 1998.

Insurance companies

In principle, the FSC will make measures for insurance companies' management improvement plan according to their ability to payout their insurance claims. The 18 life insurance companies and 4 nonlife insurance companies have submitted their management rationalization plan on June 20, to the FSC. The FSC appointed accounting firm that will review insurance companies' management rationalization plans on June 15, and the appointed accounting firm is currently conducting assessment on the insurance companies' asset and liability status. The assessment will be concluded by the end of July.

The management rationalization plan will be assessed by the assessment committee in July, and restructuring plan for insurance companies will be finalized in August.

Investment trust companies
Taking into account the fact the impact on capital market, the FSC will induce strong management rationalization efforts while implementing improvement of regulatory measures for securing financial soundness of the investment trust companies.

The FSC required investment trust companies to submit their management rationalization plan on May 22 and the FSC is currently conducting assessment on the implementation of the plans submitted by the investment trust companies.

To protect individual investors and secure the financial soundness of investment trust companies' assets, the government will make regulatory improvement in July. The timing of financially unsound investment trust companies' restructuring will be decided after taking into account the domestic stock market situation, and the government will setup laws for allowing establishment of mutual funds.

3. MONEY AND SECURITIES MARKET

☐Money Market

The money market in Korea embraces the call market and a wide range of other financial markets including those for Monetary Stabilization Bonds (MSBs), negotiable certificates of deposit (CDs), repurchase agreements (RPs), corporate bills including commercial paper (CP), and Treasury bills (TBs).

During the period from 1980 to 1997, there was a sharp increase in the outstanding balance of money market instruments. This was chiefly due to product innovation and the expansion in the number of financial institutions handling these instruments.

Securities Market

The growth of the securities market in Korea has been quite impressive. Encouraged by government efforts and the improved investment climate with sustained economic growth and the gradual opening of the stock market, the role of the securities market in mobilizing funds has been greatly strengthened.

During the period from 1980 to 1997, the traded value of listed stocks jumped more than over one hundred fold from 1.1 trillion won to 162.3 trillion won and the stock price index recorded around a four-fold increase. In line with this, direct corporate financing through the securities market showed a notable increase.

DEREGULATION IN INFORMATION AND COMMUNICATIONS

DEREGULATION AS AN IMPORTANT PART OF GOVERNMENT REFORM DRIVE

Since its inauguration as the "government of the people", the Kim administration has vigorously pushed for reforms and deregulation in its effort to cope with the current economic difficulty. The government's reform drive is getting the necessary momentum as the public began to share the realization that reforms in every sector of society are critically important in bringing a breakthrough for economic recovery and in obtaining better national credit ratings from international creditors.

The first thing the government intends to do through this effort is to abolish any laws or regulations that are in the way of promoting competition or inconsistency with the international norms. As for the rules that cannot be abolished because of their close relation to public interest, the means and standards for the rules will be rationalized so as to be more suitable to the deregulated environment. Secondly, the government will strengthen the pre-screening system to suppress the adoption of new rules and regulations and limit the scope and overall quantity of regulations. This aims at making Korea "a good place to do business and a friendly place to live."

Under this government policy, the Ministry of Information and Communication(MIC) is pushing forward deregulation to enhance national competitiveness and help the economy recovery quickly.

To remove more than half of the existing regulations in information and communication

MIC has been consistently pushing for reform to promote competition and to protect public interest under the new market environment driven by the market forces. Therefore, its campaign for reform is nothing new. The newly announced reform plan, however, is historic both in terms of its scope and nature.

Unlike the previous efforts, the campaign has reviewed the entire regulatory system to remove more than 50% of the existing rules and regulations. Any rules of regulations that hinder business activities and cause inconvenience to the people will be done away with first and those that cannot be abolished will be improved in the means and standards depolyed in their application.

Of 342 rules and regulations in information and communications, 182(53.2%) have abolished and 70 (20.5%) will be improved. In total, 252 or 73.7% of the existing regulations have been or will be subjected to change. MIC is amending related laws and regulations so as to accomplish this goal. The following is the outline of MIC's plan for amendments.

PROMOTION OF FOREIGN DIRECT INVESTMENT

MIC made regulatoy changes to promote foreign direct investment in Korea and to increase accountability of management. First, we removed the existing ceiling of 10%(wire) or 33% (wireless) on single person ownership in the netwrok service provider, and increased the percentage of stocks foreigers are allowed to own in Korea Telecom to 33% starting in 1998. The foreign ownership limit of the network service provider will increase up to 49% before 2001, earlier than originally planned.

The current law prohibits any local company of which the upwards of 33% of stocks are held by a foreigner from opening a radio station. However, this will be changed and the foreigners and the Korean citizens will be given equal treatment. In addition, the number of countries with which Korea has "mutual recognition" will be expanded so as to any radio equipment that is type-approved, type-registered or registered as electromagnetic-wave-proof in those countries can be

For additional analytical, business and investment opportunities information,
please contact Global Investment & Business Center, USA
at (202) 546-2103. Fax: (202) 546-3275. E-mail: rusric@erols.com

imported without going through additional procedures of obtaining certifications or registration in Korea.

MIC will allow any foreigner who obtains a license as an amateur radio operator in Korea to operate a radio station under the same conditions given to Korean amateur radio operators. Moreover, any foreign amateur radio operator who obtained her license outside Korea and stays in Korea temporarily will be allowed to operate on limited terms. We expect that the increased exchanges among amateur radio operators will help Korea achieve improved profile in the international community. 2. Promotion of Telecom Businesses

MIC has been overhauling rules and regulations restricting free competition in the marketplace in order to support restructuring telecom businesses and help them enhance competitiveness. Companies other than network service providers are now allowed to acquire or merge with such companies. Therefore, they are now able to enter into the network-based telecom business. Previously, corporations whose shares were owned by network service providers were unable to enter into network-based telecom business. But now they are permitted to provide network-based service, and the cross-shareholding between network service providers has been made possible.

As the initial license for network service providers was abolished, companies do not have to go through the two-phase licensing system. In addition, application for network-based telecom business license is received twice a year instead of once a year, and license application for multiple services is also allowed.

With regard to telecom construction business, only simple registration is required for the start of the business instead of government approval, and other requirements such as technical skills and amount of the capital will be greatly relaxed. Furthermore, the limit of business for each category of the business will also be removed, eliminating the possibility of conflicts among categories and promoting competition in telecom construction business.

Previously, capacity test for telecom equipment was carried out annually to incerase the efficiency of the equipment. The regulation on the test was recently abolished. MIC, also, removed other approval system for commercial telecom facilities for the convinience of service providers in using telecom facilties.

Accoring to the previous rules, a corporation that transfers its business to the other was not allowed to transfer its license for radio station. So the radio station license. In revised rules, however, the license for radio station is allowed to be transferred as corporate business is transferred, saving the cost and promotin the restructuring telecom business.

HIGHER STANDARD OF LIVING

MIC has determined to include more radio equipment in the list of the equipment that does not need approval by or reporting to the authorities in installation and to simplify the licensing system for radio stations to four phases from seven, in order to make it easier and less expensive for the public in using radio technology.

For the same purpose, technical standard authorization was abolished in July 1998 for mobile phones, PCS, TRS and data communication terminal, and will be abolished soon for radio equipment for celluar stations, mobile stations, land mobile stations, on-board communications stations and amateur stations.

For additional analytical, business and investment opportunities information, please contact Global Investment & Business Center, USA at (202) 546-2103. Fax: (202) 546-3275. E-mail: rusric@erols.com

The calculation system of radio frequency usage fee will also be reformed.
The fee will be charged in a manner that its growth rate diminished as the radio facilities are expanded instead of following the current way that the fee is decided in proportion to the expansion rate of the facilities(this way, the fee will be lowered by some 35%). MIC will also reduce radio frequency usage fee for mobile phone subscribers from 5,000 won for each quarter to 3,000 won, in hopes of promoting both consumption and investment.

The reform of the rules and regulations outlined above is wide in its coverage and revolutionary in its substance. Setting the goal of abolishing more then 50% of regulations, MIC has re-examined all the rules and regulations one by one and improved and even eliminated inappropriate ones which restrict business and public activities. Indeed, the 1998 deregulation will greatly promote telecom business and public convenience.

FOREIGN INVESTMENT CLIMATE

A host of laws, regulations and unwritten ministerial guidance makes for a challenging business environment for those who invest in Korea. The government has long sought to reverse the country's well-deserved reputation for having a difficult environment for foreign direct investment (FDI) by undertaking a series of liberalization programs which have sought to curtail the government's interference in private decision-making. The repeated nature of these liberalization campaigns indicates that the government has yet to convince the bureaucracy to limit its predilection to micro-manage the economy.

The principal law governing the terms of foreign investment -- the 1966 Foreign Capital Inducement Act (FCIA) -- was completely revamped in early 1997 and renamed the Act on Foreign Direct Investment and Capital Inducement (FDIA). The FDIA is somewhat more liberal than its predecessor, with four important improvements:

- Applications for foreign investment are now subject only to prior
  notification, regardless of whether the concerned business will
  operate in sectors which are opened fully or partially to foreign
  investment;

- Offshore commercial loans with terms of five years or more are
  redefined as foreign direct investment (FDI), with some limitations;

- The acquisition of outstanding shares of Korean companies is also
  redefined as FDI; and,

- A legal basis was provided to reduce or exempt plant site rents for
  foreign-invested firms in the manufacturing sector.

In its current form, the FDIA and related regulations categorize business activities as either "open," conditionally or partially restricted," or "completely closed" to foreign investment. As of January 1, 1997, Korea restricts foreign investment in 53 categories of activities, including the growing of cereal grains, publishing, utilities (power generation, water), transport, telecommunications, banking, insurance, securities dealing and broadcasting. Among the 53 sectors in which foreign investment is currently restricted, many are partially open to foreign investors who satisfy certain conditions.

By January 1, 2000, the number of sectors where there exist any restrictions will fall from the present level of 53 (27 fully restricted; 26 partially) to 43 (16 fully restricted; 27 partially). Interested foreign investors need to monitor the implementation of this schedule closely, however,

For additional analytical, business and investment opportunities information,
please contact Global Investment & Business Center, USA
at (202) 546-2103. Fax: (202) 546-3275. E-mail: rusric@erols.com

since the various categories of activities which a particular investment project might include may not open simultaneously.

Until 1996, applications for establishing businesses which were partially open to FDI were subject to approval by the relevant ministries. Now an investor only has to notify a designated foreign exchange bank. Among the "open" categories, an application for foreign investment must be notified in advance to any one of the 40 designated foreign exchange banks which are authorized to accept applications.

In effect, these notifications are pro forma and can be processed within three hours, if the application is complete. Applications for activities in the "open" categories may be denied only on specific grounds, including those related to national security, public order and morals, any potentially adverse impact on the national economy, health and the environment and violation of any laws and ordinances of Korea. (It is rare, however, for these grounds to be invoked.)

The acquisition of outstanding shares of Korean companies was included in the concept of FDI beginning in February 1997. The government has stated, however, that it will only allow "friendly" mergers and acquisitions (M&As) through direct transaction with shareholders of domestic companies.

Potential investors need only make notification to the Korean government of M&As of domestic enterprises with total assets of less than two trillion won (about US$2.2 billion); M&As involving enterprises with assets of two trillion won or more remain subject to approval. Approval is automatic if the ratio of acquiring
outstanding shares to total shares is 15 per cent or less and if the foreign investor does not become the largest single shareholder of the targeted company.

The government has also stated that henceforth loans with terms of five years or more which are provided to foreign-invested enterprises by their parent companies or affiliate companies abroad and which are for the importation of capital goods will henceforth be included in the legal concept of FBI.

PRIVATE OWNERSHIP

Korea fully recognizes rights of private ownership and has a well-developed body of laws governing the establishment of corporate and other business enterprises. With certain exceptions, private entities may acquire and dispose of interests in business enterprises in Korea. **The Securities and Exchange Act** provides that no legal person (individual or firm) may own more than five percent of a listed
corporation without notifying both the Securities Exchange Commission and the stock exchange; the Securities Exchange Commission may then require that any shares owned above this limit be divested. In addition, Korean law contains several provisions prohibiting cross-ownership between companies.

The purpose of these provisions is to limit the ability of a firm's directors to obtain undue influence by exercising voting rights in shares of the firm owned by a second corporation. For example, the commercial code specifies that shares in a corporation owned by another company (either jointly through related holding company, firms and subsidiaries, or solely by one entity) do not convey voting rights. The Fair Trade Act also restricts cross-ownership of shares in two or more firms if the effect is to restrict competition in a particular industry.

Foreign access to real estate is strictly controlled through the Act Relating to Acquisition of Land by Foreigners and Control Thereof. As a result of amendments to the Act, foreign-invested firms

**For additional analytical, business and investment opportunities information,
please contact Global Investment & Business Center, USA
at (202) 546-2103. Fax: (202) 546-3275. E-mail: rusric@erols.com**

may purchase land for business purposes, including staff housing. Other laws, however, require that specified minimum ratios of the land be used for the investor's stated purposes; failure to meet those requirements within a specified time can result in a heavy tax or a requirement that the undeveloped land be sold. Although foreign banks and insurance companies have the right to acquire land through foreclosure, foreign-invested firms are generally not permitted to purchase land for investment purposes.

PROTECTION OF PROPERTY RIGHTS

The Korean government in recent years has undertaken a series of legal and regulatory measures to improve the climate for the protection of property rights, particularly of intellectual property rights (IPR). Legal improvements are increasingly being implemented through more aggressive prosecution, but more remains to be done throughout the system to be consistent with international norms for a developed country.

The Korean Civil Code encompasses the concept of mortgage in the case of real property. The Code recognizes and enforces secured interests in property -- both chattel and real -- through the foreclosure and/or claims for official auction by the mortgagee. Security interests are recorded in district registry offices, which are administered by district courts.

The Civil Code provides for, protects and facilitates the acquisition and disposition of all property rights, including those of land, buildings and mortgages.

Korea has comprehensive laws protecting intellectual property rights. The Korean government has made efforts to amend its IPR laws to comply with its obligations under WTO/TRIPS. Although Korea's IPR laws are generally in line with international norms, however, they remain inconsistently applied by the Korean courts or some enforcement agencies. Foreign IPR holders also have expressed difficulty getting Korean prosecutors to act in a timely manner.

Korean patent law is fairly comprehensive, in its protection of most roducts and technology. A patent may be granted to the first applicant to file in Korea, notwithstanding proof of development or international ownership. Korea is a member country of the Patent Cooperation Treaty (PCT), and U.S. patent applicants, in case of ompeting applications, can claim priority within one year from the application date in the United States. Korean patent law was recently changed to adopt the international norm for determining the term of rotection, which is 20 years from the date of application. Patent applicants must request an examination of their application within five years of filing.

Korea maintains a system for compulsory licensing of patents, although it is very limited and there have been few cases based on it. If a patent has not been worked continuously and substantially for a period of three years, a second party may seek to work the patent by requesting a non-exclusive license from the patent holder. If no license is granted, the second party may request arbitration by the patent commissioner. The patent commissioner may decide to grant a non-exclusive license. The right of the patent holder may be canceled altogether if the patent is not continuously worked for two or more years from the date on which arbitration granted a non-exclusive license. Compulsory licenses may also be issued by the patent commissioner if the invention is deemed necessary for the national defense, for the public interest, or for the protection of a dependent patent. Violators of patent rights are liable under civil and criminal law.

Korea acceded to the Berne Convention in 1996 and is obliged to treat works from participating countries as it does its own. Copyright protection is generally provided under the Korean copyright law, i.e., books, computer programs, movies, sound recordings, etc. Korea's copyright law protects both the economic and moral rights of the author.

Economic rights include the right to produce derivative works, reproduce, distribute, broadcast, and to perform or display material publicly. Moral rights include the right to claim authorship, to maintain identity, and of release. Copyrights expire 50 years after the creation of a work by an entity other than a person and are derived from the creation of a work itself during the author's lifetime plus 50 years after death; no registration is required. Korea does not, however, provide full 50-year copyright retroactivity, as is the international norm, observed by developed countries. For parties that wish to register their rights for recorded material, registration is available through the Ministry of Culture and Sports. A 1994 copyright law amendment extended the protection of neighboring rights to 50 years after initial public display. An impediment to the effective enforcement of these laws has been the requirement that the rights-holder must file a formal complaint with the police or prosecutor's office before action can be taken against violators.

In 1993, the Korean government established a review system for approving imports for sound recordings and movies. This system has proved effective in enforcing the claims of legitimate rights-holders.

A major point of contention in the IPR field relates to retroactive copyright protection. The U.S. Government asserts that under the Berne Convention and WTO/TRIPS, copyright protection should be provided retroactively back 50 years to 1947. The Korean government provides retroactive protection for national and foreign works back to only 1957, when the first Korean copyright law was promulgated.

In 1989 the Computer Program Protection Act (CPPA) was enacted to extend copyright protection to computer software. Protection is afforded for a period of 50 years, dating from publication, and applies only to computer programs written after the law went into effect in 1989. The 1994 revision of the law recognizes data base compilations as copyrighted works and entitles authors of computer
programs to authorize rentals of their works.

Legislation to protect semiconductor mask works was passed in 1991 and
took effect at the beginning of 1994. The law provides some downstream protection. U.S. industry has expressed continuing concern over the compulsory licensing provisions of the law. It is uncertain whether such a law would qualify for reciprocal recognition by the United States.

The Trademark Law extends protection only if registration has taken place in Korea. The granting of a trademark by Korean law is based on a "first to file" basis. This provision has worked to the disadvantage of U.S. rights holders who discover that their marks have already been registered by a Korean individual or firm when they attempt to enter the local market.

The U.S.-Korea 1986 bilateral agreement obligates the Korean Industrial Property Office (KIPO) to protect (under administrative practice) U.S. trademarks not registered in Korea, whether or not they are considered "well-known." Although the Korean government has disputed this interpretation of the bilateral
agreement, KIPO has in practice shown a willingness to resolve issues on a case-by-case basis in an expeditious manner. Trademark infringement is punishable by imprisonment of up to five years and/or by a fine of up to 20 million won (about US$25,000).

As in other areas of intellectual property rights protection, the Korean government began tough, systematic enforcement of the trademark law only in 1993. Many U.S. companies have applied for and successfully won an invalidation or cancellation ruling by KIPO, which in effect nullifies the previous Korean holder's right to a trademark under Korean law. U.S. companies have sought legal remedies to protect trademarks in both the KIPO trial board process and civil and criminal court systems. Due to the appeals process in both instances, the legal battles can be long and arduous, ending up usually in the Korean Supreme Court. To avoid this long and expensive process, more and more U.S. companies and Korean companies are settling their cases out of court.

Trademark registration is good for 10 years and renewable in subsequent 10 year periods indefinitely. To retain validity, the trademarks, in theory, must be used; non-use of a registered trademark for three consecutive years may allow the filing of a cancellation trial by a third party.

U.S. companies should perform due diligence to protect their trade secrets and otherwise gain confidence in the business relationship before entering into an agreement, which should in turn be thoroughly evaluated for its legal and financial implications before signature.

This is particularly true where a transfer of license is involved. In the case of an IPR-related company-specific problem, legal counsel by a Korean law firm is a must in order to weave through the intricacies of Korean bureaucracy, regulations, court procedures and documentation which must by completed. (At present, the legal profession is closed to foreign firms).

Korea is a signatory to the World Intellectual Property Organization, the Universal Copyright Convention, the Budapest Treaty on the International Recognition of the Deposit of Microorganisms, the Paris Convention for the Protection of Industrial Property, the Patent Cooperation Treaty, WTO's Trade Related Aspects of Intellectual Property (TRIPS), and most recently, the Berne Convention (1997).

PERFORMANCE REQUIREMENTS & INCENTIVES

Korea ceased imposing performance requirements on new foreign investment in July 1989 and eliminated all preexisting performance requirements in December 1992.

TRANSPARENCY OF THE REGULATORY SYSTEM

The Korean regulatory environment is difficult for domestic firms to work through and poses an even greater challenge to foreign firms. Laws and regulations are framed in general terms and are subject to differing bureaucratic interpretations. Basic concepts of administrative procedure are not well-developed, despite the enactment of an administrative procedures law in 1996. The regulatory process is not transparent and frequent informal discussions with the bureaucracy are necessary.

Mid-level bureaucrats rely on unpublished ministerial guidelines and unwritten administrative advice for direction. No formal rule-making procedure exists. Proposed rules are often not published prior to promulgation, or are published with insufficient time to permit either full public comment or an adequate period for industry adjustment. After promulgation, rules can be applied retroactively and arbitrarily.

Laws exist regulating monopolistic practices and unfair competition, but their practical effect is limited by the long-standing economic dominance of a few large business conglomerates, referred to locally as the "chaebol." Korea's Monopoly Regulation and Fair Trade Law has been repeatedly amended to address the issue of unwieldy chaebol growth. Most recently in December 1996, the government proposed the prohibition of intra-group payment guarantees by 2001, but

For additional analytical, business and investment opportunities information,
please contact Global Investment & Business Center, USA
at (202) 546-2103. Fax: (202) 546-3275. E-mail: rusric@erols.com

has yet to take any action to effect this change. In the meantime, the ceiling on inter-group payments guarantees was reduced from 200% of equity to 100%. More drastic legal change, however, is needed if the government is to achieve its professed goal of reigning in the chaebol.

Chaebol domination of the Korean economy causes some practical business problems for foreign investors. Small- and medium-sized suppliers, for example, may be reluctant to deal with foreign firms for fear of jeopardizing a prized chaebol relationship. Distribution channels may be blocked by chaebol competitors who own or dominate them. Obtaining access to credit may be complicated by the privileged relationships competing chaebols enjoy with local banks.

CORRUPTION

The nature of Korea's historic style of governance -- a lack of transparency in the formation of laws and regulations and inadequate institutional "checks and balances" -- has traditionally provided ample opportunities for corruption. Business has been transacted along these lines for centuries here, and the habit is ingrained throughout society.

The Kim Administration resolved to break with this tradition and began a momentous reform process with the requirement that all bank accounts be made "real name" by the end of 1993. This basic change had a profound impact in an economy wherein illegal wealth traditionally was hidden through the use of multiple bank accounts established using fictitious names.

These changes are profound and likely irreversible. Yet, the original conditions which contributed to corruption, principally the lack of transparency in government actions, have yet to be fully rectified. Important steps forward have been taken, including the first public hearings held by ministries to solicit popular views on proposed changes in regulations and laws. More must be done to ensure that both petty and large-scale corruption, which has led to economic inefficiencies and the absence of public confidence in the rule of law, comes to an end.

A dramatic step towards making these changes permanent was taken in 1996, when two former presidents were found guilty for inter alia accepting bribes from businesses. The symbolic nature of these decisions will likely prove to be a powerful deterrent to otherofficials who might contemplate similar actions.

It is a criminal act for a Korean official to give or accept a bribe. The penalties for the crime range from probation to life imprisonment, depending on the amount involved. Unlike U.S. provisions of the Foreign Corrupt Practices Act which prohibit U.S. businesses from bribing foreign officials, bribing a foreign official is not a crime under Korean law, although bribes to foreigners cannot be deducted from taxes as a legitimate expense. The Supreme Prosecutor in each province is responsible for ferreting out corruption. Many government officials, including ministers and now presidents, have been found guilty of corruption in recent years, as have business leaders.

LABOR

Korea has a highly educated and hard-working labor force. Although labor-management relations can be contentious, they have improved in the past five years, with wages having increased more than two and a half times over 1987 levels. Although between 1987 and 1989 they numbered in the thousands, the number of labor disputes has declined steadily, falling to 85 cases in 1996, involving 79,495 workers. Acts of violence are on the decline, but labor relations remain highly emotional.

Labor groups are quick to escalate disputes and sometimes resort to work slowdowns, abuse of leave, and disruption of business by holding rallies, wearing casual clothes, or displaying protest signs in the work environment. These tactics fall outside the scope of Korea's labor law and usually are tolerated by the authorities. Workers have on occasion occupied company offices or factories.

Foreign-invested firms may be more vulnerable to labor disturbances than wholly Korean-owned enterprises. Employees at foreign-invested firms tend to make greater demands on management. Disputes with foreign firms have, at times, taken on an emotional, xenophobic tone in which employees have made verbal threats against expatriate managers.

Although actions by striking employees may be illegal, police are reluctant to arrest unionists unless violence occurs. Labor is quick to get its side of the story into the local papers, often portraying the dispute as an issue of nationalism. Workers at foreign-owned firms perceive, most often incorrectly, that job stability and career prospects are relatively less attractive than at Korean firms, and as a result, labor is increasingly concerned about reductions in force and issues such as severance pay. Mechanisms for peacefully resolving labor disputes remain inadequate.

Following its admission into the United Nations in December 1991, Korea joined the International Labor Organization (ILO). It has not ratified, however, the basic ILO conventions on Workers Rights (Convention no. 87 on the freedom of association, Convention no. 98 on the right to organize and collective bargaining, and Convention no. 151 on public service employees' right to organize). Before the labor laws were amended this year, a number of international and domestic labor groups filed complaints against the Korean government with the ILO's Committee on Freedom of Association.

The ILO issued a report critical of Korean labor laws and recommended that Korea amend its trade union law to allow workers to form plural trade unions of their choice without restriction, to allow public servants and teachers the right to organize trade unions and engage in collective bargaining, to repeal the ban on third-party intervention in the settlement of labor disputes, and to facilitate the release of a number of imprisoned trade unionists.

The labor law reform passed in March 1997 allowed for the establishment of plural unions and repealed the ban on third party intervention. It did not authorize teachers or white collar government employees to form unions, however.

CAPITAL MARKETS AND PORTFOLIO INVESTMENT

Many forms of capital inflows and outflows have traditionally been restricted or prohibited as a matter of law or policy in Korea. The government has also exercised tight control over its domestic credit markets, often with the goal of channeling financing to priority sectors. In some instances, banks have been carrying non-performing policy loans on their books for years, even decades. Credit ceilings on loans to the ten largest business conglomerates are now in effect.

The Korean government has pursued financial sector reform over the years, with varying degrees of effect. Under a five-year program launched in 1993, the government moved to loosen foreign exchange and capital controls, eliminate government credit schemes and began to deregulate interest rates. Most of the salient features of the program have been achieved, often well ahead of schedule. For instance, the government has removed controls on interest rates for all loans and for time deposits with maturities of over six months. In December 1995, the Korean government announced the relaxation of restrictions

For additional analytical, business and investment opportunities information, please contact Global Investment & Business Center, USA at (202) 546-2103. Fax: (202) 546-3275. E-mail: rusric@erols.com

in a number of other areas, including securities, offshore borrowing, imports on deferred payment and the holding and use of foreign exchange.

The growing perception during the recent economic downturn that the inefficiencies of the domestic financial services sectors were contributing to Korea's declining competitiveness, plus pressure from Korean firms who wished to invest overseas or borrow in international capital markets, has encouraged the government to accelerate its liberalization efforts.

Korea's successful bid to join the OECD by end-1996 helped to spur further reforms which brought Korean practice into line with basic OECD standards regarding capital movements, particularly in the areas of foreign purchases of Korean corporate bonds and in long-term borrowing abroad by Korean firms. The scandals associated with the Hanbo bankruptcy encouraged the formation of a
Presidential Financial Reform Commission, whose findings are just now
being translated into regulation and law. The trend is clearly one of greater openness in this sector, although the pace of change remains slower than many of Korea's OECD partners would prefer.

In the area of portfolio investment, Korea's stock market is partially open to foreign investors. Except in rare cases, ownership in a listed company currently remains restricted to no more than 23 percent in the aggregate for foreign investors, although the government has announced its intention to raise the aggregate ceiling for foreigners by 3.0 percent annually for the next three years and finally eliminate it in 2000. The five-percent ceiling for foreign individuals purchasing stock in a single firm will be raised to 10 percent by 2000.

In addition to its generally tight control over land use, the government also strictly limits foreign land acquisition and does not permit portfolio investment in real estate. Foreigners may purchase land only for business purposes and for use as staff housing. The government is not currently considering the opening of real estate to portfolio investment.

The government permits stock purchases on margin, requiring that transactions be settled within three business days.

Korea routinely permits the repatriation of funds, although it reserves the right to limit capital outflows in exceptional circumstances, such as situations which may harm its international balance of payments, cause excessive fluctuations in interest or exchange rates, or threaten the stability of its domestic financial
markets.

The Korean banking system is basically sound, with legal, regulatory and accounting systems which are fundamentally transparent by local standards. (Any doubts engendered by the use of local accounting standards which are not comparable to international standards are offset somewhat by the government's recent blanket commitment that "no bank will fail".) The Korean government has committed to bringing these standards into line with international norms, albeit without any fixed deadline. Roughly ten percent of the total asset base is
"non-performing", the legacy of non-economic "policy loans" made in the past at the instruction of the government. Recent disclosures of collusion between bank officials, the chaebol and government leaders has shown, though, that much remains to be done to ensure complete transparency in the sector.

The total assets of Korea's 15 nation-wide commercial banks as of the end of February 1997 was 257 trillion won, or about US$289 billion.

For additional analytical, business and investment opportunities information,
please contact Global Investment & Business Center, USA
at (202) 546-2103. Fax: (202) 546-3275. E-mail: rusric@erols.com

CONVERSION AND TRANSFER POLICIES

Financial transfers in and out of Korea are heavily regulated but have not impeded profit or other remittances associated with approved foreign direct investment. Local U.S. businesses say they have encountered no problems in remitting payments of any sort.

The Ministry of Finance and Economy strictly regulates the Korean foreign exchange market under the Foreign Exchange Control Act (FECA) and attendant regulations. The FECA governs all aspects of the foreign exchange rate system, including foreign exchange transactions and holdings. The government utilizes a "negative" system of foreign exchange controls, under which transactions are allowed to take place if not otherwise specifically prohibited.

Recent changes have permitted limited short-term offshore financing, short-term intra-company loans for high technology manufacturers, working capital increases in sectors defined as "open" to foreign investment under the FDIA and equity increases due to preferred stock issues and sale of existing stock. Despite the progress made in loosening foreign exchange controls, serious restrictions remain in certain types of offshore financing and deferred payments for imports.

The right to remit profits is obtained at the time the original investment notification is sought. This notification process has been delegated to the foreign exchange banks and is considered pro forma for investments in sectors which are "open" to foreign direct investment. Approval for both the original investment and subsequent remittances rests with the relevant ministry in the case of investments which are either conditionally or partially restricted, as defined by the FDIA.

Both the agreement and the projected payment schedule must be notified to the relevant Ministry when a firm proposes a stream of royalties or other payments to be made over an extended period of time in association with FBI in compensation for a technology licensing agreement related to R&D associated with one of the following sectors: aircraft, space vehicles, atomic energy and the defense industries.

When an investor wishes to effect a remittance, he must present an audited financial statement to the foreign exchange bank to substantiate the payment. To withdraw capital, a stock valuation report issued by a recognized securities company or the Korea appraisal board must also be presented.

Foreign companies seeking to remit funds which are not related to a FDIA-type investment must work through authorized foreign exchange banks after obtaining government approval. Approval is given when a legal source of the funds is demonstrated and proof is shown that relevant taxes have been paid. There also exist limits on the amount of funds any traveler -- whether resident in Korea or domiciled abroad -- may take out of the country per trip.

Conversion of the national currency, the won, into foreign currencies for certain international transactions such as the import of goods and services is possible with the approval of an authorized foreign exchange bank. The Korean won is generally not accepted outside of Korea. The external value of the won is managed by the Bank of Korea, which allows the currency to float daily within a limited band against a basket of hard currencies. As a reference price, the Bank of Korea uses the previous day's weighted average of won-dollar interbank transactions.

There is presently no inconvertibility coverage offered by the U.S. Overseas Private Investment Corporation (see below).

EXPROPRIATION AND COMPENSATION

For additional analytical, business and investment opportunities information,
please contact Global Investment & Business Center, USA
at (202) 546-2103. Fax: (202) 546-3275. E-mail: rusric@erols.com

Korea follows generally accepted principles of international law with respect to expropriation. The law protects all foreign-invested enterprise property from expropriation or requisition. If private property is expropriated, it can only be taken for a public purpose and then in a non-discriminatory manner. Property owners are entitled to prompt compensation at fair market value. The Embassy is not aware of any cases of uncompensated expropriation of property.

DISPUTE SETTLEMENT

There exists a body of Korean law governing commercial activities and bankruptcies which constitutes an effective means to enforce property and contractual rights, with monetary judgments usually made in the domestic currency. Judgments of foreign courts are not enforceable in Korea.

Although commercial disputes can be adjudicated in a civil court, foreign businesses often feel that this is not a practical means to resolve disputes in the local context. For example, proceedings are conducted in the Korean language, often with inadequate translation. Foreign lawyers are banned from Korean courts. Civil procedures common in the United States, such as pretrial discovery, do not exist in Korea. During litigation of a dispute, foreigners may be barred from leaving the country until a decision is reached. Legal proceedings are expensive and time-consuming; if successful, enforcement is uncertain. A lawsuit is often considered a last resort, signaling the end of a business relationship.

Disputes may also be taken to the Korean Commercial Arbitration Board (KCAB), the only officially recognized arbitration center in Korea. To date, only 26 such cases involving foreigners have been arbitrated since the system's inception in 1971. The process is governed by the Arbitration Law of Korea and the Commercial Arbitration Rules of the KCAB: -

(1) Parties may request that the KCAB conduct an informal intermediary proceeding, a negotiation between the two parties in dispute which is mediated by an unbiased administrator from the KCAB. There is only a small fee charged for this service. Several hundred such mediations are conducted annually by the KCAB. -

(2) If the informal proceeding Step #1 proves unsuccessful, either or both parties may request formal arbitration. Ideally, an arbitration clause should be in a contract drawn up prior to the business arrangement, so that the arbitration can be conducted with only one party's agreement. Once arbitration is decided upon, the KCAB may appoint a conciliator who conducts the proceedings. -

(3) If the conciliation is unsuccessful after 30 days, then an arbitration proceeding is begun. One to three arbitrators are chosen by the parties in dispute from a 800-person Panel of Arbitrators (which also comprises 140 foreign arbitration experts), who will meet with the parties and ultimately render an arbitral award. If one party in the dispute is not a resident of Korea, arbitration rules allow that either party can request an arbitrator from a neutral country, who can be selected from the Panel of Arbitrators.

In drafting contracts, it is likely a good idea to provide for arbitration by a neutral body such as the International Court of Arbitration of the ICC or both the KCAB and American Arbitration Association (AAA). U.S. firms should seek local expert legal counsel when drawing up any type of contract with a Korean entity.

Arbitral awards will be upheld in all countries that are signatories of the Convention on the Settlement of Investment Disputes between States and Nationals of Other States (the so-called "Washington Convention") and the "United Nations Convention on the Recognition and

For additional analytical, business and investment opportunities information, please contact Global Investment & Business Center, USA at (202) 546-2103. Fax: (202) 546-3275. E-mail: rusric@erols.com

Enforcement of Foreign Arbitral Awards" (the so-called "1958 New York Convention"), of which the United States and Korea are both members.

Korea is also a member of the International Federation of Commercial Arbitration Institutions (IFCAI) and the World Bank's Multilateral Investment Guarantee Agency (MIGA). Korea has also signed over 45 arbitration agreements with other arbitration institutions around the world.

POLITICAL VIOLENCE

Korea does not have a history of political violence directed against foreign direct investment. The Embassy is unaware of any politically motivated threats of damage to foreign projects and/or installations of any sort nor of any incidents which might be interpreted as having targeted foreign investments. Labor violence unrelated to the issue of foreign ownership, however, has occurred in foreign-owned facilities.

Tensions on the Korean peninsula have remained relatively high due to the ongoing threat from North Korean conventional military forces. In a U.S.-DPRK agreement signed in Geneva in October 1994, North Korea agreed to freeze and eventually dismantle its nuclear weapons program in return for improved relations with the United States and a program to provide substitute energy in the form of heavy fuel oil and the construction of light water reactors, which are less subject to use for weapons development. It is hoped that this program, in conjunction with improved inter-Korean relations, will ease the DPRK's international isolation and reduce tensions on the peninsula.

BILATERAL INVESTMENT AGREEMENTS

The United States has a bilateral Treaty of Friendship, Commerce, and Navigation with Korea which contains general provisions pertaining to business relations and investment. So far, Korea has entered into bilateral investment agreements with 42 nations, including the United States, Germany, France, the United Kingdom, the Netherlands, Belgium, Switzerland, Denmark, Hungary, Thailand, Bangladesh, Sri Lanka, Senegal, Tunisia, the Russian Federation, Austria, Spain, China, Argentina and Vietnam.

OPIC AND OTHER INVESTMENT INSURANCE PROGRAMS

Since a 1991 determination under the Workers Rights provisions (Section 23la) of the Foreign Assistance Act, the Overseas Private Investment Corporation (OPIC) has refrained from writing policies under its insurance programs for companies making new investments in Korea. Coverage issued prior to this determination is still in force. Lack of OPIC coverage is not regarded as a serious obstacle to U.S. investors, since OPIC has never had to cover claims for expropriation, political risk or currency inconvertibility.

Korea has been a member of the IBRD's Multilateral Investment Guarantee Agency (MIGA) since November 1987.

FOREIGN DIRECT INVESTMENT STATISTICS

The largest group of foreign investors in Korea as of December 31, 1996 is Japanese, with US$5.6 billion invested, or about 32 percent of Korea's total stock of foreign direct investment. The second largest group is U.S.-based: US$5.1 billion, or 29 percent of the total. Europe as a whole comes in third, with US$4.6 billion, or 26 percent; the leading EU investors come from the Netherlands, Ireland, Germany, France and the United Kingdom. The ranking of these investors is measured through monitoring applications for transfers and are booked at their nominal value; retained and/or reinvested earnings are not

For additional analytical, business and investment opportunities information, please contact Global Investment & Business Center, USA at (202) 546-2103. Fax: (202) 546-3275. E-mail: rusric@erols.com

FOREIGN DIRECT INVESTMENT STATISTICS

Foreign Direct Investment Flows - Into and Out of Korea
(in US$ millions)

	Flow			Stock
	1998	1999	2000	
Total Inflow	8,852	15,541	15,690	64,730
United States	2,973	3,739	2,916	17,909
Japan	504	1,750	2,449	10,540
EU	2,885	6,261	4,607	10,540
Others	2,973	3,791	6,159	16,202
Total Outflow	5,133	4,625	4,819	29,470
North America	1,227	1,578	1,182	9,068
Asia	2,225	1,753	1,614	11,728
Europe	916	797	202	3,861
Others	765	497	1,821	4,813

Source: The Export-Import Bank of Korea and Ministry of Commerce, Industry and Energy

MAJOR U.S. INVESTORS IN KOREA

U.S. Investor------------------	Products-------------------
Amkor Technology Inc.	Electric/Electronics
S&K Development Co., Ltd.	Hotel/Ski Resort
Wal-Mart Stores Inc.	Wholesale/Retail
Microsoft Corporation	Other Services
Asia Recovery Fund LP	Life Insurance
Bowater Incorporated	Wood and Paper
E.I. Du Point De Nemours & Co.	Chemicals
Fairchild Semiconductor Corp.	Electric/Electronics
Caltex (Overseas) Ltd.	Oil Refining
Morgan Guaranty Co.	Finance
Procter & Gamble Far East. Inc.	Wood and Paper
Seminis Vegetable Seeds Inc.	Agriculture/Forestry
The Gillette Company	Electric/Electronics
3M Co. Ltd.	Electric/Electronics
J. Lyons Inc.	Foods
Ford Motor Company	Transport Equipment
Airtouch Communications Inc.	Other Services
World CI USA. Inc.	Resort

**For additional analytical, business and investment opportunities information,
please contact Global Investment & Business Center, USA
at (202) 546-2103. Fax: (202) 546-3275. E-mail: rusric@erols.com**

ECONOMIC REFORMS & FOREIGN INVESTMENTS REGULATIONS

The Korea of today is a completely different country following the onset of instability in the foreign exchange market in November of 1997. It is a country that has recognized and addressed the fundamental weaknesses created during the rapid economic development of the past four decades.

As Korea is fully committed to implementing the economic programs agreed upon with the IMF, it embarks today on a new road to economic recovery. Korea, now, in looking to the next millennium, embraces a new paradigm of development based on the principles of the free market competition and democracy, and seeks further integration with the global economy.

To go beyond the simple correction of past mistakes and regain the confidence of international investors, the Korean economy is undergoing a comprehensive reform and restructuring process. The process focuses on four major areas of change: *financial sector restructuring, corporate sector restructuring, labor market reform,* and *public sector reform.* Through this large initial step, in a series of changes to come, the Korean economy will bring business standards to the highest international levels.

Today, as a result of the strict implementation of necessary adjustments, the fundamentals of Korea's market economy have been enhanced and recovery is being pursued

Despite these signs of returning economic stability, the comprehensive reform and restructuring process will continue to be one of great difficulty. A severe economic contraction has griped the nation, while unemployment has risen. Serious pains have already had to be endured by a great deal of the Korean people and more are hardships, before relief, are expected. Moreover, recent trends in the external economic environment surrounding Korea, such as the possibility of devaluation of the yuan, the economic instability of Russia, and the continued economic difficulties faced by the nations of South East Asia, seem to be unfavorable to the recovery of the Korean economy

In spite of such formidable problems, however, under the strong democratic leadership of President Kim and with the whole-hearted public support of the entire Korean population, Korea stands strong in its uncompromising commitment to reform and restructure its economy and economic practices. President Kim's "Second Nation Building" commemoration address on the 50th Anniversary of the Republic, has clearly symbolized this.

In line with such thought, Korea grasps this challenge of today as an opportunity to change and improve. The lessons of times past will be firmly embraced and Korea shall work ever-harder to successfully overcome and re-emerge as another symbol of history that proves difficult times lead to new and better days.

REINVENTING THE ECONOMY THROUGH REFORMS AND RESTRUCTURING

In order to address the fundamental causes of the economic difficulties and to revitalize the economy, the Korean government has taken bold and decisive measures towards comprehensive structural reform.

Restructuring and related institutional reforms are being carried out in a swift and prudent manner, with strict adherence to market principles and democratic due process.

FINANCIAL SECTOR RESTRUCTURING

The main purpose of financial sector restructuring is to stabilize the financial system and to enhance the soundness and efficiency of financial institutions.

To this end, first, it is necessary to normalize the financial system as early as possible through swift and extensive reform. Second, restructuring costs must be met primarily by financial institutions, and fiscal support has been linked to their own restructuring and recapitalization plans to minimize the taxpayer's burden and eliminate the moral hazard problem. Finally, in the resolution process of financially non-viable institutions, transparent burden sharing rules are being established and strictly applied.

Furthermore, different restructuring approaches are being applied depending on the financial status of individual financial institutions. Sound institutions are being encouraged to improve their capital adequacy ratios by reducing non-performing loans and enhancing their operational efficiency. Non-viable institutions will face pressure to exit the market while unhealthy but viable institutions will be encouraged to clean up their balance and recapitalize.

Along these lines, the liquidation of five non-viable banks through P&As in banking sector took place at the end of June. Viable banks are also following through on the strong corrective actions imposed by the Financial Supervisory Commission (FSC) to further improve their soundness. The government is providing fiscal support to viable banks for the disposal of non-performing loans and recapitalization, as well as depositor protection. Meanwhile, large commercial banks are, on a voluntary basis, proceeding with mergers so as to increase their scale economies and efficiency.

For non-bank financial institutions, self-rehabilitation under the initiative of major shareholders is being encouraged, but is closely being monitored by the FSC. If self-rehabilitation steps are deemed inadequate, the institutions will either be subject to corrective actions or face closure.

The first round of financial sector restructuring was completed at the end of September.

CORPORATE SECTOR RESTRUCTURING

The objectives of restructuring the corporate sector are two-fold. The first is the reduction of corporate debt, while the second involves improving management transparency and governance structure. The government's role centers on instituting the proper institutional framework to facilitate and monitor the restructuring process.

In order to reduce debt-equity ratios, corporations are either raising additional equity capital in the capital market or sell-off their assets and subsidiaries.

To this end, Korea has been moving rapidly toward a complete liberalization of the capital market. Domestic securities markets, short-term money market instruments, foreign exchange transactions and capital flows, and M&A (both friendly and hostile), and foreign ownership of land have been full liberalized to foreign investment. Also, both domestic and foreign investors are allowed to freely establish mutual investment funds in Korea.

With regard to the issue of corporate governance, transparency and accountability are being facilitated by a number of recent measures. No new cross-debt guarantees have been allowed as of April 1, while existing cross-debt guarantees are set to be eliminated by the year 2000. Furthermore, consolidated financial statements will be required as of 1999. The rights of share holder's voting rights are allowed, and all listed companies are required to appoint outside directors. These new standards continue to be strictly enforced.

The five largest chaebols, which lie at the heart of these reforms, and their creditor banks have already reached an agreement on debt reduction and other restructuring measures. Recently, with assistance of the government, chaebol leaders announced a framework for mergers and business swaps. Before long, chaebol's strong self-rehabilitation measures are to be taken toward five restructuring objectives chaebols have already pledged, (1) enhance transparency, (2) eliminate cross-debt guarantees, (3) improve financial structure, (4) streamline business activities, (5) strengthen accountability.

ENHANCING LABOR MARKET FLEXIBILITY

An efficient labor market is directly related to the productivity of the Korean economy. Recognizing this, the Korean government seeks a labor market in which labor allocation and wage determination are efficiently governed through market mechanisms by enhancing labor market flexibility and establishing stable labor-management relations.

With the revised Labor Standard Act, passed last February, labor market flexibility was legally instituted and this amendment is facilitating necessary corporate sector restructuring and will allow firms to rebound more competitively. The Korean government will continue to work toward increase of labor market flexibility by strictly enforcing legal standards and labor practices.

In order to maintain social stability over the reform process, the Korean government has already launched a second round tripartite dialogue so that all sectors of the Korean society are equally represented with respect to burden-sharing. And the government is expanding the social safety net, including adjustments in unemployment insurance. More fiscal resources are being allocated for unemployment benefits that are commensurate with the needs of displaced workers.

PUBLIC SECTOR REFORM

Public sector reform is also important to lead the whole process of reform by setting a good example on the one hand, and by saving financial resources needed for the adjustment process on the other. Without the leading role of the government, it is difficult to persuade people to accept the pains of restructuring and higher tax burdens.

Public sector reform is being geared toward a small but efficient government. In this regard, restructuring and reduction of central and local government has been implemented, and state-owned enterprises and other government-funded institutes will be restructured or privatized so as to increase efficiency.

To increase transparency and efficiency, fiscal expenditure management will be based on the principle of "budgeting for results," and a number of special accounts and government funds are being reduced.

Foreign investment will play a major role in making the Korean Economy more efficient and allow for further integration with the global economy.

Foreign investment, first and foremost, provides stable long term foreign capital, which is so vital to Korean economy at this time. Foreign investment will also help stimulate corporate restructuring, alleviate unemployment, and induce advanced technologies and managerial skills.

Recognizing the importance of foreign investment and open economic system, the newly inaugurated "Government of the People" has made a strong commitment to creating a most favorable environment for foreign direct investment.

THE IMPROVING INVESTMENT CLIMATE IN KOREA

Through extensive restructuring, Korea is transforming its economy into a truly open and market-based system with increased efficiency that is able to complete and cooperate with the rest of the world.

In this context, the government has recently taken significant steps toward liberalizing capital flows as well as establishing a simple and transparent legal framework of foreign investment.

MEASURES COMPLETED TO PROMOTE FOREIGN INVESTMENT

Market Liberalization
Liberalization of Business Sectors
Full Liberalization of Cross-Border M&As
Capital Market Liberalization
Full Opening of the Real Estate Market
Enactment of the New "Foreign Investment Promotion Act"
These measures to open capital markets and lower barriers to foreign investment are critical steps to improving the investment environment , and the restructuring process now taking place in Korea is indicative of the country's commitment to forming long-lasting international investment partnerships.

LIBERALIZING OF BUSINESS SECTOR

The government has made significant progress to date in the implementation of measures to attract foreign direct investment. Seven sectors have been fully liberalized as of April this year, including rental of residential buildings, and eleven sectors were liberalized in May. Further liberalization in other sectors will continue.

Only 31 sectors remain closed or partially open to foreign investors out of the total of 1,148 sectors. **This means, 98.9% of all industries are open to foreign investment.**
Full Liberalization of Cross-Border M&As
The government fully liberalized mergers and acquisitions domestic firms by foreign corporations in May of this year.
Foreign investors are now allowed to purchase 100 percent of the targeted company's outstanding stock without the consent of its board of directors (previously required until May of 1998).
Previously, any investor who wished to purchase 25 percent or more of a publicly-traded company's shares was obliged to make a tender offer bid (T.O.B.) to purchase more than 50 percent of the company's shares. This regulation has now been abolished.
The government has also revised the assessment criterion for corporate purchases to enable smooth mergers or acquisition between foreign and domestic companies, while introducing a

For additional analytical, business and investment opportunities information,
please contact Global Investment & Business Center, USA
at (202) 546-2103. Fax: (202) 546-3275. E-mail: rusric@erols.com

corporate divestiture system to facilitate spilt-ups and restructuring of business sectors within a company. Tax incentives to this end have been expanded accordingly.

CAPITAL MARKET LIBERALIZATION

The Korean government has recently expanded the opening of its capital market to attract more foreign capital.

The ceilings on aggregate foreign equity ownership and individual foreign ownership were eliminated

All limits on foreign investment into the government, corporate, and special bond markets have been lifted. According to the action, foreigners can invest without limit in the gamut of bonds available

Foreign purchases of the short term financial instruments issued by corporate and financial institutions such as corporate paper, commercial paper, trade bills, CDs, repurchase agreements (RPs), notes and cover bills, etc., have been fully liberalized

ENACTMENT OF THE NEW "FOREIGN INVESTMENT PROMOTION ACT"

The government recently enacted the "Foreign Investment Promotion Act" in order to reshape the foreign investment system totally from a "regulatory and administrative system" to a "promotion and support" oriented system. The new Act was streamlined and reorganized to increase investor convenience and now provides greater autonomy to the local governments in the arena of courting FDI. The new regime will provide foreign investors with a One-Stop service by the Korean Investment Service Center (KISC), which was newly established on July 1 for the purpose of carrying out FDI inducement activities and offering various incentives such as tax exemptions or reductions (please refer to chapter III).

RESHAPING LABOR MARKET FLEXIBILITY

To regain economic vitality, it is essential to increase the labor market flexibility and establish stable labor-management relationships. These two factors will be of great help to recovery of corporate competitiveness, an increase of foreign direct investment.

Recent labor market reform, in principle, centers on the application of previously introduced institutional measures for increasing labor market flexibility as stated by law.

The second tripartite committee, which was launched in June, focuses on reviewing the implementation of the agreement reached in the first round of discussions and addresses other labor market issues related to the improvement of working conditions and the expansion of unemployment benefits.

In order to promote job creation, the government is not only expanding the job training system, but also strengthening job placement services through privatization.

However, in the process of comprehensive and painful restructuring, the unemployment rate has increased from 2.6 percent in 1997 to 7.6 percent in July this year. To address this problem, the social safety net is being strengthened and the tripartite dialogue will encourage fair burden sharing among business, labor and government. The government will not tolerate illegal or inappropriate labor practices while encouraging the institutionalized labor market reform measures.

PROMOTING LABOR MARKET FLEXIBILITY

With the amendment of the Labor Standards Act, layoffs off will no longer be an ominous prospect for workers but a necessary and efficiency-enhancing step.

MEASURES TAKEN TO ENHANCE LABOR MARKET FLEXIBILITY

Introduction of Layoffs: Enhancing the flexibility of the Korean labor market
The Flexible Work-Hour System: Lowering labor costs and encouraging part-time work
The Dispatch of employees: Enhancing the efficiency of human resource management
The Improved Legal Retirement Pay System: Payment is made in advance for the period of continuous employment of the worker before the previously set date of retirement

The significant rise in unemployment and reduced real wages clearly demonstrate that the employment adjustment is occurring in Korea at this time.

MAJOR EXAMPLES OF INCREASED LABOR FLEXIBILITY

Of 3,3347 work places which have concluded wage bargains, 68 percent, or 2,259 workplaces, have agreed on wage freezes and 559 workplaces even agreed on wage cuts Even with wage bargaining during the year, agreed wages decreased by 2.4 percent as of July

The real wage is predicted to have decreased by more than 10 percent this year as inflation is expected to be around 8 percent

Furthermore, disputes between organized labor and management have been settled with equitable burden-sharing. The settlement of the industrial dispute at Hyundai Motor Co. is a meaningful case wherein layoffs were, for the first time after the legalization of layoffs, agreed upon by labor and management.

STRENGTHENING THE SOCIAL SAFETY NET

Unemployment problems, which inevitably occur in the process of structural reform, are being addressed with the highest priority to ensure that social cohesion and societal support for the overall reform process is not undermined.

MAJOR POLICIES TO ALLEVIATE UNEMPLOYMENT

Job creation through public sector projects. With the launch of such projects, an expected 380,000 jobs will be created

Promoting re-employment through job placement services

A vocational training system to develop the abilities of the unemployed. This system will continue in the post-restructuring era

Expansion of employment insurance to include every workplace from October this year, as a result, an additional 2.3 million unemployed workers will be covered by unemployment benefits

The Korean government has and continues to provide targeted support to facilitate the readjustment of the labor market. The government forecasts the total budget used in 1998 for unemployment will amount to 10.1 trillion won. This total unemployment budget, equivalent to 2.5 percent of the GDP, is very generous in comparison with other OECD countries.

IMPROVING LABOR MANAGEMENT RELATIONS

The Korean government has been pursuing reforms through mutual understanding and participation of labor leaders, business leaders, and public officials to create a labor market in which labor allocation and wage determination are efficiently governed through market mechanisms.

The first tripartite committee accorded 90 detailed measures that have been introduced to enhance corporate governance transparency, and to increase unemployment benefits and labor market flexibility, and the second round is engaging in more detailed and extensive discussions to solidify the Accord of the first round.

The Tripartite Commission is drawing lessons from the recent settlement of the Hyundai strike, and will devise measures for enhancing a new business-labor culture.

Such cooperation helps to reaching a social consensus on burden-sharing and facilitates successful restructuring.

In the event of unfair labor practices of employers or unlawful collective actions and violence by workers, the government will meet its legal mandate to bring about a resolution of conflicts between labor and management.

FULLY LIBERALIZATION OF THE FOREIGN EXCHANGE MARKET

The Korean government has taken additional and significant steps toward liberalizing foreign exchange and capital flows as well as establishing a simple, transparent legal framework.

This process involves abolishing the old "Foreign Exchange Control Act" and replacing it with new "Foreign Exchange Transactions Act," which is expected to fully liberalize the current cumbersome set of regulations on foreign exchange transaction.

As the new Act was approved by the National Assembly on September 2, the regulatory framework for foreign exchange flows has been revised from the partial positive-list system to a new full negative-list system. Furthermore, the old system of *ex-ante* and direct regulations has been transformed into one of *ex-post facto* management centered on prudential supervision.

The liberalization plan is scheduled to be implemented by two stages. The first is scheduled to start on April 1, 1999. The second-stage of liberalization measures are planned to be completed by the end of 2000. However, even before the enactment of the new Act, some urgent liberalization measures have already gone into effect from July 1, 1998, where legal amendments were not needed, in order to increase foreign capital inflow, promote the recently sluggish exports, and provide business enterprises broader access to international capital markets.

These reforms will strengthen prudential regulatory and supervisory standards for financial institutions, and also ensure that firms behave according to market principles, primarily through improvements in corporate transparency and governance.

LIBERALIZATION

Liberalization of mid and long-term overseas borrowings with maturities of more than one year and issuance of securities with maturity of minimum one year by business enterprises

Removal of restrictions on advance payment for export, deferred payment for import and purchase and sale of local real estate properties such as commercial buildings

Abolition of regulations requiring foreign investor to maintain accounts in a single domestic foreign exchange bank for portfolio investment purpose in Korea. The revision will allow foreign investors to maintain a single investment account covering various securities as desired

The ceiling on the consolidated over-bought and over-sold positions of banks was raised to 15% of the banks net assets. Separate ceiling on spot positions was repealed

Liberalizing Financial Transactions between Companies and Banks from April 1, 1999

The new Foreign Exchange Transaction Act will fully liberalize the current cumbersome set of regulations on foreign exchange transactions. The government anticipates that this new act will revitalize the sluggish foreign exchange market by enhancing foreign investor's confidence. The resulting competition by the liberalization is expected to eliminate from the marketplace ailing financial institutions that lack the financing techniques essential to survive in a globalized, market-based economy.

Liberalization of mid and long-term overseas borrowings with maturities of more than one year and issuance of securities by business enterprises with maturity of minimum of one year

Removal of restrictions on advance payments for export, deferred payment of import purchases, and sales of local real estate properties, such as commercial buildings

Abolition of regulations requiring foreign investors to maintain accounts in a single domestic foreign exchange bank for portfolio investment purposes in Korea. The revision will allow foreign investors to maintain a single investment account covering various securities as desired

The ceiling on the consolidated over-bought and over-sold positions of banks has been raised to 15 percent of the net asset of the banks. Separate ceilings on spot positions were repealed.

UPGRADING STANDARDS TO INTERNATIONAL LEVELS BY THE END OF 2000

By the end of 2000, the government will have upgraded prudential regulatory and accounting standards to international levels, and market surveillance will have been established. This will allow substantial liberalization of capital account transactions.

At this stage, by meeting 85 of the 91 standards in the OECD Liberalization Code of Capital Movements, Korea's capital account liberalization ratio will be brought to the mid-group level of OECD member countries. The government's setting the ultimate target schedule for the second stage liberalization represents its determination to expedite the process.

LIBERALIZATION BY THE END OF 2000

Non-residents will be permitted to open domestic won deposit accounts (including trust accounts) with maturities of less than one year

Firms and financial institutions will be permitted to deposit or extend credits abroad without restriction.

Resident individuals will be permitted to deal in derivatives transactions directly with overseas financial institutions.

Full liberalization of capital account transactions of resident individuals, including investments in overseas deposits (currently permitted up to US$50,000) and overseas real estate (currently permitted up to US$300,000).

For additional analytical, business and investment opportunities information, please contact Global Investment & Business Center, USA at (202) 546-2103. Fax: (202) 546-3275. E-mail: rusric@erols.com

COMPLETE OPENING OF THE REAL ESTATE MARKET

The government has changed the paradigm of the real estate policies on the basis of free market principles and has completely opened the real estate market to the global community, recognizing anti-speculative measures in 1970s and 1980s have proven to be inconvenient to business activities and investment.

ABROGATION OF RESTRICTIONS ON FOREIGN LAND ACQUISITION

The Korean government has amended the "Foreigner's Land Acquisition Act" and has now completely abrogated foreign land acquisition limits from June 26, 1998. Accordingly, under the new Act, foreigners, including nonresidents, are now given national treatment in the acquisition of land, without any limits such as land use and land size.

Entity	Before June 26, 1998	After June 26, 1998
Foreign Individual	Only foreigners of more than 5 years' residence in Korea with a visa were allowed to acquire land Foreigners were allowed to acquire under 660m (squared) land for residence and under 165m (squared) land for commerce	All foreigners including nonresidents are allowed to acquire land All limits on foreign land acquisition are abrogated
Foreign Corporation	Land acquisition was allowed only for business purposes, such as for factories, offices, and warehouse	Land acquisition is allowed even for non-businesses purposes All limits on foreign land acquisition were abrogated

SIMPLIFICATION OF FOREIGN LAND ACQUISITION PROCEDURE

In the prior "Foreigner's Land Acquisition Act", all purchasing of land by foreigners had to be approved before the conclusion of a contract. The new Act doesn't require approval any more except "military installation reservations, cultural properties and ecological reserves." All foreigners may simply report their purchases upon the conclusion of a contract.

OPENING OF BUSINESSES RELATED TO REAL ESTATE

Now, businesses related to the real estate, which were closed to foreigners previously, have already been fully open.

Businesses related to the real estate:

The "building rental and lotting-out /sale business" has been completely liberalized as of April 1, 1998
The "land lease and land development/sale business" has been completely liberalized as of May 8, 1998

INCREASE IN FOREIGN LAND ACQUISITION

For additional analytical, business and investment opportunities information, please contact Global Investment & Business Center, USA at (202) 546-2103. Fax: (202) 546-3275. E-mail: rusric@erols.com

Following the revision of the Foreigner's Land Acquisition Act on June 26, land acquisitions by foreigners amounted to 483 separate cases, involved 4.41 million square meters, and were worth a total of US$386 million during the two month from June 26, 1998.

The number of acquisitions during the two months sharply increased to 241, representing transactions worth US$196 million. These totals are 4.5-fold in cases and 5-fold in amount, the monthly average of the period from January 1994 to June 1998 The tremendous increase in land acquisitions by foreigners is traced to be a result of the liberalization of land acquisition and the rising overseas confidence in the Korean economy.

Trends of Foreigner Land Acquisition

(1000m squared, US$ million)

Entity	Monthly Avg. (Jan.'94 - June'98)		Monthly Avg. June 26 August 25		Total June 26 August 25		
	Case	Area(m^2)	Case	Area(m^2)	Case	Area(m^2)	Amount ($ mil)
USA	25.2	324	138.5	646	277	1293	73.5
EU	2.8	40	15.5	668	31	1336	130
Japan	1.3	4.0	20.5	420	41	839	13.4
Asia	18.9	2.6	40	99	80	198	36.1
Others	7.1	69	27	374	54	747	135
Total	55.3	439.6	241.5	2207	483	4413	388

OTHER RELAXATION OF RESTRICTIONS ON REAL ESTATE

Three representative restrictions imposed on the real estate sector for the purpose of anti-speculative measures on the real estate: (1) the Land Transaction Permit System, (2) the Residential Land Holding Ceiling System, and (3) Development Charges, have now been drastically abrogated or relaxed.

Also, with establishment of the new "Act on Asset Securitization" on September 1998, Mortgage Backed Securities (MBS) have been introduced. Agencies to provide the smooth flow of MBS will be set up in the near future.

ADDITIONAL INCENTIVES FOR FOREIGN INVESTORS

To revitalize the real estate market and accelerate the corporate restructuring, the government plans to reduce or exempt acquisition, registration and capital gains taxes, and obligation of buying housing bond by December 30, 1999, and exempt the obligation of buying housing bonds by June 30, 1999.

In addition, a special-purpose company will be founded to receive the rights to the land currently held as collateral by financial institutions, and issue asset-backed securities (ABS) based on such real estate. The Korea Asset Management Corporation will establish the Real Estate Information Service. It will register and keep track of pieces of real estate offered for sale by corporations.

For additional analytical, business and investment opportunities information, please contact Global Investment & Business Center, USA at (202) 546-2103. Fax: (202) 546-3275. E-mail: rusric@erols.com

The Real Estate Information Service will provide a one-stop service to foreigners who wish to purchase real estate.

PROTECTING INTELLECTUAL PROPERTY RIGHTS

The government has made and will continue to make concerted efforts to enhance the protection of intellectual property. The Korean government revised its IPR-related laws in 1995 to bring them into conformity with the WTO/TRIPs Agreement and continue to push to further enhance IPR laws to ensure the protection of the newly emerging fields, such as IPR on internet and trade secrets.

The Protection of IPRs

Type	Definition	Term of Protection	Relevant Office
Patent	A highly advanced technological idea based on the laws of nature (major invention)	20 years from the filing date	Korean Industrial Property Office
Utility Model	A technological idea based on the laws of nature (minor invention)	15 years from the filing date	Korean Industrial Property Office
Industrial Design	A shape, pattern, color, or any combination of an article which produces an aesthetic impression in the sense of sight	10 years from the date of registration	Korean Industrial Property Office
Trademark	A sign, character, figure, three dimensional shape, or any combination thereof, with its colors, which is used on goods or services in order to distinguish their identify	10 years from the date of registration (the protection will be semi-permanent if renewal is made every 10 years)	Korean Industrial Property Office
Semiconductor Chip Layout Design	-	10 years from the date of registration	Semiconductor Division of the Korean Industrial Property Office
Computer Program	-	50 years	Korea computer Program Protection Foundation
Copyright	Creative works in the literary or artistic domain	The lifetime of the rightholder and 50 years posthumously	Copyright Division of the Ministry of Culture and Tourism

For additional analytical, business and investment opportunities information, please contact Global Investment & Business Center, USA at (202) 546-2103. Fax: (202) 546-3275. E-mail: rusric@erols.com

Source: The Korea Industrial Property Office

JOINING OF INTERNATIONAL AGREEMENTS

Korea has joined numerous international agreements to protect the intellectual property rights.

International agreements relevant to Industrial Property Rights:

> 1979: World Intellectual Property Organization (WIPO)
> 1980: Paris Convention for Protection of Industrial Property
> 1984: Patent Cooperation Treaty (PCT)
> 1988: Budapest Treaty International agreements relevant to Copyrights

International agreements relevant to Industrial Copyrights:

> 1987: Universal Copyright Convention (UCC)
> 1996: Berne Convention

The Korea Industrial Property Office (KIPO) is planning to join the Strasbourg Agreement Concerning International Patent Classification and the Nice Agreement Concerning the International Classification of Goods and Services for the Purpose of Registration of Marks to meet the international standardization of the patent and trademark systems within this year. By joining these agreements, Korea will have a regime of intellectual property rights more transparent to foreign investors and regulate itself according to international standards.

THE NEW FOREIGN DIRECT INVESTMENT REGIME

The Korean government has now, in order to create a more supportive and convenient system of foreign direct investment, replaced the old system of regulating and administering foreign investment with a new paradigm of policies. The new paradigm is symbolized in the new Foreign Investment Promotion Act (hereinafter "the new Act").

As the new Act was passed on September 2, 1998, by the National Assembly, it will become effective on November 17, 1998, subsequently abolishing the previous Act on Foreign Direct Investment and Foreign Capital Inducement. The new FDI regime is based on two major principles.

THE TWO MAJOR PRINCIPLES OF THE NEW FDI REGIME

Formulating policies to design the most supportive and convenient FDI system possible for foreign investment from the perspective of the foreign investor

Establishing a FDI system in which local governments, in efforts to advance regional development, play the central role in competitively courting FDI

To this end, the new Act has been developed to create a more transparent and liberalized system, abolish the cumbersome regulations and augment incentives, and to provide One-Stop service through the Korea Investment Service Center. It incorporates seven major objectives.

THE SEVEN MAJOR OBJECTIVES OF THE FOREIGN INVESTMENT PROMOTION ACT

Liberalization and Protection of FDI
Augmentation of Tax Incentives
Enhancement of Property Incentives and Subsidies
Simplification of Procedures
Provision of One-Stop Service
Establishment of Foreign Investment Zones (FIZs)
Establishment of the Commission on Foreign Direct Investment Policy

A. LIBERALIZATION AND PROTECTION OF FDI

Liberalization of FDI in Principle

In order to promote further global integration, Korea has continued to liberalize FDI. With the joining of the OECD, on December 12, 1996, previously restrictive regulations on FDI were drastically streamlined and brought to the internationally accepted level. After the onset of the foreign exchange crisis of late 1997, further efforts have been made.

The new Act proclaims that all the sectors, in principle, are liberalized and brings Koreas FDI regime to the highest international standards. Restrictions on FDI now only apply in cases where the sustainment of national security, public order, public health, environmental preservation, or social morals are threatened.

Category	1997	January 1998	September 1998
Total businesses	1,148		
Partially opened sectors	26	31	18
Closed	27	21	13
Liberalization ratio	97.6%	98.2%	98.9%

Liberalization ratio: Number of business fully and partially opened / Total business sectors x 100

Currently, as out of a total classified 1,148 sectors, only 13 remain closed to FDI, **98.9 percent of Korea's economy is open to the world.** The present 18 partially opened sectors will be further liberalized in the near future.

The Comprehensive Annual Announcement on FDI Restrictions

Under the new Act, to promote the transparency of Korea's FDI regime and provide further convenience for foreign investors, a comprehensive annual announcement on all FDI restrictions in various individual laws will be made by the Minister of Finance and Economy.

The announcement will henceforth be made every year on a yearly basis. The first comprehensive annual announcement will be made in January of 1999.

Actions to address and correct restrictive regulations in annual announcements which are deemed as not meeting international standards or unnecessarily hampering FDI will be taken as immediately.

For additional analytical, business and investment opportunities information,
please contact Global Investment & Business Center, USA
at (202) 546-2103. Fax: (202) 546-3275. E-mail: rusric@erols.com

NATIONAL TREATMENT FOR FOREIGN INVESTED ENTERPRISES

Under the new Act, foreign investors and foreign invested enterprises, in entering the Korean market and conducting business activities, will receive no less favorable treatment than domestic enterprises.

PROTECTION OF FDI AT THE INTERNATIONAL LEVEL

Korea has signed 53 bilateral investment agreements with such countries as Japan, Germany, U.K., and France, in order to protect FDI and guarantee the free flow of capital.

After the accession to the OECD, Korea has actively participated in the negotiations of the Multilateral Agreement on Investment (MAI). Koreas participation in MAI negotiations symbolizes its commitment for the highest standards of the liberalization and protection of FDI.

B. TAX INCENTIVES

To further promote FDI, the new Act has augmented the scope of businesses subject to tax reduction/exemption incentives, and the ratio and period of tax reduction/exemption incentives.

BUSINESSES SUBJECT TO TAX REDUCTION/EXEMPTION INCENTIVES

Advance-technology businesses
Service businesses that support the international competitiveness of domestic industry
Businesses located in a Foreign Investment Zone

Previously, the Korean government provided tax reduction/exemption incentives for 265 types of advanced-technology businesses. Under the new Act, to further support FDI, the number of types of advanced-technology businesses eligible to receive tax reduction/exemption incentives has been expanded from 265 to 436. In addition, 97 types of service businesses that support the international competitiveness of domestic industry are to also receive tax reduction/exemption incentives.

All in all, now, the number of types of business that may receive tax reduction/exemption incentives has increased more than double fold from 265 to 533.

NUMBER OF BUSINESS SUBJECT TO TAX REDUCTION/EXEMPTION INCENTIVES

Type of Business	Past	Present
Advance-technology business	265	436
Service business that supports the international competitiveness of domestic industry	0	97
Total	265	533

TAX REDUCTION/EXEMPTION RATIO AND PERIOD

For additional analytical, business and investment opportunities information, please contact Global Investment & Business Center, USA at (202) 546-2103. Fax: (202) 546-3275. E-mail: rusric@erols.com

Under the new Act, tax reduction/exemption incentives for corporate and income taxes have been expanded from eight years (five years at 100 percent, then three years at 50 percent) to ten years (seven years at 100 percent, then three at 50 percent).

To support the establishment of a FDI system in which local governments play the central role in courting FDI, local governments are empowered to provide tax reduction and exemption incentives for local taxes - property taxes, acquisition taxes, aggregate land taxes, and registration taxes - for 8 to 15 years as they see fit. The minimum required tax reduction/exemption by law is eight years (five years at 100 percent, then three years at 50 percent).

Customs duties, special excise tax, and value added tax, with respect to capital goods imported for 3 years from the date of notification of FDI for the purpose of operating a business of a foreign invested enterprise, are exempted.

TAX INCENTIVES FOR FOREIGN INVESTED ENTERPRISES

Type of Tax	Past	Present
Corporate tax Income tax	Full exemption for the first 5 years 50% reduction for 3 years thereafter	Full exemption for the first 7 years 50% reduction for the 3 years thereafter
Corporate tax on dividends Income tax on dividends	Full exemption for the first 5 years 50% reduction for 3 years thereafter	Full exemption for the first 7 years 50% reduction for the 3 years thereafter
Local taxes Acquisition tax Property tax Aggregate land tax Registration tax	Full exemption for the first 5 years 50% reduction for 3 years thereafter Registration tax is not reduced/exempted	Local tax incentives can be granted from 8 to 15 years The minimum required by law is: - Full exemption for the first 5 years - 50% reduction for the 3 years thereafter Registration tax is newly included

tax	Customs duty Special excise Value added tax	Full exemption on imported capital goods	Full exemption on imported capital goods

TAX EXEMPTION INCENTIVES ON ROYALTIES

Corporate and income tax of royalties on induced advanced technologies are fully exempted for 5 years. Applications for exemptions must be submitted to the government.

Introduction of the Tax Reduction or Exemption Checking System

Foreign-invested businesses eligible for tax incentives, which make investment in Korea for the first time, should request reduction/exemption of corporate tax or income tax before the end of the fiscal year in which the date of business opening falls. In the case of additional investment, such a request may be made within two years form the date of notification of FDI. Tax exemption can also be requested at the time of notification of the foreign investment.

Under the new Act, a "Tax Reduction or Exemption Checking System" has been introduced. Foreign investors or foreign invested enterprise may check with the government if their businesses are eligible for tax reduction or exemption incentives prior to deciding to invest.

If the contents of business are not changed when the notification of FDI is made, the tax reduction/exemption incentives will apply according to the check made with the government prior to the notification.

Requested tax reduction/exemption incentives will be decided upon by the Minister of Finance and Economy after consultation with the authorities concerned.

Tax Conventions

Tax conventions aim at preventing double taxation and tax evasion. They define important concepts such as tax residence, fixed business establishment, the scope of taxable income, the country of income source, and maximum tax rates.

If the tax conventions are in conflict with the domestic laws of the signing country, the tax conventions take precedence over the latter.

COUNTRIES SIGNED A TAX CONVENTION WITH KOREA

Austria, Australia, Bangladesh, Belgium, Brazil, Bulgaria, Canada, China, Czech Republic, Denmark, Egypt, Fiji, Finland, France, Germany, Great Britain, Greece, Hungary, India, Indonesia, Ireland, Italy, Japan, Luxembourg, Malaysia, Mexico, Mongolia, Netherlands, New Zealand, Norway, Pakistan, Philippines, Poland, Portugal, Russia, Rumania, Singapore, Spain, South Africa, Sri Lanka, Sweden, Switzerland, Thailand, Tunisia, Turkey, USA, Vietnam

For additional analytical, business and investment opportunities information,
please contact Global Investment & Business Center, USA
at (202) 546-2103. Fax: (202) 546-3275. E-mail: rusric@erols.com

ENHANCEMENT OF PROPERTY INCENTIVES AND SUBSIDIES

EXTENSION OF THE RENTAL PERIOD

Under the new Act, the rental period of central and local government properties have been expanded from 20 years up to 50 years. Rental periods may be renewed continuously up to 50 years at a time.

With respects to purchasing central government properties, payment, may be delayed for 1 year and installment payments up to a maximum of 20 years are possible. In respect to purchasing of local government properties, local governments will determine to time frame of payments.

RENTAL FEE REDUCTION/EXEMPTION FOR GOVERNMENT PROPERTY

Under the new Act, specific foreign invested enterprises eligible to receive rental fee reduction incentives for central government properties.

RENTAL FEE REDUCTION OR EXEMPTION RATIOS FOR CENTRAL GOVERNMENT PROPERTY

Rental fee reductions up to 100 % will be provided for:

> Foreign invested enterprises located in an Foreign Investment Zone (FIZ)
> Companies with advance-technology making a FDI over $1 million located in one of the three Industrial Parks for foreign invested enterprises
> Rental fee reductions up to 75 % will be provided for:
> Manufacturing companies located in one of the three Industrial Parks for foreign invested enterprises making a FDI over $10 million
> "Companies to be determined eligible by the Commission on Foreign Direct Investment Policy": companies which contribute to the augmentation of social overhead capital, support industrial restructuring, or support the financial independence of local governments from the central government
> Rental fee reductions up to 50% will be provided for: Foreign invested enterprises in located in a National Industrial Park (35 parks)

Under the new Act, in the process of renting, local governments have the autonomous power to grant rent reduction or exemption incentives and determine rent rates as they see fit.

REDUCTION OR EXEMPTION OF THE LAND CONVERSION FEE

Under the new Act, in the case a foreign invested enterprise seeks to convert a farm or forestry land into a factory site, the conversion fee will be reduced or exempted. The current farm or forestry conversion fee is 20 percent of the land value.

CENTRAL GOVERNMENT SUPPORT FOR LOCAL GOVERNMENT EFFORTS TO PROMOTE FDI

Under the new Act, in order to establish a FDI system in which local governments, in efforts to advance regional development, play the central role in competitively courting FDI, the central government will support local government efforts to promote FDI through the following methods:

For additional analytical, business and investment opportunities information,
please contact Global Investment & Business Center, USA
at (202) 546-2103. Fax: (202) 546-3275. E-mail: rusric@erols.com

Funds will be supplied for the development of FIZs
Capital, to purchase land to be rented to foreign invested enterprises, will be lent
Funds will be supplied to make up the loss local government incur by reducing or
exempting purchase or rental fees of property for foreign invested enterprises
Public subsides for various purposes, such as job training, will be provided

Through such measures, local governments will:
Become competitive with one another in inducing FDI
Be more capable to induce FDI
Eventually, offer various and better incentives to foreign investors

D. SIMPLIFICATION OF PROCEDURES

The New FDI Procedure: Simplification of the FDI Notification and Reporting Procedures

Prior to the new Act, there were the four regulatory and administrative required steps to make a foreign direct investment.

Under the new Act, FDI procedures have been drastically simplified by eliminating a number of steps, including the government acceptance of a FDI notification and the report of the arrival of foreign capital. This simplification of notification procedures means that the government's acceptance of a FDI notification is no longer required, except in the case of investments in the defense industry. Under the new Act, all permitted forms of foreign direct investment need simply be notified to the government via a Foreign Investment Notification and Registration Institution (FINER).

Foreign Investment Notification and Registration Institutions:
o   Branches and headquarters of the all banks in Korea dealing with foreign exchange (hereinafter Foreign Exchange Bank)

The overseas offices, local offices, and the headquarters of KOTRA's Korea Investment Service Center (KISC)

The requirement that non-residents appoint a resident of Korea as proxy to submit notification applications of FDI to the government has also been abolished. Anyone now may submit notification forms to the government. To make facilitate this process, notification forms to be submitted to the government have been published in English and Korean. Previously, notification forms were only available in Korean.

Under Technology Inducement Contract, the government's acceptance of an induced technology is no longer required. Under the new Act, notification is only required in cases of: (1) technologies eligible for tax reduction or exemption, (2) aviation related technologies, and (3) defense related technologies

Abolishment of the requirement to report the arrival of induced foreign capital: The requirement to report the arrival of induced foreign capital to the Minister of Finance and Economy within one month from its date of entrance, also has been abolished.
This means the new foreign investment system has been simplified into two major steps. Under the new Act, all that foreign investors have to do, in making an FDI in Korea, is notify the government of the FDI and register the FDI to a FINRI.

For additional analytical, business and investment opportunities information,
please contact Global Investment & Business Center, USA
at (202) 546-2103. Fax: (202) 546-3275. E-mail: rusric@erols.com

ESTABLISHMENT OF EXPEDITED APPROVAL OR AUTHORIZATION PROCEDURES FOR FDI ONE-STOP SERVICE

Newly Adopted Systems to Expedite FDI Procedures

The Comprehensive System the simultaneous approval of various applications
The Automatic Approval System the automatic approval of applications when a decision is not made within the specified time period stipulated by law
The Prior Approval System - the prior approvals of applications in cases where main documents are completed and only a few minor documents remain to be submitted

In order to provide further convenient services for foreign invested enterprises, step ?(approvals for business activities) has been provided with new measures to ensure more transparent and expedited approval or authorization procedures. Step ?has been simplified through the following measures:

1. The Organizational Process

Under the new law, all FDI related civil applications are now classified into three categories and settled according to respective procedure.
Regular applications: application settled through appropriate procedures required in the settlement of civil matters.
Immediate settlement applications: applications settled on the spot at the Korea Investment Service Center (KISC) by representatives dispatched from various administrative institutions.
Comprehensive settlement applications: applications settled through the Comprehensive Process System.

2. The Comprehensive Process System

Under the new Act, a "Comprehensive Process System" for approval or authorization has been established. Under the Comprehensive Process System, when a foreign investors simply submits a comprehensive settlement application to the Korean Investment Service Center (KISC), KISC operates as a proxy for the foreign investor through the whole procedure with relevant administrative institutions until a decision on approval is provided.
In the Comprehensive Process System, if the main approval (e.g.: Factory Establishment Permit) in a certain comprehensive process application (e.g.: approvals in relation to the Factory Establishment Permit) is approved, then remaining supplementary applications (e.g.: 26 approvals pertaining to 16 laws) are automatically approved.

TYPES OF COMPREHENSIVE APPLICATIONS AND RELATED MAJOR/SUPPLEMENTARY APPROVALS

The 5 Comprehensive Process Packages	Major Approval	Supplementary Approvals
Approvals in Relation to the Factory Establishment Permit	Factory Establishment Permit	26 approvals pertaining to 16 laws

For additional analytical, business and investment opportunities information, please contact Global Investment & Business Center, USA at (202) 546-2103. Fax: (202) 546-3275. E-mail: rusric@erols.com

Approvals in Relation to the Small-Medium Company Start-Up Permit	Medium and Small Company Establishment Business Plan Permit	26 approvals pertaining to 14 laws
Approvals in Relation to the Construction Permit	Construction Permit	30 approvals pertaining to 18 laws
Approvals in Relation to Environmental Permits	Sewage Disposal Facility and/or Air Pollution Control Facility Permit	7 approvals pertaining to 6 laws
Approvals in Relation to the Use of Constructed Materials Permit	Use of Constructed Materials Permit	12 approvals pertaining to 6 laws

The Comprehensive Process System minimizes the time and procedures needed to receive various approvals and authorizations from related administrative institutions.

3. The Automatic Authorization System

Under the Automatic Authorization System, if there is no response to an application of approval or authorization related to FDI within the time period stipulated by Presidential Decree, approval or authorization shall be automatically granted.

In the event of an automatic approval, a certificate of Approval or Authorization shall be presented to the foreign investor or foreign invested enterprise upon request.

4. The Prior Approval System

Under the new Act, with respect to comprehensive applications, prior approvals will be made in case of approvals where main documents are completed and only a few minor documents remain to be submitted, on the condition that remaining documents be submitted within the time frame stated by Presidential Decree.

5. Minimization of documents to be submitted

Various documents needed for notification, approval, and authorization have been reduced by approximately **50 percent**.

6. Transparency of the approval or authorization system

Under the new Act, when an approval or authorization is rejected by an administrative institution, the reasons and legal basis of the rejection must be informed to the applicant. If the applicant corrects the reasons for rejection approval or authorization, approval or authorization must be granted.

One-Stop Service at KISC

Submission of applications
Immediate settlement applications directly settled on the spot
Substitute settlement of approval or authorization applications (proxy request of settlement)
Approval or Non-approval of applications (automatic approval upon lapse of time period determined by law)
Notification of the settlement (Approval or Non-approval / other services)

For additional analytical, business and investment opportunities information, please contact Global Investment & Business Center, USA at (202) 546-2103. Fax: (202) 546-3275. E-mail: rusric@erols.com

Monitoring and encouragement of settlement procedures related to FDI

E. PROVISION OF ONE-STOP SERVICE AT THE KOREA INVESTMENT SERVICE CENTER (KISC)

Establishment of the Korea Investment Service Center

One of the grievances often cited by foreign investors was that there were too many contact points and administrative procedures, which often lead to red tape and delay. To solve this grievance, the Korean government launched the Korea Investment Service Center (KISC) at KOTRA as of April 30, 1998, for the purpose of eliminating this friction and supporting foreign investors through all stages of investment, from consulting to after-service.

KISC is staffed by experts from various authorities, including representatives of the Ministry of Finance and Economy, Ministry of Commerce, Industry, & Energy, Ministry of Justice, National Tax Administration, Korea Customs Service, Small and Medium Industry Promotion Corporation, and local governments.

Investment Promotion Activities by KISC
KISC operates as a proxy for the foreign investor through the whole procedure until approval is issued. In such cases, 90 percent of procedures concerned with foreign investment, except only a few matters of particular gravity, are to be undertaken by KISC.

KISC's services are provided free of charge.

KISC will save foreign investors a great deal of time and energy formerly consumed by administrative procedures.

Online Services
Information concerning the KISC and its services, as well as the related ministries and organizations, can be easily accessed on the Internet. Foreign investors can find information on the foreign direct investment administration in Korea, the investment climate and other data. The Korean government also provides an area on its web sites to address grievances.

The Ministry of Finance and Economy offers a up-to-date economic information of Korea. The site contains information on Korea's investment climate, policies regarding foreign direct investment, trade statistics and responses to grievances lodged by foreign investors.

KOTRA, offers information on the investment climate as well as on-line information on trade and foreign direct investment.

SERVICES PROVIDED BY KISC

Settlement for applications as a proxy for foreign investors
Information and data for investment feasibility studies
Consultation on policy, procedures, and incentives for investing in Korea
Matchmaking with potential Korean joint venture of M&A partners
Searches for locating for suitable plant sites and acting on behalf of foreign investors for procedures required for factory establishment
Follow-up service for businesses after establishment

Meeting coordination and arrangement for foreign investors with relevant government agencies, institutions, and local companies
Online services
Settlement of grievances and difficulties for foreign investors through the Ombudsman Institution
Other forms of administrative support, e.g., extension of the sojourn period of foreign invested company personnel

The Establishment of the Ombudsman Institution at KISC

Under the new Act, an Ombudsman institution has been established within the Korea Investment Service Center to address the grievances and difficulties of foreign investors and foreign invested enterprises.

Upon receiving a grievance from a foreign investor or foreign invested enterprise, the Ombudsman Institution will act immediately to remedy the situation by acting as middle man between the said related administrative institutions and foreign investor or foreign invested enterprise. The Ombudsman institution, by it own accord, will also be able to make direct investigations of the grievances of foreign investor.

The Ombudsman is empowered to request cooperation from related administrative institution.

Related administrative institutions, which receive a Request of Cooperation from the Ombudsman Institution, must, by law, immediately address the said issue and present a plan to solve the addressed issue within 7 days of receiving the Request.

The appointed head of the Ombudsman institution will be an individual with a great deal of experience in the arena of FDI.

Introduction of Foreign Investment Promotion Offices
Foreign Investment Promotion Offices have been established in local governments at metropolitan cities and provinces for the FDI inducement activities at the local level and to support for the settlement of comprehensive applications.

Foreign Investment Promotion Offices shall work to settle the approval and authorization application of their respective city and provincial governments and cooperate to settle applications requested by KISC and relevant administrative institutions.

ESTABLISHMENT OF FOREIGN INVESTMENT ZONES (FIZS)

To develop large-scale FDI projects, the Korean government has introduced the establishment of Foreign Investment Zones.

Unlike the previous system in which the location of industrial parks for foreigners were pre-designated by the government. Under the new Act, FIZs will be designated by the local government where the foreign investors expresses a preference. The criteria to designate an FIZ will be the amount of FDI and the number of jobs created by the foreign invested enterprise

DESIGNATION OF AN FIZ

Designation procedure:

The foreign investor will request the designation of an FIZ in a specified location of preference

The Governor of the region will note the preferred site of the foreign investor and develop a FIZ designation plan to be submitted to the Commission on Foreign Direct Investment Policy (CFDIP)

The CFDIP shall decide whether to approve the proposed FZI designation plan.

Upon approval from the CFDIP, the Governor will designate the selected site as an FIZ

GOVERNMENT SUPPORT FOR FOREIGN INVESTED ENTERPRISES LOCATED IN FIZS

Tax reduction or exemption incentives

Corporate tax, and income tax on dividends: the first 7 years at 100% and the remaining 3 years at 50%

Local taxes (acquisition tax, property tax, aggregate land tax, and registration tax): 8 to 15 years

Custom duties: exemption

Exemption from the mandatory fee for the creation of traffic congestion due to the establishment of a building/factory

Providing support for medical facilities, housing, and educational facilities (to be determined by the Commission on Foreign Direct Investment Policy)

Allowing all firms to engage in sectors previously restricted solely for small and medium sized companies

Exception from the requirement to employee National Meritorious Persons (e.g., war veterans and their family) till 2003

Granting automatic approval of imports and exports business operations and deregulation of restrictions on imports and exports, such as import diversification

Allowing the omission of the mandatory approval of the Mayor when dividing land in an FIZ

ESTABLISHMENT OF THE COMMISSION ON FOREIGN DIRECT INVESTMENT POLICY

Under the new Act, the Commission on Foreign Direct Investment Policy will be established to deliberate upon and make swift decisions in regards to the following issues:

Basic policy and affairs in the of the FDI regime

Affairs in the improvement of the FDI environment

Affairs in the tax reduction/exemption criteria for foreign invested enterprises

Affairs in the cooperation and reconciliation of opinions and conflicts of the central government and other municipalities in relations to foreign direct investment

Affairs in the designation and support of FIZs

Affairs in determining the support for local government efforts to induce FDI

Other major affairs in the inducement of FDI

Under the new Act, the chairman of the commission shall be the Minister of Finance and Economy and members of the commission shall be the ministers and heads of relevant administrative institutions.

RECENT TRENDS IN FDI

The Steady Increase of Foreign Direct Investment

In response to Korea's continued efforts to offer a favorable investment environment, foreign investment has sharply increased by an average of 64% each year since 1993. Especially, the large increase in 1997 (see table) is traced to be a result of joining the OECD and liberalizing the Korean market to OECD

The chief contributions in FDI have come mainly from advanced nations, such as the US, Japan, and the countries of the European Union. Since 1996, when the three economies accounted for their lowest total of 68% of all FDI in Korea, their share has drastically risen to record 84% in 1997 and 88% for this year. In 1998, the sharp increase in Japanese ratio of FDI has played a major role in the upward tendency.

Although last year's foreign exchange crisis brought the temporary downfall, foreign investment has once again steadily increased since February of this year. The most substantial pick up of FDI was in the month of July. In July alone, foreign direct investments increased to US$1.2 billion, well exceeding the July 1997 total by almost 203 percent.

Observers in government and industry are ascribing the favorable trend in FDI to a rise in investor confidence following the stabilization of the won in foreign exchange markets and the implementation of a sweeping range of liberalization measures. Especially, the increase of FDI in the manufacturing sector is seen as proof of the optimism foreign investors have in regards to the prospects of the Korean economy.

Although there is a temporary drop in FDI in August resulting from seasonal factors, such as the summer holidays, and the recent turbulence in the world financial markets, FDI for September once again shows rising signs. With the enactment of the Foreign Investment Promotion Act in November, FDI in Korea looks to continue to substantially increase.

Increase of M&As

A salient feature of the overall pattern of FDI this year is that M&A related investments via acquisition of shares of existing Korea companies increased substantially. Between January and August, such M&A related investments reached US$930 million, accounting for 22.7 percent of total investments (versus 10 percent in 1997). Particularly, out of 83 cases in which the investment amount exceeded US$10 million, 31 cases were M&A related. Thus, the considerable rise in corporate restructuring via sales of shares is evident.

Foreign Investor (Nationality)	Korean Counterpart	Business Sector	Amount (US$ mil.)
Commerz Bank A.G. (Germany)	Korea Exchange Bank	Finance	276
BASF (Germany)	Hyosung BASF	Chemical	43
Seagram Co., Ltd (Canada)	Doosan Seagram Co., Ltd	Food	41
Fuji Xerox	Korea Xerox	Electronics	50

For additional analytical, business and investment opportunities information, please contact Global Investment & Business Center, USA at (202) 546-2103. Fax: (202) 546-3275. E-mail: rusric@erols.com

(Japan)			
Pfizer Holdings Ireland (Ireland)	Pfizer Korea	Pharmacy	34
Interbrew Int'l B.V. (Holland)	Doosan Brewery Co. Ltd.	Brewery	250
Bowater Incorporated (USA)	Bowater-Halla Paper co.	Paper	230
Glaxo Group Ltd. (UK)	Glaxo-Welcom, Korea	Pharmacy	75
Wal-Mart Stores (USA)	Korea Makro Co.	Wholesale	181
Vetrotex finance S.A. (France)	Vetrotex Korea	Ceramics	40
Societe d'Administrationet de Gestion (France)	Hanglass Co.	Ceramics	61
Volvo Korea Holding A.B. (Sweden)	Volvo Construction Equipment Korea	Transportation Equipment	180
Norske Skog Asia Pacific Pte. (Singapore)	Norske Skog Korea Co.	Paper	175
Bank of America (USA)	Koram Bank	Finance	30
Air Products & Chemicals Inc. (USA)	Air Products Korea	Chemical	31
Costco Wholesale Int'l Inc. (USA)	Costco Wholesale Korea Ltd.	Wholesale	104
Clark Material Handling Co. (USA)	Clark Material Handling Asia	Transportation Equipment	37
Kimberly Clark Corp. (USA)	Yuhan Kimberly	Paper	32
CRI Financial Corp. (USA)	Coca-Cola, Korea	Foods	123
IR. G. Passchier Management B.V.(Holland)	AES Inchon Generating Co.	Generation	100

PROSPECTS FOR THE KOREAN ECONOMY

With the challenges presented by the economic difficulties of today, Korea's government, businesses, and people are rallying together, under the leadership of President Kim, to overcome the economic hardships in the process of restructuring and reform.

Korea acknowledges that there continues to be a possibility of a decrease in economic growth in 1998 due to contractions in domestic and international demands, a domestic credit crunch, and the impact of restructuring efforts. However, in 1999, Korea expects the real GDP growth rate to be 2 percent, as the benefits of restructuring and economic reforms are borne, and confidence and domestic demand return.

For additional analytical, business and investment opportunities information, please contact Global Investment & Business Center, USA at (202) 546-2103. Fax: (202) 546-3275. E-mail: rusric@erols.com

The current account surplus in 1998 will be about US$ 37 billion. The size of the surplus will be reduced in 1999 to around US$ 18 billion, due to rise in imports. Inflation is also expected to be subdued in 1999 to about 5 percent by dint of exchange rate stabilization.

By 2000, the structural reforms will be largely completed, and the economy should resume its potential growth rate. In particular, financial restructuring will allow more credit at lower interest rates, thereby promoting domestic demand through private consumption and fixed investment. Furthermore, the sustained current account surplus will significantly improve Korea's foreign debt position and further stabilize the exchange rate. With financial market stability restored, the economy is predicted to grow to its potential.

Opening a New Horizon of Opportunities

Across time and countries, successful reform is quite rare and it is not an easy process, nor does it produce results overnight. Even nations that do achieve their reform goals are inevitably subject to occasional bumps in the road. Korea is no exception in this regard.

However, despite the obstacles, the Korean government and the Korean people's commitment to implement reform is strong. As the immediate liquidity problem has been stabilized under a short period of time, Korea now looks to set upon a path towards recovery

By way of structural reforms, Korea is not only increasing efficiency, but enhance economic growth potential as well. Financial sector reform will establish the principle of management responsibility based on sound financial structures, resulting in more efficient allocation of financial resources. Corporate sector reforms will not only improve investor confidence and induce investment, but also enhance corporate resiliency against external shocks. Public sector reform will provide customer-oriented public services through more competition and managerial innovation. The labor market will be more flexible and cooperative in industrial relations.

These reforms will also set new horizons for investment and business opportunities for foreign investors. In turn, such measures will prove greatly beneficial to Korea, as foreign investment in Korea country will help the country to pay back foreign debt and overcome the current economic difficulties.

In addition, Korea today presents many exemplary advantages for foreign investment. To stimulate our investment climate, as mentioned above, numerous regulations and restrictions related to foreign investment have been streamlined and incorporated into a single legal framework, represented by the Foreign Investment Promotion Act.

This will enable the government to provide One-Stop service and national treatment for foreign investors, in sharp contrast to the previously cumbersome set of complex procedures and selective treatment.

The government has also made significant progress to date in the implementation of measures to open the capital market and reduce barriers to portfolio and real estate investment.

With regard to the labor market, which potential foreign investors are keeping a watchful eye on, the government has already increased flexibility, and is carefully examining all the issues raised in the process of consultations between labor and management. A standardized system for labor-management relations is also being developed.

For additional analytical, business and investment opportunities information, please contact Global Investment & Business Center, USA at (202) 546-2103. Fax: (202) 546-3275. E-mail: rusric@erols.com

Beyond such efforts made by the government to overcome current economic difficulties and reform the FDI system, Korea offers a great many inherent benefits to foreign investors.

First, Korea's proximity to China - potentially the largest market in the world, Japan the second largest economy in the world, and Russia the largest country in the world, offers a prime central geographic location for investors who wish to develop a foothold in the potentially largest global market of the coming 21st century.

Second, Korea, offers a variety of factors, such a highly productive and educated workforce (which is immeasurably important to foreign investors) and a business environment which is based upon and ensures free market principles.

Third, considering the enormous potential growth of Korea's domestic firms to come, the present price of shares in the Korean stock market is highly undervalued. This will provide foreign investors with high returns.

Fourth, Korea's economic fundamentals remain sound, including high savings, an advanced industrial base, and prudent macroeconomic policies - all elements which are noted as key ingredients to sustained growth.

Last, Koreans have always shown a strong sense of national purpose in overcoming difficulties. Emerging from the ruins of war, Korea has risen to be the 11th largest economy in the world.

The recent tripartite agreement between labor, business and government also signifies in concrete terms the Korean people's realistic understanding of the effects of the current crisis, as well as their determination to work together toward recovery under the strong and democratic leadership of President Kim.

Furthermore, the Korean people generally understand and support the responsible participation of foreign investors based on a uniform set of rules and procedures that apply to and protect the interests of all parties. Thus, the Korean public's support, in this regard, has been reflected in a recent poll, whereby 87 percent of those polled believe that foreign participation is important to the Korean economy.

Now, Korea ushers in the new millennium by establishing a new economic paradigm that advocates both sustainable growth and full integration into the world economy. Through it, Korea's new economic system will surely open a broader horizon of opportunities for its citizens and foreigners alike.

President Kim stated that "under the WTO system, capital doesn't have nationality, thus, Toyota USA is more American than IBM Korea," Korea is transforming its economic system and investment environment for foreign businessmen to feel Korea is the best place to do business in this world.

BASIC REGULATIONS AND PROCEDURES FOR FOREIGN INVESTMENTS IN KOREA

"FOREIGN INVESTMENT PROMOTION ACT"

The Foreign Investment Promotion Act was approved at the National Assembly on September 2, 1998. The new law is expected to play a key role in making Korea's foreign investment environment more internationally competitive and attractive to foreign investors by providing simplified procedures, one-stop foreign direct investment service, and reinforced tax incentives.

BASIC DIRECTION

Foreign direct investment (FDI) policies will be restructured to support foreign investment from the perspective of the foreign investor and an investment environment based on the competitive inducement of FDI by local governments will be established. And laws will be transformed from a regulatory and administrative nature to focus on promoting and supporting FDI.

Greater autonomy will be given to local governments in the fields of tax reduction or exemption and rent reduction or exemption (as in the case of land). Furthermore, local governments will also be given greater autonomy in the designation, development, and maintenance of Foreign Investment Zones (FIZs) to enhance entrepreneurial efforts in inducing of FDI.

Efforts taken and accomplishments in inducing FDI will be the criteria by which the central government allocates fiscal support to local governments.

Administrative provisions in the Foreign Investment Promotion Act will be minimized.

Approval and authorization procedures being facilitated to expedite FDI and current number of provisions regulating FDI will be reduced from 66 to 36.

The Investment Promotion Center will be established at the Korea Trade/Investment Promotion Agency (KOTRA) to provide One-Stop service for FDI.

Investor support will be enhanced through a system of various incentives, such as tax reduction or exemption and job training subsidies.

FIZs will be established in order to induce large scale FDI.

MAJOR POINTS

1. Simplification of FDI Procedures

A. Simplification of notification and registration procedures

The Acceptance of Foreign Direct Investment Notification System will be changed to a simple Notification System.

Notification and applications for registration can be submitted to the branches and headquarters of the Foreign Exchange Bank and the overseas offices, local offices, and the headquarters of KOTRA's Investment Promotion Center.

Previously, applications could only be submitted to the headquarters of the Foreign Exchange Banks.

Notification forms will be provided in Korean and English (Working Rule). Previously, notification forms were only available in Korean.

B. Abolition of the report on customs clearance of foreign capital and the resident agent notification requirement

Abolition of the report on customs clearance of foreign capital : The law requiring notification to the Minister of Finance and Economy within one month of the customs clearance of induced foreign capital will be abolished. (Current Law Article 38)

For additional analytical, business and investment opportunities information, please contact Global Investment & Business Center, USA at (202) 546-2103. Fax: (202) 546-3275. E-mail: rusric@erols.com

Abolition of the resident agent notification requirement : The law requiring a non-resident to appoint a resident as an agent to submit notifications, applications, or reports regarding FDI transactions will be abolished. (Current Law Article 10)

LIBERALIZATION OF FOREIGN DIRECT INVESTMENT

Proclamation that there are, in principle, no restrictions on FDI
Restrictions on FDI can only be applied if the national security, public order, public health, environmental preservation, or social morals are threatened.
The Minister of Finance and Economy will make comprehensive annual announcements of all restrictions provided in other laws related to FDI, which are not stated in the Foreign Investment Promotion Act.

3. Augmentation of Foreign Direct Investment Incentive System

A. Augmentation of tax reduction or exemption

1) Expansion of tax reduction or exemption

National Tax(Reduction or Exemption of Corporate and Income Taxes)

Present	New
A business accompanying advanced technology: reduction and exemption of taxes for 8 years 5 years at 100% the remaining 3 years at 50%	A business accompanying advanced technology, or service industries that support the manufacturing sector which strengthen the international competitiveness of a domestic business reduction and exemption of taxes for 10 years (7 years at 100%, 3 years at 50%)
A business located in a Free Export Zone (FEZ) 8 years for a business accompanying advanced technology 5 years for all other types of companies - 3 years at 100% - the remaining 2 years at 50%	A business located in a FIZ reduction or exemption of taxes for 10 years * The augmentation of FIZ incentives apply to the Masan and Iksan FEZs.

* Tax reduction or exemption on corporate and income tax on dividends for 10 years

Local tax (acquisition tax, property tax, aggregate land tax, and registration tax. Previously, registration tax was not included) : Local governments will have the autonomous power to grant tax reduction or exemption from anywhere between 8 to 15 years. However, the tax reduction or exemption period and ratio will be higher than that of the previous law (5 years at 100 percent, the remaining 3 years at 50 percent). Candidates for tax reduction or exemption for corporate and income taxes will also be eligible to apply for local tax reduction or exemption.

Customs duties, special excise tax, and value added tax : Capital goods used in business operations already receiving tax reduction or exemption will be exempted from customs duties, special excise taxes, and value added taxes.

2) Tax reduction or exemption when a foreign invested enterprise changes its content of business

- o If a foreign invested enterprise changes its content of business during a determined tax reduction or exemption incentive period, it will continue to receive the remaining tax reduction or exemption as long as the incentives still apply to the reported change in its content of business when authorized.

3) Introduction of the Tax Reduction or Exemption Checking System

- o A Foreign investor may check potential tax reduction or exemption incentives prior to deciding to invest. Presently, foreign investors may apply for tax reduction or exemption only after giving notification of their investment.

B. Augmentation of incentives for the renting of national and local government properties

1) National government properties

Expansion on the rent period from 20 years to 50 years (Draft Article 13, Paragraph 1) : Continuous renewal of rental periods, up to 50 years at a time, will be made possible. (Draft Article 13, Paragraph 7)

Rent fees will be stipulated by Presidential Decree. (Draft Article 13, Paragraph 3)

Reduction or exemption of rental fees (Draft Article 13, Paragraph 4) : Rent reduction or exemption is possible for national government   properties in Foreign Investor's Industrial Parks, National Industrial Parks, and FIZs. The Ratio and criteria for rent reduction or exemption will be   stipulated by Presidential Decree.

2) Local government properties

As in the case of national government properties, the rental period of local government properties will be expanded to 50 years.

Businesses eligible for rent reduction or exemption, as well as the rates to be applied, will be autonomously determined by local governments. In the Present Local Government Property Rental System, the rent period is 3 years for Administrative Properties, 5 years for Miscellaneous Properties (Rents can be renewed). Renting fees Must be more than 5 percent of the value of the properties

3) Private contracts

Under the Foreign Investment Promotion Act, national and local government properties can be rented on the basis of private contracts. Previously, this was not allowed.

Installment payments and delayed payments for the purchase of national and local government properties will be permitted

C. Central government support for local government activities to induce FDI

For additional analytical, business and investment opportunities information, please contact Global Investment & Business Center, USA at (202) 546-2103. Fax: (202) 546-3275. E-mail: rusric@erols.com

The central government will support local government activities to induce FDI through the following methods

1. Funds will be supplied for the creation of FIZs;
2. Capital to purchase land, to be rented to foreign invested enterprises will be lent;
3. Purchase and rental fees of land will be reduced or exempted for foreign investors and foreign invested enterprises;
4. Public subsidies for various purposes, such as job training, will be provided.

D. Reduction or exemption of land conversion fee

In the case a foreign invested enterprise seeks to convert a farm or forestry land into a factory site, conversion fee shall be reduced or exempted. The criteria and ratio for reduction or exemption shall be stipulated by Presidential Decree.

ESTABLISHMENT OF A ONE-STOP SERVICE

ESTABLISHMENT OF AN EXPEDITED APPROVAL OR AUTHORIZATION PROCEDURES FOR RELATED TO FDI

A. Establishment of a "Comprehensive Process System" for approval or authorization

If the main approval in a certain comprehensive process package is approved, the remaining supplementary approvals will also be approved. (Draft Article 17, Paragraph 1 and Paragraph 2)

Types of Comprehensive Applications and their Major Applications(Draft Announcement 1)

The 5 Comprehensive Process Packages	Major Approval	Supplementary Approvals
Approvals in relation to the Factory Establishment Permit	Factory Establishment Permit	26 approvals pertaining to 16 laws
Approvals in relation to the Small-Medium Company Start Up Permit	Medium and Small Company Establishment Business Plan Permit	26 approvals pertaining to 14 laws
Approvals in relation to the Construction Permit	Construction Permit	30 approvals pertaining to 18 laws
Approvals in relation to the environment	Sewage Disposal Facility and/or Air Pollution Control Facility Permit	7 approvals pertaining to 6 laws
Approvals in relation to the Use of Constructed Materials Permit	Use of Constructed Materials Permit	12 approvals pertaining to 6 laws

For additional analytical, business and investment opportunities information,
please contact Global Investment & Business Center, USA
at (202) 546-2103. Fax: (202) 546-3275. E-mail: rusric@erols.com

B. Measures to expedite approval or authorization procedures

The Automatic Authorization System will be introduced.

- If there is no response to an application of approval or authorization related to FDI within the time period stipulated by law,approval or authorization shall be automatically granted.

- In the event of an automatic approval, a certificate of Proof of Approval or Authorization shall be presented to the foreign investor or foreign invested enterprise. (Draft Article 17, Paragraph 3)

Foreign Investment Promotion Officers will be introduced.

- Foreign Investment Promotion Officials will be responsible for the smooth settlement of the comprehensive process system in metropolitan cities and provinces. (Draft Article 16, Paragraph 1)

Procedures for the rejection of approval or authorization applications by related administrative institutions

- If a approval or authorization application was rejected, the factors and legal basis of the rejection shall be reported to the foreign investor and the relevant Foreign Investment Promotion Officer.

Regulations not listed under the Foreign Investment Promotion Act will not be applicable to foreign investors and foreign invested enterprises.

☐Establishment of the Investment Promotion Center

Within KOTRA, the Investment Policy Center will be established to serve as the central institution in inducing FDI. (Draft Article 15, Paragraph 1)

- The Investment Promotion Center shall deal with all matters of assistance for foreign investors and foreign investment enterprises. The Investment Promotion Center shall provide:

Substitute settlement and direct settlement of approval or authorization applications for foreign investors and foreign invested enterprises;

substitute settlement: upon submitting the appropriate application forms to KOTRA, KOTRA will settle applications with other related administrative institutions for foreign investors and foreign invested enterprises;

direct settlement: upon submitting the appropriate application forms to KOTRA, KOTRA will directly settle applications, through dispatched public officials from related ministries at KOTRA for foreign investors and foreign invested enterprises;

- Guidance and support in all matters relating to FDI;

- Other assistance in the promotion of FDI and execution of investment surveys.

Legal provisions empowering the Investment Promotion Center

- The Head of KOTRA shall hold the Right of Request to request the dispatch of public officials from related ministries.

- The Head of KOTRA shall hold the Right of Request to request cooperation in matters related to FDI.

- Related ministries and related institutions shall dispatch experienced officials to work under the Head of KOTRA .(Draft Article 15, Paragraph 2 and Paragraph 6)

Recruitment of personnel and administration of the Investment Promotion Center (Draft Article 15, Paragraph 3)

- The center will be composed of and managed by experienced KOTRA officials and civilian specialists.

- Officials dispatched from related ministries and related administrative institutions will support the logistical activities of the Investment Promotion Center to promote FDI.

e.g.: Dispatched officials will, by their own accord, directly settle approval or authorization applications in the designated civil affairs and act as administrative liaisons with related ministries.

Establishment of an Ombudsman System

An Ombudsman institution will be established within the Investment Promotion Center to address grievances and difficulties of foreign investors and foreign invested enterprises. (Draft Article 15, Paragraph 7)

The appointed head of the Ombudsman institution will be an individual with a great deal of experience in the arena of FDI. (Presidential Decree)

- The Ombudsman institution will hold the Right of Request to request cooperation from related administrative institution and related ministries.

ESTABLISHMENT OF FOREIGN INVESTMENT ZONES (FIZS)

Designation, development, and maintenance of FIZs Competent authority: Governor
- Selection criteria: Stipulated by Presidential Decree

  e.g.: large scale FDI

- Section procedure:

  A Governor will select a site
  The approval of the Foreign Direct Investment Committee will be sought
  Upon approval, the Governor will designate the selected site as an FIZ
  Development and maintenance:

For additional analytical, business and investment opportunities information,
please contact Global Investment & Business Center, USA
at (202) 546-2103. Fax: (202) 546-3275. E-mail: rusric@erols.com

New FIZs will be designated, developed, and maintained by city and provincial governors as Local Industrial Parks.

- An FIZ designated in a previously existing Industrial Parks will be maintained by the original competent authority.

☐**Support for foreign invested enterprises located in an FIZ and developers of FIZs**

Tax reduction or exemption will apply for all foreign invested enterprises located in an FIZ. (Draft Article 9, Paragraph 1)
Developers contributing to the development of an FIZ will receive construction cost and fundamental facilities support.

- Up to 50 percent support for fundamental facilities, such as roads, water facilities, and sewage

- Support for harbors, rail roads, roads, water facilities, telecommunication, and electronic energy facilities shall take priority

Tax reduction or exemption for developers contributing to the development of an FIZ

- Capital gains tax reduction and acquisition and registration tax exemption, etc.

- Exemption from 7 types of mandatory fees, such as the farm or forest land conversion fee

- The traffic inducement fee shall be exempted for the construction of buildings in FIZs.

The Foreign Direct Investment Committee will decide upon the content of support for medical care, education, housing and living environment facilities in FIZs.

Special treatment for FIZ participation

When dividing land in an FIZ, the approval of the mayor can be omitted.
Foreign invested enterprises located in an FIZ automatically receive the right to act as an import-export business.
Foreign invested enterprises located in a FIZ will be allowed to conduct business in sectors previously restricted solely for small and medium sized companies.

TECHNOLOGY INDUCEMENT CONTRACT (CONTINUATION OF THE PRESENT LAW)

In principle: Liberalization of the introduction of technology notification procedures will be abolished
Exceptions: Notification is required for the inducement of those technologies stipulated by Presidential Decree

(1) technologies eligible for tax reduction or exemption

(2) aviation related technologies

(3) defense related technologies

Tax reduction or exemption (Draft Article 26)

- 5 years exemption from corporate and income tax on royalties for high-technology stipulated by President Decree.

ESTABLISHMENT OF THE FOREIGN DIRECT INVESTMENT COMMITTEE

Organization (Draft Article 27, Paragraph 2)

Chairman: Minister of Finance and Economy
Committee members:

Minister of Foreign Affairs and Trade, Minister of Science and Technology, Minister of Culture and Tourism, Minister of Agriculture and Forestry, Minister of Commerce, Industry, and Energy, Ministry of Environment, Minister of Information Technology, Minister of Environment, Minister of Labor, Minister of Construction and Transportation, Minister of Maritime Affairs and Fisheries, city and provincial Governors, and Heads of related administrative institutions stipulated by Presidential Decree

The Head of KOTRA will be allowed to attend meetings and submit opinions.

□Function: Deliberation and decision making on the following issues

The basic policy and regime for FDI

Criteria for tax reduction or exemption incentives (e.g.: the parameters of high-technology)
Support for local government
Designation and support of FIZs

FOREIGN DIRECT INVESTMENT PROCEDURES

DEFINITION OF FOREIGN INVESTMENT

A. Foreign Investor

A "Foreign Investor" is defined as a foreign national who has subscribed for owns shares in accordance with the Foreign Investment and Foreign Capital Inducement Act (FIFCIA). A "foreign national" means an individual who has a foreign nationality, a juridical person organized under foreign laws, or an economic cooperation organization. Furthermore, the meaning of the terms " individual" includes a Korean national who has obtained permanent residency or an equivalent status from a foreign government.
B. Forms of Investment

Cash;Capital goods;Dividens or their equivalent accruing from shares acquired in accordance with the FIFCIA;Industrial property rights or any other technology equivalent thereto, or any right to use the same; andRemaining assets distributed to a foreigner following the liquidation of a Korean branch or office of a juridical person in conjunction with the transformation of such branch or office into a domestic incorporated entity.

C. Amount and Ratio of Foreign Investment

The initial foreign investment in an entity in Korea has to be at least 50 million won. However, there is no minimum requirement in the case of additional investments in the same entity.

As a general rule, the foreign direct investment ration should be 10 percent or higher.

NOTIFICATION OF FDI / APPLICATION FOR APPROVAL

A. Foreign Direct Investment through Acquisition of Newly Issued Shares

Foreign investment in all industries, excluding those closed to foreign direct investment, are subject to the notification system.

Institutions Accepting Notification Document to be Submitted (2 copies of the following documents)

Business Proposal
Types of product or service
Purpose of foreign direct investment

Summary of business plan

A copy of the Joint Venture Contract (in case of a joint venture)

Resolution of the Board of Directors of the General Stockholders Meeting and

Letter of Intent of Investment (in case of investment by a single individual)

Certificate of Nationality

For a corporation, a document certifying the nationality of the corporation issued by the foreign government or the competent public organization

For an individual, a certificate of nationality issued by the foreign government

For a Korean residing overseas, a certificate of permanent residence issued by the foreign government or a certificate of registration as an overseas Korean issued by the Korean consular in the foreign country

Documents certifying delegated authority (e.g., power of attorney) (in case of proxy only)

B. Foreign Direct Investment through Acquisition of Outstanding Shares

Documents to be Submitted (2 copies of each of the following documents)

Documents certifying the resolution of the Board of Directors approving the proposed share transfer;

One copy of the sale and purchase agreement for the outstanding stock;
Document certifying the nationality of the stock;

Document certifying any special relationship between the transferees, if there is more than one transferee;

Document certifying inheritance, testation or gift (in case of acquisition by way of inheritance, testation or gift); and

Document certifying delegated authority (e.g., power of attorney)

INCORPORATION OF FOREIGN-INVESTED COMPANIES

A. Type of Entity

There are four types of business company; general partnership, limited partnership, private company and corporation. The most common type in Korea is the corporation.

B. Introduction of Capital

Foreign currencies must be sent through foreign banks to Korea, sold and then paid into the company in Korean currency in exchange for shares issued by the company. However, if foreign currency funds are needed by the company, foreign currencies may be paid into the company without conversion into Korean won. A foreign investor may also invest in kind, such as capital goods and industrial property rights.

C. Procedures for Incorporation of a Company

A company becomes a legal business entity upon completing its registration at the Korean Court Registry. The documents to be submitted as the following.

1. Application for the formation of a company and articles of incorporation (notarized);
2. Documents certifying the subscription of shares initially issued;
3. Records of examination by director, auditor and inspector and related documentsl
4. Minutes of inaugural general meeting and minutes of the board of directors metting;
5. Document confirming the custody of the capital paid-in;
6. In the case of investment in kind, a report by an inspector or a document confirming the completion of investment in kind; and
7. Document confirming the acceptance of notification or approval of foreign direct investment

REGISTRATION OF FOREIGN-INVESTED ENTERPRISES

Application for Registration

A foreign investor who has subscribed for newly issued shares of a Korean company shall register the company with a delegated foreign exchange bank within 30 days from completion of such capital contribution. A foreign investor who has acquired existing shares of a Korean company shall register the company with a delegated foreign exchange bank as a foreign-invested enterprise within 30 days of making the payment for such acquisition.

The following documents are required for the registration of a foreign-invested enterprise :

1. Application for registration of foreign-invested enterprise;
2. Document certifying the completion of the capital contribution; and

3. Certificate of subscription of stock or a certificate of payment for shares.

APPENDIX 1. INDUSTRIES OPEN TO FOREIGN DIRECT INVESTMENT

As mentioned above, the Korean government launched the Five-Year Foreign Investment Liberalization Plan in June 1993. Through several revisions of the plan, the government continuously widened the door for foreign investors. When Korea became a member of the OECD in December 1996, the government submitted a supplementary plan to open 44 industries to foreign investors. Since then the Minister of Finance and the Economy has announced each year the schedule for opening sectors of the domestic market to foreign investment.

The government fully opened seven sectors in April this year, including rental of residential buildings, and 11 sectors in May, including gasoline service stations. Again, the government broadened the business scopes of the sectors of gambling and electric power generation.

31 sectors remain closed (13) or only partially open (18) to foreign investors out of the total of 1,148 sectors, 98.9% of all industries being opened. Those residual sectors mostly involve national defense, cultural property protection, and protecting the livelihood of small-scale farmers. The Korean government will continue to move on promoting liberalization programs and additional openings of those restricted sectors.

13 FDI Restricted Industries

1. Growing of Cereal Grains
2. Farming of Cattle (Jan. 2000, partial liberalization)
3. Inshore Fishing
4. Coastal Fishing
5. Wholesale of Meats (Jan. 2001, partial liberalization)
6. Air Traffic Control
7. Medical Insurance
8. Workmen's Accident Compensation Insurance and Other Social Security Insurance
9. Radio Broadcasting
10. Television Broadcasting
11. News Agency Activities (Jan. 1, 2000, partial liberalization, less than 25% ownership allowed)
12. Horse Racing Track and Similar Stadium Operation
13. Gambling (May 1, 1999 only casinos allowed)

18 Partially Liberalized Industries

1. Distilling of ethyl alcohol (will be fully liberalized on Jan. 1. 1999)
2. Manufacturing of tobacco products (allowed for foreign equity ratio not exceeding 25%)
3. Publishing of books, brochures musical books and other publications (allowed for foreign equity ratio not exceeding 50%)
4. Publishing of news papers (allowed for less than 25% and scheduled to expand to 33% in 1999)
5. Publishing periodicals (allowed for less than 25% and scheduled to expand to 50% in 1999)
6. Manufacture of biological products (allowed except for manufacturing of blood preparation)
7. Coastal water passenger transport (allowed for foreign equity ratio less than 50%)
8. Coastal water freight transport (allowed for foreign equity ratio less than 50%)
9. Deep sea foreign freight transport (will be fully liberalized on . Jan. 1. 1999)
10. Scheduled air transport (less than 50%)

11. Non scheduled air transport (less than 50%)
12. Wire telegraph and telephone (less than 33% and will be more liberalized on Jan. 1.1999, and also on Jan. 1. 2001)
13. Wireless telegraph and telephone (less than 33% and will be more liberalized on Jan. 1.1999, and also on Jan. 1. 2001)
14. Telecommunications n.e.c.
15. Domestic banking (allowed only for commercial banks)
16. Trust and trust companies (further liberalization on Dec. 1, 1998)
17. Cable broadcasting (less than 30%)
18. Electricity power generation (Private power generation business is fully opened, and public power generation business is allowed less than 50%)

By the year 2000, nearly all business lines in Korea will be open to foreign investment, except for 16 line such as Medical Care insurance, Television broadcasting, and Gambling.

Number of business areas restricted form FDI

Category	1997	1998	1999	2000
Total number of businesses	1,148			
Partially opened businesses	26	18	18	26
Restricted businesses	27	13	11	3
Liberalization rate(%)*	97.6	98.9	99.0	99.7

* Liberalization rate = (Number of businesses fully and partially opened) / (Total Businesses(1,148)) * 100
*Source : Ministry of Finance and Economy

APPENDIX 2. INSTITUTIONS ACCEPTING NOTICE

Main Offices of Domestic Banks

Korea Development Bank
Industrial Bank of Korea
Citizens National Bank
Korea Housing Bank
Cho Heung Bank
Commenical Bank of Korea
Korea First Bank
Hanil Bank
Seoul Bank
Korea Exchange Bank
Shinhan Bank
KorAm Bank
Hana Bank
Boram Bank
Peace Bank of Korea

The Daegu Bank Ltd.
Pusan Bank
The Kwang Ju Bank Ltd.
Cheju Bank
Jeon Buk Bank
The Kangwon Bank Ltd.
Kyong Nam Bank
Chung Buk Bank
Korea Long Term Credit Bank

Branches of Foreign Banks

Citibank
Bank of America
The First National Bank of Chicago
Chemical Bank
The Chase-Manhattan Bank
First National Bank of Boston
Bank of Hawaii
The Bank of Tokyo
Dai-ichi Kangyo Bank
The Sakura Bank
Sumitomo Bank
The Fuji Bank
The Sanwa Bank
The Daiwa Bank
The Asahi Bank
Long-term Credit Bank of Japan
Mitsubishi Trust and Banking
The Tokai Bank
Yamaguchi Bank
Banque Indosuez
Credit Lyonnais Bank
Banque Nationale de Paris
Banque Paribas
Societe Generale
Standard Chartered Bank
Royal Bank of Canada
National Bank of Canada
Internationale Netherland Bank
Australia & New Zealand Banking Group
National Australia Bank
The Development Bank of Singapore
Deutsche Bank
Hong Kong and Shanghai Banking
Bank of China
Arab Bank

For additional analytical, business and investment opportunities information, please contact Global Investment & Business Center, USA at (202) 546-2103. Fax: (202) 546-3275. E-mail: rusric@erols.com

APPENDIX 3. BUSINESSES ACCOMPANIED BY ADVANCED TECHNOLOGY ELIGIBLE FOR TAX EXEMPTION OR REDUCTION

1. Electronic, Information and Electric Technology Branch

Electronic and Information Technology Section

1-1. Information Processing and Computer Operating System

System Integration, system management & operation and technology consultation
LAN, MAN, WAN and digital communication network technology
Data base design & retrival and management technology

1-2. Development of Software and Production Technology

System software(distribution data processing technology, communication processing and management, operating technology, automatic processing large data, groupware technology, security management program)
Application software(application specific software, presentation software, package technology, multimedia software for game, video and audio, scientific computation technology, natural language processing technology, machine language translation compiler technology, self-diagnose and recovery technology)
Development tool design

1-3. Computer Aided Automatic Management System Technology

Automatic management system for production & operation and related technology(CAD, CAM, CAE, CIM, CAI)
Intelligent building communication service and OA system operation management
Automation system of logistics such as POS, auto recognition device etc. and security management system

1-4. Technology of Computer Manufacture and Design for 32bits and over {personal computer(lap-top, notebook, pen input, cordless communication PC, PDA), high performance workstation(office, engineering), intellignt multimedia computer, high-speed parallel processing computer(1 GIPS over), optical computer, neural network computer, medium and large size server & parallel vector processing computer}

1-5. Computer Peripheral Device

Input device{high-resolution and high speed image scanner, pen input device, tablet(digitizer), touch pannel, 3-D mouse}
Output device(color LCD, ultra-thin LCD, 3D display, color printer, 600 DPI LBPor more
Memory device{3.5" less HDD, 8" or more HDD, 2.5" MODD/ODD, optical card, optical tape drive, flash memory, IC card, four CD-ROM drive, CD-1 drive, tape drive(QIC, 8mm, 4mm), CD/OD autochanger}

1-6. Communication Device and Associated Technology

For additional analytical, business and investment opportunities information, please contact Global Investment & Business Center, USA at (202) 546-2103. Fax: (202) 546-3275. E-mail: rusric@erols.com

Digital mobile communication system (base station equipment, switching station equipment), its operating technology and digital terminal

GPS, earth observation satellite system and its operating technology and terminal

Satellite system and its operation technology and terminal

Optical communication system and its operating technology

Digital broadcasting system(digital and wireless CATV system, HDTV transmission and receiver system) and its operation technology and terminal(subscriber settop box)

Ultra-speed data-communication system(high-speed and large capacity data communication device, high-speed intelligent switching system etc.) and its operating technology and terminal(G3 FAX, G4 FAX, video phone)

Other digital communication device(digital keyphone system)

1-7. Semiconductor Materials and Manufacturing Equipment

Semiconductor device{discrete divice(diode, transistor, thyristor), IC(bipolar, analog, logic, micro component, memory), compound semiconductor(optical device, high frequency electronic), flip chip bond technology, packaging liquid encapsulation technology}

Semiconductor material(poly silicon, silicon wafer, compound semiconductor wafer, photo mask, photo resist, die attach material, TAB tape, target, lead frame, bonding wire, molding material, process chemical, specialty gas)

Equipment and its parts for specialty gas manufacturing(including mixing, refining and fill analysis)

> fill manifold
> manifold controls
> life safety system
> burn box
> Particle collector
> purifier
> evacuation pump
> R.G.A. vacuum gauge
> gas analyzer
> piping parts
> stainless valve

Semiconductor manufacturing equipment

1-8. Automatic Control Equipment for Industrial Purpose and Related Accessories

1-9. Precision Measuring Instruments and machinery for test & measurements

1-10. Video and Audio Instruments

Digital signal processing-type video instruments(HDTV, flat TV, LDP, MDP, video projector, camcorder)

Digital signal processing-type audio instruments(CDP, DCC, mini disc player)

Digital radio(including sending and receiving equipments)

Audio instrument techniques(disc recording film plating technique, blue laser diode

For additional analytical, business and investment opportunities information, please contact Global Investment & Business Center, USA at (202) 546-2103. Fax: (202) 546-3275. E-mail: rusric@erols.com

technique, optical pick-up technique, high-density disc technique)

1-11. Home Automatic System

Electrics Section

1-12. Electric Apparatus Requiring High Technology and Heating Equipment

Transmission & distribution equip. & facility(345 KV and above)

Application equip. & facility for superconductors(generators, transformers, cables)

Power conversion system & technology

Electric equip. & facility for high speed railway system(Power Supply equip., switchgear & substation equip. for train-set, monitoring, signaling system)

Heating equipment{DC arc electrical furnace, electrical furnace for high frequency induction furnace(30KHz~50KHz), high frequency inverter welder & plasma cutting machine, soldering & cutting machine for surface mounted accessories, laser welder, welding equipment for electrical railroad, heating equipment for surface processing, far infrared rags heating equipment(heater, dryer), microwave & ultrasound machine}

1-13. Electronic Domestic Appliances

{Non-CFS refrigerant refrigerator, high frequency electronic induction heater, non-detergent power saving type washing machine, electric heating equipment(using plasma discharge halogen lamp), DSP(Digital Signal Process) type vending machine.}

1-14. Lighting Appliances

(3-band/5-band phosphor powder, high power factor and low THD electronic ballast, luminous tube for discharge lamp electrodeless discharge metal halide lamp, halogen lamp for optics, compact fluorescent lamp, digital signal control method of flash system)

Electronic, Electric and Material Section

1-15. Core Parts of Communication Device

Core parts of digital mobile communication system(base station equipment, switching station equipment etc.) and digital terminal

Core parts of satellite using system such as GPS, earth observation etc. and terminal

Core parts of satellite system and digital terminal

Core parts of optical communication system

Core parts of digital broadcasting system(digital and cordless CATV system, HDTV transmission receiver system) and terminal(subscriber set-top box etc.)

Core parts of ultra-speed data-communication system(high-speed and large capacity data communication device, high-speed and intellignt switching system etc.) and terminal(G3 FAX, G4 FAX, video phone)

Core parts of other digital communication device(digital key-phone system)

1-16. Computer Peripheral Device

CPU chip set with greater than 200MIPs
High performance magnetic-head
Engine and head of output device

1-17. Display and Component

LCD and related component, material, equipment(except for TN-LCD)
Flat panel display and special component(PDP, EL, VFD, FED)

1-18. Optical and Magnetic Recorder Techniques(digital and disc-type only)

1-19. Electron Tube and Other Essential Components(except for CRTs for TV monitor smaller than 20")

1-20. High Performance Transformer{rotary transformer, high frequency (>=150khz) transformer, amorphous transformer}

1-21. Precision Motor(including industrial motors)

AC, DC servo motor
Stepping motor
Brush-less DC motor
Driving motors for electric cars and trains
Linear motor
High efficiency motor
Ultrasound motor

1-22. Electronic-Ceramics Materials and Components
Piezo-ceramic materials and components{piezo-actuator(pump, fan etc.)}

1-23. Other Electronic & Electric Related Components and Materials

Components for manufacturing equipment
Optical fiber, optical fiber cable and related accessories
Communication cable
Power cable(345KV grade or more and for submarine)
High performance battery(non-polluting, high performance, miniaturized battery only)
Antenna(>=3GHz)
Charge-combining device(CCD design, manufacturing, CCD application module)
Special components for precise tests and measuring equipment
Special components for controlling equipment and systems
SMD and chip-type components
Power supplier(>=1KW)
High precision switch and connector, relay and high density quartz vibrator(VCO, TCXO)
Super conducting materials(high temperature super conducting coil)
Head lamp for automobile
Essential components for detectors
Sensor(device sensing some specified changes and transforming them to electrical signals)
Printed circuit board(circuit distance <= 0.15mm, hole size <=0.15, flexible PCB, PCB

For additional analytical, business and investment opportunities information,
please contact Global Investment & Business Center, USA
at (202) 546-2103. Fax: (202) 546-3275. E-mail: rusric@erols.com

with more than 6 layers)
Electronic analog for wrist-watch movement

2. Precise Machinery and Advanced Process Branch

2-1. Automation, Precise Textile Machinery and Parts

High speed winder
Texture M/C
Programmable M/C for preparing textiles
Loom or knitting M/C
Automation for production process flow equipment system
Clothing for paper making M/C(forming fabrics only)
Polymerization M/C(for man-made textile materials only)
Textile winding or reeling M/C
Spinning M/C
Autoembroidery M/C

2-2. Precise Offset Printing M/C and Rotary Press M/C

Printing M/C(offset printing M/C over 480 x 660mm in printing size)
Rotary press M/C(rotary offset printing M/C for commercial and printing newspaper)

2-3. Numerically Controlled(NC) Precision Machinery

NC plastic forming M/C(injection moulding M/C, extruder moulding M/C, vacuum moulding M/C, thermoforming M/C)
NC precise working M/C and its core parts
NC machine tool and its parts

2-4. Industrial Robots and Core Parts

2-5. Computer Production System and Its Components(operation controlling systems, automatically logistic management system and communication, CAD, CAM, CAE)

2-6. Advanced Transportation and Stevedoring Machinery, Construction Machinery and Mining Machinery(in the field of automatically controlled technology)

2-7. Precision Machinery and Parts

Precise bearing
High performance cutting tool(except ceramic cutting tool)
Precision mold
Rolling mills(tube mills, hot mills, cold mills)
Machinery using wind and water power(liquid pump, gas pump, vacuum pump and fan)
Shaft, gear, gear box
Diecasting machine
Winding machine
Dryer(except agricultural products, lumber and paper)
Coating machine

For additional analytical, business and investment opportunities information,
please contact Global Investment & Business Center, USA
at (202) 546-2103. Fax: (202) 546-3275. E-mail: rusric@erols.com

Filter and cleaner(types for domestic use are excluded)

2-8. **Hydraulic M/C with High Function and Refrigerating and Air Conditioning Apparatus with High Efficiency**

2-9. **Hydraulic Parts for Construction Machinery**

2-10. **Industrial Diesel Engines**

2-11. **Automatic Control System and Facilities for Green House**

Automatic climate control system which control growing conditions by computer and sensor

Fertilizer and irrigation system which supply plant nutrients and water by using computer and sensor

Combine and its parts

3. Material

3-1. **Advanced Metallic Material**

Metallic Magnetic Material(except sintering of ferrite, alnico, Nd and bond magnetic)
Conductive Material
Dielectric Material(metal thin film vapor deposition technology)
Insulating Material(including polymer concrete)
Spark erosion resistant Material(Cr, Cu-Cr-Bi, sintered alloy)
Functional Material
Structural Material(weight-reducing material for vehicles and component)
Rare metal(only refining process in case of producing with by-product made by smelting)
Welding Material(only flux cored wire)

3-2. **Advanced Metal Technology**

Advanced smelting and refining technology
Advanced casting and rolling technology
Valuable metal recovery & metal recycling technology
Advanced surface treatment technology and equipment
Surface defect detection technology and equipment
Advanced machining technology(extrusion, pipe production)
Molten steel trace element analysis technology

3-3. **Polymeric Advanced Materials**

Polymer composites
Polymer membranes
Polymeric medical materials
Polymeric materials for information industries
Polymeric materials for electric applications
Specialty polymers

Multi-phase polymers
Engineering plastics

3-4. **Tire or rubber Waste Recycling Technology (generating, utilizing heat or electricity, recovery, powdering)**

3-5. **Plastics Recycling Technology, Plastics Waste classfication Technology or Recycling Technology**

3-6. **High Performance and High Touch Fibers**

High tensile fibers(high tensile polyester fiber, high tensile poly acrylonitrile fiber, high tensile polyethelene fiber, high tensile polypropylene fiber)

Special high performance fibers(carbon fiber, polyphenylensulfide fiber, boron fiber, silicon nitride fiber, silicon carbide fiber, polyimide fiber, polyacetal fiber, alumina fiber, aramid fiber)

Multi-functional fibers(thermocromic fiber, light-thermal-electric response elastic fiber, shape memory fiber, ultraviolet cut fiber(substitute for urethans foam), substitutive fiber for asbestos, filtration material(active carbon fiber), fiber materials for prevention of environmental contamination, ultra-high speed spinning yarn(above 5,500m/min.), ultrafine denier flashspinning yarn(below 0.05 denier)

3-7. **Manufacturing Technology for High Performance Non©woven Fabrics(flashspun, melt blown, spunlace process)**

3-8. **Paper for G4 Grade Facsimile(resolution 500DPI over)**

3-9. **Specialty adhesives(anaerobic adhesives, amide and acrylate type hot melt adhesives, polyamide based adhesives, electrical conducting adhesives, flexible super glues)**

3-10. **Advanced Ceramics(fine ceramics) Synthesis, Evaluation, Application Technology**

4. New Materials and Biological Industries Branch

New Materials Section

4-1. **Intermediates for Pharmaceuticals and Diagnostic Agents**

Pharmaceutical precursors and intermediates(substance patents)
Process technology for experimental reagents(chemical and biological)
Process technology for diagnostic reagents(substance patents)
Supporting technologies for new pharmaceuticals development(evaluation system for new pharmaceuticals, development of animal models, animal/plants breeding technology, pre- clinical evaluation system, clinical evaluation system)

4-2. **Organic Pigments(condensed and fused-ring system), Dyestuffs(quinoxaline and multi-functional reaction dyestuff high fastness dyestuff), Paints(elastomeric silicon eased water proof paint, fluorocarbon resin paint, electrical insulating varnish, ceramic paint, elastomeric urethane paint, non-volatile paint, waterborne paint, nontoxic paint and other specialty paint)**

4-3. **Catalysts and Additives**

Catalyst technologies(catalyst manufacture, reaction initiator, polymerization initiator)

For additional analytical, business and investment opportunities information,
please contact Global Investment & Business Center, USA
at (202) 546-2103. Fax: (202) 546-3275. E-mail: rusric@erols.com

Additives(new rubber curing accelerators, fluidity improvers, phenolic and phosphite anti-oxidants, antistatic agents, UV stabilizers, flame retardant, anti-fogging agents, additives for engine oils and industrial lubricants, chelating agents)

4-4. Chemicals for Electronic Industries and Photographs(ultra-purity gases for semi-conductor industry, high-purity organic and inorganic chemicals for electronic industry, plating chemicals, chemicals for photograph)

4-5. Manufacturing and Formulation of Fragrances and Flavors

Formulated Fragrances and Flavors(fragrance and flavor fixers, musk fragrance, macrocyclic fragrances, synthetic fragrances and flavors)

Manufacturing Fragrances and Flavors{analysis of fragrance and flavor constituents, production technology for fragrances and flavors, development of reaction flavor technology, technology of supercritical carnbon dioxide extraction, development of long -lasting fragrances, sysnthesis of fragrances and flavors(menthol, artificial musk), technology for the use of aromacalogy}

4-6. Specialty and Intermediate and Chemicals

Intermediate chemicals for dyestuffs, pigments, fragrances, flavors, surfactants, adhesives and additives

Alternate chemicals for CFC and Halon

Bioindustry

4-7. Biopharmarceuticals Manufacturing Technology(patented biopharmaceuticals excluding those in clinical trial)

Therapeutic new proteins, carbohydrates and peptides

Gene therapy

Brain disease therapeutics(senile dementia therapeutic), aging control agent, autoimmune disease therapeutics, cancer therapeutics using antibody

4-8. Advanced Biotechnology(patented)

Artificial enzymes and organs

Biochip

4-9. Bioenvironment, Biochemicals, and Biofood

Bioleaching technology

Biocatalytic technology

Biological mass production of hydrogen

Biodegradable polymer

5. Optical and Medical equipment branch

5-1. Laser Oscillators, Applications, and Their Core Parts

Laser oscillators(gas laser, solid-state laser, semiconductor laser, dye laser, chemical

laser, free-electron laser)
Application lasers(cutting, welding, boring, marking, micro-fabrication, laser CVD, laser etching)
Semiconductor processing lasers(lithography, trimming, repair, scribing, annealing)
Laser generator and component technology

5-2. Instruments for Image Formation and Optical Information Recording and Playback

Picture recording machine(instant printing camera, 35mm camera for roll film, still video camera, infrared camera, movie camera, VTR camera, camcorder)
Picture playback instruments(indirect process electrostatic transfer system in electric copy machine, mini-lab, movie projector)
Picture observation and inspection instruments(zoom binocular, high resolution microscope)

5-3. Optical Materials, Parts, and Optical Fiber Sensing

Advanced optical parts and materials
Optical fiber sensing(sensor for temperature, pressure, vibration, displacement, magnetic field, electric current, electric voltage, acoustic sound, security and optical fiber gyroscope)

5-4. Electronic and Accurate Medical Equipment

Biomedical equipment(less than 5ch ECG except less than wire & wireless patient monitor), audiometer
Electric, electronic surgical apparatus & equipment and cure apparatus & equipment
Near throsis & artificial organ
Diagnostic imaging equipment
Medical rehabilitation

6. Aerospace and Transportation Branch

Aerospace

6-1. Aircraft Parts and Manufacturing Technology

Airframe design and manufacturing technology
Aircraft engine design and manufacturing technology(engine assembly, compressor, combustor, turbine, nozzle)
Rotorcraft transmission design and manufacturing technology(transmission)
Avionics design and manufacturing technology
Development of aircraft materials and forming technology

6-2. Spacecraft Parts

Launcher manufacturing and design technology(rocket motor, engine design and manufacturing technology)

Satellite manufacturing and design technology(attitude and orbit control subsystem, structure subsystem, thermal subsystem, power subsystem, propulsion subsystem, telemetry command and ranging subsystem, payload)

Spacecraft materials

6-3. Parts and Equipment for the use by the Defense Industry

6-4. Automobile Parts

Power generation system(Electronic control engine, Light & advanced material applied engine, Alternative fuel engine, Compressive ignition engine, Fuel injection system and electric pumping system, Low emission lean burning engine, Catalytic converter, Super charger system, Turbo charger system)

Drive System(Hydraulic clutch, Manual transmission, Auto transmission, Continuous variable transmission, Drive shaft, Constant velocity joint, Electronic control clutch)

Suspension system(Adjustable damping system & electronic control suspension system)

Driving Safety Information System {Distance warning & control system, Voice information system, Auto cruising system, Head-up display system, Intelligent cockpit system, Fuel tank(plastic material), Impact absorbing material, Air bag, Seat belt, Electric power rear view mirror}

Steering System(Hydraulic power steering system, 4 wheel steering system, Electronic power steering system)

Body System {Aero-dynamics type(air drag coefficient below 0.45 with painting process), NVH(noise vibration harshness) technology(active noise control), High safety advanced material applied}

Air Conditioning & Heating System (CFC-free air conditioning system, Air conditioning system for electric vehicle, Electro-magnetic clutch)

Brake ystem {Hydro-pneumatic brake, Braking force distribution brake, ABS(Anti-lock brake system), TCS(traction control system)}

Particulate trap system with filter regeneration technology

Motor & controller for electric vehicle

Intelligent vehicle & parts

6-5. Electronic & Electrical System {Alternator, starter, Motors(control type, intelligent type or brush-less type), Multi-plex wire harness, Electronic control unit, Battery for electric vehicle, Quick charger system for electric vehicle, Sensors, Emission reduction system & on board diagnosis system}

6-6. Train and Parts

Electric multiple unit(VVVF control type)

High Speed Train(high speed >= 200km/H) & parts

Magnetic levitation vehicle & parts

6-7. High Speed Elevator {driving system(devices), speed control system(devices)}, Linear Motor Elevator, Super High Speed Elevator

6-8. High Technology Ship and Offshore Structures

Extremely-low-temperature liquified gas carrier-super-high-speed ship(applied more than 40 knots)

For additional analytical, business and investment opportunities information, please contact Global Investment & Business Center, USA at (202) 546-2103. Fax: (202) 546-3275. E-mail: rusric@erols.com

Next generation ship(superconducting electromagnetic propulsion ship, fuel-cell propulsion ship), special purpose ship(submersible vehicle, research vessel)
Computerized ship production technologies
Advanced system design and manufacturing technologies for offshore structures

6-9. **Advanced Engines{fuel cell engines, alternative fuel engines(only fuel system), electro-magnetic hydraulic engines(applied only to electromagnetic hydraulic parts) & marine gas turbine}, Main Functional Component.**

6-10. **Advanced Marine Equipment**

Loading and unloading facilities and control system for hyper low-temperature liquided tanks
Controllable pitch propeller, ducted propeller, contra-rotating propeller
Advanced technologies for high performance marine engine systems

7. Environment, Energy and Construction

Environment Section

7-1. **Air pollution control equipment and technology.**

Dust precipitator with ceramic filter for high temperature technology.
Automobile catalytic converter with honeycomb type ceramic.
Catalyst manufacturing technology for desulfurization equipment and waste gas treatment facility.
Minimization of CO_2 generation and CO_2 application technology(except biological and chemical CO_2 fixation technology, separation and recovery technology for COt, and hydrogen production technology)

7-2. **Water Pollution Control Equipment and Technology**

Robotic auto sampling equipment for water quality.
Membrane production technology for water and wastewater treatment.
Heavy metal recovery equipment for wastewater.

7-3. **Development of Technology and Facilities for Intemediate, Final Disposing of Special Waste(Waste Acides, Waste Alkali, Waste Organic Solvent, Waste Oil, Other special hazardous wastes)**

7-4. **Other Environment, ©Related Products, Equipment and Technology**

Pollution monitoring technology and related equipment.
Clean technology (green products development, clean production technology, resources recovery technology)

Energy and Resources Section

7-5. **New & Renewable Energy Technology**

Power generation(photovoltaic power, wind power, fuel cell, small hydro power,

For additional analytical, business and investment opportunities information, please contact Global Investment & Business Center, USA at (202) 546-2103. Fax: (202) 546-3275. E-mail: rusric@erols.com

IGCC, tidal power, wave power)
New fuel production(bioalcohol, hydrogen)
Heat utilization(solar collector, solar heating, solar heating system controller, geothermal, waste incineration system)

7-6. Power Generating Facilities

Nuclear power(nuclear vapor producer, turbine generator)
Thermal power(boiler, turbine generator)
Composite thermal power{gas turbine, turbine generator, HRSG(heat recovery steam generator)}
Hydraulic power(pump turbine, generator motor, hydraulic turbine, generator)

7-7. Power Generating Technology

Fluidized bed combusting technology
Magnetohydrodynamic power generating technology

7-8. Equipment & Technology for Energy Conservation

Dyeing technology for energy saving(dyeing technology for energy saving, ultra-sonic application dyeing technology, low temp & low liquor ratios dyeing technology, one-bath dyeing technology, high-frequency dyeing technology, plasma application finishing technology, foam dyeing technology)
Light-controlling window technology
Non-contact temperature measuring technology
High efficiency transfer technology
Hybrid-Type reactor equipped with advanced separation membranes
Aluminum scrap refining technology
Raw material of fine ceramic technology for energy conservation
2-Component thermal medium composite power generation

7-9. Underground Energy Storage Technology

Compressed air & gas energy storage underground cavern
Heat storage
Hot water storage in aquifer

7-10. Energy & Mineral Resources Exploration Technology

Ground water monitoring system technology
TBM cutter technology
Geothermal reservoir exploration technology

Construction Sector
7-11. Technology Development of New Materials on Construction

Substitute materials for asbestos
Substitute aggregates for concrete

For additional analytical, business and investment opportunities information, please contact Global Investment & Business Center, USA at (202) 546-2103. Fax: (202) 546-3275. E-mail: rusric@erols.com

Manufacture and construction technology on super tensile strength concrete

7-12. Automation of Construction Machinery and Ground Exploring Technology

Remote control technology of construction machinery

Application technology on a precision ground stereophotograph

7-13. Building and Facilities Technology

Reduced pollution demolition and dismantling technology

Intelligent building technology (information communication and office building Automation facilities)

Export system for facilities system control

7-14. Technology Related to Advanced Transportation

Obstacle and lane sensing technology

Transmission and analysis of high speed traffic information technology

KOREA EXPORT-IMPORT AND TRADE REGULATIONS

1. TRADE POLICY

Korea is drastically liberalizing Trade regulation.

Korea recognized the importance of international trade, has adopted a policy of globalization and liberalization.

Korea is working to liberalize historically restricted sectors.

For example, many of the service sectors including distribution, telecommunications, banking and insurance are on their way to incremental deregulation.

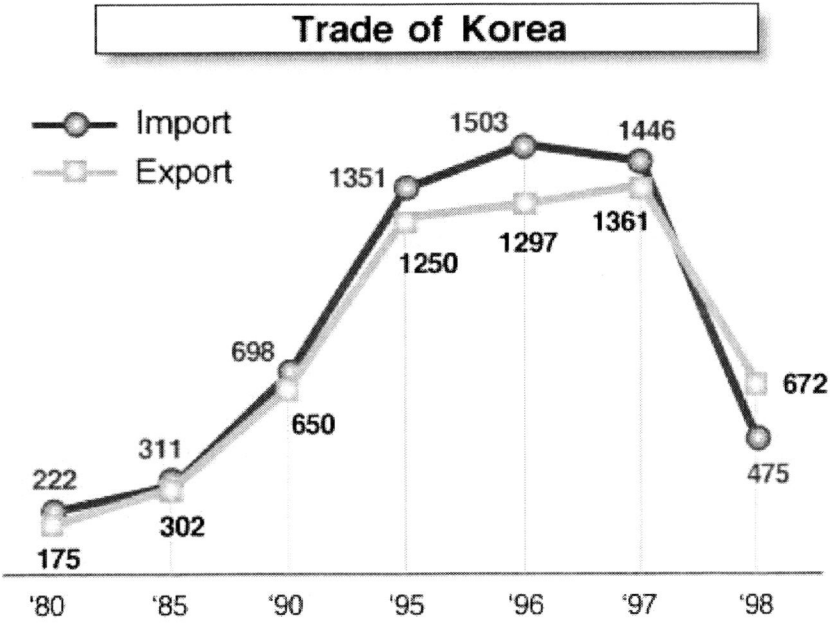

Trade of Korea

Source: Korea International Trade Assorciation (1998 Jan.-Jun.)

Korea has accomplished the following:

- Reduced tariff rates dramatically for a current trade-weighted tariff average of 6.2 percent on manufactured goods, the equivalent of tariff rates in the world's most advanced nations.

- Fully opened the domestic market to all import items except rice and beef, which are partially liberalized under the minimum market access requirements agreed upon in the Uruguay Round trade negotiations.

- As a result, Korea's import liberalization rate increased from 99.3 percent in 1996 to 99.9 percent in 1998.

- Reorganized export-import approvals to create a negative list system and abolished registration qualifications for trading businesses, both effective since 1997.

- Liberalized 1,117 of 1,148 business lines for foreign direct investment, for a liberalization rate of 98.8 percent.

 In addition, a specific liberalization program is in place to open more industries to foreign investment, including a variety of service industries.

Between 1998 and 2000, an additional 11 business lines, including publishing of newspapers, leasing of residential buildings and insurance appraisal, will be newly liberalized.

The percentage ratio of business liberalization is expected to increase from the current 98.8 percent to 99.4 percent by the year 2000.

For additional analytical, business and investment opportunities information,
please contact Global Investment & Business Center, USA
at (202) 546-2103. Fax: (202) 546-3275. E-mail: rusric@erols.com

TRADE POLICY DIRECTIONS

To provide full support in the promotion of a strong multilateral trade structure under the WTO regime.
-
To accommodate new trade issues such as intellectual property rights, intangible services and the liberalization of agricultural produce trading.
-
To restructure domestic trade-related systems in accordance with international standards.

TRADE-RELATED LAWS

External Trade Law : A primary law which regulates exports and imports and includes a range of provisions regarding overseas trade, trade agency, export and import permits, impact of import on industry, and maintenance of the trade structure.

Foreign Exchange Law : A law which regulates credits and liabilities in relation to foreign exchange and other overseas transactions. Enacted in 1961, it has been amended five times as of December 1995, To promote foreign investment it changed to a law named "foreign exchange transactions Act" which is expected to fully liberalize the current set of regulations. The liberalization plan is scheduled to be implemented in two stages. The first is scheduled to start on April 1, 1999. The second -stage of liberalization measures is planned to be completed by the end of 2000.

Customs Tariff Law : A law which regulates all goods imported and exported through customs. Its objective is to contribute to the development of the national economy and obtain income from tariffs, by levying and collecting tariffs and also to ensure appropriate control over import and export items.

3. EXPORT-IMPORT APPROVAL SYSTEM

In principle the export and import system of Korea is free trade, but there are restrictions on the amounts of certain items for import and export, and goods' quality and trade systems are under government control in order to achieve specific strategic goals. An export and import business requires a license, which is granted to those who meet necessary qualifications.

Liberalization of trade business (effective Jan. 1, 1997)
As the overseas credit rating and self-regulation of the Korean trading industry have improved greatly, the Korean government has decided to abolish regulating systems such as the licensing or registration of trade business starting in 1997, through the amendment of External Trade Law..

Accordingly, no restrictions will apply when an individual or a corporation wishes to participate in trade.

In addition, the approval system which regulates individual import and export items has been reformed to a "negative system," only a limited number of excepted areas will be subject to regulation.

Registration of a trade and agency business : As a means to maintain the overseas credit rating of Korea at a desirable level overall and supervise the trade industry, trading companies are required to obtain licenses under the notification system for trading companies.

The Minister of Trade, Industry and Energy has the principal authority to grant the license; however, in practice the authority is delegated to the Korea International Trade Association.

Registration & Information
Member Services Office, Korea International Trade Association
(Trade Tower Center 1F) 159-1 Samsung-dong, Kangnam-gu Seoul
Tel : 02-551-5334~9 Fax : 02-551-5130

The trade business is largely divided into the "offer" trade business and the "buying" trade business, by the criteria of registration and the scope of import and export activities.

Offer trade business The scope of import and export activities is not limited, and includes agency activities. The corporation with company capital of 10 million won or more, and the individual who has maintained a daily account balance of 10 million won or more consecutively for at least the last month are eligible to register.

Buying trade business The buying trade business is restricted to the import of raw materials and machinery for one's own use in the manufacture of goods for domestic sale or export. Eligible for registration are those engaged in the fields of manufacturing, mining, fisheries, in-shore fisheries, military supplies, agriculture and forestry.

Registration of trade business An individual as well as a corporation, regardless of company size, can be an applicant for an offer or buying trade business license. The applicant makes the decision whether to apply for an offer or buying license, depending on the proposed scope of import and export business and qualification requirements. All applications must be made directly to the main office or regional branch of Korea International Trade Association.

Registration of trade agency Trading agents may purchase goods to be exported, negotiate trade deals, and conduct similar activities, on behalf of overseas importers and exporters. The agency is mainly divided into offering agent and buying agent.

Registration & Information
Korea Foreign Trade Agent Association
218, 2ga Hankangro, Yongsan-gu Seoul, Korea Tel: 02-792-1581 Fax: 02-798-5461

Offering agent This is the agent delegated by the overseas exporter who wishes to export to Korea or the Korean branch or agency of the overseas exporter whose functions are primarily the issuance of sales offers on behalf of the overseas exporter and secondarily the negotiation of export items.

Only those defined as above are eligible for registration as offering agents. Registration is made at the Korea Foreign Trade Agent Assocition.

Buying agent This is the agent delegated by the overseas importer or the Korean branch or agency of the overseas importer, whose main activities include purchasing and negotiating goods to be exported and conducting market surveys. Registration is made at the Korea Export Buying Office Association.

EXPORT APPROVAL SYSTEM

Endorsement for export and advance approval If the item to be exported is listed as restricted in a government-issued public notice, the exporter requires endorsement from the relevant export association. If the item is restricted by a special law, other than public notice based on External Trade Law, the exporter should acquire an advanced export approval or endorsement from the relevant government office before applying for the export permit.

All the items not listed in the public notice restricting export & import items are designated as automatic approval items which only require a permit issued by a bank, without any additional approval or endorsement.

Import/Export Notice In compliance with the external trade law, the Minister of Trade, Industry & Energy is required to make public a notice containing

☐ distinction between import & export items requiring approval or permit and restricted items,
☐ restrictions on the amounts of import & export, the ceiling amount of transactions, standards and trading countries, and
☐ requirements such as recommendation or confirmation regarding the said restrictions.

Even automatic approval items may be restricted and required by other laws to meet certain criteria. There are a total of 49 applicable laws including the Cosmetics and Medical Instruments Law and the Food Sanitation Act, which put forward different restrictions and requirements. For this reason the Minister of Trade, Industry & Energy collects relevant information and issues a public notice, called a general notice, so that the tax offices, trade-related organizations and trade companies can easily find out which restrictions apply to a specific item.

In case the item to be exported is restricted by a set quota, the exporter must obtain endorsement for export from the relevant authority, and the necessary visa for customs clearance at the importing country, which is then dispatched together with shipping documents to the buyer.

If a company not entitled to a quota wishes to export an item restricted as a quota item, the company should first check by which export association the regulates proposed item and whether any quota is currently available. If no quota is available, the company may negotiate with another company with a quota to assign the quota or to become the exporting agent for the item.

Quota Information Centers

Export approval In principle the exporter is still required to get a permit for each export item, even though he/she has already obtained an export licence. The exporter must comply with the requirements as instructed in the course of acquiring export approval. Export items are inspected at the time of customs clearance, and the receipt of payment is confirmed by the corresponding bank.

Automatic approval items may be exported without export approval, if the payment is made with an irrevocable documentary bill payable at sight letter of credit or the payment does not exceed US$ 30,000.

Export approval authorities External trade law empowers the Minister of Trade, Industry & Energy to issue export permits; however, the power is delegated to the heads of foreign exchange banks in order to simplify and speed up the export process.

EXPORT APPROVAL AUTHORITIES

> Loan   for production fund based on past performance : amount assessed in the certificate of export performance X average increment rate X loan unit per US dollar

Effective term of export approval The effective term of export approval is determined so as to facilitate exports and maintain credit overseas; Once export approval is obtained, the exporter must carry out the planned export and collect payment within the set period.

In general, the term is set at one year starting from the approval issuing date. However, for the following exceptions, it may be increase to a maximum of 20 years;

☐
if the total time required is expected to exceed one year when including time taken for the manufacture and processing of export items,

☐
if the total time required is expected to exceed one year when including time required for shipping and the agreed date of payment,

☐
if the head of the relevant approving authority considers it necessary to allow more than a year, for example, when imports and exports take place concurrently or consecutively.

Exemption of export approval The exporter must obtain an export license, and apply for export approval for each transaction. However, license and permit requirements may be exempted in special cases of a non-commercial nature. Simplified inspection by the superintendent of Customs will suffice. Exempted items are as follows:

free samples or promotional goods
goods to make up for deficiency in an export transaction, repaired goods being returned to the owner, goods sent abroad for repair or examination,
unsatisfactory imported items being returned to the seller, or
reusable materials which are used for the transportation of container cargo.

Export Approval Information Centers

Oraganization	Telephone	Facsimile	Remarks
Export Division, Ministry of Trade, Industry & Energy	503-7171	503-9438	Operation of the quota system, allocation of quota, General information, GATT Textiles Agreement, endorsement for export, issuance of visa, etc.
International Affairs Department, Korea International Trade Association	551-5324	551-5181	
Apparels Industry Association	551-1512	551-1479	
Korea Export Association of Textiles	551-1885	551-1867	
Korea Consumer Goods Export Association	551-1867	551-1870	

Approval (authorization) of the terms of payment Currently the negative system is employed to define the terms of payment for import & export. No additional approval or permission is required unless the items are specified as exceptions that require certification from the head of a foreign exchange bank, or permission from the Governor of the Bank of Korea or the Minister of the Ministry of Finance and Economy.

Import of raw materials to be manufactured for export

Assistance in purchasing raw materials for re-export As a strategic measure to minimize the financial burden of exporting manufacturers regarding purchase of raw materials and thus strengthening the international competitiveness of Korean products, financial, commercial and tax benefits are given to manufacturing companies when they purchase raw materials not for domestic consumption but for the manufacture of export goods.

Under this provision, except in few special circumstances, it is possible to import raw materials which are restricted in the public notice or by regulations.
Trade-related financial assistance
Rebate on customs tariff

The scope of raw materials entitled to financial assistance Raw materials (including packaging materials) used to produce goods for export; raw materials used to produce military supplies with a foreign currency increment rate of over 30%; raw materials required for overseas construction and services; raw materials used to manufacture goods which are defined in International Trade Administration Regulation as earning foreign currencies; raw materials needed for the repair and after-sales service of goods which have been manufactured for export with the raw materials as defined above, and for which payment has already been received.

Restrictions in the import of raw materials to be manufactured for export Appropriate procedures need to be taken for the following items to be approved for import; selected items the import of which is restricted in order to promote replacement industries, and restricted items specified in general notice, such as agriculture, forestry & fishery produce, narcotics, and hemp.

Import approval and approving authority The Minister of Trade, Industry & Energy is the authority empowered to issue import approval; however the power is delegated to the head of foreign exchange banks, except in exceptional cases such as trade with North Korea which is placed under the jurisdiction of the Minister of The Board of National Unification.

Information about the import and purchase of raw materials

Type of transaction	Relevant authority
⚬ General export	foreign exchange bank
⚬ Export of strategic items	
- general industrial goods	Ministry of Trade, Industry & Energy
- defense-related items	Ministry of Defense
- nuclear and related items	Ministry of Science & Technology
⚬ Intermediate trade	Foreign Exchange Bank
⚬ Trade between North & South Korea	The Board of National Unification
(restricted approval items)	(Exchange Division II)
⚬ Export of industrial facilities	
- financial assistance on	Export-Imjport Bank of Korea
deferred payment basis	
- outsourcing method	Ministry of Trade, Industry & Energy
- others	Foreign Exchange Bank

Import approval system

The licensed importer is still required to obtain import approval from relevant authorities for each import transaction. This import approval system is designed to ensure proper supervision of import activities and the performance of the obligation of the overseas seller (i.e., the transfer of goods to the importer).

Recommendation of import, and advance approval The importer must obtain recommendation from the relevant government office if restricted by special laws, or from the relevant organization if restricted in import/export notice or general notice, before applying for import approval.

Import Approving Authorities

Relevant office	Telephone	Facsimile
Trade Policy Division, Ministry of Trade, Industry & Eenergy	503-9432/3	502-1754
Certification Section of Each Foreign Exchange Bank	-	-
Trade Promotion Division, Korea International Trade Association	551-5203-7	551-5237
Trade Inquiry Office, Korea International Trade Association	551-5354/8	551-5161

Effective period of import approval Once import approval is granted, the contracted goods must be received and payment made as agreed within the effective period of import approval. Under the current external trade law, the period is set at 1 year, which may be extended up to 20 years when deemed necessary to take into consideration, for example, the delivery time and the date of payment.

Exemption of import approval For speedy, smooth import process, import approval is exempted for small transactions and samples which are believed to generate no problems regarding the management of foreign exchange.

Inquiries on Import Approval

Special excise tax : (taxable price + customs duty) X special excise tax rate

Liquor tax : spirits kl X 57,000 won/kl

(add 600 won per degree of alcohol content exceeding 95)

alcoholic beverages (taxable price + customs duty) X liquor tax rate

Education tax : 30% of special excise tax or liquor tax (10% of liquor tax if the liquor tax rate is below 80% for the item subject to liquor tax)

Value-added tax : (taxable price + customs duty + special excise tax or liquor tax) X VAT rate (10%)

Special tax for rural development : 20% of tax reductions if tariff reductions are given or 10% of special excise tax for a selected list of items subject to special excise tax

Authorization (approval) of the methods of payment The approval system has been restructured into a negative system from the previous positive system, effective as of Sept. 1,

1992. In other words, no specific approval or permission is required as to the methods of payment, unless the imported goods are included in the negative list, which are those that require approval or authorization from the head of a foreign exchange bank, the Governor of the Bank of Korea, or the Minister of the Ministry of Finance and Economy.

Payment of customs tariff and related taxes

The tax system of Korea is basically payment by self-assessment. Payment must be made within 15 days from the date of income tax returns.

Calculation method for customs duties and tax Taxes levied on imported goods are customs dues, special excise tax, liquor tax, education tax, special tax for rural development, and value-added tax.

Types of customs tariff The tariff rates currently employed in Korea are the statutory (national) tariff and the conventional tariff.

Order of priority of customs tariffs 1) Dumping Prevention Duties, retaliatory tariff, Emergency Duties, Countervailing Duties, Special Emergency Duties, 2) Benefit Duties, International Cooperation Duties, 3) Adjustment Duties, Price Stabilization Duties, Seasonal Duties, Quota Duties, 4) Provisional Tax Rate, 5) Basic Tax Rate (basic tariff)

Calculation of customs duties

Relevant office	Telephone	Facsimile
Trade Policy Division, Ministry of Trade, Industry & Eenergy	503-9432/3	502-1754
Certification Section of Each Foreign Exchange Bank	-	-
Trade Promotion Division, Korea International Trade Association	551-5203-7	551-5237
Trade Inquiry Office, Korea International Trade Association	551-5354/8	551-5161

Calculation of Tax

Oraganization	Telephone	Facsimile	Remarks
Export Division, Ministry of Trade, Industry & Energy	503-7171	503-9438	Operation of the quota system, allocation of quota, General information, GATT Textiles Agreement, endorsement for export, issuance of visa, etc.
International Affairs Department, Korea International Trade Association	551-5324	551-5181	
Apparels Industry Association	551-1512	551-1479	
Korea Export Association of Textiles	551-1885	551-1867	
Korea Consumer Goods Export Association	551-1867	551-1870	

Determination of taxable price for imported goods The most widely employed method to determine taxable basis is to calculate the taxable basis based on the actual value paid; i.e., by adding to or subtracting from the actual price to pay several adjusting elements, and then adding freight charge and insurance.

4. TRADE FINANCING

Trade financing Financial assistance for exporting is arranged to contribute to export growth.

Eligibility for loans The holder of commercial papers or documents which affirms an export transaction in progress, such as export letter of credit, D/P, D/A, contracts drawn up in foreign currency about the supply of goods (e.g., export of industrial supplies).

Types and time of loans Loans are available for manufacture, import of raw materials, purchase of raw materials, and general financing. Financing on the security of the L/C is available for the acquisition of raw materials, and financing based on past export performance, which is not limited to the acquisition of raw materials, is normally arranged within 15 days of the issuance of the certificate of export performance by the corresponding foreign exchange bank.

Financing process

Financing based on the L/C: On an individual basis, an application for a loan will be processed and the amount of loan will be determined on the basis of documentary evidence submitted with each application, within the loan limit calculated in reference to previous export performance.

Financing based on past performance : Financing is arranged within the loan limit calculated in reference to previous export performance, regardless of the presence of the L/C or other materials. This financing method, used by most trading companies (90%), is designed to provide simplified loan application, for loan application and evaluation becomes complicated as companies expand in size and exports grow.

Period of loan

Financing based on past performance : maximum 90 days, but only 60 days will be given when the recipient of the loan is importing raw materials from countries like Japan, Hong Kong, Taiwan and the Philippines from which the sea trip takes on average not more than 10 days.

Financing based on the L/C : maximum 180 days. The period of loan is calculated by adding 7 days to the shipping date or the date of delivery, where applicable, and determined within the effective period of the L/C.

Loan Repayment The loan financing export activities must be repaid when the payment for the exported goods is received or when the note issued on the security of the L/C is sold. In the case of financing based on past performance, the loan is repaid at the date of loan maturity.

LEADING SECTORS FOR INVESTMENTS & BUSINESS

DEFENSE INDUSTRY EQUIPMENT

ITA CODE: DFN

	2005	2006	2007 (estimated)
TOTAL MARKET SIZE	4,468	4,900	5,292
Total Local Production	4,100	4,200	4,536
Total Exports	262	300	324
Total Imports	630	1,000	1,080

(Unit: USD million)

[Source: Ministry of National Defense (MND), Korea Defense Industry Association (KDIA), Joint US Military Affairs Group-Korea (JUSMAG-K)]

[USD 1= 1,000 Won (2005), 950 Won (2006), 930 Won (2007)]

The Republic of Korea (ROK) is currently modernizing the armed forces to a level commensurate with the country's economic strength. The ROK is in need of significant materiel modernization and replacements that will involve major investments. Although U.S. defense companies have been very successful in selling their products to Korea, European and Middle East competitors who are becoming increasingly prominent in the market could influence future sales. Nevertheless, Korea should continue to be a good market for U.S. defense companies especially when competitive products and services are offered.

The 2006-2010 mid-term plan was developed in 2005 with an emphasis on securing a self-reliant national defense. The Korean military plans to obtain an independent intelligence gathering capability focusing on the peninsula and the surrounding area by securing Airborne Early Warning (AWACS) aircraft, high-altitude Unmanned Aerial Vehicles (UAV), and long-range intelligence equipment by 2010. The Ministry of National Defense (MND) plans to steadily raise defense spending to 3.5 percent of Gross Domestic Product (GDP), from the current 2.85 percent level, in the next few years. Economic constraints, steadily rising O&M costs, and payment schedules for past acquisitions complicate force development. Korea plans to invest about USD 54 billion in force improvement programs 2006 - 2010.

Recently interoperability has become less of a factor when purchasing equipment due to Korea's desire to increase competition and diversify sources of supply. It is also expected that there will continue to be tension between indigenous development and cost-effective acquisition. The MND is trying to solve this dilemma by demanding a high degree of technology transfer and offsets for projects. Currently the most important elements for purchasing decisions by MND are price, technology transfer and offsets. U.S. industry must closely follow any and all developments in programs and be prepared to move quickly if the need arises. The Korean government has made it clear that they will procure leading edge technologies to defend Korea, which presents opportunities for the U.S. defense industry.

South Korea plans to increase defense spending to USD 28.9 billion in 2008, which is a 9% increase vis-à-vis the year before. The defense budget will account for over 15% of overall government spending in Korea. The ROK has signaled that it will increase operating expenditures to USD 20.5 billion, while setting spending of USD 8.6 billion for expenditures leading to improvements in defense capabilities. The Defense Ministry has identified key projects in the 2008 budget including the purchase or development of unmanned aerial vehicles, helicopters, infantry fighting vehicles and other ongoing projects like AEW&C, SAM-X surface to air missile and the Korean Multipurpose Helicopter.

Korean Air Force

Just like the Army and Navy, the Korean armed forces are gearing up to command its defense by 2012. With respect to the Air Force, this includes current negotiations to add an additional 20 F-15K fighters to the air fleet to replace ageing F-4 and F-5 legacy aircraft. The signing in 2006 for the purchase of Boeing E-737 AEW&C (AWAC) aircraft and development and production of up to 800 Korean Aerospace Industry T-50 jet fighter trainers in cooperation with Lockheed Martin signals Koreas intention to 1) increase air power and 2) develop a more indigenous aerospace industry for the local production of fixed wing, rotor wing, and UAV assets.

The Republic of Korea continues to negotiate the potential sale of its KAI T-50 trainer to the United Arab Emirates, and during the recently concluded Dubai Air Show, the UAE announced that the BAE Hawk was no longer being considered for the contract and that Alenia (Italy/Brazil/Switzerland) and KAI (Korea/USA) were the remaining contender for the contract.

Korean Navy

The Republic of Korea Navy plans to move to a full blue-water role by 2012, with a full range of vessels including transports, frigates, corvettes and submarine systems. Vessels like the Dokdo-class transport ship (built by Hanjin Heavy Industries) would be able to carry 700 marines, ten helos, and two LCACs. Likewise Hyundai is looking to build a 7,000 tonne destroyer with the Aegis combat system. With expenditures increasing for the Navy and Air Force, and Korea assuming its role of taking full command of its defense, the market for defense systems is improving.

BEST PRODUCTS/SERVICES

- Military Aerospace (fighters)
- Avionics
- C4ISR
- Missile technology
- Maritime Defense Electronics and Systems

OPPORTUNITIES

Airborne Mine-sweeping Counter Measures (AMCM; est. $500 million)
The ROKN plans to procure eight MH-60 class mine warfare helicopters by 2011.
Next Generation Frigates (FFX)
The ROKN plans to deploy a total of nine 2,500 ton class frigates by 2018. The delivery of one ship per year will begin from 2010-2018.

RESOURCES

Korea Aerospace & Defense Exhibition (Seoul Air Show 2009)

For additional analytical, business and investment opportunities information, please contact Global Investment & Business Center, USA at (202) 546-2103. Fax: (202) 546-3275. E-mail: rusric@erols.com

Bi-annual: dates to be determined
Naval & Defense 2009
Bi-annual: dates to be determined
Key Contacts
Ministry of National Defense (MND)
www.mnd.go.kr
Defense Acquisition Program Agency

LOCAL CONTACT

(Mrs.) Myoung Soo Lah
Commercial Specialist
Commercial Service Korea
U.S. Embassy
32 Sejong-ro Jongro-gu
Seoul 110-710 Korea
Tel: 82-2-397-4516
Fax: 82-2-739-1628
Email: myoung.soo.lah@mail.doc.gov
Website: www.buyusa.gov/korea

SECURITY SERVICES AND PRODUCTS

ITA CODE: SEC

	2005	2006	2007 (estimated)
TOTAL MARKET SIZE	1,964	2,134	2,176
Total Local Production	838	9,112	9,294
Total Exports	N/A	N/A	N/A
Total Imports	1,069	1,158	1,181

* Demand for building security in 2007 is status-quo due to limited demand from new residential/commercial buildings while demand from existing residential/commercial and government buildings remains same as 2006.

(Unit: USD million)

(Source: The above statistics are unofficial estimates by CS Korea. The total market size includes services and equipment. Statistics for local production and import data do not include security services.)

[USD 1= 1,000 Won (2005), 950 Won (2006), 930 Won (2007)]

In 2006, the overall size of Korea's security industry, including equipment and services, exceeded USD 2.1 billion. Provision of security guard services continued to account for over 50 percent of the total security market followed by leased and installed security equipment, which accounted for 25 percent of the market. Security devices took a 15 percent share. In 2006, the size of the security industry market increased by around 10%. In that year, airports and ports started to replace existing security systems while large private companies showed increasing interest in

For additional analytical, business and investment opportunities information,
please contact Global Investment & Business Center, USA
at (202) 546-2103. Fax: (202) 546-3275. E-mail: rusric@erols.com

installing integrated security systems. The security industry is projected to grow by an average of 10 percent per year for the next few years.

Total imports of security equipment and related products in 2006 were estimated at USD1.2 billion. U.S. firms are the major suppliers of airport and port security equipment, which includes X-ray scanning systems, computerized tomography X-rays, magnetometers, hand-held detectors and explosive trace detectors. Total imports of airport and port security equipment in 2006 were estimated at USD 617.5 million. U.S. imports accounted for 25 percent at USD 154 million. CS Korea expects that U.S. imports will maintain a steady market share in Korea's import security industry for the foreseeable future.

OPPORTUNITIES

The local security equipment manufacturing industry's technology level lags behind that of the major NATO member countries, especially in the area of providing high-end security solutions and C4ISR infrastructure to meet end-user requirements. As a result, the industry's major Korean players, who are also systems integrators, are seeking opportunities to develop top-notch technology in cooperation with foreign companies.

Government agencies are end-users for integrated systems for security devices and command and control infrastructure. In particular, airports, ports, and customs offices are seeking advanced integrated security systems devices. U.S. companies have a larger share of the Korean market for X-ray detection systems and container inspection systems than European and Japanese firms. U.S. systems, certified by the Transportation Security Administration (TSA) and the Federal Aviation Administration (FAA), should have growing market opportunities in Korea due to confidence in the quality of systems with these certifications. U.S. companies are encouraged to monitor government procurement plans and establish consortia with prime Korean contractors in systems integration.

RESOURCES

SecuWorld 2008
June 25-27, 2008
http://www.secuexpo.com/
Korea International Safety & Security Exhibition
June 30-July 3, 2008
www.KISS21C.org
Key Contacts
Civil Aviation Safety Authority
www.casa.go.kr
Incheon International Airport Corporation (IIAC)
www.airport.or.kr
Korea Fire Equipment Inspection Corporation
http://www.kfi.or.kr/
Korea Occupational Safety & Health Agency
www.kosha.net
Civil Defense and Disaster Management Bureau
Ministry of Government Administration and Home Affairs
http://www.mogaha.go.kr
Fire Administration Bureau
Ministry of Government Administration and Home Affairs
http://www.mogaha.go.kr

Anti Terror Division
National Police Agency
http://www.npa.go.kr/eng/index.jsp
Local Contact:
(Mrs.) Myoung Soo Lah
Commercial Specialist
Commercial Service Korea
U.S. Embassy
32 Sejong-ro Jongro-gu
Seoul 110-710 Korea
Tel: 82-2-397-4516
Fax: 82-2-739-1628
Email: myoung.soo.lah@mail.doc.gov
Website: www.buyusa.gov/korea

SPECIALTY CHEMICALS

ITA CODE: ICH

	2004	2005	2006 (estimated)
	25,093	25,775	27,292
Total Local Production	20,139	20,563	22,000
Total Exports	2,934	3,042	3,612
Total Imports	7,889	8,254	8,903

(Unit: USD million)

Korean demand for high quality, sophisticated chemical products and associated substances for the development of new products is steadily increasing. In 2006, the total market size of Korea's specialty chemicals was USD 33.4 billion, a 6 percent increase over 2005. Total imports of specialty chemicals increased by 18 percent in 2006, during which time imports from the U.S. increased by 12 percent to reach 1.57 billion. The U.S. has a 15 percent share of the specialty chemical import market.

The specialty chemical industry is projected to grow by seven percent over the next few years and is expected to result in a nine percent annual increase in demand for specialty chemical imports. In the specialty chemicals area, Korea lacks advanced chemical materials and technology, and has not made significant investments in R&D despite growing demand in the pharmaceutical, cosmetic/perfume, photochemical, and paint and ink industry sectors. As a result, Korea continues to heavily depend on imports to meet demand for intermediate raw materials and newly developed chemical products.

BEST PRODUCTS/SERVICES

- **Specialty chemicals for the medical and pharmaceutical industries**
- **Specialty chemicals for the cosmetics industry**

OPPORTUNITIES

Market demand continues to grow especially from Korean companies in the medical, pharmaceutical and cosmetic industries. These companies are very interested in using advanced chemical materials to produce new products. The technological level of domestic producers appears to be on par with advanced countries in terms of basic science and technology; consequently, newer technology is also very welcome. Korean government agencies continue to actively pursue alliances with multinational companies in countries with an advanced chemicals industry to secure know-how for the production of high-end medical, pharmaceutical, cosmetics and biochemistry products.

RESOURCES

XpoChem Conference 2008 (Annual)
Date to be determined www.kscia.or.kr
American Association of Clinical Chemistry
July 27-31 in Washington, DC
http://www.aacc.org/AACC/events/ann_meet/
Key Contact
Ministry of Environment
www.me.go.kr Ministry of Labor
www.molab.go.kr
Local Contact
(Mrs.) Myoung Soo Lah
Commercial Specialist
Commercial Service Korea
U.S. Embassy
32 Sejong-ro Jongro-gu
Seoul 110-710 Korea
Tel: 82-2-397-4516
Fax: 82-2-739-1628
Email: myoung.soo.lah@mail.doc.gov
Website: www.buyusa.gov/korea

DRUGS AND PHARMACEUTICALS

ITA CODE: DRG

	2005	2006	2007 (estimated)
	10,495	12,359	13,711
*Total Local Production	9,670	11,102	12,362
**Total Exports	419	493	562
**Total Imports	1,244	1,749	1,912
**Imports from the U.S.	152	225	246

(Unit: USD million)

The Korean market, the 12th largest pharmaceutical markets in the world, was valued at USD 9.2 billion in 2006. According to industry sources, Korean market demand for pharmaceuticals is estimated to have grown by approximately 10 percent in 2007 to reach USD 10.2 billion and is forecast to grow at an average annual rate of 10 percent over the next several years since the need for medical treatment for senior citizens is increasing rapidly.

The Korean pharmaceutical market has continued to experience unprecedented restructuring since 1999, when the Korean government implemented significant reforms to improve the transparency of the health care system. These reforms have helped increase have helped increase transparency in the reimbursement system and have, to some degree, leveled the playing field for multinationals. There have also been positive changes in the regulatory climate that have allowed smoother and earlier market access for new, innovative drugs. Multinationals have expanded their share of the total therapeutic (ethical and over-the-counter) pharmaceutical market from 35.7 percent in 2005 to 36.6 percent in 2006.

Over the next few years, one important factor that may slow the growth rate in overall market demand and hamper patient access to innovative pharmaceuticals will be the measures taken by the Korean government to finance the national healthcare insurance system. The Korean government has implemented the National Health (NHI) Insurance Drug Expenditure Rational Plan (DERP) as of December 29, 2006. The key contents of the DERP included a change in the management system from a Negative List System in which all medicines were, in principle, covered by insurance, to a Positive List System in which mainly the medicines that are superior in cost effectiveness are covered by insurance. Additionally, the National Health Insurance Corporation (NHIC), the single payer, has introduced a price negotiation procedure which determines whether a new drug should be listed and at what price.

Notwithstanding the Korean government's cost containment measures, the U.S. government will continue to work closely with and advocate on behalf of U.S. exporters' market access concerns. This includes continuing to encourage the Korean Government to make the market more transparent, to reimburse innovative drugs at appropriate levels, and to ensure Korean patients' access to innovative pharmaceuticals. Industry sources speculate that the Korean government's need to reduce costs will be balanced by satisfying consumer demands for advanced health care over the next few years. We advise U.S. exporters of research-based, innovative drugs to evaluate the impact of the new reimbursement system on their potential sales before entering this lucrative and growing, but challenging, market.

With the Korean government's encouragement, the Korean biotech pharmaceutical industry is striving to invest more in R&D (currently only 4-5 percent based on sales revenue) and diversify from the production of generics and antibiotics. This trend presents excellent opportunities for U.S. biotech firms to participate in Korea's strategic biotech sector. Although Korea's pharmaceutical industry is competitive in terms of chemical synthesizing technologies, it is much less competitive in drug screening, safety evaluation and clinical trials. Korean companies are pursuing strategic alliances with multinational firms to finance R&D for new products or for cross licensing of existing technologies. Industry experts predict that the U.S. market share will increase as more U.S. biotechnology-based products become commercially available over the next few years.

BEST PRODUCTS/SERVICES

-Therapeutic pharmaceuticals

OPPORTUNITIES

The Osong Bio-Technopolis, a program within the Korean Ministry of Health and Welfare, is seeking foreign investment for biotechnology industry development in the high-tech science park at Osong. The 4,633,000 square meter science park will have two major focuses: pharmaceuticals and cosmetics (59.7 percent) and medical devices (25.8 percent). Since the

For additional analytical, business and investment opportunities information,
please contact Global Investment & Business Center, USA
at (202) 546-2103. Fax: (202) 546-3275. E-mail: rusric@erols.com

Korean biotech industry is still relatively undeveloped, the timing may be good for U.S. companies interested in getting in on the ground floor.

RESOURCES

Key Contacts
Ministry of Health and Welfare
www.mohw.go.kr
Korea Food & Drug Administration
www.kfda.go.kr
Health Insurance Review Agency
www.hira.or.kr

LOCAL CONTACT

(Ms.) Yoon-Shil Chay
Senior Commercial Specialist
Commercial Service Korea
U.S. Embassy
32 Sejong-ro Jongro-gu
Seoul 110-710 Korea
Tel: 82-2-397-4439
Fax: 82-2-739-1628
Email: yoon.shil.chay@mail.doc.gov
Website: www.buyusa.gov/korea

MEDICAL EQUIPMENT AND DEVICES

ITA CODE: MED

	2005	2006	2007 (estimated)
Total Market Size	2,534.0	3,038.8	3,379.7
Total Local Production	1,704.1	2,051.7	2,263.1
Total Exports	715.8	821.7	914.4
Total Imports	1,545.6	1,808.8	2,031.0
Imports from the U.S.	520.1	609.8	690.5

(Unit: USD million)

One of the largest Asian markets for medical devices, the Korean market was valued at USD 3.0 billion in 2006 and is expected to increase to approximately USD3.4 billion in 2007. According to industry sources, the medical equipment market is forecast to grow at an average annual rate of 10-15 percent over the next few years. However, one important factor that may slow the growth rate will be the pricing and reimbursement measures that the Korean government grapples with the national healthcare system. For example, the Korean government implemented two-phase price cut for medical devices as of November 1, 2007

Korea depends on advanced medical devices from the U.S., Japan, and the EU to supply about 60 percent of total market demand. In 2007, total imports of medical devices were estimated at USD 2.0 billion, with U.S. imports, estimated to be USD 691.2 million, representing a 34 percent import market share. Market demand for advanced and innovative medical devices is forecast to remain strong in 2007 and over the next several years as Korea's hospitals continue to purchase advanced technology products from abroad and as increasing numbers of elderly Korean patients require sophisticated medical procedures. In general, Koreans are increasingly demanding better care from their national healthcare system as the standard of living continues to improve in the world's eleventh largest economy. Another factor favoring the use of imported advanced medical equipment and devices is the growing number of Korean doctors educated in the U.S. and Europe.

BEST PRODUCTS/SERVICES

- Cardiovascular devices (e.g. stents, angio cath) - CT units - MRI units

- Dental Implants

- Orthopedic implants and joints - Hemodialysis - Laser surgical apparatus - Ultrasonic imaging system - Sight corrective ophthalmic lens - etc.

OPPORTUNITIES

The Korean government is constructing world-class hospitals with 600-800 beds in the Incheon Free Economic Zone (FEZ). The first hospital at the FEZ is targeted to open in 2010. Since this is the first time that Korea has invited foreign capital participation in healthcare, the development of the Incheon FEZ provides a good export opportunity for U.S. suppliers of high-end medical equipment and devices.

RESOURCES

Key Contacts Ministry of Health and Welfare
www.mohw.go.kr
Korea Food & Drug Administration
www.kfda.go.kr
Health Insurance Review Agency
www.hira.or.kr

LOCAL CONTACT

(Ms.) Yoon-Shil Chay
Commercial Specialist
Commercial Service Korea
U.S. Embassy
32 Sejong-ro Jongro-gu
Seoul 110-710 Korea
Tel: 82-2-397-4439
Fax: 82-2-739-1628
Email: yoon.shil.chay@mail.doc.gov
Website: www.buyusa.gov/korea

WIRELESS BROADBAND INTERNET EQUIPMENT AND SERVICES

ITA CODE: CSV

	2005	2006	2007 (estimated)
	N/A	610.5	801.9
Total Local Production	N/A	463.2	628.2
Total Exports	N/A	10.5	20.4
Total Imports	N/A	157.9	194.1

(Unit: USD million)

Korea ranks among the top countries in the world for Internet usage and broadband penetration and has one of the highest numbers of broadband subscribers among all OECD countries. Korea's total number of broadband subscribers is estimated to have reached 98 percent of the nation's 15 million households as of the end of 2007 and therefore, service providers are planning for more valued-added services including wireless broadband service and Internet protocol television (IPTV).

Wireless Internet access service in Korea can be categorized into two major services; fixed wireless Internet (WLAN) based on WiFi or Wimax technology, and mobile internet based on code division multiple access (CDMA) technology. Mobile and WLAN services enable users to access all Internet services on handheld devices without cable connections, allowing mobility and convenience. However, in order to satisfy demand for higher bandwidth and mobility over the existing wireless Internet, new "mobile Wimax," or "Wireless Broadband" (WiBro), service was commercialized in June 2006 by KT and SK Telecom using the 2.3 GHz spectrum with limited coverage in Seoul. WiBro will become the foundation of "Ubiquitous-Korea," a seamless Internet access/communication environment planned by the Korean government in cooperation with industry. The WiBro service market is expected to attract 600,000 subscribers in 2008, up from 100,000 subscribers in 2007, driving more demand for hardware and applications.

WiBro technology is part of the IEEE802.16 family of wireless Internet specifications, Wimax, and is expected to offer up to 5-15 Mbps bandwidth to mobile devices traveling at over 60 kilometers per hour (about 37 miles per hour). Major local companies, including Samsung, LG, and PosData, as well as the Electronic Technology Research Institute (ETRI), a Ministry of Information and Communication (MIC)-sponsored R&D think tank, are developing a new standard with the help of the Telecom Technology Association (TTA). The development includes the evaluation and adaptation of different types of foreign and local technologies. ETRI will play a major role in developing and localizing WiBro core technology. The institute plans to make at least 20 percent of the technology homegrown in order to minimize the payment of licensing fees to foreign firms. This aggressive agenda calls for immediate R&D and infrastructure investment for new WiBro technologies by foreign companies since the Korean government has realized the importance of global standardization in order to export new technologies.

Korea's global leadership in wireless communications and broadband Internet access services has spawned tremendous demand for all types of equipment, contents, and solutions, especially for specialized and innovative technologies, providing opportunities for sales of advanced and highly specialized U.S. telecommunications equipment, solutions, and contents.

BEST PROSPECTS/SERVICES

-
-
-

For additional analytical, business and investment opportunities information,
please contact Global Investment & Business Center, USA
at (202) 546-2103. Fax: (202) 546-3275. E-mail: rusric@erols.com

OPPORTUNITIES

Market demand for WiBro services should drive investment in the telecom sector for the next five years. Nationwide infrastructure installation for WiBro will be deployed in 2008, and more "killer applications" and relevant services including triple play services (TPS), Internet protocol TV, and video on demand (VoD) are expected to be introduced by KT, SK Telecom, Hanaro Telecom, etc. triggering more service and content demand.

According to MIC, the market demand for WiBro service is expected to reach USD 1 billion by 2011 with nine million subscribers and will eventually transition to the 4th generation next generation network (NGN) telecom network. The total market demand for mobile WiMax equipment and solutions is expected to reach a total of USD 2 billion over the next three years.

RESOURCES

TRADE SHOWS

http://www.sek.co.kr

http://www.wisexpso.co.kr

Smart Home Network Show (June 10-12, 2008)

http://www.smarthomeshow.com/en

2008 IT EXPO BUSAN (September 3-6, 2008)

http://www.itexpo.or.kr/2007/english/index

KES 2008 (October 14-18, 2008)

http://www.kes.org

IT-SoC Fair 2008 (October 15-16, 2008)

http://www.it-soc.org/English/index.asp

KEY CONTACTS

Ministry of Information and Communication (MIC)

http://www.mic.go.kr/index.jsp

Radio Research Lab (RRL)

http://www.rrl.go.kr/eng/index.jsp

Telecommunications Technology Association (TTA)

http://www.tta.or.kr/English/new/main/index.htm

Electronics and Telecommunications Research Institute (ETRI)

http://www.etri.re.kr/www 05/e etri/

Local Contact
(Mr.) Chris Ahn

Senior Commercial Specialist
Commercial Service Korea
U.S. Embassy
32 Sejong-ro Jongro-gu
Seoul 110-710 Korea
Tel: 82-2-397-4186
Fax: 82-2-737-5357
Email: chris.ahn@mail.doc.gov
Website: www.buyusa.gov/korea

COMPUTER SOFTWARE

ITA CODE: CSF

	2005	2006	2007 (estimated)
Total Market Size	5,992	5,786	6,023
Total Local Production	5,603	5,368	5,568
Total Korean Exports	125	123	123
Total Imports into Korea	514	541	577

(Unit: USD million)

The Korean market for packaged software, including systems infrastructure software (e.g. operating systems, security software), application software (e.g. Word, Excel, enterprise solution packages), and application development/deployment software, was valued at USD 5.9 billion in 2007. Forecasts are for the market to reach USD 6.33 billion in 2008 and grow at an average annual rate of 8 percent for the next three years. Korea's global leadership in wireless communications and broadband Internet access services has spawned tremendous demand for all types of software, especially for specialized and innovative technologies, providing opportunities for sales of advanced and highly specialized U.S. software solutions. U.S. suppliers' willingness to customize their software to meet specific user needs is a critical factor in end-user purchase decisions. Although U.S. software is considered superior, Korean end-users, more often than not, will avoid purchasing from U.S. suppliers if localization cannot be achieved.

In 2007, the total import market for packaged software represented 3.1 percent of the total market demand valued at USD 19 billion, which, in general, consists of packaged software, computing-related services/software, and digital contents. Although the statistics show the import market share to be relatively low, in reality, the substantial amount of localized or customized software and systems integration (SI) services provided by major U.S. subsidiaries that participate in large projects as strategic partners are counted in the total Korean software market share.

U.S.-sourced packaged software accounts for more than 80 percent of Korea's software import market, and U.S. suppliers are expected to remain the principal suppliers of packaged software to Korea for the next several years. Technological advancements in Korea's software sector are still behind that of the U.S. and Japan, a result of Korea's relatively recent computerization and an acute shortage of highly qualified software engineers. Korea's systems integration companies and software developers are actively trying to develop partnerships with global leaders in every segment of IT services and solutions to deliver total solutions to clients in a time-to-market manner and to target the domestic and global market at the same time. U.S. suppliers will continue to enjoy the competitive advantages of strong project management and marketing skills, compared to Korean firms and third-country suppliers.

The overall market demand for packaged software has been growing in relation to the development of Korea's advanced IT infrastructure and related services in the e-commerce and telecom segments and will continue to grow at an average annual rate of 8 percent for the next three years. The fact that the Korean government has increased efforts to strengthen its IPR protection and enforcement through the Computer Program Protection Law (CPPL) has also contributed to the strong growth in demand for both Korean and imported packaged software.

OPPORTUNITIES

The market demand for IT services, digital content, and security software are forecast to experience strong growth, driven by mergers and acquisitions among Korea's financial institutions. Companies should expect continued investment in wireline/wireless broadband convergence infrastructure, as well as by growing demand for upcoming Internet Protocol TV.

RESOURCES

Key Contacts
Ministry of Commerce, Industry and Energy (MOCIE)
http://www.mocie.go.kr/eng/default.asp

Ministry of Information and Communication (MIC)
http://www.mic.go.kr/index.jsp

Radio Research Lab (RRL)
http://www.rrl.go.kr/eng/index.jsp

Korea Association of RFID/USN (KARUS)
http://karus.or.kr/eng/index.asp

Local Contact
(Mr.) Chris Ahn
Senior Commercial Specialist
Commercial Service Korea
U.S. Embassy
32 Sejong-ro Jongro-gu
Seoul 110-710 Korea
Tel: 82-2-397-4186
Fax: 82-2-737-5357
E-mail: chris.ahn@mail.doc.gov
Website: www.buyusa.gov/korea

COSMETICS

ITA CODE: COS

UNIT: USD MILLION

	2005	2006	2007

			(Estimated)
	4,631	5,041	N/A
Exports	269	302	334
Imports	500	597	N/A
Imports from U.S.	115	145	N/A
(Included in imports)			
Total Market	5,400	5,941	6,172

[USD1= 1,000 Won (2005), 950 Won (2006), 930 Won (2007)]

During the last few years, Korean women have become more receptive to western health and beauty items. As more Korean women enter the labor force and experience rising incomes, they have become avid users of imported cosmetics, yielding significant gains for U.S. suppliers. Other trends have developed in tandem with the continued strong expansion of the Korean market for imported cosmetics. As Koreans tend to be more health-conscious, following the "well-being" trend, they prefer natural and "green" cosmetics products. Also, since Korean women want to look younger and healthier, functional cosmetics, so-called cosmeceuticals, focusing on anti-aging, whitening, and anti-ultraviolet care have become very popular. Another trend is that Korean men are also becoming significant consumers of cosmetics, providing opportunities for cosmetics companies featuring men's lines. As the Korean cosmetics market continues to be polarized, with products focused at the premium end and at the lower-priced, mass-market end, two distinct groups of consumers are the target audiences: those shopping at low-cost cosmetics franchise stores and those shopping for very expensive and luxurious cosmetics at department stores. The U.S. - Korea Free Trade Agreement (KORUS FTA) signed between both nations in June 2007 has the potential to bring further advantages for U.S. exporters as Korean tariffs on imported U.S. cosmetics are eliminated over three to ten years. These market trends portend good opportunities for U.S. companies in the years ahead.

Some foreign cosmetics companies claim that the importation process is unnecessarily complex and time-consuming. The Korean government has announced that it will increase the budget to hire more personnel to handle the Korea Food and Drug Administration's (KFDA) testing and approval process due to the increasing number of cosmeceutical products entering the market.

Sales of men's cosmetics in Korea have increased significantly, to approximately USD 520 million or about nine percent of the overall market in 2007. This market segment is estimated to continue healthy growth in 2008 to USD 563 million (source: Amore Pacific). This growth reflects the trend that men have expanded their interest from simple skincare to other cosmetics, such as facial scrubs, facial masks, congealers, SPF products, and other cosmeceutical products. With this trend, men's skincare salons have opened in business districts, providing one-stop total beauty and hair care services including hair cutting, perms, treatments, as well as facials. To meet this increasing demand for men's skincare products, many department stores have opened men's cosmetics counters on the men's floor featuring multiple brands, such as Clinique, Clarins, and Biotherm with after-shave lotions, cleaning foams, facial scrubs, facial packs, essences, and other functional cosmetics.

According to research from the Korea Cosmetic News, skin care products make up about 15 percent of the total cosmetics market, or about USD 903 million. Imported cosmetic skin care products accounted for about 50 percent of the USD 903 million, or USD 451.7 million. The most sought after products by consumers are cosmeceuticals such as whitening and anti-wrinkle products. Also, as more consumers become aware of natural ingredients, and as their preference for natural/organic products increases, local industry is focusing on developing natural/organic products.

BEST PROSPECTS/SERVICES

- **Men's Cosmetics**

- **Natural/Organic Skincare Products**

- **Cosmeceuticals**

OPPORTUNITIES

The cosmetics/cosmeceuticals industry's retail distribution channels have expanded in the last several years. The recent introduction of on-line shopping malls, television home-shopping channels such as QVC, pharmacies/drug stores, and catalogue orders have emerged as challengers to traditional retail channels such as direct selling, multi-level marketing, "mom and pop" stores, specialty retail establishments, department stores, discount stores, etc.

There are currently three major franchised drug stores competing in the local market, Olive Young by CJ, W-Store by Kolon, and GS Watson's by GS in partnership with Watson's. These retailers target customers focusing on wellness products by providing organic/natural cosmetics, nutritional supplements, OTC drugs, and general consumer goods. U.S. companies should seek opportunities in line with this new retail concept.

RESOURCES

Major Show
Name: Cosmobeauty Seoul
http://www.cosmobeautyseoul.com/en/index.php
Key Contacts
Korea Food & Drug Association (KFDA)
http://www.kfda.go.kr/
Korea Pharmaceutical Traders Association (KPTA)
http://www.kpta.or.kr/E_main.asp
Local Contact
Grace Sung
Commercial Specialist
Commercial Service Korea
U.S. Embassy in Korea
32 Sejong-ro Jongro-gu
Seoul 110-710 Korea
Tel: 82-2-397-4324
Fax: 82-2-739-1628
Email: grace.sung@mail.doc.gov
Website: www.buyusa.gov/korea

TRAVEL AND TOURISM

ITA Industry Code: TRA

For additional analytical, business and investment opportunities information,
please contact Global Investment & Business Center, USA
at (202) 546-2103. Fax: (202) 546-3275. E-mail: rusric@erols.com

	2005	2006	2007
			(Estimated)
Outbound Travel	10,080,143	11,609,878	13,000,000
Outbound Travel to the U.S.	665,181	800,000	880,000
Inbound Travel	4,347,318	6,155,047	6,350,000

Interest in international travel by Koreans has been spurred by rapidly rising GDP, gradual increases in leisure time, heightened globalization, and greater awareness and interest in developments outside the Korean peninsula. Korea's per capita GDP has risen to almost USD 24,000, placing it securely in the ranks of middle-income countries. Korean consumer confidence also has increased along with a sharp rise in discretionary spending for such activities as overseas travel for both business and leisure. Korea also has begun to upgrade its domestic tourism sector infrastructure.

With these changing cultural and income factors, conditions look promising for more growth in the outbound Korean travel market. Koreans are showing an increased desire to travel to the U.S. despite the lengthy travel time and the relatively high airfares required to make the trip. The Korean mass media is influenced by U.S. movies, advertising, popular culture, and most recently, the Internet, which continue to stimulate Koreans' interest in U.S. travel destinations. Koreans overwhelmingly choose the U.S. as a non-Asian destination because of the diversity of tourism opportunities not easily available back home, including U.S.-style shopping, theme parks, cultural attractions in major U.S. cities, relatively inexpensive golfing experiences, and the major U.S. national parks.

In 2007, 13 million Koreans traveled abroad, an increase of 10.6 percent over 2006. The Korean Tourism Organization (KTO) estimates that 880,000 Koreans traveled to the U.S. in 2007, a 10 percent increase over 2006, when 800,000 visited the U.S. The number of Korean travelers to the U.S. has varied greatly over the past decade. Prior to the Asian financial crisis in 1997, 806,264 Koreans traveled to the U.S., then sharply decreased. Since then, the numbers slowly picked up back to 719,227 by 2000. However, the September 11, 2001, terrorist attacks caused the number of travelers to the U.S. to decrease. Only recently are the numbers beginning to surpass 1997 levels. Competition from other destinations that do not require visas, such as Japan and Southeast Asian countries, is strong. Thailand is becoming a popular honeymoon destination. The stricter U.S. visa regime put in place following 9/11, which requires the U.S. Embassy to fingerprint and interview all applicants for U.S. visas, has dampened some interest in leisure travel to the U.S. However, recent legislative changes in the U.S. make it likely that Korea will join the Visa Waiver Program within a few years, which will increase the number of Korean travelers to the U.S.

As reported by the U.S. International Trade Administration, Korea is currently the seventh-largest source of inbound travel to the U.S., behind Canada, Mexico, the United Kingdom, Japan, Germany, and France. In 2006, Korea accounted for a modest one percent of the total 51 million foreign visitors to the U.S.

BEST PROSPECTS/SERVICES

- High quality group package tours to the U.S.

- Family/leisure trips

For additional analytical, business and investment opportunities information,
please contact Global Investment & Business Center, USA
at (202) 546-2103. Fax: (202) 546-3275. E-mail: rusric@erols.com

OPPORTUNITIES

Following traditional travel patterns and because the U.S. is a country that offers a variety of activities, climates, and cultural experiences, the U.S. is by far the leading non-Asian destination for Koreas. KTO figures indicate that in 2007, a record 13 million Koreans traveled to other countries. Out of the top five destinations for Koreans, China ranked number one, followed by Japan and the U.S. Travelers to the U.S. account for 6.5 percent of the Korean outbound tourism market. Korean travel industry sources indicate that Los Angeles, San Francisco, Las Vegas, and Seattle are the most popular U.S. destinations, followed by the East Coast New York-Washington D.C corridor. United Airlines expanded its routes to include non-stop service between Seoul and San Francisco in March 2006; Korean Air inaugurated direct non-stop flights between Seoul and Las Vegas in September 2006; Delta Air Lines launched its direct link between Seoul and Atlanta in June 2007; and Korean Air has increased the frequency of service from Seoul to its Honolulu and Dallas markets.

Koreans usually travel to the U.S. on package group tours or individually to visit their friends, families, and relatives. The market for group tours has untapped demand for higher-class services that provide a variety of activities and cater to the more sophisticated tastes of seasoned Korean travelers. Koreans who travel to the U.S. are very much interested in visiting not only museums and amusement parks, but in looking for bargains at fashion outlets, playing golf, and visiting wineries.

RESOURCES

Major Show
Name: Korea World Travel Fair
http://www.kotfa.co.kr/eng/main/main.htm

KEY CONTACTS

Korea Tourism Organization
http://english.tour2korea.com/07T2KZone/aboutUs/top_tour2korea.asp?konum=1&kosm=m7_7
Ministry of Culture and Tourism (MCT)
http://www.mct.go.kr/english/index.jsp
Local Contact
Grace Sung
Commercial Specialist
Commercial Service Korea
U.S. Embassy in Korea
32 Sejong-ro Jongro-gu
Seoul 110-710 Korea
Tel: 82-2-397-4324
Fax: 82-2-739-1628
Email: **grace.sung@mail.doc.gov**
Website: **www.buyusa.gov/korea**

BROADCASTING SERVICES AND EQUIPMENT

ITA CODE: AUV

	2005	2006	2007 (E)

	253	238	245
Total Local Production	26	27	30
Total Exports	N/A	10	15
Total Imports	217	201	200

(Unit: USD million)

Driving the development of digital content are new and potentially exclusive channels, basic and premium tier channels, plus on-demand content from domestic and foreign program suppliers. The business of digital programming and content is made highly attractive by significant competition from cable, the rise in direct to home (DTH) services, the advent of Internet protocol television (IPTV), a projection that the digital TV universe will be almost all-pay by 2015, and major gains in consumer purchases of digital set-top-boxes (STBs). It is forecast that total subscription revenues for pay TV will grow from USD 131 million in 2004 to over USD 427 million by 2010 and will be USD 658 million by 2015.

Cable TV was launched in Korea with analog broadcasting service in 1995 featuring 24 channels (program providers) delivered by 54 cable system operators (SOs). Currently, 103 SOs are transmitting cable TV content. Digital terrestrial TV was introduced in 2001, and digital cable TV services launched in 2004. As a result, Korean cable TV SOs and program providers need to digitize most of their broadcasting facilities from 2003 to 2010. After the introduction of DTH services in 2000, the Korea Digital Satellite Broadcasting consortium (KDB) acquired the necessary license and launched pay TV services in March 2002 via its DTH satellite platform SkyLife. SkyLife acquired more than 1.96 million digital DTH subscribers in 2007, a 10.7 percent penetration rate of TV households in Korea.

Attracting portable TV viewers is becoming more competitive. Since December 2005, terrestrial providers have moved into digital multimedia broadcasting (DMB), which allows viewers to watch TV via a cell phone. The rapid growth of DMB has become a hot trend, drawing the attention of the media and consumers. According to the Ministry of Information and Communication (MIC), the number of satellite DMB subscribers reached over two million as of October 2007. These new satellite DMB services enable viewers to consume different types of video content, but they are discovering that content is severely lacking. Lack of available content has forced providers to show amateur videos – to fill time, a provider broadcast the finalists of a university student video contest. According to the Korea IT Industry Promotion Agency, the market demand for digital video content is relatively small, at approximately 5.5 billion Won, around USD 5.4 million, in 2005. However, the industry is forecast to grow to be worth several billion dollars by 2010 as new service platforms are implemented.

In 2005, market demand for TV broadcasting equipment and services reached an estimated USD 240 million. Although equipment is currently being procured primarily for terrestrial TV broadcasting, the market demand for digital equipment for cable and satellite TV services is forecast to be very strong over the next three to five years. There are no major market access barriers for broadcasting equipment, and most categories of equipment enter Korea with an eight percent duty based on cost-insurance-freight (c.i.f.) value.

Spending among the multi-station operators (MSO) has driven opportunities for suppliers of digital equipment for terrestrial broadcasting. In March 2004, the National Assembly revised the broadcasting law allowing for the establishment of digital services. The law also allows increased foreign investment in Korean SOs and program providers. This investment will speed up the deployment of digital cable TV, which in turn means increased opportunities for equipment suppliers and program providers.

OPPORTUNITIES

Korea maintains certain broadcasting quotas (e.g., cable companies are limited to using no more than 20 percent of their channels for foreign channel retransmissions, and local content must account for 35 percent of animation channel programming). While these are market barriers, there is a general dearth of local content, so foreign content is still in demand.

The surge of investment in new broadcasting services represents important opportunities for U.S. program providers (PPs). Korea currently has four terrestrial TV networks, 160 satellite TV channels, and approximately 70 cable TV channels. After the launch of digital satellite and digital cable TV services, the current total number of Korea's satellite and cable channels reached approximately 200. Also, the number of subscribers to the satellite and expanded cable TV services reached more than 80 percent of all households in Korea and will create great demand for foreign programming. Currently, U.S. programming accounts for approximately 70 percent of all imported programming. With the popularity of U.S. programming in Korea and the enormous projected increase in channels, U.S. PPs are well positioned to expand rapidly in Korea's growing market. As of December 2007, there were about 200 registered PPs in Korea. Among this number, approximately 70 PPs are responsible for the majority of activity in the market, providing programming both to satellite and cable TV channels. Although digital broadcasting equipment for terrestrial TV services is forecast to remain the largest market segment through 2010, Korea's launch of digital satellite and digital cable TV broadcasts will continue to bolster strong market demand over the next three years.

KDB, the platform operator for satellite TV in Korea, projects purchases of digital broadcasting system equipment to average USD 14.5 million annually over the next seven years. However, the investment plan is contingent upon increases in the numbers of subscribers. KT (Mega TV), Hanaro Telecom (Hana TV), and LG Dacom (My LG TV) launched and aggressively promote digital video services (or IPTV) over ADSL, VDSL, and fiber to the home (FTTH) networks. Also, non-network operator Daum plans to launch service soon, in cooperation with Microsoft. This may take longer to execute due to regulatory restrictions, but the threat of an integrated product bundle will clearly be a challenge to cable. As a result, SOs are increasingly focusing their efforts on deploying digital set-top-boxes in volume, bundled with both Internet and, in the future, VoIP services.

RESOURCES

Local Contact
(Ms.) Alex Choi
Commercial Specialist
Commercial Service Korea
U.S. Embassy
32 Sejong-ro Jongro-gu
Seoul 110-710 Korea
Tel: 82-2-397-4466
Fax: 82-2-739-1628
Email: alex.choi@mail.doc.gov
Website: www.buyusa.gov/korea

For additional analytical, business and investment opportunities information,
please contact Global Investment & Business Center, USA
at (202) 546-2103. Fax: (202) 546-3275. E-mail: rusric@erols.com

EDUCATION AND TRAINING SERVICES

ITA CODE: EDS

	2005	2006	2007 (E)
	107,525	104,018	114,420
Total Local Production	102,320	98,740	108,720
Total Exports	N/A	2	3
Total Imports	5,205	5,275	5,697

(Unit: USD million)

Korea's education market plays a significant role in the country's overall economy and offers exceptionally good opportunities for the U.S. education sector. According to the Organization for Economic Cooperation and Development (OECD), Korea is one of the largest investors in education among developed countries. Korea's education sector offers good opportunities for U.S. educational institutions because Koreans still prefer the U.S. to other nations competing for education dollars. The Korean market also looks promising for cooperative programs involving e-learning and educational training in the fields of language training, business administration, and technical programs.

Higher education throughout Korean history has been synonymous with privilege and power. A degree from a well-known institution is a status symbol and essential for finding the right job in the right company. Coveted spaces in Korea's top schools are open for competition from all students, but are attainable only by a few. Many talented students opt for the best schools overseas. The desire to obtain a diploma from an accredited overseas school translates into opportunities for U.S. schools to recruit some of Korea's most talented students, and Koreans remain willing to spend a substantial portion of their incomes on education.

The market for overseas education continues to grow and is being augmented by

e-learning as well as business training. According to the Student and Exchange Visitor Information System (SEVIS), U.S. Immigration and Customs Enforcement, as of October 2007, 107,834 students from Korea were studying in the U.S. Korea is the leading supplier of foreign students to the U.S., followed by India and China, for the third year in a row.

Rank	Place of Origin	2005	2006	October, 2007
1	Korea	81,616	93,728	107,834
2	India	67,761	76,708	95,525
3	China	54,562	60,850	75,744
4	Japan	49,422	45,820	45,207

The Korean Ministry of Education statistics indicate that as of April 2007, a total of 217,959 Korean students were studying abroad. The U.S. (27.1 percent), China (19.4 percent), U.K. (8.4 percent), Australia (7.6 percent), Japan (8.7 percent), Canada (5.9 percent), and other countries (2.9 percent) host most of these Korean students. Over the past few years, the U.S. share of the Korean study abroad market has remained fairly constant, although from 2001 it began to see a slight erosion as some Korean students considered other options to U.S. schools, primarily because of relatively higher costs to attend U.S. schools and perceived challenges to receiving a

U.S. F-1 student visa. Although U.S. schools and institutes remain very popular with Koreans, other countries such as Britain, China, Australia, Japan, and Canada are also vigorously promoting themselves as attractive destinations for Korean students.

OPPORTUNITIES

Market demand continues to grow for short-term (four weeks to two months) or long-term (one year) English language training in U.S. schools for college students during summer (typically from the middle of June until the end of August) and/or winter breaks (typically from the end of December until the end of February). Among Korean college students, English language training in the U.S. not only improves language skills but also provides a U.S. school and cultural experience. This experience leads many students to choose the U.S. for subsequent academic study.

Participation in education fairs held in Korea is one way to recruit. The fairs are categorized by level of schools (high schools, community colleges, four-year colleges and graduate programs). Almost all education fairs are held during the spring (March) and fall (September and October).

Utilizing educational consulting agents is the most efficient way to recruit Korean students. As Korea sends the largest number of students to the U.S., choosing the right partners in Korea is key for U.S. higher education institutions to enter the Korean market.

RESOURCES

KEY CONTACTS

Ministry of Education and Human Resources
http://english.moe.go.kr/
Fulbright (Korean-American Educational Commission)
http://www.fulbright.or.kr/en.php
KOSA (Korea Overseas Studying Agencies)
http://www.kosaworld.org/
Local Contact
(Ms.) Alex Choi
Commercial Specialist
Commercial Service Korea
U.S. Embassy
32 Sejong-ro Jongro-gu
Seoul 110-710 Korea
Tel: 82-2-397-4466
Fax: 82-2-739-1628
Email: **alex.choi@mail.doc.gov**

AUTOMOTIVE PARTS AND ACCESSORIES

ITA CODE: APS

	2,005	2,006	2007 (Estimate)
Total Market Size	36,667	41,741	45,999
Total Local Production	41,732	48,432	54,546

Total Exports	7,860	10,014	12,380
Total Imports	2,796	3,323	3,832

(Unit: USD million)

In 2007, Korea manufactured 4 million automotive vehicles, making it the fifth largest car manufacturer in the world after the Japan, the U.S., China, and Germany. The total size of the automotive parts market was estimated at USD 46 billion in 2007, a 8 percent increase from 2006. The OEM market segment accounted for about 94 percent of total market demand and the aftermarket represented about the remaining 6 percent.

Imports increased to USD 3.8 billion in 2007 from 3.4 billion in 2006 to account for 8 percent of the total market demand. Asian countries, including Japan, are the principal exporters to Korea, accounting for 46 percent of the total import. EU and North America follow Japan with a 38 percent and 14 percent market share, respectively. CS Korea forecasts that imports will continue to grow over the next two years to reach a value of USD 4.7 billion in 2009.

Major U.S. exports items for OEM market include gear boxes, wheels, steering parts, and engine parts, among others. For aftermarket, road wheels, spark plugs, ignition cables among others are well-received U.S. products.

In the era of global competition in the automotive industry, Korean OEMs are expected to expand global outsourcing practices for the procurement of parts and accessories. Industry sources predict that the launch of Hyundai Motors' manufacturing plant in Alabama, and the planned launch of KIA Motors' Georgia plant in 2009 will accelerate the trend. As import passenger cars gain more market share in Korea, the aftermarket for replacement parts is forecast to grow as well.

BEST PRODUCTS/SERVICES

For OEMs:
- **leading-edge engine designing, engine control units (ECU), electronic engine parts**
- **advanced core parts including automatic transmissions, anti-lock brake systems and air bags**
- **hybrid car and pollution-free car related technologies**
For aftermarket:
- **replacement parts**
- **spark plugs**
- **ignition cables**
- **timing belts**
- **wiper blades**
- **high-end car audio systems and components**
- **high-performance automotive chemicals, such as wax and rust-proofing solutions and accessories like window films.**

OPPORTUNITIES

U.S. suppliers need to be aware of the competition, and offer products with a technological advantage vis-à-vis the competition. Exporters must also educate end-users about the advanced features of their products. It is strongly recommended to partner with qualified and capable Korean distributors who maintain their existing sales network to serve end-users. Exhibiting at

For additional analytical, business and investment opportunities information,
please contact Global Investment & Business Center, USA
at (202) 546-2103. Fax: (202) 546-3275. E-mail: rusric@erols.com

local automotive trade shows can be a useful platform to explore the market and gain exposure to end-users.

Doing business with the Hyundai plant in the U.S. and U.S. parts suppliers with a manufacturing base in Korea is highly recommended to gain access to the Korean market. Most of the major auto parts suppliers including Delphi, Visteon, TRW, Johnson Automotive Controls, etc. have a manufacturing base in Korea.

To supply to aftermarket, U.S. exporters are recommended to explore opportunities to supply using existing OEM's after-sales service networks, automotive service franchises, independent auto service shops, etc.

KEY CONTACT

Ministry of Construction and Transportation
http://www.moct.go.kr/EngHome/

Local Contact
(Mr.) Young Wan Park
Commercial Specialist
Commercial Service Korea
U.S. Embassy
32 Sejong-ro Jongro-gu
Seoul 110-710 Korea
Tel: 82-2-397-4164
Fax: 82-2-739-1628
Email: **young.park@mail.doc.gov**
Website: **www.buyusa.gov/korea**

POLLUTION CONTROL EQUIPMENT

ITA CODE: POL

	2005	2006	2007 (estimate)
Total Market Size	5,394	6,253	7,142
Total Local Production	5,177	6,015	6,882
Total Exports	301	364	428
Total Imports	518	601	688

Korea, like most industrialized and urbanized states, is concerned about pollution and is strengthening regulations in order to improve the environment. The Government of Korea continues to initiate and introduce national environmental projects as well as strengthening the enforcement regime. Therefore, it is government policy and action that is the driving force in the pollution control market in Korea.

CS Korea estimates the size of pollution control equipment industry at USD 7 billion in 2007. According to industry experts, imports account for about 10 percent of the total market. Japan is the principal foreign supplier with about 47 percent market share, followed by the U.S. with 32 percent market share, Germany and France.

Local environmental equipment manufacturers in Korea have supplied a major portion of environmental projects with medium-level technology and medium-cost products. While they have significantly improved their technology prowess mostly through technology transfer and merger with non-Korean suppliers, they still lack the core technologies to supply the products that meet the government's stringent regulatory requirements, and are seeking more advanced import products and technologies.

OPPORTUNITIES

The Korean government plays a key role in the pollution control equipment industry, as the regulatory body and also as the biggest end-user. According to Bank of Korea statistics, the Korean government's expenditure for environmental protection was estimated at about USD 9.8 billion in 2007, near half of the total national expenditures of USD 21 billion. The general industry and pollution control service providers followed spending USD 6.5 billion, and USD 3.8 billion, respectively. For government projects, the tenders are announced on the Korean government procurement (PPS) website with detailed information on the project scope and contact information.

To enter the pollution control equipment market, U.S. suppliers are strongly recommended to partner with qualified and capable Korean companies who maintain their existing sales network to serve end-users, and are fully aware of regulatory changes that drive the market. Exhibiting at local environmental trade shows can be a good platform to explore market as well as gain exposure to end-users.

RESOURCES

LOCAL CONTACT

(Mr.) Young Wan Park
Commercial Specialist
Commercial Service Korea
U.S. Embassy
32 Sejong-ro Jongro-gu
Seoul 110-710 Korea
Tel: 82-2-397-4164
Fax: 82-2-739-1628
Email: **young.park@mail.doc.gov**
Website: **www.buyusa.gov/korea**

CNC MACHINE TOOLS

ITA CODE: MTL

	2005	2006	2007(estimated)
Total Market Size	4,180	3,800	4,200
Total Local Production	3,190	3,300	3,900
Total Exports	1,265	1,350	1,650
Total Imports	2,200	1,800	1,900

(Unit: USD million)

Korea's market for machine tools has shifted from standard, cost-effective or general products to high-precision, high-speed and high-powered machine tools. In 2007, computerized numerically controlled (CNC) cutting machine tools, including lathes, milling machines, and machining centers, represented 79 percent of total domestic machine tools demand while non-CNC and metal forming machines, including presses, represented the remaining 21 percent. The biggest demand for machine tools exists in the automotive production, metal processing, electronics and precision machine industries.

The Korean Machine Tools Manufacturers Association estimates that the import market increased 5 percent from 2006 - 2007. This is largely due to the increasing demand for parts in the automotive and shipbuilding industry. According to the Korean Customs Service, the United States is the second largest importer of machine tools to Korea, with a 37 percent market share. Japan maintains a 38 percent market share and Germany holds a distant 10 share of the market. Trends over the past three years have shown the import market to be highly volatile. For example, imports increased 20 percent in 2005 to USD 2 billion only to see a 10 decline in 2006 and a slight recovery to USD 1.9 billion in 2007.

The Korean CNC machine tools industry continues to be led by investment in production facilities by major manufacturing industries, such as automobiles, shipbuilding, telecommunications, construction equipment and electronics, including the semiconductor sector. In particular, many companies are investing in factory automation that will account for growing market demand in advanced machine tools. Given the volatility of the market and the ability of Korean competitors to produce quality machine tools, US importers are most successful where they offer a cost or technological edge.

OPPORTUNITIES

For exporters of U.S. products to Korea, establishing strategic alliances, such as joint ventures or licensing agreements, with leading Korean machine tool manufacturers is recommended. Hiring local agents or distributors also is one of the most effective ways to sell U.S. products in the Korean market. Large machine tool manufacturers have expressed interest in partnering with U.S. CNC machine tool manufacturers.

RESOURCES

Seoul International Tool & Related Equipment Exhibition
www.tool.or.kr

Korea Machinery Fair (KOMAF) 2007
www.komaf.org

Seoul International Machine Tool Show (SIMTOS) 2007
www.komma.org

Key Contacts
Industrial Machinery Division of the Ministry of Commerce, Industry & Energy: **www.mocie.go.kr**
Korea Machine Tool Manufacturers Association:
www.komma.org

Korea Tools Industry Cooperative:
www.tool.or.kr

Korea Association of Machinery Industry:
www.koami.or.kr

Korea Construction Equipment Manufacturers Association:
www.kocema.org

Korea Automobile Manufacturers Association:
www.kama.or.kr

Korea Automotive (Auto Parts) Industries Cooperative Association:
www.kaica.or.kr

Korea Aerospace Industries Association:
www.aerospace.or.kr

Korea Aerospace Research Institute:
www.kari.re.kr

Local Contact
Nathan Huh
Commercial Specialist
Commercial Service Korea
U.S. Embassy
32 Sejong-ro Jongro-gu
Seoul 110-710 Korea
Tel: 82-2-397-4130
Fax: 82-2-737-5357
E-mail: nathan.huh@mail.doc.gov
Website: www.buyusa.gov/korea

CONSTRUCTION

ITA CODE: ACE

	99,400	112,947	114,731
Total Local Production	103,279	129,568	154,135
Total Exports	4,076	16,730	39,800
Total Imports	197	109	397

(Unit: USD Million)

Continued and strong economic growth plus increased real estate development and continued work on large-scale infrastructure projects will bring strong market opportunities in real-estate development, project and construction management, supervision, supplying construction materials, architectural design, urban planning, and civil engineering consulting services.

Korea seeks to position the nation as a logistics and financial hub of Northeast Asia. As such construction and the building of large infrastructure to meet its requirements has led to a 2007 construction bill estimated at over USD 114 billion. With Korea's accession to the World Trade

Organization in 1997, the construction and civil engineering market was opened to international firms.

Korean demand for construction services is driven by demand in the following four diverse, yet closely linked construction sub-sectors: construction of residential apartment buildings, civil engineering services, construction work of commercial/ industrial facilities and government-initiated infrastructure. In 2007, Korea's spending on constructing residential buildings was estimated to be USD 55 billion and Korea's civil engineering projects was estimated to be USD 30 billion; government infrastructure projects was estimated to be USD 33 billion; while Korean investment in commercial/industrial facilities stood at USD 15 billion. Korea anticipates that spending will continue to increase due to increased residential redevelopment and government projects, which are estimated at USD 114 billion.

One significant government construction project is the government-backed Ubiquitous City development, which should add an additional USD 36 billion in projects by 2010. The Ubiquitous City development will also lead to additional technology to be incorporated as these new urban development projects will be linked with the latest information systems technology including wireless networking and RFID.

The total value of imported construction and civil engineering services was USD397 million in 2007. However, the Korean market will require higher financing capabilities and new design and engineering technologies for major urban developments. Generally these are not available in Korea and foreign real-estate developers, project management companies and engineering companies will have opportunities to fill these important gaps. Key engineering technologies will be in demand for tourism as well as ubiquitous infrastructure, information and telecommunications, urban planning, green building, water supply, sewage and waste treatment and disposal, earthquake-proof buildings, and industrial processing facilities.

As the Korean engineering services market evolves, the demand for technically advanced services continues to rise, creating additional demand for very creative and innovative services and technologies from the U.S, Europe, and Japan. U.S. engineering firms working in Korea are expected to expand their activities into the future as U.S. companies continue to hold a strong position in advanced engineering and soft technologies.

BEST PRODUCTS/SERVICES

New Songdo City development project --- Construction of the International Business Complex, the High-Tech Industry Park and the Biological Industry Complex.

U.S. Base Relocation Project --- U.S. Forces-Korea (USFK) relocation project is consolidated into the Land Partnership Plan (LPP) and the relocation of the Yongsan US Army Garrison. The USFK will surrender 36 bases and training facilities to the Korean government. DOD will consolidate numerous small garrisons and camps and have USFK operations move from the center of Seoul and the surrounding region to a new facility in Pyongtaek region. The prime management contract has been awarded to the U.S. engineering firm CH2M Hill and scope of work requirements and timelines are being developed.

Seoul Subway Line No. 9 Project Phase II --- Construction of a 12.5 kilometers subway in the southeast area of Seoul.

Ubiquitous City Infrastructures---There are currently 7 key Ubiquitous City development projects underway: Incheon Free Economic Zone, Busan U-City, Pankyo U-Healthcare Town, Jeju Telematics, Suwon Techno Valley, Osong U-Bio City, Changwon U-City and U-Jeonju .

KEY CONTACTS

Ministry of Construction & Transportation
www.moct.go.kr

Seoul Metropolitan City Government
www.seoul.go.kr

Incheon Metropolitan City Government
www.incheon.go.kr

Gyunggi Provincial Government
www.gg.go.kr

Construction Association of Korea
http://www.cak.or.kr/

Korea Engineering & Consulting Association
www.kenca.or.kr

Korea Institute of Construction Technology
www.kict.re.kr

Construction & Economy Research Institute of Korea
www.cerik.re.kr/

Local Contact
Nathan Huh
Commercial Specialist
Commercial Service Korea
U.S. Embassy
32 Sejong-ro Jongro-gu
Seoul 110-710 Korea
Tel: 82-2-397-4130
Fax: 82-2-739-1628
E-mail: nathan.huh@mail.doc.gov
Website: www.buyusa.gov/korea

**For additional analytical, business and investment opportunities information,
please contact Global Investment & Business Center, USA
at (202) 546-2103. Fax: (202) 546-3275. E-mail: rusric@erols.com**

PRACTICAL INFORMATION FOR CONDUCTING BUSINESS

MARKET OVERVIEW

Korea is the 13th largest economy in the world and is an outstanding trading partner for the United States. With its high-tech industry, a sophisticated consumer market, and a long history of successful trade with the United States, Korea is an excellent market for U.S. companies to enter or expand their Asian presence. The United States and Korea concluded negotiations for a Free Trade Agreement in 2007, which will remove 95% of all tariffs and establish a framework for a more transparent and robust commercial environment that would increase an already strong bilateral relationship by more than USD 20 billion.

In 2007, the U.S. exported USD 34.7 billion in goods and services, making Korea the seventh largest export market for the United States in the world. As a center for high technology, 36% of U.S. exports to Korea are categorized as "advanced technology products." Though our trade relationship is based on high technology, U.S.-Korean trade is also diversified and represents a broad range of consumer and agricultural products.

U.S.-Korean trade is also diversified with respect to trade from all points within the United States. Twenty-nine U.S. States record Korea as one of their top ten trading partners and nine states experienced export growth in 2007 of USD 100 million more over the previous year. Last year total U.S. exports grew by nearly USD 3 billion and significant growth is anticipated upon ratification of the Korea-U.S. Free Trade Agreement (KORUS FTA)—a trade agreement that Secretary of Commerce Carlos Gutierrez noted as the most significant trade agreement for the United States in 15 years.

MARKET CHALLENGES

The negotiation of the Korea-U.S. Free Trade Agreement and the eventual ratification of the largest trade agreement in fifteen years, will lead to a significant change in the market climate in Korea and the United States. The FTA will bring about stronger IPR protections, greater transparency in procurement and contracting processes, closer harmonization and acceptance of standards, and stronger trade facilitation.

Onerous and unique testing requirements for a full range of manufactured products, a less than transparent regulatory environment, and significant market pressures for price reductions and discounting continue to affect U.S. businesses. The Free Trade Agreement would significantly improve market conditions, and by some estimates, provide a stimulus to U.S. exports and the increase of sales by as much as 50%.

STARTING A BUSINESS

COMPANY REGISTRATION

Procedure	Time to complete:	Cost to complete:
1 Check the availability of trade name and	1 day	no charge

For additional analytical, business and investment opportunities information, please contact Global Investment & Business Center, USA at (202) 546-2103. Fax: (202) 546-3275. E-mail: rusric@erols.com

	obtain a certificate of name availability		
2	Make company seal	1 day	KRW 30,000
3	Obtain bank statement from a bank	1 day	KRW 2,000-5,000 depending on bank
4	File the application package for incorporation registered with the District Government Office and obtain a corporate registration tax bill.	1 day	KRW 24000
5	Registered with the Commercial Registry Office in the Seoul District Court and obtain certificate of seal impression of corporation.	1-2 days	1.2% capital registration tax + education tax (20% of the registration tax)+ KRW 10,000 (e-registration form) or KRW 20,000 (non-e-registration form) of Supreme Court stamps
6	Register with the District Tax office for a business certificate within 20 days of commencement of business and get a tax identification number under the Value Added Tax Act	5-10 days	no charge
7	Register electronically for Public Health Insurance Program, National Pension Fund, and Employment Insurance and Industrial Accident Compensation Insurance	1 day	no charge
8	Submit the rules of employmentto the local labor office of Labor Minister	1 day	no charge

REGISTRATION REQUIREMENTS DETAILS

Procedure 1.

Check the availability of trade name and obtain a certificate of name availability

Time to complete:

1 day

Cost to complete:

no charge

Name of Agency:

Comment:

No trade name that has been registered by another person shall be registered as a trade name by the same kind of business, in the same city, metropolitan area, or kun. The name search can be done through the Supreme Court Web site (www.iros.go.kr).

Procedure 2.

Make company seal

Time to complete:

1 day

Cost to complete:

KRW 30,000

Name of Agency:

Comment:

The promoters may use their personal seal and thus there is no need to make a new one

Procedure 3.

Obtain bank statement from a bank

Time to complete:

1 day

Cost to complete:

KRW 2,000-5,000 depending on bank

Name of Agency:
Comment:

> According to new government reforms, a bank certificate is not required, but a bank statement, as a simpler and less expensive method, is still necessary.

Procedure 4.

> File the application package for incorporation registered with the District Government Office and obtain a corporate registration tax bill.

Time to complete:

> 1 day

Cost to complete:

> KRW 24000

Name of Agency:
Comment:

Procedure 5.

> Registered with the Commercial Registry Office in the Seoul District Court and obtain certificate of seal impression of corporation.

Time to complete:

> 1-2 days

Cost to complete:

> 1.2% capital registration tax + education tax (20% of the registration tax)+ KRW 10,000 (e-registration form) or KRW 20,000 (non-e-registration form) of Supreme Court stamps

Name of Agency:
Comment:

> The company's incorporation is registered with the Commercial Registry Office in the Seoul District Court. Documents to be filed include the application form; the articles of incorporation; the application for shares; the record of examinations by directors, auditors, and inspectors, together with related documents; the minutes of inaugural general meetings and the minutes of board of director meetings on the appointment of directors; the inspector reports, confirming completion of in-kind investments; and documents confirming custody of paid-in capital.
>
> The corporate registration tax is 0.4% of capital unless the corporation is located in a major city, where the registration tax is higher. For example, in Seoul, the registration tax is 1.2% of capital, and the education tax is 20% of the registration tax. The amount of bond to be purchased is 0.1% of capital.

Procedure 6.

> Register with the District Tax office for a business certificate within 20 days of commencement of business and get a tax identification number under the Value Added Tax Act

Time to complete:

> 5-10 days

Cost to complete:

> no charge

Name of Agency:
Comment:

> To register for a business certificate, the company must complete registration forms for VAT and corporate income tax. The following documents must be submitted in person to the Tax Office: the certificate of incorporation; the articles of incorporation; the promoter's names, addresses, and share portions; a detailed list of property and assets; the office space lease agreement (if any); the company's registered seal of the company; the certificate of payment for shares on deposit in a bank; and list of directors.

For additional analytical, business and investment opportunities information, please contact Global Investment & Business Center, USA at (202) 546-2103. Fax: (202) 546-3275. E-mail: rusric@erols.com

Procedure 7.
Register electronically for Public Health Insurance Program, National Pension Fund, and Employment Insurance and Industrial Accident Compensation Insurance
Time to complete:
1 day
Cost to complete:
no charge
Name of Agency:
Comment:
Company founder fills out an electronic form, which gets forwarded to the respective agencies. The registration is obligatory for firms with 1 or more employees. A certificate of authenticity must be obtained, using the company's tax identification, to file via the Internet.
Procedure 8.
Submit the rules of employmentto the local labor office of Labor Minister
Time to complete:
1 day
Cost to complete:
no charge
Name of Agency:
Comment:
The rules are submitted along with proof of accident insurance. The procedure is required for companies hiring 10 or more employees.

PROPERTY REGISTRATION

Procedure	Time to complete:	Cost to complete:
1 Obtain their commercial registry extracts and the registry extract of the concerned land and building from the commercial registry	1 day	KW 4000
2 Obtain a copy of the Land Cadastre Certificate and the Building Management Certificate	1 day	KW 500 1st page + KW 100 each additional page for the Land Cadastre Certificate + KW 1000 for the Building Management Certificate
3 Obtain a statement of taxes from the tax department of the jurisdictional district office	1 day	no cost
4 Buyer buys and affixes a National Revenue stamp	1-2 days	Fee for real estate agent (between 0.2-0.8% of sale price) + National Revenue Stamp, according to the following schedule: Property value (in KW) NRS From 10 to 30 millions
5 Buyer pays taxes at a commercial bank and obtains receipt	1 day	2 % of sale price for the Acquisition tax (transfer tax) 2 % of sale price for the Registration tax 20% of registration tax (0.4% of sale price) for the Education tax 10% of Acquisition tax (0.2% of sale price) for the Agricultural and Fisheries Tax
6 The buyer buys Housing Bonds	1-3 days	5% of sale price (not included in calculation of total cost)
7 Buyer applies for the registration of the titles	3 days	KW 9,000 per real property (land + building) for court registry stamp

REGISTRATION REQUIREMENT DETAILS

Procedure 1.

Obtain their commercial registry extracts and the registry extract of the concerned land and building from the commercial registry

Time to complete:

1 day

Cost to complete:

KW 4000

Name of Agency:

Commercial Registry

Comment:

The buyer obtains a certificate of its registered corporate seal issued by the commercial registry office (KW 1000). The buyer obtains its commercial registry from the commercial registry office (KW 1000). The seller obtains its commercial registry extract from the commercial registry office (KW 1000). The seller also obtains the registry extract of the concerned land and building from the commercial registry office (KW 1000). There is more than one way (in person, via website, through an unattended machine) to obtain the certificates. Most people obtain the extract through an unattended machine placed in a governmental district office or from the website of the Supreme Court.

Procedure 2.

Obtain a copy of the Land Cadastre Certificate and the Building Management Certificate

Time to complete:

1 day

Cost to complete:

KW 500 1st page + KW 100 each additional page for the Land Cadastre Certificate
KW 1000 for the Building Management Certificate
(It is assumed that all certificates have 5 pages each)

Name of Agency:

Land Registry and Building Registry

Comment:

The seller obtains from the jurisdictional district office an official copy of the extract from the land registry, or the Land Cadastre Certificate and an official copy of the extract from the building registry or the Building Management Certificate. The actual sale price is currently used as the standard real property price. Both buyer and seller should obtain the jurisdictional district office's stamp of the original copy of the contract executed by both parties. Prices for certificates can be found on the website www.onnara.go.kr

Procedure 3.

Obtain a statement of taxes from the tax department of the jurisdictional district office

Time to complete:

1 day

Cost to complete:

no cost

Name of Agency:

Tax department of jurisdictional district office

Comment:

The parties need to obtain a statement of taxes due from the tax department of jurisdictional district office after calculating the taxes payable:
- Registration Tax: 2% of the sale price
- Education Tax: 20% of the registration tax
- Acquisition Tax: 2% of the purchase price
- Agricultural and Fisheries Tax: 10% of the acquisition tax

**For additional analytical, business and investment opportunities information,
please contact Global Investment & Business Center, USA
at (202) 546-2103. Fax: (202) 546-3275. E-mail: rusric@erols.com**

- Stamp Duties: KW 150,000 for KW 500 millions; KW 350,000 if above KW 1 billion

The Local Tax Law was amended effective January 5, 2005. According to the newly amended Local Tax Law, registration tax for sale and purchase of property between legal entities is 2% (1% for transfers between individuals)

Procedure 4.

Buyer buys and affixes a National Revenue stamp

Time to complete:

1-2 days

Cost to complete:

Fee for real estate agent (between 0.2-0.8% of sale price) + National Revenue Stamp, according to the following schedule:

Property value (in KW)
NRS

From

Name of Agency:

District government office

Comment:

The buyer buys and affixes a National Revenue stamp to obtain an approval for the sale agreement from the district government office.

The lawyer or real estate agent had previously prepared the sale agreement. The seller was responsible for gathering all the documents to be presented to the lawyer or real estate agent.

For small operations, the real estate agent will connect the parties and prepare the sale agreement. For more important operations such as the one analyzed here, both a lawyer and the real estate agent will be used. The real estate agent will help connect the parties and the lawyer will prepare the sale agreement.

Official rate of 0.2-0.8% of the sale price for the real estate agent. In most cases the real estate agent fee is more than the official rate.

Lawyer fees will be between KW 100,000 and KW 250,000 per hour of work. It is estimated that on average a lawyer will charge between 5 and 10 hours to prepare the sale agreement.

The documentation shall include:

For the preparation of the sale agreement, the following documentation is needed:
• The Certificate of Registration that is in the possession of the seller
• A copy of Property Register to show the owner and encumbrances (obtained in Step 1)
• Land Cadastre Certificate and Building Management Certificate (obtained in Step 2)
• Seller ID (a copy of Corporate Commercial Register)
• Official Chop/Seal of the seller company
• Property tax clearance

Procedure 5.

Buyer pays taxes at a commercial bank and obtains receipt

Time to complete:

1 day

Cost to complete:

2 % of sale price for the Acquisition tax (transfer tax)
2 % of sale price for the Registration tax
20% of registration tax (0.4% of sale price) for the Education tax
10% of Acquisition tax (0.2% of sale price) for the Agricultural and Fish

Name of Agency:

Commercial Bank

For additional analytical, business and investment opportunities information, please contact Global Investment & Business Center, USA at (202) 546-2103. Fax: (202) 546-3275. E-mail: rusric@erols.com

Comment:
>The buyer pays the Acquisition tax, Registration tax, Education tax, and the Agricultural and Fisheries Tax at a commercial bank, and the bank issues to the buyer a confirmation of tax receipt and notice.

Procedure 6.
>The buyer buys Housing Bonds

Time to complete:
>1-3 days

Cost to complete:
>5% of sale price (not included in calculation of total cost)

Name of Agency:

Comment:
>The buyer buys Housing Bonds and determines to sell them at a discounted price. Housing Bonds are bonds issued by the National Government to support a national program to supply housing to the poor. It is mandatory to buy these bonds in an amount equal to 5% of the actual sale price. These bonds are then usually sold in the secondary market with a discount of about 10%, but depend on market conditions.

>(Procedure 6 is not included in the calculation of total cost.)

Procedure 7.
>Buyer applies for the registration of the titles

Time to complete:
>3 days

Cost to complete:
>KW 9,000 per real property (land + building) for court registry stamp

Name of Agency:
>Court Registry

Comment:
>The buyer prepares an application form and applies for the registration of the title to a competent court registry under the buyer's name. Parties must purchase the required revenue stamp and attach it to the title transfer registration application. Land and building are registered separately.

>The documentation shall include:
>• Certificate of buyer's registered corporate seal (obtained in Procedure 1)
>• Buyer and seller's commercial registry extracts (obtained in Procedure 1)
>• Seller's registry extract of the concerned land and building (obtained in Procedure 1)
>• Land Cadastre Certificate (obtained in Procedure 2)
>• Building Management Certificate (obtained in Procedure 2)
>• Sale agreement with the National Revenue Stamp affixed (obtained in Procedure 4)
>• Tax payments' receipts (paid in Procedure 5)
>• Receipt of purchase of Housing Bonds (bought in Procedure 6)

MARKETING PRODUCTS AND SERVICES

DISTRIBUTION AND SALES CHANNELS

Local representation is essential for the success of foreign firms in the Korean market. This is especially true in considering the fact that in Korea, business relationships are built upon personal ties and social introductions, and that much of the major third-country competition is only a few flight-hours away. In addition, for sectors that involve any type of government procurement, an entity must be registered with the Korean government in order to bid on the procurement projects.

Hence, many American firms enter into a consortium with a Korean company or enter into a representative agreement, especially for the purposes of market entry. Finally, the language barrier and established social/ business circles make it extremely difficult to enter the Korean market without a qualified Korean representative.

Distribution methods and the number and functions of intermediaries vary widely by product area and local conditions. The market for most consumer products is concentrated in major cities. Retail distribution is accomplished through a highly complex network, the majority of which are small family-run stores, stalls in markets, and street vendors, though this traditional distribution method is changing rapidly toward large-sized discount stores. There are many large retail stores in the major cities, especially Seoul, Il-san, Taejon and Busan, and their outer-lying suburbs. This distribution channel is one of the best ways to market foreign products to Korean consumers. Recently, retailing concepts such as Full-Line Discount Stores (FDS) including Price Costco (USA), Wal-Mart (USA), Carrefour (France), and E-mart (Korea) have gained tremendous popularity in Korea. Rapid expansion of these discount chain stores are planned nation-wide, with suburban satellite cities attracting the greatest number of stores.

In November 1995, regulations from the Korean Ministry of Finance and Economy (MFE) took effect, which allowed the legal entry of parallel imports. Prior to this legislation, distribution was disciplined with exclusive distributor/agents agreements where besides an authorized and registered distributor/agent, no other importer could legally clear goods through Korean customs. Often times, importers that were not the exclusive distributor/agent found their shipments held up at customs.

The effect of parallel imports is to marginally reduce the value of an exclusive distribution agreement. Many American companies continue to give exclusives, since they have in place territorial limits in neighboring countries that enhance the value of the exclusive in any one country. Likewise, any parallel importer in Korea is not getting the support of the OEM, cannot provide after sales service, etc. in the same manner, probably doesn't deal in the same volume, cannot be guaranteed a steady source of supply, and if the trademark is registered, should not be able to display it in a store (though this still occurs). As noted above, the legitimate exclusive distributor still has considerable advantages in Korea.

INFORMATION ON TYPICAL PRODUCT PRICING STRUCTURES

The rate of commission for using an agent or distributor varies depending on the type of product and the amount of transaction. On average, Korean agents require 10% commission, particularly when a transaction is conducted on a spot basis, but this varies for different products. Generally, 7% commission applies to product categories such as general machinery including packaging, construction, and material handling equipment. Meanwhile more sophisticated products such as medical/laboratory/scientific analytical instruments usually require a commission of 15-18% or more, since these are products in which after-sales service is very important.

On August 1, 2000, the Ministry of Commerce, Industry, and Energy passed consumer-protection legislation requiring consumer items, in general, to be labeled with both the manufacturer's sales price to the retailer and the marked-up retailer's price to the consumer. The mark-up from manufacturer to consumer ranges from as low as 50% to up to 150%.

USE OF AGENTS/DISTRIBUTORS; FINDING A PARTNER

The most common means of representation include: 1) appointing a registered commissioned agent (or more commonly known by Koreans as an "offer agent") on an exclusive or non-exclusive basis, 2) naming a registered trading company as an agent, or 3) establishing a branch sales office managed by home office personnel with Korean staff.

Any traders registered with the Korea International Trade Association (KITA) can import goods in their own names. Appointing a registered trading company (rather than an "offer agent") as an agent has the advantage of these agents being able to handle all of the importing paperwork and import for their own account. Registered trading companies tend to be larger firms and hence split their business between exports and imports. However, these larger firms may be less attentive to building the U.S. supplier's business, placing a higher emphasis on diversifying their portfolio of products from different countries. Similarly, while the larger general trading companies may be influential and well known in the market, they also may not devote as much attention to a single product as smaller firms do.

To find a local representative, a good place to begin is with a fee-based service called the International Partner Search (IPS) through U.S. Export Assistance Centers (USEAC) located throughout the U.S. and the U.S. Commercial Service Korea (CS Korea). For a modest fee, industry specialists of CS Korea's local staff tap into their well-established network of industry contacts and trade associations. The client will soon receive an annotated list of three to five potential, qualified representatives. The next step would be to plan a visit to Korea, perhaps calling upon CS Korea to arrange market briefings, a meeting schedule, and an interpreter/secretary under another fee-based service, Korea Gold Key (KGK).

Another good source of contacts is the Association of Foreign Trading Agents of Korea (AFTAK), a well-established, private trade association founded under government auspices uniquely dedicated to increasing imports into Korea. To fulfill its original mission of promoting balanced trade, AFTAK helps to execute Korea's import diversification plan, leads annual purchasing missions to the United States, Latin America, and Europe, and holds monthly meetings between member agents and the foreign commercial services of various embassies in Korea.

In the past Korean law stipulated that a sales agent must be a member of AFTAK to be able to issue and make price quotations, or pro forma invoices in their own names. However, since the beginning of January 2000, this mandatory registration requirement is now voluntary. Quotations, locally used as 'offers,' issued directly by foreign suppliers are no longer subject to case-by-case approval by AFTAK. A commissioned agent/distributor does not have to be registered with AFTAK. American businesses can contact AFTAK by sending their catalog with a letter specifying the items for which they are seeking an agent or visit the AFTAK office directly. Catalogs are displayed in the AFTAK library and inquiries are published free of charge in the association's web site or monthly AFTAK Magazine (AFTAK contact information is listed at the end of this section). The U.S. Commercial Service of the U.S. Embassy also works closely with AFTAK to advertise requests for agents received from American companies.

Usually an agency contract specifies the terms applicable to terminating an agent's contract. When there are no specific provisions in a contract on agent termination, the Korean Commercial Arbitration Code can specify the provisions for terminating an agent contract. This compensation clause allows the agent to claim compensation from the principal. The amount of compensation is usually determined as the total year average of one year's sales commission (i.e. total sales commission over the years divided by the number of years). As a mutually signed contract between supplier and agent/distributor overrules the default Korean provisions of claims for a commercial agent, U.S. companies are advised to specifically include provisions on agent termination.

The U.S. Commercial Service in Korea recommends that U.S. companies seek legal counsel prior to signing a contract in Korea. The legal advice that law firms with international experience can provide can prove to be very important. Most experts advise engaging a local attorney before making major business decisions in dealing with Korean companies.

U.S. companies should also seek legal counsel with regards to protecting their intellectual property. Trademark and patent (if applicable) registration with the Korea Industrial Property Office (KIPO) is the minimum safeguard for your intellectual property rights to be protected in Korea. U.S. companies are advised to seek the services of a local attorney to directly register their trademarks and/or patents in their own names, not the Korean agent's name. In order to have control over these important intellectual property rights, registration must be done in the U.S. company's name. Korean law requires that only local attorneys be allowed to make applications to KIPO. A list of major attorney firms in Korea is listed at the end of this chapter in the section entitled "Need for a Local Attorney."

USEFUL CONTACTS REGARDING AGENTS/DISTRIBUTORS

(Note: Telephone dialing information when calling from outside of Korea:
82 is the country code for Korea, followed by 2, which is the city code for Seoul)

Association of Foreign Trading Agents of Korea
AFTAK Bldg., 218 Hankangro 2-ka
Yongsan-ku, Seoul 140-012, Korea
TEL: 82-2-792-1581/4
FAX: 82-2-785-4373
Website: www.aftak.or.kr

The Korean Commercial Arbitration Board (KCAB)
43rd Floor, Trade Tower 159 Samsung-dong,
Kangnam-ku, Seoul 135-729 Korea
Trade Center P.O.Box 50,
TEL: 82-2-551-2000/19
FAX: 82-2-551-2020
Website: www.kcab.or.kr

Branch Office, Pusan Korea (KCAB)
Rm. 805, Daehan Tongun bldg., 1211-1,
Choryang-dong, Dong-ku,
Pusan 601-714 Korea
TEL: 82-51- 441-7036/8
FAX: 82-51-441-7039
Website: www.kcab.or.kr

Korea International Trade Association (KITA)
Trade Inquiry Office, 6th floor, Trade Tower, KWTC
159-1, Samsung-dong, Kangnam-gu, Seoul, Korea
Tel: 82-2-6000-5267
Fax: 82-2-6000-5161
Website: www.kita.or.kr

FRANCHISING

Potential Korean franchisees often favor doing business with American franchisers since the American companies can successfully market their established brand names to the Korean consumer as well as bring in an American-style of systematic management. Conversely, U.S. firms consider financing and marketing acumen to be the two most important qualities to look for when selecting their Korean master franchisee. A Korean master franchisee can be either a large

For additional analytical, business and investment opportunities information,
please contact Global Investment & Business Center, USA
at (202) 546-2103. Fax: (202) 546-3275. E-mail: rusric@erols.com

corporation or a small-sized enterprise. A large corporation may be strong in financial support but can be less aggressive in marketing since the corporation runs the franchise as one of its operation units. A small-sized enterprise, on the other hand, can be more aggressive in marketing, but may not present well-organized management skills or adequate financial resources.

In Korea, the franchise industry is divided into three main areas: food service, retail, and the service sectors;

Food Service: Franchising in Korea developed primarily in the restaurant market, an area that requires large investment to cover start-up and market development costs. Korean business partners seek U.S. franchisers who can offer marketing expertise and brand name recognition.

Retail: Franchise operations currently account for approximately 8% of the Korean retail industry. Korea's continued economic growth has helped spur a domestic retail industry that grew by 7%, to US $90 billion, in 2000. Korea's retail franchise market is expected to further expand over the next few years as a result of the Korean government's targeted financial support for small and medium-sized businesses and venture capital businesses.

Service: Korea offers a potentially good market for this business segment, and U.S.- based service franchise operations in Korea have attracted favorable attention from Korean investors who are looking for new investment opportunities, especially small office/home office (SOHO) businesses. For example, San Diego-based Mail Boxes Etc. (MBE) opened its first MBE center in downtown Seoul in June, 1999 and MBE plans to open more than 300 locations altogether in Korea by the end of 2003.

As new-to-market U.S. franchisors consider the Korean market they should be cognizant of the Korean business culture and remain flexible regarding franchising fees and marketing standards. For example, in order to justify Korean franchisees' earning claims on their business franchise, U.S. business partners are often asked to wave the royalty fees for the first several months. To expedite transactions, U.S. franchisors should seek the counsel of private franchise consultants or CS Korea prior to making a decision.

Currently there are five qualified franchise consulting firms in Korea. The following is contact information for those firms:

Franchise Information Co., Ltd.
Room 301, Hyundaiparkville 108, Guro 5-dong
Guro-gu, Seoul
Phone: 82-2-855-6006; Fax: 82-2-855-6788
E-mail: kfcpark@chollian.net
Web: www.franchise.co.kr

Franchise Plaza
Room 402, Seochang Bldg., 941-22,
Bangbae 1-dong, Seocho-ku, Seoul
Phone: 82-2-523-4307; Fax: 82-2-523-5069
E-mail: ibnet@franchiseplaza.co.kr
Web: www.franchiseplaza.co.kr

Frannet Korea Corp.
2nd Floor, Yonghyun Bldg., 50-1
Yongkang-dong, Mapo-ku, Seoul

Phone: 82-2-701-6373; Fax: 82-2-701-6376
E-mail: frannetkorea@netsgo.com
Web: www.frannetkorea.com

Jason FMP Consulting Co.
Hyundai 210-503, 288 Hagye, Nowon-ku, Seoul
Phone: 82-2-949-2453; Fax: 82-2-6223-2454
E-mail: jasonfmp@korea.com
Web: www.jasonfmp.com
www.restaurantdoctor.co.kr

Korea Business Information Development Institute
5th Floor, Kumsan Bldg., 17-1, Yoido-dong
Youngdungpo-ku, Seoul
Phone: 82-2-761-3511; Fax: 82-2-761-3510
E-mail: hslee@businessun.com
Web: www.businessun.com

DIRECT SELLING AND MARKETING

DIRECT SELLING

Door-to-Door Sales:

There are 11,025 door-to-door sales firms in Korea as of February 1, 2001. The major door-to-door sales items include home education materials, books, household consumer goods, cosmetics, health foods, sporting goods, and service products such as insurance and travel counseling. According to the Korea Direct Selling Association (KDSA), the Korean door-to-door sales market for 2000 totaled $1.17 billion.

Multi-level Marketing

Korea's multi-level sales for 2000 totaled $1.67 billion. As of December 31, 2000, the multi-level marketing (MLM) industry employed about 2 million active distributors. Over the years, the Korean government has derided MLM as an "undesirable or inappropriate business form" for Korea, claiming that it neglects consumer safety, profits "excessively," and threatens the Korean social fabric through its "pyramid schemes." However, MLM's negative image in Korea appears to be changing due to the combined efforts of U.S. firms, Commercial Service Korea, and KDSA. KDSA is a member of the World Federation of Direct Selling Associations in Washington, D.C.

In keeping with its deregulation plan, the Korean Ministry of Commerce, Industry and Energy (MOCIE) reduced the restrictions on MLM companies by amending its Door-to-Door Sales Act (DDSA), which the Korean National Assembly passed on January 5, 1999. The new legislation eliminated existing market barriers in the MLM industry such as the obligation to disclose retail prices on the MLM product label. In addition, on May 25, 1999, the authority to enforce this new legislation was transferred from MOCIE to the Fair Trade Commission (FTC) by the newly revised Government Reorganization Law.

Despite these recent changes, the current Door-to-Door Sales Act still contains some restrictive provisions, which the MLM industry is working on modifying in order to further open the Korean market. For example, the Act includes price ceilings on any product priced below 1 million won (about $830) and a ceiling on sponsoring bonuses equal to 35% of the selling price. On behalf of its U.S. and Korean colleagues, the KDSA recently proposed that these restrictions be deleted from the Act. New DDSA legislation is expected to clear the Korean National Assembly this year and the MLM industry is closely monitoring the situation to see if its requested revisions are included.

As a result of these market liberalization measures, multi-level marketing activities by U.S. firms in the cosmetic, cleaning product, and kitchenware sectors have been expanding. In order to garner further successes, however, U.S. multi-level sales firms should promote their products and services appropriately and efficiently by carefully analyzing Korean market trends. Prior knowledge of the market conditions can help prevent unnecessary conflicts with government officials, consumer 'watchdog' groups, or industry groups.

DIRECT MARKETING

By December 31, 2000, there were 6,232 direct marketing firms in Korea. Gross revenues for the Korean direct marketing industry in 2000, including catalog sales and TV and Internet shopping, are as follows:

Catalog Sales	$ 673 million
TV Shopping	1,122 million
Internet Shopping	383 million
Total	$2,178 million

JOINT VENTURES/LICENSING

Since the late 1997 economic crisis, the Korean government has made a dramatic and high-profile effort to attract foreign investment for the purposes of restructuring the Korean economy and bringing in much needed foreign capital. In its efforts to counter the economic downturn, the government has not only publicly encouraged foreign investment, but it has also implemented liberalization policy measures, including an increase in foreign equity ownership, in order to accommodate its goals. Though a group of high-level officials- headed by President Kim and the Prime Minister's Office- have spearheaded efforts to de-regulate and liberalize the economy, some foreign companies have responded negatively to the initiatives, with claims that the policies block restrictive regulations that would eliminate trade and investment barriers at the working level.

Nevertheless, many foreign companies that already have operations in Korea chose this opportunity to increase their involvement in Korea, such as Coca-Cola and Pfizer. Meanwhile, other U.S. investors continue to be cautious because of continued concerns over corporate transparency and indebtedness. Opportunities exist for such prudent investors though it may be some time before many investors have regained former levels of confidence.

Foreign investment approval is controlled by the Ministry of Finance and Economy (MFE) and governed by the Foreign Capital Inducement Act (FCIA), which was replaced by the Foreign Investment Promotion Act (FIPA) in 1998. The FIPA is anticipated to enhance investor rights and incentives as well as remove bureaucratic obstacles to investment.

Selecting the appropriate partner is one of the most difficult and crucial aspects of initiating a joint

For additional analytical, business and investment opportunities information,
please contact Global Investment & Business Center, USA
at (202) 546-2103. Fax: (202) 546-3275. E-mail: rusric@erols.com

venture in Korea. On the one hand, the large Korean conglomerate "chaebols" still exercise considerable influence in Korea, permeating throughout the country's government and financial institutions. On the other hand, the Korean government's attempts at a policy shift toward the support of small- and medium-sized businesses mean that the participation of a "chaebol" in a joint venture could create additional obstacles in terms of obtaining necessary approvals and local financing. This is further compounded because of the recent government policy shift towards anti-monopoly behavior. In addition, "chaebols" tend to insist on operating a joint venture in accordance with the overall policies and business culture of the group, sometimes to the detriment of the foreign shareholder's interest. Though an injection of foreign capital may be deemed necessary for the survival of a company, there is a tendency inherent in Korean business culture to maintain local control, regardless of the percentage invested by foreign entities. A U.S. company may therefore consider assigning its headquarters staff to Korea in order to closely monitor and influence the activities of a newly established joint venture company.

Management control must be evaluated on three levels: 1) shareholder equity; 2) representation on the board of directors; and 3) active management (Representative Director and subordinate management). Legally, Korean board meetings require the physical presence of all members as well as a quorum of the directors. Therefore, if a foreign investor intends to exercise day-to-day management, he/she must appoint a Representative Director who resides in Korea. Moreover, the Representative Director will need the support of and access to key functional areas of the company in order to manage in accordance with the foreign investor's wishes. Therefore, the internal organization of a joint venture company as well as key management appointments should be worked out and agreed upon by all involved parties as early as possible.

The compatibility of goals between the Korean and foreign partners is also crucial to the joint venture's success. Problems may arise due to conflicting goals. For example, the foreign investor's primary goal may be to send profit dividends offshore while his/her Korean counterpart may be most concerned with corporate growth in Korea, particularly through exporting to overseas markets.

To most Koreans, a contract represents the current understanding of a "deal" and is the beginning of rather than an end to negotiations with a Korean partner. If changing circumstances result in omissions or points that no longer accurately reflect the original agreement, then problems will arise. The same is true if the contracting parties change. This type of experiences in Korea has led many foreigners to believe that Koreans place less importance on a written contract than Westerners. Though Americans may regard a written contract as legally binding, Koreans may regard the same contract as a "gentlemen's agreement" that is subject to further negotiations should conditions change. Therefore, contract negotiations with Koreans should be viewed as a process of extensive dialogue and as having the following objectives: 1) reaching a common understanding of the deal that includes each party's responsibilities; 2) recording that detailed understanding; and 3) being prepared to modify the terms of the agreement should there be a change in circumstances.

Certain terms of the commercial relationship between the joint venture partners, such as technology transfer, raw material supply, marketing and distribution, should be agreed upon in detail in the joint venture agreement. Though circumstances are slowly changing, Korean companies have not invested a great portion of their operating funds towards research and development. For this reason, there is a large Korean demand for technology transfer licensing agreements from foreign countries, particularly the United States, whose companies have a comparative advantage in the high technology area.

American companies should proceed with caution when they enter into a transfer technology licensing agreement. A company's intellectual property is not necessarily protected and may be

For additional analytical, business and investment opportunities information,
please contact Global Investment & Business Center, USA
at (202) 546-2103. Fax: (202) 546-3275. E-mail: rusric@erols.com

particularly vulnerable in the later stages of a business relationship when the survival of a Korean company is dependent on the technology. Though U.S. companies oftentimes register their patented technology with the Korean Industrial Property Office (KIPO) before entering into a licensing agreement, the most successful American companies intentionally withhold a small but key component of the manufacturing process or component from their Korean partner. This preventative strategy allows the U.S. company to control the use of the licensed technology as well as maintain the integrity of the licensing agreement.

If a contract is violated in Korea, the country's legal procedures can be lengthy, cumbersome and expensive. Hence, if at all possible, the best strategy to employ is to prevent all possible conflicts. The identification of a viable and trustworthy business partner from the outset is essential; therefore, foreign investors should exercise due diligence when selecting a business partner.

One precautionary approach is to consult with attorneys throughout negotiations of a contract. (Please refer to a list of attorneys in Korea at the end of this chapter.) In addition to consulting with an attorney, foreign investors should also consult with the Korean Commercial Arbitration Board (KCAB). The KCAB is staffed with counselors who advise U.S. companies on contract guidelines. At the company's request, an assigned KCAB counselor can review the contract and stress the importance of an arbitration clause in the contract. The KCAB contact information is as follows:

Mr. Lee, Joo-Won, Manager
Public Information Section
The Korean Commercial Arbitration Board
43rd Floor, Trade Tower (Korea World Trade Center)
159 Samsung-dong, Kangnam-ku
Seoul 135-729, Korea
Tel. 82-2-551-2073
Fax. 82-2-551-2020

ESTABLISHING AN OFFICE

The following section provides some basic step-by-step guidelines on how to set up an office in Korea. In addition, a list of real estate and real estate consultancy, taxation and human resource search services in Korea is provided in this section.

Step 1: Assess Your Company's Ability to Conduct Business in Korea

Depending on your company's particular industry sector, each investment will be different in terms of its size and complexity. Investment is also dependent on any relevant Korean laws and regulations. Because the Ministry of Finance and Economy (MOFE) continually revises its negative list, the best way to verify that you may establish your business in Korea is to contact the "Investing in Korea Service Center."

The Korea Investment Service Center (KISC), formerly the Investing in Korea Service Center (and before that, the Comprehensive Center for Foreign Investment), provides general counseling for potential investors who wish to establish an office in Korea. The Center not only studies the feasibility of such an endeavor but also provides general assistance both prior to and during the set up of the office once it is approved. Under the auspices of the Ministry of Commerce, Industry and Energy, the Center provides both assistance and advice to foreign investors, including information and consultations regarding trade and investment regulations, taxation, financing, customs clearance, plant/office site location, and the resolution of any problems related to foreign investment.

For additional analytical, business and investment opportunities information,
please contact Global Investment & Business Center, USA
at (202) 546-2103. Fax: (202) 546-3275. E-mail: rusric@erols.com

The Center is located in an active business area of southern Seoul. The contact information for the KISC is as follows:

Kim, Doo-Hwan, Director
Korea Investment Service Center (KISC)
6th Fl., #300-9, Yumgok-dong, Seocho-ku
Seoul 137-170, Korea
Tel: 82-2-3460-7500
Fax: 82-2-3460-7940
E-Mail: dhkim@kotra.or.kr
Website: www.kisc.org

Step 2: Receive Authorization to Proceed with an Investment

Once you are approved to conduct business in Korea, the next step is to complete and submit the necessary notification documents. Approved foreign investment projects are subject to notification from the Ministry of Commerce, Industry, & Energy (MOCIE), which delegates its authority to the head office of a major commercial bank in Korea. (A list of major banks in Korea can be found at the end of Chapter VIII - Trade and Project Financing.)

The head office of any major commercial bank has the ability to accept notification from companies proposing to engage in business in a liberalized sector. In practice, a commercial bank's head office will also generally accept notification of partially liberalized sectors provided that the foreign investment meets the criteria for the specific business. However, the bank will reject those notifications in sectors that prohibit foreign entry.

Your company's designated representative should visit a commercial bank's head office and consult with staffers who deal with foreign clients and foreign investment. The bank provides application documents that are to be completed then re-submitted to the bank for authorization. Once all the documents have been submitted, along with Korean translations, the authorization process should be completed within three hours.

Step 3: Search for an Office Site

Companies are required to submit notification documents to the head office of a Korean commercial bank for approval prior to setting up an office. However, as finding and negotiating an office site may take more time than completing the necessary documents, companies should consider completing steps 2 and 3 simultaneously. To a company unfamiliar with Korean real estate, it is vital that the company locate a reputable real estate agent or real estate consulting firm with experience in foreign investment in order to locate a suitable office site. A list of select real estate agents and real estate consulting firms can be found at the end of this section.

Due to the scarcity of and high demand for land, property in Seoul is expensive even by U.S. and Asian standards and has remained so despite the economic downturn. The rental rates for office space in Seoul, by comparison, are not as high as other East Asian capitals such as Tokyo or Hong Kong. A recent spot survey indicated that the range of monthly rents in popular Seoul commercial buildings is from $50 to $85 per pyong (equal to 3.3 square meters). These rates are inclusive of maintenance fees and are based on gross floor area, which include common areas. Compared to a 1996 spot survey, the rates in 2000 decreased by 30%. However, from 1999 to 2000, the rates increased by roughly 7%.

In addition to the monthly rent, another major expense is the substantial deposit payment (or "key money"), which is a one-time charge that is refundable upon termination of the lease. Nearly all Korean landlords require key money, which ranges from $3,000 to $6,000 per pyong. However, due to the present economic situation in Korea, the rental fee may be negotiable. There are various combinations of monthly rental fees and key money deposits, and the price per pyong varies based on the negotiated terms. Office parking, another scarce commodity in Seoul, is usually available with monthly charges.

Most foreign companies in Seoul are located in the following four well-known districts: 1) City Hall -- the historic downtown area where the U.S. Embassy and a few Korean ministries are located; 2) Yoido -- or "Manhattan Island," which is adjacent to the Han River, where many financial firms and the National Assembly can be found; 3) Kangnam -- the expansive, bustling, new city center south of the river where one can find the World Trade Center complex and the American Chamber of Commerce in Korea; and 4) Mapo District -- which is halfway between Yoido and City Hall. While heavy urban traffic is an ongoing source of frustration and delay, Seoul has an excellent public transportation grid that allows foreign investors to consider various locales for their Korean offices.

In the past, the Korean government limited the foreign acquisition of Korean land under the Enforcement Decree of the Alien Land Acquisition and Management Law. Under the former law, foreign investors were required to obtain permission from the government in order to acquire land. However, according to the revised Foreign Land Acquisition Law that is presently in effect, the Korean government allows foreigners to purchase land regardless of the size and purpose. Local zoning laws- which restrict certain types of activity- should also be taken into consideration by the investor before making the final purchase.

Step 4: Register with the Nearest Tax Office

After locating the site for the branch office and providing notification to the Bank, the investor must register with the nearest tax office within the jurisdiction of the site area for tax reporting purposes. Local Korean tax authorities, in addition to performing tax audits, provide new tax information and counseling at the request of the company. However, the complexity of Korean tax laws and the language barrier make it difficult for foreign companies to file taxes with Korean authorities. Therefore, foreign companies should consider hiring a local accountant firm to file taxes. A list of local accountants is provided at the end of the section entitled "Steps to Establishing an Office."

Step 5: Seek Qualified Employees

One of the final steps in setting up an office in Korea is to locate and hire qualified employees, whether local or foreign, to staff your office. Oftentimes, a U.S. company's headquarters designates one or two Americans to head the company's Korean office, while the remainder of the staff in the office are usually local nationals or Koreans educated in the U.S. Some major factors that attract local Koreans to work at the Korean branch office are a high salary, prestige in position, opportunities for travel, the ability to both use and learn English, and finally, the possibility of transferring to the company's home office or other foreign branch office.

Korea has a large pool of conscientious, highly educated, enthusiastic, and underutilized women workers who are usually unable to find equivalent employment in Korean companies due to traditional cultural attitudes toward women in the work force and the prevalence of the "old boy network" in Korea's corporate culture. Due to the rarity and infrequency of opportunities for professional advancement in many Korean companies, frustrated Korean women- particularly professionally qualified Korean women- often welcome employment offers from foreign firms.

Korean employees' complete dedication and loyalty to the company is slowly decreasing. Company loyalty still exists, but it, along with high productivity, should not be taken for granted. It is essential that the employer first earn the respect of his/her Korean employees. Many foreign managers have successfully used recognition and increased pay to reward increased productivity.

Whether seeking to hire local or foreign staff or obtaining consultation and information on the local labor laws, a foreign investor should consult an employment agency in Korea. A list of employment agencies is shown below.

MAJOR REAL ESTATE AND REAL ESTATE CONSULTANCY FIRMS IN KOREA

(Note: Telephone dialing information when calling from outside of Korea: 82 is the country code for Korea, followed by 2, which is the city code for Seoul)

Century 21 Korea Co., Ltd.
3/F., Daewon Bldg.,
946-18, Daechi-dong, Kangnam-ku, Seoul 135-280
Phone: 82-2-561-0021; Fax: 82-2-561-0361
www.century 21korea.co.kr
Contact: Mr. O.J. Kwon, CEO & Regional Director
(Specialized in commercial & residential real estate)

ERA Korea Co., Ltd.
8/F, Hojung Building, 1327-35, Seocho-dong, Seocho-ku, Seoul 137-070
Phone: 82-2-3472-9114; Fax: 82-2-3472-9113
www.erakorea.co.kr
Contact: Mr. Young-Suk Lee, Chairman
(Specialized in commercial & residential real estate)

Kearny Global, Inc.
9/F., Sam Hwan Bldg.,
98-5, Unni-dong, Chongro-ku, Seoul 110-742
Phone: 82-2-3668-8300; Fax: 82-2-3668-8301
Contacts: Mr. Pietro A. Doran, President & CEO; Mr. David Yoon, Senior Director
(Specialized in commercial, retail, location analysis, project & construction management and development consulting)

KIRA Consulting
18/F., Construction Bldg.,
71-2, Nonhyun-dong, Kangnam-ku, Seoul 135-701
Phone: 82-2-544-8400; Fax: 82-2-547-8480
www.kira.co.kr
Contacts: Mr. Won-Jae Chun, President; Mr. Won-Kyum Kim, Manager
(Specialized in commercial real estate)

Korealand Co.
Room 3603, Trade Tower, KWTC,
159, Samsung-dong, Kangnam-ku, Seoul 135-090
Phone: 82-2-548-4900; Fax: 82-2-551-6611
www.koreailand.com
Contact: Mr. Young-Dae Kang, Planning Director

(Specialized in real estate development/ REITS)

Le Meilleur Co., Ltd.
15/F., F.K.I. Bldg.,
28-1, Yoido-dong, Youngdungpo-ku, Seoul 150-756
Phone: 82-2-761-0600; Fax: 82-2-786-0901
Contacts: Mr. K. T. Chung, President; Mr. Choi, Soo Young, General Manager
(Specialized in real estate marketing)

Pacific Consulting Co., Ltd.
2/F, Namdo building, 52-6, Banpo-dong, Seocho-gu, Seoul 137-040
Phone: 82-2-785-1818; Fax: 82-2-3478-0039
www.land8.com
Contact: Mr. Jae-Wan Yang, President
(Specialized in commercial real estate consulting/marketing)

ACCOUNTING CORPORATIONS

Ahn Kwon Accounting Corp.
4-7, 10,11 &13 /F., Tae Young Bldg.,
252-5, Gongduk-dong, Mapo-ku, Seoul 121-717
Phone: 82-2-3271-3114; Fax: 82-2-3271-3200
www.ahnkwon.co.kr
Foreign Partner: Deloitte Touche Tohmatsu

Anjin Accounting Corp.
14/F., Hanhwa Security Bldg.,
23-5, Yoido-dong, Youngdungpo-ku, Seoul 150-010
www.anjin.co.kr
Phone: 82-2-784-6901; Fax: 82-2-785-4753
Foreign Partner: Arthur Andersen (U.S.A)

Daejoo Accounting Corp.
6/F., Dongha Building,
629, Daechi-dong, Kangnam-ku, Seoul 135-081
Phone: 82-2-2263-2868; Fax: 82-2-2267-0470
Foreign Partner: BDO International (Netherlands)

Samduk Accounting Corp.
12/F., Seohung Bldg.,
68, Gyunji-dong, Chongro-ku, Seoul 110-170
Phone: 82-2-735-0241; Fax: 82-2-730-9559
Foreign Partner: Nexia International (Netherlands; has several business networks in the U.S.A)

Samil Accounting Corp.
21/F., Hanil Group Bldg.,
191, 2-ka, Hangangro, Yongsan-ku, Seoul, 140-702
Phone: 82-2-709-0800; Fax: 82-2-796-7027
www.samil.co.kr
Foreign Partner: PriceWaterhouseCoopers(U.S.A.)

KPMG Samjong Accounting Corp.

For additional analytical, business and investment opportunities information,
please contact Global Investment & Business Center, USA
at (202) 546-2103. Fax: (202) 546-3275. E-mail: rusric@erols.com

15/F., Construction Center,
71-2, Nonhyun-dong, Kangnam-ku, Seoul 135-701
www.kr.kpmg.com
Phone: 82-2-3438-3800; Fax: 82-2-3445-4455
Foreign Partner: Klynveld Peat Marwick Goerdeler (U.S.A)

Shin Han Accounting Corp.
5/F., Samwhan Camus Bldg.,
17-3, Yoido-dong, Youngdungpo-ku, Seoul 150-010
Phone: 82-2-782-9200; Fax: 82-2-786-1890
Foreign Partner: Robinson Rhodes, Salustro Reydel, McGladrey & Pullen (multi-national)

Young Wha Accounting Corp.
7-14/F., Daeyoo Securities Bldg.,
25-15, Yoido-dong, Youngdungpo-ku, Seoul 150-010
Phone: 82-2-783-1100; Fax: 82-2-783-5890
www.youngwha.co.kr
Foreign Partner: Ernst & Young Int'l (U.S.A)

HUMAN RESOURCES/EXECUTIVE SEARCH AGENCIES

Adecco Korea
10/F., KyungAm Bldg.,
157-27, Samsung-dong, Kangnam-ku, Seoul 135-090
Phone: 82-2-555-0606; Fax: 82-2-3452-1911
www.adecco.co.kr
Contact: Ms. Jung-A Choe, President

AMROP International
14/F., Jongkeundang Building,
368, Chungjungro 3-ka, Seodaemun-ku, Seoul 120-756
Phone: 82-2-393-3701; Fax: 82-2-393-1811
www.amrop.co.kr
Contact: Mr. Theodore In-Shig Shim, President

Boyden International, Inc.
Room 1105, Changkyo Bldg.,
1, Changkyo-dong, Chung-ku, Seoul 100-760
Phone: 82-2-756-9305; Fax: 82-2-755-4632
www.boyden.co.kr
Contact: Mr. Ki-Soon Yim, Managing Director

Dream Search Inc
9/F Hosan Bldg.,
823-23, Yeoksam-dong, Kangnam-ku, Seoul 135-080
Phone: 82-2-569-3833; Fax: 82-2-569-3834
www.dreamsearchkorea.com
Contact: Ms. Byung-Sook Lee, President

Global Human Bank
15/F., YooWon Bldg., 75-95,
Seosomun-dong, Chung-ku, Seoul 100-110

For additional analytical, business and investment opportunities information,
please contact Global Investment & Business Center, USA
at (202) 546-2103. Fax: (202) 546-3275. E-mail: rusric@erols.com

Phone: 82-2-7750-113; Fax: 82-2-7750-112
www.jobghb.co.kr
Contact: Mr. David H. Lim, President

IBK Consulting Group
20 & 22/F., Hanhwa Building,
23-5, Yoido-dong, Youngdungpo-ku, Seoul 150-010
Phone: 82-2-782-2807; Fax: 82-2-786-6743
www.ibkconsulting.com
Contact: Mr. Han-Seok Kim, President

I-tec Consulting Co., Ltd.
7/F., Seoul Bldg.,
Yeoksam-dong, Kangnam-ku, Seoul 135-080
Phone: 82-2-3453-3058/9; Fax: 82-2-554-8374
www.itec-consulting.co.kr
Contact: Mr. Dae-Shik Kim, President

KK Consulting, Inc.
Suite 514, City Air Terminal,
159-6, Samsung-dong, Kangnam-ku, Seoul 135-728
Phone: 82-2-551-0203; Fax: 82-2-551-0220
www.kkconsulting.com
Contact: Mr. Kuk-Kil Kim, President

Norman Braodbent International
Suite 630, Royal Bldg.,
5, Dangjoo-dong, Chongro-ku, Seoul 110-721
Phone: 82-2-735-4565; Fax: 82-2-735-4562
www.normanbroadbent.co.kr
Contact: Mr. Hak-Bum Lee, Managing Director

P & E Consulting, Inc.
#1007, Ilshin Bldg.,
541, Dowha-dong, Mapo-ku, Seoul 121-040
Phone: 82-2-719-7902; Fax: 82-2-719-7907
www.pneconsulting.co.kr
Contact: Sunnie Hong, Rep. Director & Sr. Consultant

Search International
2/F., Myounghwa Bldg.,
629-31, Shinsa-dong, Kangnam-ku, Seoul 135-120
Phone: 82-2-514-3522; Fax: 82-2-514-3044
www.searchi.co.kr
Contact: Ms. Hyuk-Hee Kwon, President

ServeCorp.
13/F., Woonam Bldg.,
824-22, Yeoksam-dong, Kangnam-ku, Seoul 135-080
Phone: 82-2-508-0073; Fax: 82-2-508-1007
www.i-servcorp.co.kr
Contact: Ms. Sung-Hee Song, President

**For additional analytical, business and investment opportunities information,
please contact Global Investment & Business Center, USA
at (202) 546-2103. Fax: (202) 546-3275. E-mail: rusric@erols.com**

Solution Inc.
15/F., Dongshin Bldg.,
141-26, Samsung-dong, Kangnam-ku, Seoul 135-090
Phone: 82-2-565-5362; Fax: 82-2-565-5599
www.solution.co.kr
Contact: Mr. Sang-Hoon Han, President

Star Communications, Inc.
16/F., Songchon Bldg.,
642-9, Yeoksam-dong, Kangnam-ku, Seoul 135-080
Phone: 82-2-2185-5450; Fax: 82-2-756-0755
Contact: Ms. Joanne Lee, President

Tack International, Inc.
Room 303, Hyunjin Bldg.,
798-30, Yeoksam-dong, Kangnam-ku, Seoul 135-080
Phone: 82-2-564-0581; Fax: 82-2-564-0584
www.tack.co.kr
Contact: Mr. Sang-Tack Choi, President

Top Business Consultant Service
Room 3501, KWTC,
159-1, Samsung-dong, Kangnam-ku, Seoul 135-729
Phone: 82-2-551-0361; Fax: 82-2-551-0369
www.headhunter.co.kr
Contact: Mr. Kang-Shik Koh, President

Unico Search Inc.
Suite 1705, City Air Tower,
159-9, Samsung-dong, Kangnam-ku, Seoul 135-973
Phone: 82-2-551-0313; Fax: 82-2-551-4959
www.unicosearch.com
Contact: Mr. Soon-Shin Yoo, President

SELLING FACTORS/TECHNIQUES

Three practices are essential for success in the Korean market: (1) adapting products and procedures to Korean tastes and conditions, (2) regular communication with Korean business partners and customers, and (3) consistently exhibiting a firm commitment to the Korean market over the long run.

In selling to manufacturers, personal contact is important not only because of the value placed on direct discussion and on building long-term relationships but also because such contact brings the end-user in touch with new processes and equipment. In light of the competition offered by Japanese suppliers, who often visit potential and existing customers throughout Korea, U.S. suppliers should consider (1) making visits to Korea to augment the efforts of the local representative; (2) bringing representatives back to the home office periodically to ensure they are fully informed, motivated and up-to-date on the supplier and its offerings; (3) allowing the distributor or agent to appropriately choose among the U.S. company's full product line selection for sale in the Korean market, (4) holding more demonstrations, seminars and exhibitions of their products in Korea; (5) increasing the distribution of technical data and descriptive brochures; and (6) improving follow-up of initial sales leads.

ADVERTISING

In 1991, Korea's advertising market was completely opened to 100% foreign equity participation. As a result, a large number of joint venture agreements between major international advertising agencies and local Korean advertising firms have been established. Foreign advertising agencies have been able to take advantage of the current economic boom following the 1997 financial crisis, and they now control more than 33% of the Korean advertising market. Today, all the major international agencies are present in Korea.

There are four major broadcast networks (television and radio) in Korea. KBS I and KBS II are owned and operated by the Korean government, while MBS and SBS are independently operated. However, government influence remains since advertising time on these and other broadcast networks is sold exclusively through the government selling organization, the Korea Broadcast Advertising Corporation (KOBACO) and companies must register with this corporation if they intend to advertise in either of these two media. As of April 2001, approximately 200 foreign and Korean agencies are registered with this corporation.

However, KOBACO's exclusive control over advertising may soon change since as one of the government's efforts to privatize government-owned firms, the Korean National assembly is currently considering legislation that would end KOBACO's monopoly. When in effect, this "Broadcasting Advertising Law" would allow the creation of a competing media agency whose ownership would include non-governmental organizations and corporations, in effect giving the sales back to the broadcasting companies.

Though censorship in advertisement is still practiced in Korea, it is not as strict as in the past. The Korean Broadcasting Committee is the government authority that approves local broadcast advertising. But, in August of 2000, the Korea Advertising Review Board (KARB), which is organized by advertising associations, societies and industry associations, took control of advertising censorship procedures from the Committee. In addition, the governmental Korean Fair Trade Commission is responsible for determining whether an advertisement makes accurate claims.

Several local TV stations have been established in recent years. This development as well as the opening of cable television in 1995 has expanded advertising's potential reach to Korean audiences. As of June 2001, the Korean cable industry is served by 77 system operators, and 44 program providers providing such diverse cable programs as business news, sports, music, Buddhist programming, shows on the Korean board game, baduk ("Go"), and so forth. There are also two shopping channels among these program providers, and three more will be created by 2002.

Advertising market opportunities are predicted to show strong growth as more Koreans gain access to electronic media. For example, while cable television in Korea currently has an audience of 1.5 million households, industry specialists have estimated that by the end of 2001, this figure will grow to 5 million households. In addition, the government has been taking steps for Korea to broadcast satellite television in digital format by the end of 2001, with expectations of nationwide coverage by 2010. Korea Digital Broadcasting, a subsidiary of state-run Korea Telecom, was awarded the contract for digital broadcast in December of 2000 and by 2002 it is expected that Korea will be broadcasting 60-70 satellite channels, and about 120 by 2005.

Internet advertising also offers significant market growth potential, since the number of computer users will further increase in the coming years. There are currently 19 million Internet users in Korea, which amounts to more than 40% of the population.

For additional analytical, business and investment opportunities information, please contact Global Investment & Business Center, USA at (202) 546-2103. Fax: (202) 546-3275. E-mail: rusric@erols.com

TRADE PROMOTION

Seoul has several world-class trade resources including a government trade promotion agency and several modern exhibition venues. The Korea Trade-Investment Promotion Agency (KOTRA), a wholly-owned corporation of the Korean Ministry of Commerce, Industry and Energy, operates a Buyer Service Center. This Center provides assistance to foreign buyers visiting Korea in arranging business meetings with Korean companies and collecting information on Korean products and suppliers. KOTRA has built an extensive worldwide network of domestic and overseas Korea Trade Centers (KTC), with locations in 12 Korean cities, including Busan, Inchon, Ulsan, and many others. KOTRA also has 11 offices in the United States.

The Korea International Trade Association (KITA) is the largest trade association in Korea. As a member of the World Trade Centers Association (WTCA), KITA explores new trade opportunities for Korea by dispatching trade missions and market survey teams to a number of foreign countries on a regular basis. KITA's Trade Service Center also assists any potential foreign buyer or seller by responding to written inquiries from all over the world. The Center also offers on-the-spot consultation and personalized advisory service regarding trade rules and regulations, export and import procedures, business management, market research, technology development, and taxation. In addition, KITA's maintains six overseas branch offices, two of which are based in Washington D.C. and New York.

Seoul also touts the largest trade show venue in Korea, the Convention and Exhibition Center, popularly known as "COEX." Covering 36,027 square meters of exhibition space, COEX is a full-service trade organization offering multi-lingual simultaneous translation, world-class audio-visual equipment, state-of-the-art lighting and sound systems, and up-to-the-minute information services. Also in Seoul is the newly built Seoul Trade Exhibition Center (SETEC) which is operated by KOTRA.

In addition, Busan, the second largest city in Korea located in the far southern part of the Korean peninsula, currently has one exhibition hall called the Busan Exhibition & Convention Center (BEXCO). BEXCO is directly run by BEXCO, Inc., a Busan City-invested firm, which finished construction this year and was opened in May, 2001. This new hall will more than double Busan's trade exhibition capacity. The indoor exhibition hall has a floor space of 26,446 square meters. There is also an outdoor exhibition site, that is 13,223 square meters in size.

MAJOR NEWSPAPERS AND BUSINESS JOURNALS

Major Newspapers in Korea

Chosun Ilbo
(Korean newspaper)
General: Tel: 82-2-724-5114 Fax: 82-2-724-5329 (Int'l Div.)
Advertising: Tel: 82-2-724-5824 Fax: 82-2-724-5809
Address: 61, 1-ka, Taepyung-ro
Chung-ku, Seoul 100-756 Korea
Web site: www.chosun.com

Dong Ah Ilbo
(Korean newspaper)
General: Tel: 82-2-2020-0114 Fax: 82-2-2020-1239 (Int'l Div.)
Advertising: Tel: 82-2-2020-0777 Fax: 82-2-2020-1409
Address: 139, Sejong-ro
Chongro-ku, Seoul 110-715 Korea
Web site: www.donga.com

Hankuk Ilbo
(Korean newspaper)
General: Tel: 82-2-724-2114 Fax: 82-2-732-9288 (Int'l Div.)
Advertising: Tel: 82-2-724-2802 Fax: 82-2-720-7222
Address: 14, Chunghak-dong
Chongro-ku, Seoul 110-150 Korea
Web site: www.hankooki.com

Hankyoreh Shinmun
(Korean newspaper)
General: Tel: 82-2-710-0114 Fax: 82-2-715-6184 (Int'l Div.)
Advertising: Tel: 82-2-710-0417 Fax: 82-2-710-0410
Address: 116-25 Gongduk-dong
Mapo-ku, Seoul 121-750 Korea
Web site: www.hani.co.kr

Joong-ang Ilbo
(Korean newspaper)
General: Tel: 82-2-751-5114 Fax: 82-2-751- 5420 (Int'l Div.)
Advertising: Tel: 82-2-751-5076 Fax: 82-2-751-5806
Address: 7, Soonhwa-dong
Chung-ku, Seoul 100-130 Korea
Web site: www.joins.com

Korea Economic Daily
(Korean newspaper)
General: Tel: 82-2-360-4114 Fax: 82-2-360-4319 (Int'l Div.)
Advertising: Tel: 82-2-3604-477 Fax: 82-2-392-4168
Address: 441, Joonglim-dong,
Chung-ku, Seoul 100-360
Web site: www.hankyung.com

Korea Herald
(English newspaper)
General: Tel: 82-2-727-0114 Fax: 82-2-727-0670
Advertising: Tel: 82-2-727-0333 Fax: 82-2-727-0676
Address: 1-12, 3-ka, Hoehyun-dong
Chung-ku, Seoul 100-771 Korea
Web site: www.koreaherald.co.kr

Korea Times
(English newspaper)
General: Tel: 82-2-724-2114 Fax: 82-2-732-4125
Advertising: Tel: 82-2-724-2827 Fax: 82-2-732-4110
Address: 14, Chunghak-dong,
Chongro-ku, Seoul 110-792 Korea
Web site: www.koreatimes.co.kr

Kuk Min Ilbo
(Korean newspaper)
General: Tel: 82-2-781-9114 Fax: 82-2-7819-380 (Int'l Div.)
Advertising: Tel: 82-2-781-9818 Fax: 82-2-781-9830

**For additional analytical, business and investment opportunities information,
please contact Global Investment & Business Center, USA
at (202) 546-2103. Fax: (202) 546-3275. E-mail: rusric@erols.com**

Address: 12, Yoido-dong, Youngdungpo-ku
Seoul 150-010 Korea
Web site: www.kukmimnilbo.co.kr

Kyunghyang Shinmun
(Korean newspaper)
General: Tel: 82-2-3701-1114 Fax: 82-2-735-6140 (Int'l Div.)
Advertising: Tel: 82-2-3701-1500 Fax: 82-2-736-4985
Address: 22, Jung-dong
Chung-ku, Seoul 100-702
Web site: www.kyunghyang.com

Maeil Kyungjae
(Korean newspaper)
General: Tel: 82-2-2000-2114 Fax: 82-2-2000-2287 (Int'l Div.)
Advertising: Tel: 82-2-2000-2250/1 Fax: 82-2-2000-2219
Address: 30,, Pil-dong 1-ka
Chung-ku, Seoul 100-728 Korea
Web site: www.mk.co.kr

Munhwa Ilbo
(Korean newspaper)
General: Tel: 82-2-3701-5114 Fax: 82-2-3701-5187 (Int'l Div.)
Advertising Tel: 82-2-3701-5566 Fax: 82-2-730-0674/5
Address: 68, 1-ka, Choongjung-ro
Chung-ku, Seoul 100-151 Korea
Web site: www.munhwa.co.kr

Naeway Economic Daily
(Korean newspaper)
General: Tel: 82-2-727-0114 Fax: 82-2-727-0661 (Int'l Div.)
Advertising Tel: 82-2-727-0303 Fax: 82-2-727-0674/5
Address: 1-12, 3-ka, Hoehyun-dong
Chung-ku, Seoul 100-053 Korea
Web site: www.naeway.co.kr

Segye Ilbo
(Korean newspaper)
General Tel: 82-2-2000-1234 Fax: 82-2-2000-1341 (Int'l Div.)
Advertising Tel: 82-2-2000-1405 Fax: 82-2-793-7125
Address: 63-1, Hangangro 3-ka
Yongsan-ku, Seoul
Web site:

Daehan Maeil
(Korean newspaper)
General: Tel: 82-2-2000-9000 Fax: 82-2-2000-9239 (Int'l Div.)
Advertising: Tel: 82-2-2000-9383 Fax: 82-2-2000-9399
Address: 25, 1-ka, Taepyung-ro
Chung-ku, Seoul 100-101 Korea
Web site: www.seoul.co.kr

Seoul Kyungjae Shinmun

For additional analytical, business and investment opportunities information,
please contact Global Investment & Business Center, USA
at (202) 546-2103. Fax: (202) 546-3275. E-mail: rusric@erols.com

(Korean newspaper)
General: Tel: 82-2-724-2114 Fax: 82-2-730-0688 (Int'l Div.)
Advertising: Tel: 82-2-724-2829 Fax: 82-2-734-9009
Address: 19, Chunghak-dong
Chongro-ku, Seoul 110-150 Korea
Web site: www.sed.co.kr

Important Newspapers and Business Journals

Korea Economic Report
(monthly magazine)
General: Tel: 82-2-783-5283/7 Fax: 82-2-780-1717
Address: Suite 903, Shinsong Bldg.
25-4 Yoido- dong, Youngdungpo-ku
Seoul 150-010 Korea
Web site: www.economicreport.co.kr

Korea Trade and Investment
(bi-monthly magazine)
General: Tel: 82-2-3460-7524~6 Fax: 82-2-3460-7940
Address: Investment Public Relations
KOTRA
300-9, Yomgok-dong
Seocho-ku, Seoul 137-170 Korea
Web site: www.kt-i.com

Travel Trade Journal
General: Tel: 82-2-744-4010 Fax: 82-2-742-1881
Address: 10th Fl., Koryo Bldg.
66-21, Wonnam-dong
Chongro-ku Seoul 110-450 Korea
Web site: www.ttj.co.kr

PRICING A PRODUCT

U.S. goods have a reputation among Korean buyers of high quality and performance; however, Korean manufacturers often regard U.S. input products as very expensive since they are very price-conscious. In an export-oriented economy where finished products must meet keen competition in the world market, many Korean manufacturers believe that it is essential to buy the cheapest raw materials and equipment, even at the expense of quality. Goods from Japan and elsewhere are often considered to be better buys than goods from the U.S., though their quality and durability are poorer. In addition, Korean manufacturers often seek to offset labor wages with low-cost inputs. However, as Korea continues to move toward exporting higher-end and manufacturer-branded products, and as it tries to combat criticisms of poor quality control of certain Korean products in recent years, the precedence manufacturers give to price as a buying factor may be somewhat tempered. Other characteristics in Korean price considerations are the tendency to seek "bundled" prices, as well as to undervalue "software" (engineering and other services components), particularly in the procurement of major systems.

Considering the factors outlined above, U.S. exporters might consider: 1) adapting their products to Korea by marketing basic units, 2) taking into account in their price quotations the likelihood of repeat business for spare parts and auxiliary equipment, and most importantly, 3) emphasizing and marketing the idea that the superior quality of U.S. manufactured input products ultimately results in lower production costs.

SALES SERVICE/CUSTOMER SUPPORT

In determining the long-term success of U.S. suppliers in the Korean market, sales and after-sales service, or A/S, are second only to the selection of the appropriate product and price. Immediately following the Korean War, at a time when foreign exchange was exceedingly scarce, Korean plant operators learned to rely on their own resources or on the many small machine shops in order to service machinery. This tradition of self-reliance and improvisation is still evident in contemporary Korean business practices. However, with heavy competition among foreign suppliers in the Korean market, servicing has become an increasingly important component of selling.

Private traders and offer agents often hire available in-house engineers to install equipment. For specialized installations, however, the best sources of assistance include resident and offshore foreign engineers in coordination with local engineers, whose services are available for contract.

Japan's geographical proximity to Korea as well as the similarities in business culture between the two countries allow Japan to send teams of specialists to Korea at minimal cost and effort in order to offer skilled advice in installation, maintenance and repair. U.S. firms should consider establishing regional servicing facilities that can effectively service and support equipment sold in Korea. The emphasis given recently by some U.S. firms on the training of personnel, often through American programs, has proven beneficial.

SELLING TO THE GOVERNMENT

The purpose of the World Trade Organization's Government Procurement Agreement (GPA) is to establish non-discriminatory procedures for the procurement process so that a maximum number of qualified suppliers can fairly compete. The GPA defines steps to be followed regarding qualification of suppliers, publication, opening and award of tenders, and specifies minimum bid deadlines. It also limits circumstances under which open and competitive tendering procedures may be waived, such as cases of extreme urgency or follow-on procurement of spare parts. The GPA strives for greater transparency by requiring Korea and other signatories to publish laws, regulations, and detailed statistics regarding government procurement. The Agreement also requires procuring entities to make public basic information about contract awards, including (if requested and if not deemed contrary to the public interest) an explanation of why a supplier failed to qualify or was disqualified from competing on a bid, why its tender was not selected, or the reasons why the winning tenderer was selected. Another novel feature about the GPA is that it establishes bid challenge procedures in cases where a supplier believes a procuring entity has breached the Agreement. While such procedures have yet to be tested in Korea's case, they have been successfully used in other GPA signatory countries to the benefit of U.S. suppliers.

Korea began implementing the GPA on January 1, 1997. In its accession offer, Korea agreed to cover procurements valued over certain "threshold" amounts made by Korean central government agencies, their subordinate entities, Korean provincial and municipal governments, and some two dozen government-invested companies. In addition, procurement of services--including construction services--by covered Korean entities is included. Other features of the GPA for Korea include a prohibition against offsets as a condition for awarding contracts on covered procurements, and a provision requiring procuring entities to allow suppliers to pursue alleged violations of the Agreement through GPA-defined bid challenge procedures. Accordingly, the Korean Ministry of Finance & Economy (MOFE) has established an International Contract Dispute Settlement Committee to deal with any challenges by foreign suppliers that Korean procuring entities have not complied with GPA provisions.

The annexes to Korea's accession document specify certain thresholds, below which GPA rules do not apply. Thus, the threshold for Annex 1 (central government) entities for supplies and services is approximately $180,000, and for construction services approximately $7 million. Thresholds for supplies/services and construction services are considerably higher for Annex 2 (sub-central government entities) and Annex 3 (government-invested corporations). Korea also specified certain categories of purchases that would be exempt from GPA coverage altogether, including procurement related to national security and defense, Korea Telecom's purchases of telecommunications commodity products and network equipment, procurement of satellites, and purchase by the Korea Electric Power Corporation (KEPCO) of certain equipment related to electrical transmission and distribution.

The Supply Administration of the Republic of Korea (SAROK, formerly the Office of Supply or OSROK) is responsible for the purchase of goods and incidental services required by central and sub-central government entities, government construction contracts and related services, and stockpiling raw materials. Not all GPA-covered procurement is handled by SAROK. In the case of Korean government-invested corporations (listed in Annex 3 of Korea's accession agreement), procurement is handled in-house, with these entities following the same GPA rules. Thus, tendering under open, formal procedures is required.

U.S. suppliers are required to register in advance with SAROK (or any other procuring entity), which maintain lists of pre-qualified suppliers for given materials, equipment and services. Invitations to bid are announced 40 calendar days in advance of the bid deadlines. As required by the GPA, the procuring entity must publish information on bid opportunities in at least two sources: the daily newspaper Seoul Shinmun (daily newspaper) and the Korean Government Gazette. While these sources are published in the Korean language, any given tender announcement must be accompanied by a summary in English, including the subject matter of the contract, the deadline for submission of tenders, and the address and contact point from which full documents relating to the contracts may be obtained. The tender announcement must contain a statement that the bid is covered by the GPA.

While SAROK features tender information in English on its internet home page at http://www.sarok.go.kr, other procuring entities only sporadically publish information on their respective web sites (if available) and the information is not always timely. While not required in order for foreign firms to be eligible to bid on Korean Government contracts, any foreign firm with local representation tends to have a competitive advantage on Korean tenders, since it can better track tender notices, arrange for translation, and ensure that bids are properly submitted.

PROTECTING YOUR PRODUCT FROM IPR INFRINGEMENT

The protection of intellectual property rights, with regards to patents and copyrights and their policy implications, is further addressed in Chapter VII (Investment Climate). For the purposes of this chapter on marketing U.S. products and services, however, the protection of a valuable marketing tool, such as a trademark, is addressed in this section.

U.S. companies encountering problems in the intellectual property rights (IPR) area or wishing to register their trademark, patent or copyrights should engage the services of an attorney firm (a list of law firms in Korea can be found at the end of this chapter). U.S. companies can seek trademark and patent registration from the Korea Industrial Property Office (KIPO). Foreign applicants are required to retain a licensed local attorney in order to prepare applications in Korean and to conduct necessary follow-up correspondences locally. Under international law, copyrights do not have to be registered in order to be protected; however, like in the U.S. where copyright registration is possible, registration is also possible in Korea with the Ministry of Culture and Tourism. Enforcement of legally registered copyrights, trademarks, and patents are under the jurisdiction of the Prosecutor's Office in Korea.

If a U.S. company wanted to see if their trademark were registered without authorization, they would have to employ the services of a qualified Korean attorney because Korean law requires that foreign applicants designate a qualified attorney to represent them at legal proceedings in the Korean language (e.g. at trials to revoke or invalidate unauthorized registrations). In addition, if a U.S. company wanted to pursue legal avenues in the Korean legal system or in the KIPO Trial Board System, the intricacies of Korean IPR law in addition to the immense paperwork and documentation needed to be completed and compiled in the Korean language can be a daunting task for a U.S. firm that has neither full time local presence nor any contacts in the Korean government. Hence, in order to attempt to remedy most IPR problems in Korea, an effective local attorney is a key asset.

One of the most frequent IPR problems facing U.S. businesses in Korea is trademark protection. Unlike the trademark registration system in the United States, which is based on "first commercial use" or "first intent to use," the trademark registration system in Korea is based on "first-to-file," or more accurately, first to successfully register with KIPO. If a U.S. company is fortunate enough to have the foresight to consider entering into the Korean market, and no one has yet filed to register the same or similar trademark in Korea, it is highly advised that the U.S. company register its trademark first before another unauthorized party registers it. The company will save a lot of time, energy, resources, and legal fees in the long run. In order to successfully register a trademark, one must hire a qualified local attorney who is familiar with registration procedures. To have maximal effect using this prevention strategy, the company should be prepared to register the trademark in each product class category which is applicable for the product(s); should the trademark be challenged, protection is not generally provided under the Korean legal system if the company does not register in the pertinent particular product class category. Again, U.S. companies should be the first to file their trademark in Korea, and file in every applicable class category.

During the course of trademark registration, information on registration pending applications becomes initially available from publications of the Korea Invention and Patent Association two to three months after the initial application. Official announcements of pending applications are published for comment by KIPO in its Official Gazette. Generally, U.S. companies hire a local attorney and ask the firm to look into the status of the company's trademark in Korea. Sometimes, the U.S. company discovers from the aforementioned publications that an unauthorized party has already filed the trademark and is awaiting registration. In this case the company is eligible to file an Opposition Action Petition within a 30-day period of official publication. In an opposition action petition, the company states their case as to why the unauthorized party's application should be rejected during the course of initial review. After reviewing the opposition action petition, KIPO can decide either to proceed to successfully register the unauthorized trademark application, or, KIPO can decide to reject the trademark application, enabling the U.S. company to clear the path for the American company's successful registration at a later date.

If the American company is not yet fully engaged in the process of registration but plans to enter the Korean market in the distant future, then the company may at least want to monitor KIPO's public notices to see if someone tries to register the mark. If the company cannot monitor the situation from America, then the U.S. company should consider hiring someone in Korea, such as an attorney, who can.

The March 1998 Trademark Act includes a new provision to increase the possibilities of a successful action of U.S. trademark holders. It provides KIPO, grounds to reject a third-party application of the same or similar trademark application if KIPO is convinced that the registration is done in "bad faith." Even if an unauthorized party has filed for a U.S. company's trademark, hopefully, the capable trademark examiner at KIPO will have done his/her homework and have the knowledge to reject a famous/well-known trademark application.

As capable as trademark examiners can be, some trademark registrations by unauthorized registrants have slipped through the cracks and have been successfully registered. A registration by an unauthorized party is particularly unscrupulous in cases where the party registers the mark without intent to use the mark in a "predatory registration" (i.e., knowing that the mark belongs to another company, the unauthorized applicant registers the mark in hopes of cashing in when the legitimate trademark owner tries to enter the Korean market).

In this case, because the Korean legal system is based on first to file, and because the unauthorized registrant successfully registered with KIPO, the unauthorized registrant is the legal owner of the trademark in Korea—even if it is the U.S. company's mark and the American company has been using it in international commerce for the past several years! Provided that the mark was not used in commerce by the successful but unauthorized registrant in Korea for the past three years, the company can file a Cancellation Action petition to cancel the existing mark. If the cancellation action is successful and there is no appeal, the company can immediately file to register the trademark with KIPO, therefore, reclaiming the trademark.

The most onerous scenario takes place when an unauthorized trademark application has been successfully registered with KIPO, and the party is actually using the U.S. company's trademark in commerce in Korea. In this case, the legal remedy available is an Invalidation Action. An invalidation action petition can be filed anytime during the course of the 10-year life of a trademark, provided the trademark is actually being used by the unauthorized registrant. The American company's petition would outline why the unauthorized trademark owner's registration should be voided (invalidated), i.e. that the American company is the legitimate and original trademark owner, and that consumers know the trademark to be associated with the U.S. company.

If the company follows either the invalidation or cancellation action routes, the burden of proof lies with the petitioner. U.S. companies should be prepared to provide all kinds of documentation showing commercial use (include samples of the product and show the uniqueness of the trademark and product); to substantiate financial investment in advertisements (include advertisements in every way, shape, or form); even to provide the results of a survey conducted to show that the brand name is recognized by the public at large in Korea and that the company is the source of the legitimate goods touting the trademark.

Provided that the company and their attorneys put forth a convincing argument with meticulously documented details as to why the company is the legitimate trademark owner, the company has a good chance of winning the case before the KIPO Trial Board. However it may not be over as cancellation and invalidation actions have an appeals process from the KIPO Tribunal Board to the Korean Patent Court and finally, to the Supreme Court of Korea. The rule of thumb for trial date is first come, first served; petitions are filed by date with the trial dates occurring in order of the date of petition.

Unlike the case of a successful cancellation action where the company may file for the trademark immediately with KIPO, in the event an invalidation action is successful and there are no appeals, the U.S. company cannot officially file to register the trademark until one year has passed from the invalidation action date. However, U.S. companies can seek enforcement measures from the date of invalidation of the Korean registration.

**For additional analytical, business and investment opportunities information,
please contact Global Investment & Business Center, USA
at (202) 546-2103. Fax: (202) 546-3275. E-mail: rusric@erols.com**

Suffice it to say that the above means are legal means. There is always the possibility of settling out of court. And, because of the lengthy time it takes to go from the KIPO Tribunal Board to the Korean Patent Court, all the way up to the Supreme Court of Korea, some companies just cannot wait that long to re-claim their trademark. Time is money. Four years or more is not unheard of for a final decision using the legal process, and even then, there is no guarantee that the U.S. company would win. Because the opportunity cost of not entering the lucrative Korean market is so great, some companies have opted to settle out of court, i.e., to buy their own trademark from the unauthorized (but legal) registrant for use in the Korean market. However, some companies have strictly limited themselves to legal battles based on moral principle; in either case, good legal counsel is an absolute must. Ultimately, the decision is up to the U.S. company with good legal counsel as to how to proceed.

When registering for a copyright, trademark or patent, US companies, should maintain control of their intellectual property, even if they request their Korean agent to do the processing. This control is particularly relevant should the Korean-American partnership dissolve. In such previous cases where the Korean agent maintained control of the intellectual property, long, costly legal battles have ensued. The legal system is structured on an appeals process which could take at a minimum three to four years in the courts should a case go to the Supreme Court of Korea or to the Supreme Civil/Criminal Court. Again, even then, there is no guarantee that the US party would win. Hence, to avoid such legal disputes and hefty legal fees, US companies are urged to do their due diligence when choosing a potential Korean partner.

NEED FOR A LOCAL ATTORNEY

Although the industry is in the process of liberalization, the legal services sector is presently closed to foreign firms. Though in theory, foreign citizens may sit for the Korean judicial exam and eventually become a licensed attorney, in practice there are no licensed non-Korean attorneys. However, an increasing number of foreign attorneys are hired as consultants by Korean law firms. In international transactions, many so-called "foreign consultants" are essentially practicing law, with the exception of a final approval signature, which must be completed by a Korean attorney.

Out of a population of nearly 45 million people, the present Korean examination system establishes a limit of eight hundred newly graduated law students to enter into the ranks of practicing attorneys each year. Over the last several decades, the Korean government has worked to liberalize the sector by allowing more graduates to enter into the profession. Since 1996, the quota has been raised from 300 per year to the current 800 per year, and further liberalization to 1,000 new attorneys per year is expected soon. Due to the limits placed on the number of new attorneys accredited each year, experienced counsel is at a premium.

The Korean legal community has divergent opinions on liberalizing the market. The large established firms, which have a virtual monopoly on lucrative international transactions, resolutely oppose opening to foreign competition, which may drive legal fees down and provide more choices for Korean and foreign consumers. On the other side of the argument is an emerging group of small law firms that see the arrival of foreign firms in Seoul as an opportunity to forge new partnerships and capture some of the established business of the larger firms.

A large proportion of the practice by Korean law firms focuses on international business and transactions. Most experts advise engaging a local attorney before making major business decisions in dealing with Korean companies. The legal advice that Korean firms with international experience can provide can be very important. In addition to advice on structuring deals or arranging contracts, Korean law firms are usually well connected into the power structure and have extensive contacts in the government ministries that can determine the fate of foreign companies and international transactions.

For additional analytical, business and investment opportunities information, please contact Global Investment & Business Center, USA at (202) 546-2103. Fax: (202) 546-3275. E-mail: rusric@erols.com

Although it is important to have legal representation when a business in Korea reaches even a modest level of complexity, it is important to remember two things. First, as a matter of legal culture, Korean lawyers do not see themselves as businessmen and try to avoid intruding on business judgments. It is rather rare for Korean lawyers to venture far from recitation of applicable statutes. This is one reason why it is a good idea to seek a Korean firm employing foreign legal consultants who tend to provide a proactive, commercial-oriented practice philosophy. Second, although major Korean firms have extensive and excellent contacts with the Korean bureaucracy, for anyone planning long-term business involvement in Korea, it is often useful to establish direct contacts with the officials who oversee any given industry.

LIST OF MAJOR LAW FIRMS IN KOREA

(Note: Telephone dialing information when calling from outside of Korea: 82 is the country code for Korea, followed by 2, which is the city code for Seoul)

Aram International Law Offices
5th Fl., Hoesung Building, 51-7, Banpo-dong, Seocho-ku, Seoul 137-040
Tel: 82-2-592-0892; Fax: 82-2-596-6081
Web site: www.aramlaw.com

Aurora Law Offices
15th Fl. Se-Ah venture Tower, 946-12, Daechi-dong, Kangnam-ku, Seoul 135-280
Tel: 82-2-501-1811; Fax: 82-2-501-1812
Web site: www. auroralaw.co.kr

Bae, Kim & Lee, P.C.
6th - 12th Fl., Hankuk Tire Building, 647-15, Yuksam-dong, Kangnam-ku, Seoul 135-080
Tel: 82-2-3404-0000 Fax: 82-2-3404-0001
Web site: www. bkl.co.kr

Central International Law Firm
5th Fl., Korea Re-insurance Bldg., 80 Soosong-dong, Chongro-ku, Seoul 110-140
Tel: 82-2-735-5621/6; Fax: 82-2-733-5206/7
Web site: www.cilf.co.kr

Chin, Ahn, Ha & Seo
8th Fl, Il-Heung Building, 1490-25, Seocho-Dong, Seocho-Ku, Seoul 137-870
Tel: 82-2-586-2240; Fax: 82-2-586-3184
Web site:www.tllawyer.co.kr

C.J. International Law Offices
8th Floor, Daedong Bldg., 51-5, Banpo 4-dong, Soecho-ku, Seoul 137-044
Tel: 82-2-736-0145; Fax: 82-2-3476-5995
www.barunlaw.com

First Law Offices of Korea
275-7, 17th Fl., KEC building
Yangjae-dong, Seocho-ku, Seoul 137-130
Tel: 82-2-589-0001; Fax: 82-2-589-0002
Web site: www.firstlaw.co.kr

Hwang Mok Park & Jin Law Offices
9th Fl., Daekyung Building, 120, 2-ka, Taepyong-ro, Chung-ku, Seoul 100-724
Tel: 82-2-772-2700; Fax: 82-2-772-2800
Web site: www.hmpj.com

Kim & Chang Law Offices
Seyang Building, 223, Naeja-dong, Chongro-ku, Seoul 110-720
Tel: 82-2-737-4455; Fax: 82-2-737-9091/3

Kim, Chang & Lee
171, 5th Fl., Wonseo building, Wonseo-dong, Chongro-ku, Seoul 110-280
Tel: 82-2-397-9800 Fax: 82-2-725-8727
Web site: www.kimchanglee.co.kr

Kim, Shin & Yu
12th Fl., Leema Bldg., 146-1, Susong-song, Chongro-ku, Seoul 110-755
Tel: 82-2-2000-5000 Fax: 82-2-739-6606, 82-2-739-6182
Web site: www.ksy.co.kr

Law Offices of Lee & Ko
17th-20th Fl. Marine Center Main Bldg., 118, 2-ka, Namdaemun-ro, Chung-ku, Seoul 100-770
Tel: 82-2-772-4000 Fax: 82-2-772-4001/4002
Web site: www.lawleeko.com

Shin & Kim
Samdo Bldg., 4th Fl., 1-170, Soonhwa-dong, Chung-ku, Seoul 100-130
Tel: 82-2-316-4114; Fax: 82-2-756-6226
Web site: www.shinkim.com

Shin & Shin: Suite 1913 Champs Elysees Center Building
#889-5, Daechi-dong, Kangnam-Ku, Seoul 135-280
Tel: 82-2-565-6300; Fax: 82-2-565-7400

Wonjon Intellectual Property Law Firm
8th Fl., Poong Lim Bldg. 823-1
Yeoksam-dong, Kangnam-ku, Seoul 135-784
Tel: 82-2-553-1246 to 1250; Fax: 82-2-553-0990 or 0987
Web site: www.wonjon.co.kr

Yoon & Partners: Suite 831,
Korea Chamber of Commerce & Industry Bldg.
45, Namdaemunro 4-ka, Chung-ku, Seoul 100-743
Tel: 82-2-773-0161; Fax: 82-2-773-4947; 82-2-773-4948
Website: www.yoonpartners.co.kr

TRADE REGULATIONS, CUSTOMS AND STANDARDS

Korea continues a process of economic liberalization and deregulation, but the Korea government (ROKG) has yet to adopt a hands-off policy where the economy and trade are concerned. The U.S. Embassy, in addition to the American Chamber of Commerce (AmCham) in Korea, works actively to liberalize the many regulatory trade barriers that currently exist.

In its annual Improving Korea's Business Climate, AmCham Korea lists the following areas of concern: market access for imported goods; advertising; aerospace and defense; agricultural/food products; animal health; automobiles; chemicals; construction and engineering; environment; financial services (banking, capital markets, insurance); information technology; intellectual property rights; investment; labor and employment; legal services; medical devices; pharmaceuticals; real estate; taxation; telecommunications; travel and tourism; venture; and competitive issues affecting American companies' ability to do business abroad. Those interested in the specifics of the above issues may purchase the comprehensive book from the American Chamber of Commerce in Korea. Address: #4501 Trade Tower 159-1, Samsung-dong, Kangnam-gu, Seoul 135-731, Korea; Tel. 564-2040; Fax. 564-2050; E-mail: info@amchamkorea.org. Also, for a full description of trade barriers in Korea the annual National Trade Estimate (NTE) report produced by USTR should be consulted.

TRADE BARRIERS, CUSTOMS REGULATIONS, TARIFFS RATES AND IMPORT TAXES

Korea bound 92% of its tariff-line items as a result of the Uruguay Round negotiations. Korea's average basic tariff in 2000 is about 7.9%. Duties still remain very high on a large number of high-value agricultural and fisheries products. Korea imposes tariff rates of 30-100% on many agricultural and horticultural products of interest to U.S. suppliers. Under WTO "Zero for Zero" initiatives, Korea is in the process of reducing tariffs to zero on most or all products in the following sectors: paper, toys, steel, furniture, semiconductors and farm equipment.

Korea also maintains a tariff quota system designed to stabilize domestic commodity markets. Customs duties can be adjusted every six months within the limit of the basic rate plus or minus 40%. As of July 1, 2001, 70 items were selected, up from 60 items as of year-end 2000 and 55 items as of July 1, 2000. Among the 70 items, 20 items are agricultural, forestry and fishery related. In operating the quota rate system, the government has agreed to notify foreign business associations like AmCham when local industry recommends items for quota rate designation to the government. Korea also uses "adjustment tariffs" at the four-digit H.S. code level to respond to import surges and to protect domestic producers. The system is adjusted on an annual basis. Effective January 1, 2001, Korea reduced the number of items subject to adjustment tariffs from 27 items to 26 items, 20 of which are agricultural, forestry and fishery related.

In accordance with the Information Technology Agreement (ITA), Korea is reducing to zero tariffs on 203 types of telecommunication and information related equipment. The tariff reduction was completed for most tariffs in 2000, but implementation will be phased in for 10 categories (six by 2002 and four by 2004). Korea has also participated in the ITA - 2 negotiations aimed at eliminating tariffs on 108 other items with a target year of 2002.

Korea has a flat 10% Value Added Tax on all imports and domestically manufactured goods. A special excise tax of 10%-20% is also levied on the import of certain luxury items and durable consumer goods. Tariffs and taxes must be paid in Korean won within 15 days after goods have cleared customs.

CUSTOMS VALUATION

Most duties are assessed on an ad valorem basis. Specific rates apply to some goods, while both ad valorem and specific rates apply on a few others. The dutiable value of imported goods is the cost, insurance, and freight (C.I.F.) price at the time of import declaration.

Import duties are not assessed on capital goods and raw materials imported in connection with foreign investment projects. Authorization to import on a duty-free basis those items and supplies designated in a foreign investment application usually accompanies the Ministry of Finance and Economy's approval of a foreign investment project. In addition, raw materials used in the production of export goods are often exempt from duty, and certain machinery, materials, and parts used in designated industries such as high-technology and aerospace may enter Korea either duty free or at reduced rates. Tariffs are zero on materials used for educational purposes and on computer software.

IMPORT LICENSE REQUIREMENTS/ SPECIAL IMPORT-EXPORT REQUIREMENTS

Following a revision of the Customs Act and its Enforcement Decree, import procedures and the required documentation were simplified effective January 1, 1997. Goods entering Korea no longer require an import license (I/L) issued by a foreign exchange bank. Separate approval for payment in foreign currency is also no longer required. All commodities can be freely imported, subject to special registrations and import approvals for categories like pharmaceuticals and medical devices, unless they are included on the Negative List, which includes commodities that are either prohibited or restricted.

The Negative List is officially known as the Export and Import Notice. Fifty-four individual laws stipulate requirements and procedures for importing certain products (1,074 items, or 1% of all items) to ensure the protection of public health and sanitation, national security, safety, and the environment.

Applications for licenses to import items on the Negative List are approved on a case-by-case basis after screening and approval by the government agencies concerned, or by the relevant manufacturer's association. Typically, health or safety related products, such as pharmaceutical and medicines, require additional testing or certification by recommended organizations before clearing customs. In addition, special items defined by the Ministry of Commerce, Industry and Energy (MOCIE) in its Annual Trade Plan (firearms, illicit drugs, endangered species, etc.) require approval by the Minister of MOCIE. In most cases, the supplier's qualified local agent completes the registration process. In accordance with the amendment of the Foreign Trade Act, all restrictions on trading companies were eliminated by changing from the previous approval system to a new system under which firms simply file import notifications with MOCIE.

The IMF program called on Korea to improve the transparency of its import certification procedures. The government has reviewed 54 laws and regulations to identify necessary improvements in transparency. Amendment of the relevant laws and regulations was completed in 2000. Streamlining efforts on import certification continues through amendment of the Export and Import Notice. Whether or not these changes are liberalizing trade remains to be seen.

IMPORT/EXPORT DOCUMENTATION

Customs clearance procedures were simplified by the revision of the Customs Act and its Enforcement Decree in December 1995. The import license system was replaced by the import declaration system so that an import declaration filed without defect is immediately accepted for release of goods. With the exception of high-risk items related to public health and sanitation, national security, and the environment, which often require additional documentation and technical tests, goods imported by companies with no record of trade law violations are to be released upon the acceptance of the import declaration, without customs inspection. The Korean Customs Administration's EDI (Electronic Data Interchange) system for paperless import clearance came on line in July 1999 and allows importers to make an import declaration by computer, without visiting the customs house. Another noteworthy change in customs clearance effective January 1, 1999, is that goods can be released even before the filing of an import declaration and payment of tariffs. In 1999, the KCA linked its computer database with all the agencies dealing with exports and imports, allowing all exchanges of documents (approval, issuing recommendation, inspection and quarantine) to be done electronically.

Import declarations may be filed at the Customs House before a vessel enters the ports, or before the goods are unloaded into bonded areas. In both cases, goods are released directly from the port without being stored in a bonded area if the import declaration is accepted.

Along with import procedures, export procedures and documentation were also simplified effective January 1, 1997. Exported goods no longer require an export license (E/L) issued by a foreign exchange bank. Exporters can file their export notices to Korean Customs by computer based on their shipping documents at the time of export clearance. All commodities can be freely exported unless they are included on the negative list.

TEMPORARY GOODS ENTRY REQUIREMENTS

Pursuant to Korean Customs Law, advertising material and samples of merchandise are exempt from customs duties, provided that such items are used solely for that purpose and are valued at less than 100,000 won (about $75). Some U.S. firms, however, have reported problems in receiving duty exemptions. In practice, duty-free entry of these items is left to the discretion of the customs officials at the port of entry. Valuable samples or goods for re-export may be admitted temporarily on a duty-free basis under deposit for the amount of the duty. Careful documentation and handling of samples are essential to minimize problems.

With rare exceptions, Korean Customs allows free customs entry of goods brought into Korea that are hand-carried by foreign business persons (such as laptop personal computers) for use during their stay in Korea. In such a case, Korean Customs makes a note on the travelers' passport and then requires the traveler to take them out of Korea.

Goods entering Korea for exhibition purposes must be stored in a bonded area. For example, the Korea Exhibition Center (COEX) is a bonded area. Exhibition goods will be kept without charge at COEX during the exhibition period, after which they must be either: 1) reshipped directly out of Korea without payment of duty; 2) presented at Customs for payment of regular duty on value declared at time of entry; or, 3) transferred to the Seoul Customs house bonded storage area. Goods stored in a bonded warehouse can incur, if applicable, storage costs, customs brokerage charges, local transportation costs, and moving equipment fees.

LABELING, MARKING REQUIREMENTS

Country of origin labeling is required for commercial shipments entering Korea. The Korean Customs Service (KCS) publishes a list of the country of origin labeling requirements by Harmonized System Code number. Further labeling and marking requirements for specific products, such as pharmaceutical and food products, are covered by specific regulations from the Korean Government agencies responsible for these items. Korean language labels, except for country of origin markings that must be shown at the time of customs clearance, can be attached locally on products in the bonded area either before or after clearance. The Korea Food & Drug Administration (KFDA) is responsible for setting and enforcing Korean labels for food products other than livestock products. The Ministry of Agriculture and Forestry (MAF) regulates livestock products. MAF also has its own set of standards for markings for the country of origin labeling of agricultural products. Detailed information on country of origin labeling is provided in the guideline for country of origin labeling. Local importers usually print Korean language labels when imported quantities are not large, and can consult with the KCS as to where they can be attached to the product.

For additional analytical, business and investment opportunities information, please contact Global Investment & Business Center, USA at (202) 546-2103. Fax: (202) 546-3275. E-mail: rusric@erols.com

Effective April 1, 1998, the government made the following changes in relation to country of origin listing requirements: (1) defined "minimum processing" in more detail to increase transparency; (2) gave a more concrete description of when country of origin listing is required; and, (3) replaced value added reports with Harmonized System Code Number when determining the country of origin for six items.

For pharmaceuticals, all imported containers and packages must be conspicuously marked to show:
1) country of origin and manufacturer's and importer's names and addresses;
2) name of product;
3) date of production and batch number;
4) names and weights of ingredients;
5) quantity;
6) number of units;
7) storage method;
8) distribution validity date;
9) instructions for use;
10) import license number;
11) effectiveness;
12) import price and suggested retail price.

All imported food products (livestock products are regulated by MAF standards) are required to have Korean language labels. (Stickers may be used instead of Korean language labels, but such stickers must be in Korean. The sticker should not be easily removable and should not cover the original labeling). Labels should have the following inscriptions printed in letters large enough to be readily legible:

1) Product name: The label should state the name of product. This product name should be identical to the product's name as declared to the licensing/inspection authority.
2) Product type: Only the designated products are required to provide the information.
3) Importer's name and address and the address where products may be returned or exchanged in the event of defects.
4) Manufacturing date, month, and year: This is mandatory only for specially designated products such as lunch box and sugar. The shelf-life for these designated products must also be labeled. It is not required to label liquor with a shelf life but the manufacturing date is required. However, such requirement for liquor may be exempted if it has a manufacturing number (lot number) or bottling date.
5) Shelf life: Food products should identify their shelf-life as determined by the manufacturer. If various kinds of products having different shelf-lives are packaged together, the shelf-life of the product that has the shortest shelf-life should be used on the label. The products that are subject to mandatory shelf-life limits, in accordance with the Korea Food Code, should meet such standards.
6) Contents: Weight, volume or number of pieces (if the number of pieces is shown, the weight or volume must be indicated in parentheses).
7) Ingredient(s) or raw material(s) and a percent content of the ingredient(s) should be included on the label (contents of the ingredients are included only when certain ingredients are used in the product name or as a part of the product name). The name of the major ingredient in accordance with the Article 7 of the Act must be included on the label as well as the names of at least the next four principle ingredients. These should be listed with the highest percentage first followed by the others. Artificially added purified water does not count as one of the five major ingredients.
8) Component name and content: When labeling the name of a component that was not added but is contained in one of the ingredients, the actual amount of the component contained in the

product can be labeled.

9) Nutrients: Only special nutritional foods, health supplementary foods, products wishing to carry nutritional labels and products wishing to carry a nutrients emphasis mark are subject to nutritional labeling.

10) Other items designated by the detailed labeling standards for food et al.: This includes cautions and standards for use or preservation (e.g. drained weight for canned products, radiation-processed products, etc.). Products that must be kept at low temperatures, such temperatures should be indicated.

Please note that KFDA revised the Labeling Standards for Food et al on July 28, 2000.

Note: Labeling standards for livestock products, food additives, equipment, container and packaging for food products are set separately. Information covering labeling standards for livestock products and nutritional labeling is available from Food & Agricultural Import Regulations and Standards Report 1999 provided on the USDA website. "Labeling Standards for Food et al" is also available from the American Chamber of Commerce in Seoul.

In August 1998, the requirement to list the import prices on the label was eliminated. Retail price marking is still required for both imported and domestic products for goods sold in shops with a floor-space greater than 33 square meters.

GMO LABELING REQUIREMENTS

As of March 1, 2001, under the Agricultural and Fisheries Product Quality Control Act, Korea requires that products that are produced using biotechnology must be labeled indicating that they are genetically modified agricultural products. Soybeans, corn and soybean sprouts are subject to this regulation, with potatoes to be added as of March 2002.

As of July 13, 2001, Korea will require labeling of foods or food additives that are manufactured or processed using, as major raw materials, one or more of the raw materials subject to the GMO labeling in accordance with the provisions of the Agricultural and Fisheries Product Quality Control Act. Details for these regulations are also available on the USDA website.

PROHIBITED IMPORTS

In principle, all commodities, subject to specific conditions, may be freely imported into Korea unless they are included on the negative list of prohibited or restricted items. The negative list is published by the Ministry of Commerce, Industry and Energy as the Annual Trade Plan (Export and Import Notice). Restricted items include firearms, illicit drugs, endangered species, etc. More important than the negative list, however, are market access barriers related to imports prohibited from entry into Korea due to non-compliance with standards and/or testing as set by the relevant Korean ministries responsible for the particular industry/agricultural category. Pharmaceuticals (including over-the-counter products), medical devices, cosmetics and food products are particularly vulnerable to lengthy, cumbersome and costly testing requirements. See the "Standards" section which follows.

EXPORT CONTROLS

Although not a member of COCOM, Korea observed COCOM licensing procedures since 1993. In 1995, the Korean government became a member of the post-COCOM regime, known as the "Wassenaar Arrangement." Korea is also a signatory to the Chemical Weapons Convention (CWC). Under the Foreign Trade Act, if an export control is deemed necessary for the maintenance of international peace and security, national security, or other national interests, an exporter or importer is required to obtain a certificate or permit from the head of the related administrative agency or MOCIE. The list of controlled items is published, and includes nuclear products, arms, chemical weapons, and missiles.

On its negative export list, Korea also prohibits the export of 13 items by Harmonized System 6 digit classification, including whale meat, uncut pieces of stone (granite, etc), and dog fur or skin products.

In accordance with the elimination of "gray area measures" under the WTO/Safeguards Agreement, the number of items that require export licenses was reduced from 834 items to 782 items. Out of 782 items, 778 items are related to quota and bilateral agreements on textiles and vehicles and the remaining four are voluntary restraints aimed at protecting natural resources like sand.

STANDARDS

The Korean Government adopted the ISO 9000 system (modified into the KSA 9000) as its official standard system as of April 1992, and published related regulations in September 1993. In 1997, Korean companies also adopted the ISO 14000 environment management system. However, there are still concerns about Korea's implementation of commitments made when it signed the GATT Agreement on Technical Barriers to Trade (the "Standards Code") in 1980. Korea seems to develop standards that effectively block imported goods by affecting only imported goods, or which are not applied in an equal manner to domestic products. In addition, the Korean government sometimes issues new regulations without adequate public rule-making procedures. The absence of a comment period and adequate time for industry to adjust can be a significant barrier to trade. Finally, implementation periods sometimes do not give foreign exporters sufficient time to comply, which lead to unnecessary and costly interruptions in trade.

In light of the fact that Korean firms consider compliance with the ISO 9000 necessary in order to compete in the international market, the Korean government has indicated that it will work to address such problems and reduce barriers. From Jan. 1, 2000, National Standard Basic stipulates that any new national standards shall be in compliance with ISO international standards. The Korean Industrial Standardization Act was also amended to require 60 days notice before announcing new standards. Whenever there is a change of standards, the government is required to notify the WTO's Committee on Technical Barriers to Trade (TBT). The Korean Agency for Technology and Standard is undertaking a program from 2000 through 2005 to make Korean standards consistent with international standards.

There are local testing laboratories authorized to certify firms under the ISO 9000 system. As Korea has joined the IAF-MLA (International Accreditation Forum-Multilateral Recognition Arrangement), local certificate on ISO 9000 system is recognized in 27 member countries of IAF-MLA.

In 2000, the Korean Laboratory Accreditation Scheme (KORAS) signed a multilateral mutual recognition agreement with International Laboratory Accreditation Cooperation (ILAC) on testing and calibration. As a result, tests that are done in laboratories of member countries of ILAC can be mutually recognized by 28 countries and 38 accreditation entities.

FREE TRADE AREAS/WAREHOUSES

The government has designated several free trade zones (MOCIE changed the name from "free export zones" to "free trade zones" in 2000) for the bonded processing of imported materials into finished goods for export. The free trade zones are specially established industrial areas where foreign invested firms can manufacture, assemble, or process export products using freely imported, tax-free raw materials, or semi-finished goods. Tax incentives are provided for foreign invested firms.

The Masan Free Trade Zone is located near Busan in southern Korea. The Iksan (formerly Iri) Free Trade Zone is located near Gunsan on the western coast. The Kunsan Free Trade Zone will be opened in July 2001. There are three industrial parks specifically for foreign firms in Gwangju and Cheonan (for high technology industries) and Daebul, offering incentives including large discounts on land rental fees and self-contained shopping and educational facilities. To encourage foreign investment, the government set the minimum foreign ownership requirement at 10% for Gwangju and Daebul and 30% for Cheonan.

Following the revision of the Foreign Investment Promotion Act in November 1998, there are now four ways in which a foreign investor can request designation as a Foreign Investment Zone (FIZ). For example, any foreign investor whose investment exceeds $100 million can request designation as a Foreign Investment Zone (FIZ). From 2000, more than two investors in similar industrial sectors can apply for a designation as a FIZ. (In the past only one investor can be designated for one FIZ.) This new system is aimed at attracting large-scale foreign direct investment by providing various incentives. Once designated as an FIZ, national taxes on the investment (income tax and corporate tax) are waived for the first seven years and reduced by 50% for the following three years. Local taxes (acquisition tax, registration and property tax) can also be waived for 8-15 years in accordance with a decree by local authorities. In addition, national property can be rented free of charge and financial support for infrastructure construction can be given.

As of January 1, 1999, six separate types of bonded facilities which previously required individual licenses can be designated as an integrated bonded area. A Foreign Investment Zone can also be designated as an integrated bonded area by simply filing a notice, which does not require approval. There is no restriction on the types of business and goods as long as those goods are not deemed to threaten national security, health and environment. The storage period is unlimited. Within the bonded area, goods can be stored, manufactured, processed, sold, constructed or exhibited without going through customs clearance.

Bonded storage facilities in Korea are under the supervision of the Collector of Customs. With the introduction of the new comprehensive bonded area, Korea has three kinds of bonded areas: 1) designated bonded areas (designated storage sites and customs inspection sites); 2) licensed bonded areas (bonded storage sites, bonded warehouses, bonded factories, bonded exhibition sites, bonded construction sites, and bonded sales sites); and, 3) integrated bonded areas. The period for which goods may be stored in a licensed bonded warehouse is one year and can be extended for another year. Duties are payable only when goods are cleared through customs. Storage fees are high, and the use of a bonded warehouse to maintain inventories is limited. The storage period does not apply to the storage of live animals or plants, perishable merchandise, or other commodities that may cause damage to other merchandise or to the warehouse. The Collector of Customs bears no responsibility for goods while they are stored in customs facilities. Integrated bonding areas however, have no time limit for storage. At this type of bonded area, storage, manufacturing, processing, building, sales and exhibition can be comprehensively carried out.

In addition to the Integrated Bonded Area designated as a Foreign Investment Zone, bonded warehouses are the facilities available in Korea to foreign companies where a U.S. exporter can store shipped goods and still maintain title until they are cleared through customs by normal import procedures. Korea's customs laws specify that any person who wishes to establish a bonded warehouse shall obtain a license from the director of each Customs Zone. Applications must include the name of the bonded warehouse, location, structure, numbers and sizes of

For additional analytical, business and investment opportunities information,
please contact Global Investment & Business Center, USA
at (202) 546-2103. Fax: (202) 546-3275. E-mail: rusric@erols.com

buildings, storage capacity and types of products to be stored. In addition, articles of incorporation and corporate register must be submitted, when applicable.

MEMBERSHIP IN FREE TRADE AGREEMENTS

The Republic of Korea is a member of the Asia-Pacific Economic Cooperation (APEC) forum. One goal of APEC, as outlined in its 1994 declaration, is to establish a Free Trade Area among its member countries by the year 2020. Substantive principles which are encompassed in the APEC forum include investment liberalization, tariff reduction, deregulation, government procurement, and strengthening IPR protection.

The Republic of Korea is a member of the World Trade Organization (WTO) and has signed subsidiary agreements including TRIPs (Trade Related Aspects of Intellectual Property) and the Government Procurement Agreement. In December 1996, Korea joined the Organization for Economic Cooperation and Development (OECD).

CUSTOMS CONTACT INFORMATION

The International Cooperation Division of the Korean Customs Administration can provide assistance with general customs questions. Contacts are Mr. Park, Jae Hong, Director General, International Cooperation Division, Korea Customs Service based in Taejon, Tel. 82-42-481-7950, Fax. 82-42-481-7969 and Mr. Sohn, Byung Jo, Director, Cargo Control Division, Korea Customs Service, Tel. 82-42-481-7860; Fax. 82-42-481-7869.

TRADE AND PROJECT FINANCING

In response to the 1997-98 financial crisis, the Korean government closed or merged scores of insolvent banks and financial institutions; by 2001 had injected upwards of $119 billion into the banking system, with plans to spend $22 billion more; set up the Korean Asset Management Corporation (KAMCO) to dispose of non-performing assets; required banks to raise their capital adequacy ratios to the BIS standard of 8%; introduced strengthened asset classification standards for banks; and imposed "forward-looking" criteria (FLC) to force the banks to provision adequately for non-performing loans, among other reforms. More stringent prudential oversight has generally tightened bank credit.

The government has exercised tight control over its domestic credit markets, largely to reduce inflationary pressures, but also to meet other economic policy objectives. In the 1970's, the government allocated credit (so-called "policy loans") through Korean banks at subsidized interest rates to priority export industries and the agriculture sector. In the 1980's the Korean economy grew rapidly. Growth-oriented Korean chaebol (conglomerates) expanded domestically and overseas, often without regard for profitability and accumulating debt. The government slowly abandoned its policy-loan approach, but did not use its financial supervisory authority to pressure banks and other financial institutions to adequately assess credit risk. In the 1990's the government tried without apparent success to limit loans to 30 large business conglomerates to reduce economic concentration. The result was high levels of non-performing loans in the Korean banking system, due to distortions in credit allocation due to government controls; limited risk-analysis; weak prudential oversight; tightly bound societal relationships; and moral hazard arising from the widespread belief that the government would make good any and all losses.

Traditionally, most trade and project financing has gone to large Korean conglomerates (chaebol), due to their perceived financial security and immense capital base. The banking industry gave scant attention to domestic small and medium-sized companies. This attitude has changed, particularly since the spectacular mid-1999 collapse of Daewoo Group, at that time

Korea's second-largest chaebol. Daewoo's demise, which involved around $80 billion of unpaid debt, was easily the world's biggest corporate bankruptcy. Since then, banks have moved to modernize their lending capabilities. SMEs, particularly information-technology firms, have benefited from easier access to bank lending.

Korean companies often request or insist on extended credit terms for international trade, such as open account, even for the first transaction. U.S. exporters might want to resist granting too favorable terms to Korean businesses until they have carried out some initial transactions on a secured basis and established mutual business confidence.

The Daewoo bankruptcy and following liquidity crisis suffered by Hyundai affiliates further aggravated conditions in the financial sector, which was already undergoing restructuring initiated as result of the 1997 financial crisis. Non-performing loans at banking and non-banking financial institutions amounted to 50.2 trillion won ($38.6 billion) at the end-March 2001. The government has encouraged mergers among banks by offering government support and enacted a financial holding company law.

Effective July 1, 2000, Investment Trust Companies (ITC's) must use "mark-to-market" accounting (instead of par value) for new investment into existing funds and for funds launched after November 1998.

BANKING SYSTEM

Korea's financial system consists of banking and non-bank financial institutions. The Financial Supervisory Commission (FSC) and the Financial Supervisory Service (FSS), its regulatory arm, are responsible for supervising and examining all banks, including specialized and government-owned banks, as well as securities and insurance companies. The FSC has played a key role in financial restructuring and has strengthened the regulatory and supervisory framework governing the entire financial sector. Oversight standards are improving but they will need more time to meet international standards. Audits generally are performed by the Korean branches of international accounting firms. Audit quality also is improving. The government reduced the unlimited guarantee for bank deposits to 50 million won ($38,000) per account beginning in 2001 to further activate market disciplines.

FOREIGN EXCHANGE CONTROLS AFFECTING TRADE

The 1998 Foreign Exchange Transaction Act liberalized foreign exchange controls, easing restrictions on capital movements in two phases over two years. The Ministry of Finance and Economy (MOFE) described its guiding reform principles as creating a simplified and transparent framework in line with OECD benchmarks. The first phase of liberalization, implemented on April 1, 1999, included five major changes: (1) a negative list system replaced the previous positive system for capital account transactions; (2) all capital account transactions related to business activities of firms and financial institutions were liberalized, including a firm's short-term borrowings from abroad; (3) non-residents were allowed to issue won-denominated securities abroad; (4) all qualified financial institutions were permitted to engage in the foreign exchange business, with most remaining restrictions on the foreign exchange business to be removed; and, (5) participants in the spot and forward markets no longer had to demonstrate their business purpose to purchase forward currency contracts. Also, a commercial foreign currency brokerage system was introduced.

Second stage measures, effective January 1, 2001, liberalized most capital account transactions that were not liberalized in the first stage, including those related to national security and crime prevention. Non-residents are now able to invest in won-denominated domestic deposits with maturities of less than one year, and residents will have the right to invest in foreign-currency-denominated overseas deposits. Some foreign investors complain that MOFE's foreign-exchange-transaction reporting requirements are burdensome.

According to the revised Foreign Exchange Management Regulations, limits on foreign exchange purchases by Korean overseas travelers as well as on monthly overseas expenses were removed. Korean residents living offshore longer than two years can purchase foreign real estate without any limit. In addition, Korean residents are now permitted to hold deposits abroad; however, individuals should inform the BOK of the transaction if the deposit is more than $50,000.

Proposed foreign capital remittances are guaranteed when investment approval is obtained.

A foreign firm that invests under the terms of the Foreign Capital Promotion Act (FCPA) is permitted to remit a substantial portion of its profits, providing it submits an audited financial statement to its foreign exchange bank. To withdraw capital, a stock valuation report issued by a recognized securities company or the Korean Appraisal Board must also be presented. Foreign companies not investing under the FCPA must repatriate funds through authorized foreign exchange banks after obtaining government approval. Although Korea does not routinely limit the repatriation of funds, it reserves the right to do so in exceptional circumstances, such as in situations which may harm its international balance of payments, cause excessive fluctuations in interest or exchange rates, or threaten the stability of its domestic financial markets. To date, the Korean government has had no instances of limiting repatriation for these reasons, even during and after the 1997-98 financial crisis.

GENERAL FINANCING AVAILABILITY

Medium and short-term credit is available from Korean and foreign banks and through the issuance of debentures. Domestic companies generally have better access to local funding as well as informal and secondary financial markets charging higher interest rates. Debentures are a financing alternate, although slightly more expensive than bank financing. Long-term debt is available from the Korea Development Bank, but generally for high priority industries.

After the 1997-98 economic shock, the government decided that its foreign loan system was distorted, and eased its restrictions on foreign long-term credit. In the past, Korean companies were obliged to obtain approval from MOFE for loans over $10 million with maturities of over one year. As of July 1, 1998, companies need only to notify MOFE of loans over $50 million with maturities over one year.

HOW TO FINANCE EXPORTS/METHODS OF PAYMENT

The Korean financial system is perennially hard-pressed to meet the demand for financing and capital. Foreign companies in a start-up operation with a Korean partner often invest financial resources for the joint venture, while their Korean partner makes an investment in kind, i.e., land or facilities, as the Korean share of equity. Joint-venture companies and foreign firms often work with branches of foreign banks for local-currency financing, although the branches of foreign banks control a small portion of won availability. Other potential sources of won financing include domestic nationwide commercial banks, regional banks and specialized banks including the Korea Development Bank, the National Agricultural Cooperative Federation, the Industrial Bank of Korea, and Korea Housing Bank.

There are three documentary practices in settling Korea's imports: (1) sight and usance Letters of Credit, (2) Documents against Acceptance (D/A) and Documents against Payment (D/P); and, (3) Open Account Transactions. D/A and usance LCs are forms of extended credit in which the importer makes no payment for the goods until the date called for in the credit; however, the importer may clear the goods from customs prior to payment. D/P is the same as D/A except that

For additional analytical, business and investment opportunities information,
please contact Global Investment & Business Center, USA
at (202) 546-2103. Fax: (202) 546-3275. E-mail: rusric@erols.com

the importer cannot clear the goods from customs prior to payment. In some cases an importer can clear goods prior to payment under a sight LC. LC transactions generally follow standard international UCP codes.

Limitations on the use of deferred payment terms for imports, D/A and usance L/Cs were abolished in July 1998.

The Commercial Service of the U.S. Embassy in Seoul recommends that U.S. companies consider dealing on a confirmed letter of credit basis with new and even familiar clientele. A confirmed L/C through a U.S. bank is recommended because it prevents unwanted changes of the original L/C, and it shifts responsibility for collection onto the familiar banks involved, rather than onto the seller. This may cost a bit more, but may be well worth it.

TYPES OF AVAILABLE EXPORT FINANCING AND INSURANCE

In 1991, the Overseas Private Investment Corporation (OPIC) stopped writing insurance policies for companies making new investments in Korea under Section 231A of the Foreign Assistance Act. In light of economic difficulties in Korea, OPIC announced in June of 1998 that it would resume operations in Korea. OPIC has never had to cover claims for expropriation, political risk or currency inconvertibility in Korea. Further, the United States and Korea are negotiating a Bilateral Investment Treaty (BIT). The conclusion of a BIT would provide greater confidence to the American investment community.

Prior to the economic crisis, loans and guarantees from the U.S. Export-Import Bank (Eximbank) of the United States were not commonplace because international trade transactions were being conducted in a stable environment. At the height of the economic crisis, when many foreign banks reduced their exposure to Korea, Eximbank agreed to provide short and medium-term credit guarantees for capital goods and services to help to ensure confidence in the Korean market.

Since 1987, Korea has been a member of the Multilateral Investment Guarantee Agency of the World Bank Group. The Republic of Korea (ROK) is a recent graduate of the International Bank for Reconstruction and Development (The World Bank), though it is again a recipient of World Bank loans. Within the World Bank Group, the ROK is a member of the International Bank for Reconstruction and Development (IBRD), the International Development Association (IDA), the International Finance Corporation (IFC), and the Multilateral Investment Guarantee Agency (MIGA). The Commercial Service of the U.S. Department of Commerce has a presence at the World Bank Group within the Office of the U.S. Executive Director. Contact information at the World Bank is as follows:

Janice Mazur, The World Bank, The Commercial Service Liaison Staff
Office of the U.S. Executive Director, 1818 H Street, NW, Washington, DC 20433
Tel. 202-458-0120/0118, Fax. 202-477-2967
E-mail: Jmazur@mail.doc.gov

MAJOR AMERICAN AND KOREAN BANKS IN KOREA

(Note: Telephone dialing information when calling from outside of Korea:
82 is the country code for Korea, followed by 2 which is the city code for Seoul)

American Banks in Seoul

American Express Bank Ltd. (Seoul Branch)

15th Floor, Kwangwhamoon Bldg.,
#64-8, Taipyungro 1-ka, Chung-ku, Seoul 100-101
Mailing Address: KPO Box 1390, Seoul, Telex: K24484, Tel: 399-2900, Fax: 399-2967
Web site: www.aexp.com

Fleet National Bank (Seoul Branch)
15th Floor, Kyobo Bldg.,
#1, 1-ka Chongro, Chongro-ku, Seoul 110-714
Mailing Address: same as above, Telex: K23750, Tel: 397-3300, Fax: 733-6989
Web site: www.fleet.com

Bank of America NA & SA (Seoul Branch)
9th Floor, Hanhwa Bldg.,
#1, Jangkyo-dong, Chung-ku, Seoul 100-797
Mailing Address: CPO Box 3026, Seoul, Telex: K23294, Tel: 729-4500, Fax: 729-4525
Web site: www.Bankamerica.com

Bank of California, N.A. (Seoul Branch)
12th Floor, Kyobo Bldg.,
#1, 1-ka Chongro, Chongro-ku, Seoul 110-714.
Mailing Address: same as above, Telex: K22815, Tel: 721-1830, Fax: 732-9526
Web site: www.uboc.com

Bank of Hawaii (Seoul Branch)
10th Floor, OCI Bldg.,
#50, Sogong-dong, Chung-ku, Seoul 100-070
Mailing Address: CPO Box 5146, Seoul, Telex: K23589, Tel: 3179-114, Fax: 757-3516
Web site: www.boh.com

Bank of New York (Seoul Branch)
23rd Floor, Young Poong Bldg.,
#33, Seorin-dong, Chongro-ku, Seoul 100-752
Mailing Address: CPO Box 4906, Seoul, Telex: K29553, Tel: 399-0001/6, Fax: 399-0055
Web site: www.bankofny.com

Chase Manhattan (Seoul Branch)
Chase Plaza Bldg.,
#34-35, Jung-dong, Chung-ku, Seoul 100-120
Mailing Address: CPO Box 2249, Seoul, Tel: 758-5114, Fax: 758-5423
Web site: www.chase.com

Citibank, N.A. (Seoul Branch)
CitiCorp Center Bldg.,
#89-29, Shinmoonro 2-ka, Chongro-ku, Seoul 110-062
Mailing Address: KPO Box 749, Seoul, Telex: K23293, Tel: 2004-2004, Fax: 2004-1013
Web site: www.citibank.co.kr

First Chicago NBD (Seoul Branch)
15th Floor, Oriental Chemical Bldg.,
#50, Sokong-dong, Chung-ku, Seoul 100-718
Mailing Address: CPO Box 7239, Seoul, Telex: K27534, Tel: 316-9700, Fax: 753-7917
Web site: www.bankone.com

**For additional analytical, business and investment opportunities information,
please contact Global Investment & Business Center, USA
at (202) 546-2103. Fax: (202) 546-3275. E-mail: rusric@erols.com**

American Banks with a Representative Office in Seoul

First Union National Bank, NA (Representative Office)
10th Floor, Samhwa Bldg.,
#21, Sogong-dong, Chung-ku, Seoul 100-070
Telex: K27966, Tel: 3706-3114, Fax: 3706-3141~3
Web site: www.firstunion.com

Major Korean Banks in Seoul

Chohung Bank
#14, amdaemoonro 1-ka, Choong-ku, Seoul 100-757
Telephone: 3700-4037, Fax: 3700-4971/4972
Web site: www.chb.co.kr

Hana Bank
#101-1, Ulchiro 1-ka, Choong-ku, Seoul 100-191
Telephone: 2002-1111, Fax: 775-7472
Web site: www.hanabank.co.kr

Hanvit Bank
#203, 1-ga, Hoihyun-dong, Jung-ku, Seoul 100-792
Telephone: 2002-3000, Fax: 2002-5685/5686
Web site: www.hanvitbank.co.kr

Housing & Commercial Bank
#36-3, Yoido-dong, Youngdeungpo-ku, Seoul 150-886
Telephone: 769-8114/7114, Fax: 769-8350
Web site: www.hncbworld.com

Kookmin Bank
#9-1, Namdaemoonro 2-ka, Choong-ku, Seoul 100-703
Telephone: 317-2114, Fax: 317-2704
Web site: www.kookmin.co.kr

Koram Bank
#39, Da-dong, Chung-ku, Seoul 100-180
Telephone: 3455-2545, Fax: 3455-2966
Web site: www.goodbank.com

Korea Exchange Bank: #181,
Ulchiro 2-ka, Choong-ku, Seoul 100-793
Telephone: 729-8986, Fax: 775-9819
Web site: www.keb.co.kr

Korea First Bank
#100, Gongpyoung-dong, Chongno-ku, Seoul 100-702
Telephone: 3702-3114, Fax: 3702-4936
Web site: www.kfb.co.kr

Peace Bank
#647-9, Yoksam-dong, Kangnam-ku, Seoul 135-080
Telephone: 2222-2210, Fax: 564-8464

For additional analytical, business and investment opportunities information,
please contact Global Investment & Business Center, USA
at (202) 546-2103. Fax: (202) 546-3275. E-mail: rusric@erols.com

Web site: www.pbk.co.kr

Seoul Bank
#10-1, Namdaemoonro 2-ka, Choong-ku, Seoul 100-746
Telephone: 3709-5114, Fax: 3709-6443/6445
Web site: www.seoulbank.co.kr

Shinhan Bank
#120, Taepyoungro 2-ka, Choong-ku, Seoul 100-865
Telephone: 756-0505, Fax: 774-7013
Web site: www.shinhanbank.com

FOREIGN EXCHANGE REGULATIONS

1. NEED FOR REFORM

Foreign capital is a crucial element in the recovery of the Korean economy. The government has recently adopted a series of measures to open our capital market and lower the barriers to portfolio and direct investment. Among the actions it has taken, it is raising the equity ownership ceiling and easing restrictions on land purchases by foreigners. Thus far, however, sufficient inflows of foreign capital have not yet materialized.

One of the key obstacles to foreign investment in Korea is the cumbersome legal and regulatory environment. The laws and regulations governing foreign exchange transactions are especially complex and cumbersome. We therefore need to take additional and significant steps toward liberalizing foreign exchange and capital flows in Korea as well as establishing a simple, transparent legal framework. This requires the replacement of the Foreign Exchange Control Act with an entirely new law which fully meets global standards. Likewise, the current Foreign Exchange Management Regulation, which consists of 512 articles in total, will be replaced by a greatly simplified set of regulations.

2. OVERALL OF LIBERALIZATION

A major part of foreign exchange liberalization concerns the deregulation of capital movements. However, because complete capital account liberalization is expected to induce subtantial inflows of short-term speculative capital, the domestic financial markets could very well be destabilized.

It is therefore important that the timing and sequencing of the implementation of the liberalization measures be carefully planned taking into account the pace and timing of other reforms which are being undertaken to minimize the undesirable side-effects of full liberalization.

Therefore, implementation of the first-stage liberalization is scheduled to start on April 1, 1999. Implementation of the second-stage of liberalization measures is planned to be completed by the end of 2000 at the latest following completion of ongoing structural reforms in the banking and corporate sectors. These reforms will strengthen prudential regulatory and supervisory standards for financial institutions, and also ensure that firms behave according to market principles, primarily through improvements in corporate transparency and governance. Even before the enactment of the new law, some urgent liberalization measures went into effect after July 1, 1998. The following sections outline the principal elements, and timing, of the foreign exchange liberalization program.

MAJOR CONTENTS OF LIBERALIZATION MEASURES

Introduction of a negative list system in place of the current positive system for capital account transactions

Liberalization of all capital account transactions related to business activities of firms and financial institutions including firms' short-term borrowings from abroad

Non-residents will be allowed to issue won-denominated securities abroad.

Foreign exchange business will be permitted to all financial institutions meeting the requirements. All restrictions on money exchange bureau businesses will be removed.

The real demand restriction on spot and forward market transactions will be removed, and the commercial foreign currency brokerage system will be introduced.

SECOND STAGE LIBERALIZATION: BY THE END OF 2000

Liberalization of those capital account transactions that remained restricted in the first stage; except for those related to national security and the prevention of criminal activities.

This stage of liberalization will include:

- non-residents' investment in won- denominated domestic deposits with maturities less than 1 year.

- resident individuals' investment in foreign-currency denominated overseas deposits, etc.

3. Immediate Liberalization measures
(Effective date : July 1, 1998)

☐Transactions related to inward foreign investments

In order to facilitate foreign investment in Korea, all foreign exchange transactions related to foreign direct investment, equity investment, or mergers and acquisitions of Korean companies by foreign investors was liberalized on July 1, 1998. The only exceptions to this sweeping liberalization measure would be those transactions involving offshore Korean won or domestic won-denominated deposits, which would have rather serious implications for the sound management of domestic money supply.

More specifically, the following liberalization measures was implemented on July 1, 1998:

¤Lift the restrictions on foreign investment in short-term financial instruments such as CDs and RPs;

¤Allow foreigners' investment in over-the-counter (OTC) stocks and local real estates (including commercial buildings);

For additional analytical, business and investment opportunities information, please contact Global Investment & Business Center, USA at (202) 546-2103. Fax: (202) 546-3275. E-mail: rusric@erols.com

¤Abolish the designated foreign exchange bank system so that foreign investors who wish to invest in equities and bonds issued by listed companies will not be required to handle all of their transactions through the same, single foreign exchange bank based in Seoul;

Transactions related to residents' foreign borrowings

All restrictions on the use of foreign borrowing for short-term trade financing was abolished on July 1, 1998. More specifically, the restrictions on the maximum maturities as well as the types of import goods eligible for deferred import payment (usance letters of credit) was completely lifted. The restriction on the receipt of down-payments for exports and the maximum period for advance payments for exports (currently 180 days) was abolished.

We also believe that, to allow unlimited access to foreign funding and thus to facilitate ongoing corporate restructuring efforts, the medium-term foreign borrowings by domestic business firms was liberalized. More specifically, the current restrictions on foreign borrowings and issuance of foreign bonds with maturities of between one and three years was lifted on July 1, 1998.

Another important area of liberalization is FX position at the foreign exchange banks. The ceiling on the consolidated over-bought and over-sold positions of banks was raised to 15% of the banks net assets. Separate ceiling on spot positions was repealed. Prior to the revision, the consolidated over-bought and over-sold positions of foreign exchange banks could not exceed 15% and 10% of their net assets respectively. However, there was a separate regulation on spot currency position, which limited the spot over-bought and spot over-sold position to below 5% of the net asset.

4. First Stage Liberalization Measures
(effective date : April 1, 1999)

☐**Current account liberalization**

Except for a few types of international current transactions, all current account transactions by business firms and banks other than individuals will be fully liberalized on April 1, 1999. This will bring the number of transaction types on the negative list down from 20 to only five. These five restrictions are mostly on individuals' transactions, such as ceilings on travel expense or gift or donation abroad. Also, some of them will remain in effect out of concerns about national security and prevention of criminal activities, such as money-laundering drug-trafficking.

Some of the noteworthy changes that will be made at this stage are as follows:

¤Payments for invisibles which previously required individual licenses, such as the payments for consulting services, commissions for trade brokering, and research and development (R&D) expenses incurred by overseas subsidiary companies;

¤Allow all Koreans living abroad to ship out their domestic wealth, subject only to the notification to local tax authority;

¤Restrictions on payment methods should also be abolished so that firms and individuals can pay and settle expenses through netting and third-party payments. This will greatly save foreign exchange transaction cost for export and import companies.

For additional analytical, business and investment opportunities information,
please contact Global Investment & Business Center, USA
at (202) 546-2103. Fax: (202) 546-3275. E-mail: rusric@erols.com

☐Capital account liberalization

In the process of capital account liberalization, two key objectives have been targeted. First, the legal, regulatory framework should be changed from a Positive List System to a Negative List System: in order to enhance transparency, all capital account transactions should be liberalized unless otherwise specifically prohibited by negative list. Second, the degree of capital account liberalization should continuously be enhanced to meet the OECD requirement, if not fully. At this stage, our goal is to liberalize 72 of the 91 types of transactions specified by the OECD Codes of Liberalization of Capital Movements. Currently, only 49 items are liberalized. More specifically:

¤ All domestic foreign exchange transactions, including forward transactions involving foreign currency or domestic currency, will be exempt from "the real demand principle" requirement. Thus businesses will no longer have to prove business purpose to purchase forward currency. This will promote the development of an efficient domestic foreign exchange forwards market and allow for the hedging of Korean investment risks.

¤ All derivative transactions through foreign exchange banks will also be permitted.

¤ Firms' short-term overseas borrowings with maturities of less than one year will be liberalized.(Borrowings with maturities of one year and above will have been liberalized in 1998.)

¤ Non-residents will be permitted to open domestic won deposit accounts with maturities of more than one year, and to freely withdraw funds from those accounts.

¤ Institutional investors (such as securities companies, insurance companies, and pension funds) will also be permitted to extend overseas loans without limit (US$300,000 currently).

¤ In order to support their global activities, business firms and financial institutions will be permitted to pursue foreign direct investment in the financial services industry in areas such as banking, insurance, leasing and finance companies. Business firms and financial institutions will also be permitted to freely open overseas branches.

¤ Business firms and financial institutions, other than individuals, will be permitted to make foreign direct investment in real estate as well.

¤ Offshore transactions in the won will be liberalized, permitting non-residents to issue won-denominated securities abroad, which is expected to contribute to the internationalization of won.

☐Expand foreign exchange banks and exchange bureaus

In order to reduce inefficiencies stemming from the selective licensing of foreign exchange banks, any financial institutions that meet the certain conditions required to maintain an effective ex-post transaction management system should be allowed to participate in foreign exchange businesses. However, the complete liberalization of foreign exchange businesses, which extends the businesses to non-financial institutions, should be undertaken in the second stage.

More specifically, the current approval system for foreign exchange banks will be replaced by a less onerous registration system.

To lower entry barrier to the money exchange bureau business, we also recommend that the current approval requirement be replaced by less stringent registration requirement. However, the participants will be required to check customers' identifications and report ex post in order to prevent such problems as money laundering.

☐Development of the foreign exchange market

An efficient, well-functioning foreign exchange market will be developed through the following measures:

¤The Fund Intermediation Office will be privatized, and other commercial foreign exchange brokerage firms will be subsequently established. This will establish a professional foreign exchange brokerage system.

¤The current exchange rate system (the Market Average Exchange Rate System) means the daily quotations of market average exchange rates do not reflect the most recent market conditions. This method of computing the daily averages will be reviewed so quoted rates reflect market conditions more accurately.

¤The internationalization of Korean won will be pursued by liberalizing overseas trade in won and allowing foreigners to issue won-denominated securities abroad. The regulations on overseas deposit accounts will be relaxed to facilitate overseas financial trade.

5. Second Stage Liberalization Measures
(Effective on January 1, 2001)

☐Current account liberalization

The ex ante reporting system will no longer be applied to all but foreign exchange transactions that may harm international peace and cause public disorder.

The examples of those current transactions that remained restrictive in the first stage are:

¤Remittance of individuals' gift money or contributions with no ceiling;

¤Travel expenses without any limit;

¤Moving and settlement expenses without any limit;

¤Importation and exportation of payment instruments without any limit.

☐Capital account liberalization

Capital account transactions that remained restricted in the first stage will be liberalized, for example:

¤Overseas borrowings by the business firms of less than one-year maturity will be completely liberalized; ¤Foreigners' investment in won-denominated domestic deposits and in OTC derivative products even without the intermediation through foreign exchange banks will be permitted;

¤Resident individuals' investment in overseas deposits, (which is currently permitted up to $50,000) and in overseas real estates (which is currently permitted up to $300,000) will be completely liberalized; As a result, Korea's liberalization ratio will improve to the mid-group level of OECD members, meeting 85 of 91 items in the OECD Liberalization Code of Capital Movements.

☐Foreign exchange businesses liberalization

The foreign exchange bank system will be completely repealed, which means that the foreign exchange businesses will be allowed to all juridical persons and natural persons, including the business firms and individuals. Also, the money exchange bureau will completely be liberalized: even the registration requirement will be eliminated.

☐Foreign exchange market liberalization

All foreign exchange transactions including those tradings of forward exchanges and derivatives not intermediated by foreign exchange banks will be liberalized. For example, resident individuals are permitted to deal directly with overseas financial institutions. Together with the complete free entry into the foreign exchange businesses, this liberalization measure will greatly contribute to the deepening of foreign exchange market.

Also in this stage, the genuine free floating exchange rate system will be introduced.

6. Post-Liberalization Management System

Managing full liberalization of foreign exchange and capital movements poses many challenges. Unless carefully overseen, rapid liberalization can also result in rapid growth in bank assets, corporate over-indebtedness and asset price bubbles.

☐Emergency Safeguard Measures

A legal framework will be introduced through which the Korean government will be permitted to take safeguard measures when necessary. However, the terms and conditions for invoking emergency safeguard measures will be very stringent and will conform to international standards, such as the balance of payment safeguard provisions in the WTO or MAI. One example of such emergency measures is:

¤ Variable Deposit Requirements(VDR) : A certain percentage of foreign borrowings will be placed with the central bank in interest-free deposits for a fixed period of one year. In some countries, this measure has been effective in discouraging short-term capital inflows.

☐Macroeconomic policy measures

Monetary policy targeting the exchange rate and the short-term interest rate through indirect and market-based investments will be complemented by fiscal tools such as government bond issues

For additional analytical, business and investment opportunities information,
please contact Global Investment & Business Center, USA
at (202) 546-2103. Fax: (202) 546-3275. E-mail: rusric@erols.com

and tax instruments. Monetary policy will be closely coordinated with fiscal policy, and there will be an appropriate policy mix between the two.

Furthermore, to improve consistency between monetary policy and fiscal position, the government will establish a joint policy committee which includes agencies involved in macroeconomic policy-making. Cross-border capital movements will be closely monitored by a comprehensive foreign exchange monitoring network, which will soon be in place. The purpose of the monitoring network will be to provide real-time information to allow the government to take timely safeguard measures. An early warning system, utilizing a range of economic forecasting models and currency crisis indicators, will be installed with technical assistance from the World Bank during this year.

Microeconomic measures

Radical changes in the operating environment for banks will mean an increase in banking risk. Therefore, liberalization will be accompanied by prior or concurrent measures to strengthen the supervisory framework.

Prudential regulations will be strictly enforced on financial institutions to reduce excessive risk exposures. They will include strict enforcement of foreign exchange exposure limits, introduction of consolidated limits for banks including their offshore branches, tighter regulation of foreign currency maturity mismatch risk, and introduction of internal liquidity control systems.

Market supervision of firms' activities will also be very tight. The disclosure system for listed companies will be made more transparent and the supervisory role of banks will be strengthened. Specifically:

¤ Improvement of management transparency through consolidated financial statements, imposition of internationally- recognized accounting standards and so on.

¤ Introduction of a separate accounting and disclosure system for firms' foreign exchange transactions.

¤ Strengthening of banks' supervisory roles on firms' foreign exchange operations.

Tax incentives, such as those to encourage the use of debt instruments that have the characteristics of long-term capital, will be established, and a legal framework will also be set up to reduce the risk of capital flight and money laundering.

Computerized network system

A comprehensive computer network will be instituted through which individual foreign exchange transactions will be recorded in the computer system in the foreign exchange information center. Information collected in the center will be accessible, at any time, to monetary and supervisory authorities.

¤ By the end of March, 1999, the construction of the computerized network system will be completed.

7. Effects of Liberalization

Liberalizing foreign exchange and capital flows in Korea will enhance the efficiency of the local financial market.

¤ The breadth and depth of the foreign exchange market will be improved as new participants enter the market, and transaction volumes are expected to increase substantially.

¤ Deregulation of the designated foreign exchange bank system will enhance competition in domestic financial markets.

¤ Abolition of "real demand principles" for forward or derivative transactions will increase liquidity in the foreign exchange market and enable market participants to manage exchange risk.

By enhancing foreign investor confidence in the Korean economy, foreign exchange liberalization is also expected to induce a substantial increase in foreign capital inflows.

To summarize, the government's guiding principles for foreign exchange reform are :

¤A simplified transparent framework

¤Full liberalization in line with OECD benchmarks

These measures can be expected to raise international confidence in the Korean financial system, and result in substantial capital inflows.

FOREIGN TRADE ACT

GENERAL PROVISIONS

Article 1 (Purpose)

The purpose of this Act is to contribute to the growth of the national economy by means of promoting foreign trade, maintaining the balance of international payments and making arrangements for the expansion of commerce by establishing the fair trade system.

Article 2 (Definitions)

The definitions of terms used in this Act shall be as follows:

1.The term "trade" means exports and imports of goods;

2.The term "goods" means movables other than documents evidencing means of payment, securities, and obligations determined by the Foreign Exchange Control Act;

3.The term "trader" means any person who is entrusted in whole or in part, with the importation or exportation of goods, or who engages, in whole or in part, in the exportation or importation of goods by himself, for instance, exporters or importers, any person who is entrusted by overseas exporters or importers, and any person who entrusts someone with the exportation or importation of goods;

4.The term "trade business" means a business of dealing with any kind of trade;

5.The term "trade agency business" means a business in which anyone entrusted by overseas importers or exporters (including branch offices or local agents of overseas importers or exporters) makes contracts or performs other functions related thereto, in Korean territory, for purchasing goods to be exported from the country or for making imports of goods; and

6.The term "design" means what can be identified by its appearance falling under any of the following items:

(a) Features of shape, configuration, or color of goods, or combination thereof; or

(b)The status of changes in the case where the functions of goods change.

Article 3 (Principle of Free and Fair Trade, etc.)

(1) Foreign trades in the Republic of Korea shall be based on the principle of free and fair trade in accordance with the treaties concerning trade which are concluded and promulgated under the Constitution of the Republic of Korea and the generally recognized international law.

(2) In case where there are provisions which restrict trade, in treaties on trade which are concluded and promulgated under this Act, other Acts, or the Constitution of the Republic of Korea and in the generally recognized international law, the Government of the Republic of Korea shall apply such restrictions within the limits necessary for achieving the purposes of such restrictions.

Article 4 (Measures for Promotion of Trade)

(1) The Minister of Trade, Industry and Energy may take measures for continuous increase of exports and imports of goods in accordance with the Presidential Decree, where it appears to him to be necessary for the promotion of trade.

(2) The Minister of Trade, Industry and Energy may provide supports for a person falling under any one of the following subparagraphs in accordance with the Presidential Decree, where it appears to him to be necessary for the promotion of trade mentioned in paragraph (1):

1.A person dealing with the business of advice, guidance, overseas advertisement, exhibition, training, consulting, etc., for the purpose of the promotion of trade;

2.A person dealing with the business of installing or operating trade exhibition grounds or trade training center, etc.; or

3.A person dealing with the business of establishing or operating the system of scientific administration of trade functions.

Article 5 (Special Measures as to Restrictions on Trade, etc.)

In case where it falls under any one of the following subparagraphs, the Minister of Trade, Industry and Energy may restrict or prohibit exports and imports of goods in accordance with the Presidential Decree:

1.In case where the Republic of Korea or its trade partner (hereinafter referred to as the "trade partner") is involved in war, or natural disaster;

2.In case in which a trade partner denies rights and benefits of the Republic of Korea recognized by treaties and the generally recognized international law;

3.In case in which trade country imposes unfair or discriminatory burdens or restrictions upon Korean trade;

4.In case where it is necessary to discharge duties for the maintenance of international peace and security under treaties on trade concluded and promulgated by the Constitution of the Republic of Korea and the generally recognized international law; or

5.In case where it is necessary for the protection of life, health and safety of human beings, the protection of life and health of animals or plants, the protection and preservation environment or the protection of domestic resources.

Article 6 (Consultation, etc. as to Acts and Subordinate Statutes on Trade)

(1) As to trade, this Act shall apply.

(2) The head of the administrative authority concerned shall seek consultation with the Minister of Trade, Industry and Energy in advance, where he intends to enact or amend Acts and subordinate statutes, directives or public notices (hereinafter referred to as the "guidelines of exports and imports") restricting exports and imports of goods. In this case, the Minister of Trade, Industry and Energy may request the head of the administrative authority concerned to adjust guidelines of exports and imports.

Article 7 (Establishment of Trade Policy Council)

(1) The Trade Policy Council (hereinafter referred to as the "Council")

shall be established in to the Ministry of Trade, Industry and Energy to deliberate important matters as to the trade policy.

(2) As to the organization and operation of the Council, the necessary matters shall be determined by the Presidential Decree.

PROMOTION OF COMMERCE

Article 8 (Establishment of Plans for Promotion of Commerce)

(1) The Minister of Trade, Industry and Energy shall establish plans for the promotion of commerce of the following year so as to promote trade and commerce every year.

(2) Plans for the promotion of commerce under paragraph (1) shall contain matters indicated in the following subparagraphs:

1. Purposes of plans for the promotion of commerce;

2. Analysis and forecast of conditions of international commerce;

3. Action plans for trade related negotiations and overseas industrial cooperation;

4. Supporting measures for exploration of foreign markets such as advice, guidance, overseas advertisement, exhibition, consulting, education and training of professional manpower, etc. for the promotion of commerce;

5. Schemes for collection, analysis, and use of commercial information; and

6. Other matters as determined by the Presidential Decree.

(3) The Minister of Trade, Industry and Energy may investigate the commerce systems and practices of trade partners, and difficulties for Korean companies doing business overseas, so as to collect primary materials necessary for the establishment of plans for the promotion of commerce under paragraph (1).

(4) The Minister of Trade, Industry and Energy may request Korean companies doing business overseas to provide necessary materials for the establishment of plans for the promotion of commerce under paragraph (1) and, if necessary, may take supporting measures.

(5) In case of the establishment of plans for the promotion of commerce under paragraph (1), the Minister of Trade, Industry and Energy shall seek, in advance, opinions from the Seoul Special Metropolitan City Mayor, Metropolitan City Mayors, or *Do* governors (hereinafter referred to as the "Mayor/*Do* governor"), and shall give notice with regard to such plans to the Mayor/*Do* governors after the establishment of plans for the promotion of commerce. The same shall also apply in case of changing such plans.

(6) The Mayor/*Do* governor shall establish and implement appropriate plans for the promotion of commerce in each jurisdictional area, when he receives the notice of plans for the promotion of commerce under paragraph (5).

(7) The Mayor/*Do* governor shall give notice to the Minister of Trade, Industry and Energy, when he has established plans for the promotion of commerce in each jurisdictional area in accordance with paragraph (6). The same shall also apply in case of changing such plans.

Article 9 (Assistance, etc. for Cooperative Activities by Private Sectors)

(1) In case where the administrative authorities or organizations involving trade and commerce conduct cooperative activities in commerce, industry, technology, energy, etc. with the Government, local governments, administrative authorities or organizations of trade partners, the Minister of Trade, Industry and Energy may provide necessary assistance pursuant to the Presidential Decree.

(2) The Minister of Trade, Industry and Energy may provide necessary information for local governments and companies by collecting and analyzing systematically information from the administrative bodies or organizations relating to trade and commerce so as to assist companies to explore foreign markets.

TRANSACTIONS OF EXPORTS OR IMPORTS

SECTION 1 Trade

Business and Trade Agency

Business

Article 10 (Notice, etc. of Trade Business)

(1) Any person who intends to do trade business or trade agency business shall give notice to the Minister of Trade, Industry and Energy. The same shall also apply in case where he intends to change important matters provided for in the Presidential Decree and indicated in the notice.

(2) In relation to contents or procedures, etc. of the notice under paragraph (1), the necessary matters shall be determined by the Presidential Decree.

(3) The Minister of Trade, Industry and Energy shall issue a certificate of complete notice of trade business or trade agency business to the person who gives notice in accordance with the provisions of paragraph (1).

Article 11 (Exemption, etc. from Giving Notice of Trade Business)

As to exports and imports of goods falling under any one of the following subparagraphs, the provisions of Article 10 shall not apply:

1. Imports of goods by government agencies, local governments, or government-invested institutions as prescribed by the Presidential Decree for their own uses;

2. Introduction of foreign capitals in accordance with the Foreign Investment and Foreign Capital Inducement Act;

3. Imports of goods by educational establishments or research institutes or other non-profit making corporations as prescribed by the Presidential Decree for their own uses;

4. Exports and imports of goods without payment of the price; or

5. Exports and imports of goods under the level determined by the Presidential Decree, or in particular circumstances.

Article 12 (Succession, etc. of Status of Trade Business)

(1) In cases where a trader or trade agency transfers his business or dies, or where a juristic person doing trade business or trade agency business has been merged into another, the

For additional analytical, business and investment opportunities information,
please contact Global Investment & Business Center, USA
at (202) 546-2103. Fax: (202) 546-3275. E-mail: rusric@erols.com

transferee or successor, or the juristic person which remains or is created after the merger, may succeed to the status of the trader or the trade agency.

(2) In cases where a trader or trade agency as an individual is converted into a juristic person, and the juristic person meets the criteria provided for in the Presidential Decree, such a juristic person may succeed to the status of the trader or trade agency as an individual.

(3) Any person who intends to succeed to the status of a trader or trade agency in accordance with the provisions of paragraph (1) or (2), shall give notice to the Minister of Trade, Industry and Energy within two months after the occurrence of grounds for succession.

SECTION 2 General Provisions as to Transactions of

Exports or Imports

Article 13 (Principles of Exports and Imports)

(1) Subject to the purposes of this Act, exports and imports of goods, and collection and payment of the price thereto shall be made free.

(2) A trader shall carry out the transactions concerned in good faith under his own responsibility so as to obtain a certain level of overseas credit and to maintain good orders in a free trade system.

Article 14 (Restrictions, etc. on Exports and Imports)

(1) The Minister of Trade, Industry and Energy may restrict exports and imports of goods, where it appears to him to be necessary to carry out duties under the treaties concluded and promulgated under the Constitution of the Republic of Korea and the generally recognized international law, and to preserve living resources.

(2) Anyone shall seek an approval of the Minister of Trade, Industry and Energy, where he intends to export or import goods which are determined by the criteria prescribed in the Presidential Decree for the purpose of promoting balance of trade, or goods designated by the Minister of Trade, Industry and Energy in order to carry out duties under treaties concluded and promulgated under the Constitution of the Republic of Korea and the generally recognized international law, and to preserve living resources: *Provided,* That this shall not apply to exports and imports of goods falling under the criteria prescribed in the Presidential Decree, such as goods for imminent purposes, or goods for which the procedures of exports or imports need to be simplified.

(3) Any person who intends to change important matters determined by the Presidential Decree from among those approved by paragraph (2) shall seek an approval of changes from the Minister of Trade, Industry and Energy, and any person who intends to change other minor contents shall give notice of such changes to the Minister of Trade, Industry and Energy.

(4) The Minister of Trade, Industry and Energy may, where it appears to him to be necessary, restrict quantity, price, and standards of each item which is subject to approval as referred to under paragraphs (1) and (2), and export and import areas.

For additional analytical, business and investment opportunities information, please contact Global Investment & Business Center, USA at (202) 546-2103. Fax: (202) 546-3275. E-mail: rusric@erols.com

(5) The Minister of Trade, Industry and Energy shall give public notice with regard to restrictions on or procedures of exports and imports determined in accordance with paragraphs (1) through (4).

(6) Any person who obtains export license or export approval pursuant to Article 21 or 22 shall be deemed to have obtained export approval under paragraph (2).

Article 15 (Consolidated Public Notice)

(1) In the case of the enactment or amendment of guidelines of exports and imports, the heads of the administrative authorities concerned shall submit the guidelines of exports and imports to the Minister of Trade, Industry and Energy so that the public notice on enactments or amendments may be given under paragraph (2) before the entry into force of the guidelines of exports and imports concerned.

(2) The Minister of Trade, Industry and Energy shall give public notice after consolidating such guidelines of exports and imports as submitted in accordance with paragraph (1).

Article 16 (Permission, etc. of Specific Forms of Trade)

(1) The Minister of Trade, Industry and Energy may permit specific forms of export or import transactions of goods provided for in the Presidential Decree so as to facilitate exports or imports of such goods.

(2) In relation to the permission of forms of export or import transactions pursuant to paragraph (1), the Minister of Trade, Industry and Energy shall seek in advance consultation with the Minister of Finance and Economy in accordance with the Presidential Decree, where the transaction form concerned is considered as falling under such categories as requiring the method of settlement of account which needs to be authorized by the Minister of Finance and Economy in accordance with Article 17 or 18 of the Foreign Exchange Control Act.

(3) The Minister of Finance and Economy shall consult in advance with the Minister of Trade, Industry and Energy, where he intends to determine the method of settlement of trade account pursuant to Acts and subordinate statutes relating to the control of foreign exchange.

Article 17 (Confirmation of Performance of Exports and Imports)

The Minister of Trade, Industry and Energy shall confirm each matter of the following subparagraphs:

1.Whether a person who has obtained approval or approval of changes as to the exportation or importation of goods in accordance with the main sentence of Article 14 (2) or paragraph (3) of the same Article, exports or imports goods as approved;

2.Whether exported or imported goods without approval (limited to goods under the main sentence of Article 14 (2)) are those goods under the proviso of Article 14 (2); or

3.Whether a person having permission by Article 16 (1) exports or imports goods as permitted.

Article 18 (Establishment of System of Scientific Administration of Trade Functions)

(1) The Minister of Trade, Industry and Energy shall make every effort to establish the system of scientific administration of trade functions, for instance, electronic document exchange system, etc. so as to maintain good order or to perform functions effectively in the export or import trade.

(2) The Minister of Trade, Industry and Energy may request the heads of the administrative authorities concerned to provide information on the export or import trade of goods, for instance, customs clearance records, where it appears to him to be necessary to establish the system of scientific administration of trade functions under paragraph (1). In this case, the heads of the administrative authorities concerned shall give assistance to the requests.

(3) The heads of administrative authorities concerned may make requests for the information on the export or import trade of goods gathered under the provisions of paragraphs (1) and (2), where it appears to him to be necessary for the purposes of this Act. In this case, the Minister of Trade, Industry and Energy shall give assistance to that.

SECTION 3 Importation of Raw Materials and

Machinery for Obtaining Foreign Currencies

Article 19 (Import Approval, etc. of Raw Materials and Machinery for Obtaining Foreign Currencies)

(1) The Minister of Trade, Industry and Energy may not apply the provisions of Article 14 (4) to imports of raw materials, equipments, machinery, and manufactured goods (hereinafter referred to as the "materials or machinery") used for obtaining foreign currencies, for instance, through exports of goods: *Provided,* That in cases where it appears to him to be necessary to encourage the use of domestic materials or machinery, this shall not apply.

(2) The Minister of Trade, Industry and Energy shall prescribe and give public notice as to categories, items, and quantity of materials or machinery under paragraph (1).

(3) Any person who imports, or entrusts importation of materials or machinery to obtain foreign currencies, shall obtain foreign currencies corresponding to the amount of such imports: *Provided,* That in cases where he acquires approval of the Minister of Trade, Industry and Energy pursuant to Article 20, this shall not apply.

(4) The target amount of foreign currencies under paragraph (3), the period during which foreign currencies shall be obtained, or other necessary matters shall be determined by the Presidential Decree.

Article 20 (Use, etc. of Materials or Machinery for Purposes Other than to Obtain Foreign Currencies)

(1) Where anyone who imported materials or machinery pursuant to Article 19 (1), intends to use, for unavoidable causes, the imported materials or machinery, or manufactured goods made of the materials or made by the machinery for other purposes for which such materials or machinery has been originally imported, he shall seek an approval from the Minister of Trade, Industry and Energy in accordance with the Presidential Decree, save for materials or machinery, or manufactured goods made of the materials or made by the machinery determined by the Presidential Decree.

(2) In cases where a person intends to transfer materials or machinery imported pursuant to Article 19 (1), or manufactured goods made of such materials or made by the machinery to a person who wants to use or export them for purposes for which such materials or machinery has been originally imported, both of them shall seek an approval from the Minister of Trade, Industry and Energy, save for such materials or machinery as determined by the Presidential Decree.

(3) The provisions of Article 19 (3) and (4) shall apply *mutatis mutandis* to the transferee of materials or machinery, or manufactured goods made of such materials or made by the machinery in accordance with paragraph (2).

SECTION 4 Exportation or Importation of Strategic

Materials

Article 21 (Export License, etc. of Strategic Materials)

(1) The Minister of Trade, Industry and Energy may make restrictions, such as requiring a person intending to export goods placed on the public notice by the Minister of Trade, Industry and Energy (hereinafter referred to as the "strategic materials") to seek an export license from the heads of the administrative bodies concerned, or may issue an import certificate to an applicant intending to import strategic materials, when it appears to him to be necessary for the maintenance of international peace and security, and the national security.

(2) In relation to the restrictions on exports or issuance of an import certificate of strategic materials under paragraph (1), necessary matters shall be determined and given public notice by the Minister of Trade, Industry and Energy.

(3) The public notice pursuant to paragraph (2) shall contain matters relating to strategic materials falling under any of the following subparagraphs:

1.Items and standards;

2.Geographic areas to which exports are not allowed;

3.Procedures of export license and issuance of import certificate; and

4.Other relevant matters as to exports and imports.

SECTION 5 Export of Industrial Plants

Article 22 (Approval, etc. of Export of Industrial Plants)

(1) In the case of application for an export approval for one of the following subparagraphs (hereinafter referred to as the "export of industrial plants"), the Minister of Trade, Industry and Energy may approve the export of the industrial plants concerned pursuant to the Presidential Decree. The same shall also apply in case of changing the matters approved:

1.Exports of industrial plants of not less than a level specified by the Minister of Trade, Industry and Energy from among plants determined by the Presidential Decree, and from among machinery and equipments to be installed to conduct agriculture, forestry, fishing, mining, manufacturing, electricity, gas and water supply, transportation, warehousing, broadcasting and telecommunications businesses; or

2.Exports of industrial plants, technical services, and construction in package (hereinafter referred to as the "exports by package order basis contracts")

(2) The Minister of Trade, Industry and Energy shall seek opinions from the heads of the administrative authorities concerned as to the validity of exports of industrial plants, when it appears to him to be necessary to decide whether he gives an approval or an approval of change, in accordance with paragraph (1). In this case, he shall give, without delay, opinions to the Minister of Trade, Industry and Energy, unless there are justifiable reasons to deny such requests.

(3) The Minister of Trade, Industry and Energy shall seek in advance the consent of the Minister of Labor and the Minister of Construction and Transportation, when he intends to give an approval or an approval of change, to exports by package order basis contracts. In this case it is deemed that a report has been made as to an offer of overseas employment pursuant to the Employment Security Act, in the case of the consent of the Minister of Labor, and that a report has been made as to action plans on overseas construction works pursuant to the of Overseas Construction Promotion Act, in the case of the consent of the Ministry of Construction and Transportation.

(4) As to exports of construction services or civil engineering sectors by a package order basis, the Minister of Trade, Industry and Energy may give an approval or an approval of change, only to contractors performing overseas construction under the Overseas Construction Promotion Act.

(5) In case where export of industrial plants is approved, or where an approval of change thereon is given pursuant to paragraph (1), the Minister of Trade, Industry and Energy shall give notice without delay to the heads of the administrative authorities concerned.

(6) A person who intends to export industrial plants may organize projects as to market research, exchange of information, reception of orders, and cooperative works in relation to such exports. In this case, the Minister of Trade, Industry and Energy may designate an administrative authority or associations relating to exports of industrial plants to carry out functions for the promotion of those projects.

SECTION 6 Marking etc. of Country of Origin

Article 23 (Marking of Country of Origin of Exported or Imported Goods)

(1) In cases where the Minister of Trade, Industry and Energy gives public notice on goods which are required to have marks of the country of origin so as to maintain the fair trade system (hereinafter referred to as the "goods requiring the mark of the country of origin"), any person intending to export those goods shall mark the country of origin of those goods.

(2) As to methods of marking or confirming the country of origin under paragraph (1), other necessary matters shall be determined by the Presidential Decree.

(3) In relation to the mark of the country of origin of goods, no trader or seller of goods may conduct activities falling under any one of the following subparagraphs:

For additional analytical, business and investment opportunities information, please contact Global Investment & Business Center, USA at (202) 546-2103. Fax: (202) 546-3275. E-mail: rusric@erols.com

1.Acts to make false or misleading marks of the country of origin; or

2.Acts to damage or modify marks of the country of origin.

(4) The Minister of Trade, Industry and Energy may inspect imported goods, when it appears to him to be necessary to confirm whether there are violations of the provisions of paragraph (1) or (3).

Article 24 (Determination, etc. of Country of Origin)

(1) The Minister of Trade, Industry and Energy may determine the country of origin of exported or imported goods, where it appears to him to be necessary.

(2) According to the Presidential Decree, standards for the determination of the country of origin shall be established and given public notice by the Minister of Trade, Industry and Energy.

(3) A trader or seller of goods may request the Minister of Trade, Industry and Energy to determine the country of origin of exported or imported goods.

(4) In relation to such requests under paragraph (3), the Minister of Trade, Industry and Energy shall give notice to the requesting person as to the determination of the country of origin of the goods concerned.

(5) In cases where a person to whom a notice has been given under paragraph (4) intends to challenge the determination of the country of origin, he may submit complaints to the Minister of Trade, Industry and Energy within thirty days after the receipt of the notice.

(6) In relation to the submission of complaints under paragraph (5), the Minister of Trade, Industry and Energy shall give notice of decisions as to complaints within a hundred and fifty days after receipt of complaints.

(7) Matters necessary for procedures of the determination of the country of origin, such as the request for determination of the country of origin, or the submission of complaints, shall be prescribed by the Presidential Decree.

Article 25 (Submission of Certificate of Country of Origin of Imported goods)

(1) The Minister of Trade, Industry and Energy may require a person intending to import goods to submit certificates of the country of origin issued by the country in which the goods concerned are produced or shipped, where it appears to him to be necessary to confirm the country of origin.

(2) Matters concerning the submission of certificates of the country of origin or the confirmation of the country origin under paragraph (1) shall be prescribed by the Presidential Decree.

INVESTIGATION, ETC. OF INJURY TO INDUSTRY CAUSED BY IMPORTS

SECTION 1 Requests and Investigation

Article 26 (Requests for Investigation as to Injury to Domestic Industry Caused by Increase of Certain Imported Goods)

(1) In cases where a domestic industry is considered to fall under any of the following subparagraphs, any person who has interest in the domestic industry, and the head of the administrative authority concerned with the domestic industry may request the Trade Committee under Article 32 (hereinafter referred to as "Trade Committee") to investigate injury to the domestic industry caused by imports of the goods concerned or supply of trade and distribution services:

1.In case where increased imports of particular goods concerned have caused or are threatening to cause serious injury to the domestic industry that produces like or directly competitive goods;

2.In case where the increased supply of trade and distribution services by foreigner (including a juristic person founded by the Acts of the Republic of Korea, more than half of whose shares or stocks is held by foreigners) has caused or is threatening to cause serious injury to the domestic industry that produces like or directly competitive trade and distribution services; or

3.In case where imports of goods in violation of patent right, utility model right, design right, trademark right, copyright, neighboring rights, program right, right on lay-out designs of integrated circuits, which are under domestic protection or are threatening to cause serious injury to the domestic industry that produces like or directly competitive goods.

(2) Matters concerning the categories of persons who have interest in the domestic industry, and the procedures of requests under paragraph (1), shall be prescribed by the Presidential Decree.

Article 27 (Investigation of Injury to Domestic Industry Caused by Increase of Certain Imported Goods)

(1) In the case of requests by Article 26 (1), the Trade Committee shall decide whether to commence investigation after consulting with the heads of the administrative authorities concerned within thirty days from the date of requests, and give notice to the requester as to the decision.

(2) In cases where the Trade Committee, after considering it necessary, upon requests under Article 26 (1), or upon the result of investigation under subparagraph 7 of Article 35, to investigate injury to the domestic industry caused by imports of particular goods or by supply of trade and distribution services, commences the investigation, the Trade Committee shall make a determination as to the existence of injury to the domestic industry concerned within 120 days after the commencement of such investigation: *Provided,* That in cases where matters to be investigated are complicated, or where the requester requests with justifiable reasons, the period above to be extended, the period of investigation may be extended within the limit of not more than 120 days.

SECTION 2 Suggestion or Application of Safeguard

Measures

Article 28 (Suggestion, etc. of Temporary Import Restriction)

(1) In case where the Trade Committee determines that there exists injury to the domestic industry according to the result of investigation of injury to the domestic industry, the Trade Committee may set a time-limit of a certain period within 45 days after the determination, and suggest that the heads of the administrative authorities concerned to take measures falling under any of the following subparagraphs (hereinafter referred to as the "safeguard measures"):

1.Quantitative restrictions on imports of goods;

2.Adjustment of the tariff rate;

3.Supports for industries, agriculture, forestry, and fishing businesses, mining industry, small and medium enterprises, and technology in accordance with relevant Acts and subordinate statutes;

4.Designation of the industry, which is under investigation, as requiring rationalization pursuant to the Industrial Development Act;

5.Suspension or prohibition of imports of particular goods, or imports by particular traders (limited to the case falling under Article 26 (1) 3); or

6.Other measures determined by the Presidential Decree as necessary for safeguarding the domestic industry.

(2) In relation to the suggestion of safeguard measures under paragraph (1), the heads of the administrative authorities concerned shall determine within 45 days whether to take safeguard measures, and shall give notice to the Trade Committee: *Provided,* That the period mentioned above shall not include a period, during which preparatory measures for application of safeguard measures, such as consultation with the major interested countries or amendment of Acts and subordinate statutes, are necessary.

(3) In the case of taking safeguard measures, the heads of the administrative authorities concerned shall take into account impacts on the international trade relations and the national economy.

(4) In the case of safeguard measures under paragraph (2), the heads of the administrative authorities concerned shall withdraw such measures, where there are grounds to withdraw safeguard measures, for instance, the disappearance of grounds for safeguard measures. In this case, he may, if necessary, seek opinions from the Trade Committee.

Article 29 (Provisional Measures)

(1) Even if an investigation is proceeding in accordance with Article 27, the Trade Committee may suggest that the heads of the administrative authorities concerned take provisional safeguard measures equivalent to those under Article 28 (1) 2, where, unless urgent safeguard measures are taken, it appears that it has caused or is threatening to cause irreparable injury to the domestic industry, under the investigation.

(2) The main sentence of Article 28 (2) and the provisions of Article 28 (3) and (4) shall be applicable *mutatis mutandis* to provisional safeguard measures under paragraph (1) above.

Article 30 (Review)

(1) The Trade Committee may examine impacts or influences upon the domestic industry by safeguard measures taken by the heads of the administrative authorities concerned in accordance with Article 28 (2) or 29 (1), and suggest that the heads to modify the contents of the safeguard measures, withdraw such measures, or extend the period of application of such measures.

(2) The provisions of Article 28 (2) and (3) shall be applicable *mutatis mutandis* to cases falling under paragraph (1).

IMPORT RESTRICTIONS ON TEXTILE AND CLOTHING

Article 31 (Import Restrictions on Textiles and Clothing)

(1) The Minister of Trade, Industry and Energy may make import restrictions, where it appears to him that the increase of imports of textiles and clothing has caused or is threatening to cause serious injury to the domestic industry that produces like or directly competitive goods.

(2) In relation to import restrictions under paragraph (1), necessary matters as to goods and countries covered by such restrictions, scope of restrictions, and investigation procedures shall be determined by the Presidential Decree.

TRADE COMMITTEE

Article 32 (Establishment of Trade Committee)

(1) The Trade Committee shall be attached to the Ministry of Trade, Industry and Energy, so as to carry out investigation, determination, and suggestion of safeguard measures, which are necessary to remedy injury to the domestic industry caused by the increase of imports of particular goods, the increase of supply of trade and distribution services, or unfair imports.

(2) There shall be a trade research division in the Trade Committee for the performance of functions and duties of the Trade Committee, such as various investigations and research on international trade system under paragraph (1).

Article 33 (Composition, etc. of Trade Committee)

(1) The Trade Committee shall consist of commissioners of not more than nine, including a chairman.

(2) There shall be permanent commissioners, the number of whom shall be determined by the Presidential Decree.

(3) The chairman and other commissioners shall be appointed by the President upon the recommendation of the Minister of Trade, Industry and Energy from among those who have vast knowledge and experiences on industry, trade, commerce, law or accounting.

(4) The tenure of chairman and commissioners shall be three years and be renewable.

(5) In cases where the chairman may not perform his functions and duties for unavoidable reasons, one of permanent commissioners nominated in advance by the chairman shall carry out his duties.

Article 34 (Security of Status of Chairman and Commissioners)

No chairman or commissioner shall be dismissed from his office against his will, save for cases falling under any one of the following subparagraphs:

1.In cases where he is sentenced to punishment of imprisonment without prison labor or heavier; or

2.In cases where he cannot perform his duties for a long period because of physical or mental incapacity.

Article 35 (Functions of Trade Committee)

The functions of the Trade Committee shall include those mentioned in the following subparagraphs:

1.To decide whether to commence investigation and to determine whether there exists injury to industry under Article 27;

2.To make a suggestion for safeguard measures under Article 28 (1);

3.To make a suggestion for provisional safeguard measures under Article 29 (1);

4.To examine impacts or influences on the domestic industry, and to make a suggestion for modification or withdrawal of the safeguard measures concerned, or for the extension of the period of application in accordance with Article 30 (1);

5.To make a suggestion for investigation and orders for corrective measures, or imposition of penalty in accordance with Article 39 (3) and (4);

6.To decide whether to commence investigation for the imposition of anti-dumping duties and countervailing duties under Articles 10 and 13 of the Customs Duties Act, to investigate into facts of dumping and subsidization, to investigate and determine injury to the industry caused by such dumping and subsidization, and to make a suggestion for anti-dumping measures and countervailing measures, and for review, etc.;

7.To investigate impacts caused by imports of particular goods or by supply of trade and distribution services upon the competitiveness of the domestic industry;

8.To investigate and research rules and systems on international trade, and cases as to disputes relating to international trade; or

9.To investigate other matters which appear to the Trade Committee to be necessary for the promotion of fair trade, or to make a suggestion thereon.

Article 36 (Disqualification of Chairman or Commissioners)

No chairman or commissioner may take part in the deliberation or decision of a case falling under any one of the following subparagraphs:

1.Where he has personal interest in the result of the case;

2.Where his spouse, or relatives by blood of not more than 8th degree of relationship by consanguinity or relatives by marriage of not more than 4th degree of relationship by affinity has interest in the result of the case; or

3.Where he is a witness, expert witness or agent.

Article 37 (Quorum)

Meetings of the Trade Committee shall be convened by a majority of all the members, and decisions shall be made by a vote of a majority of commissioners present.

Article 38 (Provisions as to Organization and Operation)

Except for those prescribed by this Act, matters necessary for the organization and operation of the Trade Committee shall be prescribed by the Presidential Decree.

MAINTENANCE OF GOOD ORDER IN EXPORTS AND IMPORTS

Article 39 (Prohibition of Unfair Practices in Exports and Imports)

(1) No trader may conduct practices falling under any one of the following subparagraphs:

1.Exports and imports of goods which violate patent right, utility model right, design right, trademark right, copyright, neighboring rights, program copyright, right on lay-out designs of integrated circuits of semiconductor protected by Acts and subordinate statutes of the Republic of Korea or of trade partners;

2.Exports and imports of goods having fraudulent marks of country of origin, or damaged or modified marks of country of origin;

3.Other practices determined by the Presidential Decree as threatening to disturb good order in exports and imports; or

4.Practices which violate this Act, or orders or measures under this Act.

(2) The Minister of Trade, Industry and Energy may give public notice with regard to categories and standards of practices as determined by paragraph (1) 1 above.

(3) The Trade Committee may make an investigation to decide as to whether a trader has violated the provisions of paragraph (1) 1 through 3 in accordance with provisions of the Presidential Decree.

(4) In cases where violations of the provisions of paragraph (1) 1 through 3 are found to exist as a result of investigation under paragraph (3), the Trade Committee may suggest that the Minister of

For additional analytical, business and investment opportunities information,
please contact Global Investment & Business Center, USA
at (202) 546-2103. Fax: (202) 546-3275. E-mail: rusric@erols.com

Trade, Industry and Energy make orders for corrective measures or impose a penalty for violation of such provisions.

(5) In cases where the Minister of Trade, Industry and Energy has found that a trader had violated any of the provisions of subparagraphs of paragraph (1), or where the Trade Committee makes a suggestion pursuant to paragraph (4), the Minister of Trade, Industry and Energy may make orders for corrective measures, or may impose a penalty less than thirty million won.

(6) The categories of violations subject to the penalty under paragraph (5), the amount of penalty in accordance with levels of violations, and other necessary matters shall be prescribed by the Presidential Decree.

(7) The Minister of Trade, Industry and Energy may collect penalties in the same way as the handling of the national taxes in arrears, unless penalties are paid within the period of payment by a person upon whom penalty has been imposed under paragraph (5).

Article 40 (Prohibition of Disguised Price of Exported or Imported Goods)

No trader may disguise import or export prices of goods so as to transfer foreign currencies to abroad unlawfully.

Article 41 (Speedy Resolution of Trade Disputes between Traders)

(1) No trader may delay in resolving disputes without justifiable reasons, where there take place disputes on exports and imports of goods between traders in the Republic of Korea or between traders in the Republic of Korea and those in trade partners.

(2) In the case of disputes under paragraph (1), the Minister of Trade, Industry and Energy may require a trader to give oral statements as to the resolution of disputes, or to submit documents relating to such disputes.

(3) The Minister of Trade, Industry and Energy may investigate facts relating to such disputes, where it appears to him to be necessary after receiving documents or hearing opinions under paragraph (2).

(4) The Minister of Trade, Industry and Energy may recommend that traders make an arbitration agreement for the resolution of disputes, where it appears to him to be necessary for speedy and fair settlement of disputes under paragraph (1).

Article 42 (Conciliation, etc. of Disputes as to Preshipment Inspection)

(1) An organ which conducts preshipment inspection of goods exported by an enterprise upon contracts or mandates by the Government of an importing country, in the territory of the Republic of Korea (hereinafter referred to as "preshipment inspection entity"), shall comply with the Agreement on Preshipment Inspection of the World Trade Organization. In this case, the preshipment inspection entity shall not carry out preshipment inspection in a way to place barriers against exporting trades by an enterprise.

For additional analytical, business and investment opportunities information, please contact Global Investment & Business Center, USA at (202) 546-2103. Fax: (202) 546-3275. E-mail: rusric@erols.com

(2) In cases where there take place disputes between exporters and the preshipment inspection entity as to preshipment inspection, the Minister of Trade, Industry and Energy may conduct conciliation to resolve such disputes.

(3) An independent arbitral institution may be established by the Presidential Decree to administer arbitration as to disputes in paragraph (2).

Article 43 (Adjustment Orders for Maintenance of Good Order in Exports and Imports)

(1) The Minister of Trade, Industry and Energy may order traders to adjust price, quantity, quality, terms of transactions, or geographic areas to which goods are exported, or from which goods are imported, within the limits of each of the following subparagraphs, where the Presidential Decree provides for maintaining good order in exports and imports:

1.To contribute to the establishment of infrastructure for exports, development of new products, or exploration of overseas markets;

2.To prohibit from impairing or discriminating rights and benefits of other traders without reasonable causes; or

3.To make adjustment orders within limits sufficient enough to maintain good order in exports and imports of goods.

(2) The Minister of Trade, Industry and Energy may not give approvals, or may have the heads of the authorities concerned cease proceedings as to giving approvals pursuant to Article 14 (2), when it appears to him to be necessary to make orders for adjustment under paragraph (1).

Article 44 (Protection of Designs of Export Goods)

(1) The Minister of Trade, Industry and Energy may designate such goods as requiring the protection of designs of goods from among goods exported by a trader (hereinafter referred to as the "goods with designated designs"), where it appears to him to be necessary to promote the development of designs by preventing designs of export goods from being copied.

(2) The Minister of Trade, Industry and Energy shall designate an institution so as to deal with functions as to the registration and certification of designs of the goods concerned, when he designates goods as goods with designated designs under paragraph (1) (hereinafter referred to as a "design certification institution").

(3) In relation to the designation of goods with designated designs and design certification institution under paragraphs (1) and (2), the Minister of Trade, Industry and Energy shall give public notice of such designation.

(4) A trader may have designs of goods with designated designs registered at the design certification institution concerned.

(5) Any person intending to export goods with designated designs shall obtain, in advance, certificates from the design certification institution to the effect that designs of the goods concerned are not identical with or similar to the designs registered by other persons in accordance with paragraph (4).

(6) In relation to the designation, or revocation of designation, of goods with designated designs and a design certification institution, or the registration of designs, other necessary matters shall be prescribed by the Presidential Decree.

EXPORT AND IMPORT

ASSOCIATION, ETC.

Article 45 (Establishment, etc. of Association)

(1) Traders may establish, upon authorization of the Minister of Trade, Industry and Energy, export associations, import associations, or export- import associations (hereinafter referred to as "each association") so as to maintain good order in exports and imports of like or similar goods, or to improve mutual benefits among partners.

(2) Each association shall satisfy requirements falling under the following subparagraphs:

1.To contribute to maintaining good orders in exports and imports of goods;

2.To allow partners to join or withdraw voluntarily;

3.To allow partners to have equal voting rights in decision and election; and

4.To forbid activities for making profits.

(3) Each association shall be a juristic person.

(4) Each association shall be established upon the registration of establishment at the place of the head office.

(5) Each association shall have in its name of association such descriptions as "export association", "import association", or "export-import association."

(6) No person other than each association may use in his name such descriptions as "export association", "import association", "export-import association", or other similar denominations.

(7) Contents of articles of association, the operating and supervising of each association, or other necessary matters shall be prescribed by the Presidential Decree.

(8) The provisions of the Civil Act relating to corporate juristic person shall be applicable *mutatis mutandis* to each association, save for such matters as are provided for in this Act.

Article 46 (Projects of Each Association)

Each association shall carry out projects falling under the following subparagraphs:

1.Projects to maintain good orders in exports and imports of goods;

For additional analytical, business and investment opportunities information,
please contact Global Investment & Business Center, USA
at (202) 546-2103. Fax: (202) 546-3275. E-mail: rusric@erols.com

2.Projects to prevent unfair exporting or importing activities of goods;

3.Projects to conduct advertising, market research, transaction brokerage, and resolution of difficulties in exports and imports of goods;

4.Projects to improve quality and designs of exported or imported goods;

5.Projects to provide facilities for common use and financing brokerage so as to improve mutual benefits of partners;

6.Projects to export or import goods within limits to improve mutual benefits of partners;

7.Projects mandated by the Minister of Trade, Industry and Energy to maintain good order in exports and imports of goods; or

8.Other relevant projects determined by articles of each association.

Article 47 (Revocation of Authorization of Establishment of Each Association)

The Minister of Trade, Industry and Energy may revoke authorization given to each association under Article 45 (1) for grounds falling under any one of the following subparagraphs:

1.In cases where each association has obtained an authorization in fraudulent or unlawful ways;

2.In cases where each association does not satisfy the requirements under Article 45 (2); or

3.In cases where each association performs projects other than those prescribed by Article 46.

Article 48 (Designation of Comprehensive Trade Enterprises)

(1) The Minister of Trade, Industry and Energy may designate a trader as a comprehensive trade enterprise for the purposes of providing assistance to trading activities by small and medium enterprises by means of systematization with small and medium enterprises exploration of overseas markets and diversification of trading functions.

(2) With respect to standards and procedures of designation under paragraph (1), necessary matters shall be determined by the Presidential Decree.

(3) In case in which criteria for designation under paragraph (2) are not satisfied, the Minister of Trade, Industry and Energy may revoke the designation of a comprehensive trade enterprise designated pursuant to paragraph (1).

CHAPTER ¥¶ SUPPLEMENTARY

PROVISIONS

Article 49 (Hearing)

The Minister of Trade, Industry and Energy shall provide opportunities to give opinions for the other party subject to the measures concerned or a person acting on his behalf in accordance with the Presidential Decree, where he intends to take measures falling under any of the following subparagraphs: *Provided,* That this shall not apply to the cases where it is impossible to provide an opportunity to give opinions because the other party or a person acting on his behalf does not respond without reasonable causes, or the address of the party is not known:

1.Order of corrective measures or imposition of penalties pursuant to the provisions of Article 39 (5);

2.Adjustment orders pursuant to the provisions of Article 43 (1);

3.Revocation of authorization of establishment of each association pursuant to the provisions of Article 47; or

4.Revocation of designation of a comprehensive trade enterprise pursuant to the provisions of Article 48 (3).

Article 50 (Report or Inspection)

(1) Either the Minister of Trade, Industry and Energy or the Trade Committee may order a trader or each association to make necessary reports.

(2) Either the Minister of Trade, Industry and Energy or the Trade Committee may have its public officials inspect books, documents, or other stuffs at offices, places of business, factories, or warehouses of the persons provided in paragraph (1).

(3) Any public official who inspects under the provisions of paragraph (2) shall present his certificate proving his authority to the person involved.

Article 51 (Relationship with Monopoly Regulation and Fair Trade Act)

(1) The Monopoly Regulation and Fair Trade Act shall not apply to the enforcement of adjustment orders made by the Minister of Trade, Industry and Energy pursuant to the provisions of Article 43.

(2) The Minister of Trade, Industry and Energy shall seek in advance consultation with the Fair Trade Committee in case where adjustment orders pursuant to the provisions of Article 43 are to restrict competition in the domestic market between enterprisers under subparagraph 1 of Article 2 of the Monopoly Regulation and Fair Trade Act.

Article 52 (Relationship with National Security Act)

As respects exporting or importing activities of goods under this Act, the National Security Act shall not apply where such activities are considered just within the extent of business conduct.

Article 53 (Delegation of Authorities)

(1) Some of the authorities of the Minister of Trade, Industry and Energy under this Act may be delegated to the heads of the administrative authorities belonging to him, and the Mayor/*Do*

governors in accordance with the Presidential Decree, or mandated to the heads of the administrative bodies concerned, the chief-officer of a customs office, the Governor of the Bank of Korea, the president of the Export-Import Bank of Korea, the president of the Foreign Exchange Bank, or other juristic persons or organizations as determined by the Presidential Decree.

(2) The Minister of Trade, Industry and Energy shall direct or supervise those delegated or mandated persons to discharge duties delegated or mandated pursuant to paragraph (1).

(3) The Minister of Trade, Industry and Energy may order a delegated or mandated person to make necessary reports in relation to the discharge of duties delegated or mandated under paragraph (1).

CHAPTER Ⅺ PENAL PROVISIONS

Article 54 (Penal Provisions)

Anyone who falls under any one of the following subparagraphs shall be punished by imprisonment less than five years, or by a fine of not more than three times the value of exported or imported goods:

1.A person who has violated measures for restricting or prohibiting exports or imports under each subparagraph of Article 5;

2.A person who has obtained export licenses of strategic materials in fraudulent or unlawful ways in contravention of the provision of Article 21 (1), or who has exported strategic materials without export licenses to geographic areas notified by the Minister of Trade, Industry and Energy pursuant to paragraph (2) of the said Article as areas to which strategic materials may not be exported;

3.A person who has disguised export or import prices of goods in contravention of the provisions of Article 40; or

4.A person who has violated adjustment orders as stipulated under Article 43 (1).

Article 55 (Penal Provisions)

Anyone who falls under any of the following subparagraphs shall be punished by imprisonment less than three years, or by a fine not exceeding thirty million won:

1.A person who has conducted trade business or trade agency business without a notice, or a notice of change in accordance with Article 10, or who has made a notice or a notice of change as to trade business or trade agency business in fraudulent or other unlawful ways;

2.A person who has exported or imported goods with approval or approval of change under Article 14 (2) or (3), or with the exemption of approval or approval of change which are obtained in fraudulent or unlawful ways;

3.A person who has not obtained foreign currencies corresponding to import pursuant to the provisions of the main sentence of Article 19 (3) (including the *mutatis mutandis* application of Article 20 (3));

4.A person who has used, without approval pursuant to the provisions of the main sentence of Article 20 (1), raw materials or machinery, or manufactured goods made of such materials or made by machinery for other purposes for which such raw materials or machinery has been imported;

5.A person who has assigned raw materials or machinery, or manufactured goods made of such raw materials or made by the machinery without approval pursuant to the provisions of Article 20 (2);

6.A person who has obtained approval or approval of change pursuant to the provisions of Article 22 in fraudulent or otherwise unlawful ways;

7.A person who has exported or imported goods without the mark of the country of origin pursuant to the provisions of Article 23 (1);

8.A person who has marked the country of origin in fraudulent or misleading ways, or has damaged or modified the mark of the country of origin in contravention of the provisions of Article 23 (3);

9.A person who has exported or imported goods with the country of origin marked in fraudulent, damaged or modified ways in contravention of the provisions of Article 39 (1) 2;

10.A person who has violated orders of corrective measures pursuant to the provisions of Article 39 (5); or

11.A person who has exported goods with designated designs without the certification of designs pursuant to the provisions of Article 44 (5).

Article 56 (Attempted Offences)

Attempts to commit offences under subparagraph 2 of Article 54, subparagraph 7 or 9 of Article 55, shall be punished as the offences in accordance with respective provisions.

Article 57 (Negligent Offences)

Any person who falls under any of the following subparagraphs shall be punished by a fine not exceeding twenty million won:

1.A person who has exported or imported with a gross negligence goods without mark of the country of origin in accordance with Article 23 (1);

2.A person who has marked with a gross negligence the country of origin for the purposes of misleading it, or has damaged or modified the mark of the country of origin in contravention of the provisions of Article 23 (3); or

3.A person who has exported or imported with a gross negligence goods with the country of origin marked in fraudulent, damaged or modified ways in contravention of Article 39 (1) 2.

Article 58 (Joint Penal Provisions)

In case where any representative of a juristic person, an agent, employee or other employed person of a juristic person or an individual, has committed offences under Articles 54 through 57 in respect of functions of the juristic person or the individual, the juristic person or the individual shall be punished by a fine under the provisions of respective articles, as well as the principal offender.

Article 59 (Presumption of Public Officials in Application of Penal Provisions)

In relation to the application of penal provisions under the Criminal Act or other relevant Acts, public officials are construed to include the chairman or commissioners of the Trade Committee, and the officers and staffs of a design certification institution, and directors or officers of the Bank of Korea, the Export-Import Bank of Korea, the Foreign Exchange Bank authorized by the Minister of Trade, Industry and Energy to deal with functions under Article 53, or other juristic persons or associations designated by the Presidential Decree.

Article 60 (Fine for Negligence)

(1) Any person who falls under any of the following subparagraphs shall be punished by a fine for negligence not exceeding twenty million won:

1.A person who has not submitted documents in contravention of the provisions of Article 41 (2);

2.A person who has refused, obstructed, or avoided inquiries into facts under Article 41 (3);

3.A person who has not made reports or has made false reports under Article 50 (1); or

4.A person who has refused, obstructed, or avoided inspection under Article 50 (2).

(2) Any person who falls under any of the following subparagraphs shall be punished by a fine for negligence not exceeding ten million won:

1.A trader or seller who has distributed goods for sale without mark of the country of origin in accordance with Article 23 (1), in case where he imports goods, on which the country of origin should be specified, and trades them after dissembling or repacking or after getting them through simple manufacturing process, or he trades them in items or pieces;

2.A person who has refused, obstructed, or avoided inspection under Article 23 (4); or

3.A person who has used descriptions of export associations, import associations, or export-import associations, or otherwise similar names in contravention of Article 45 (6).

(3) In relation to fine for negligence under paragraphs (1) and (2), the Minister of Trade, Industry and Energy shall impose and collect them in accordance with the Presidential Decree.

(4) Any person who intends to challenge fine for negligence imposed under paragraph (3) may submit complaints to the Minister of Trade, Industry and Energy within thirty days after receipt of the notice on such disposition.

(5) Where a person, subject to fine for negligence under paragraph (3), has submitted complaints pursuant to paragraph (4), the Minister of Trade, Industry and Energy shall give, without delay,

notice to the competent court, and the court shall commence proceedings with regard to fine for negligence under the Non-Contentious Case Litigation Procedure Act.

(6) Fine for negligence shall be collected in the same way as the handling of the national taxes in arrears, unless the fine for negligence is paid and complaints thereon have been submitted within the period of time under paragraph (4).

ADDENDA

Article 1 (Enforcement Date)

This Act shall enter into force on March 1, 1997: *Provided,* That the provisions of Articles 13, 14, 16, 17, and subparagraph 2 of Article 55 shall enter into force on January 1, 1997.

Article 2 (Time Limit of Application as to Notice of Trade Business, etc.)

The provisions of Articles 10 through 12, and subparagraph 1 of Article 55 shall take effect until December 31, 1999.

Article 3 (Examples of Application to Confirmation Whether to Perform Exports and Imports)

The provisions of Article 17 shall apply to imported goods approved first after the entry into force of this Act.

Article 4 (Transitional Measures as to Notice of Trade Business)

After this Act takes effect, a person who has been registered by the former provisions of this Act as conducting trade business shall be deemed to have made a notice of trade business in accordance with Article 10. In this case, "trade business registration certificate" shall be construed to be a "certificate of complete notice of trade business."

Article 5 (Transitional Measures as to Acting Institutions to Perform Market Research, etc. on Exports of Industrial Plants)

The Korean Association for the Development of Mechanical Engineering under the Industrial Development Act shall be authorized to perform functions of the administrative bodies or the associations designated by this Act, until the administrative bodies or the associations are designated to perform activities to promote projects under Article 22 (6).

Article 6 (Transitional Measures as to Penal Provisions)

In relation to acts done before this Act enters into force, the former penal provisions of this Act shall be applied.

Article 7 (Special Cases as to Penal Provisions)

As to those who fall under subparagraph 1 of Article 55, they are punished under subparagraph 1 of Article 55 even after the time limit of its application is over, despite the provisions of Article 2 of Addenda.

For additional analytical, business and investment opportunities information,
please contact Global Investment & Business Center, USA
at (202) 546-2103. Fax: (202) 546-3275. E-mail: rusric@erols.com

Article 8 Omitted.

Article 9 (Relationship with Other Acts and Subordinate Statutes)

After this Act takes effect, references to the Foreign Trade Act or to provisions of this Act in other Acts and subordinate statutes shall be construed to those to relevant provisions of this Act in the case of the existence of such provisions.

TAX SYSTEM: BASIC STRUCTURE
(Selected Abstracts)

**For a complete information on the Korean Tax System, please acquire our
"Korea Tax System Guide"
Global Investment & Business Center, USA
P.O. Box 15343, Washington, DC 20003.
E-mail rusric@rusline.com**

The current Korean tax system is comprised of both national taxes and local taxes. National taxes are collected by the government and can be divided into internal taxes, customs duties and earmarked taxes. Local taxes are collected by the local autonomous bodies and are divided into province taxes and city and county taxes.

The Korean tax system may also be divided between direct and indirect taxes. Indirect taxes are the main form of tax in the present tax system. The primary indirect tax is the value-added tax (VAT). Indirect taxes are supplemented by direct taxes such as the individual and corporate income taxes.

INDIVIDUAL INCOME TAX

TAX LIABILITY

An individual to whom income is attributable is the person to pay income tax under the Individual Income Tax Law (ITL). There are two forms of income tax obligations. The first is the responsibility of each person to report his own income and pay the tax amount due. The second places an obligation on an individual to withhold tax at the source on another person's income and pay the withheld tax amount to the government.

Individual liability

The following individuals are liable to pay income tax on their own individual income pursuant to the ITL:

a resident : an individual having a domicile or residence in Korea for one year or more;
a non-resident : an individual other than a resident who has income from sources within Korea

Liability to withhold tax on others' incomeThe following persons are liable to withhold income tax at the source and pay the amount over to the government pursuant to the ITL:

a resident;

**For additional analytical, business and investment opportunities information,
please contact Global Investment & Business Center, USA
at (202) 546-2103. Fax: (202) 546-3275. E-mail: rusric@erols.com**

a non-resident;
a domestic corporation - a corporation having its head office or principal office in Korea;
a branch or a business office in Korea of a foreign corporation - a foreign corporation means a corporation having its head office or principal office in a foreign country;
other persons as prescribed by the ITL.

TAXABLE PERIOD

Generally, income tax will be assessed for one year from January 1 to December 31. If a resident should die, however, the income tax will be assessed for the period from January 1 to the date of death.

If a resident should move out of the country, relocating the domicile or residence, the income tax shall be imposed for the period from January 1 to the date of departure from the country.

TAXABLE INCOME

A resident's income is divided into four types: global, retirement, capital gains and forestry income. Global income can be further divided into seven separate categories; namely, interest, dividends, real estate rental, business, wage and salary, casual capital gains and other income.

NONTAXABLE INCOME

In general, all types of income should be taxed. There are, however, certain types of income that are not taxable because of their peculiar nature or government policy. These types of income are classified as 'nontaxable income'. They are neither included on an income tax return nor subject to withholding.

EXEMPTION AND REDUCTION OF INCOME TAX

If the amount of global income (A) includes exempt income (B) as prescribed in the law, the income tax equivalent of the amount calculated by applying the tax rate to the tax base times the ratio of the exempt income to the total amount of global income shall be exempt.

Amount of exemption or reduction $=$ Calculated tax amount $\times$ B / A

CALCULATION OF TAX BASE AND GLOBAL INCOME DEDUCTION

The tax base of a resident shall be calculated by subtracting various global income deductions from the global income. The global income deductions consist of personal deduction and special deduction.

The personal deductions include basic exemption (1,000,000 Won a year), spousal exemption (1,000,000 Won a year), dependent exemption (1,000,000 Won per person a year), exemption for a handicapped person (500,000 Won per person a year), exemption for age sixty-five or older (500,000 Won per person a year), exemption for a female head of household (500,000 Won a year), and exemption for a dependent of age under six (500,000 Won per person a year).

If the total amount of personal deductions for the year exceeds the total amount of global income assembled by the resident for the year, the excess amount will be disregarded.

**For additional analytical, business and investment opportunities information,
please contact Global Investment & Business Center, USA
at (202) 546-2103. Fax: (202) 546-3275. E-mail: rusric@erols.com**

The special deductions include:

Insurance premium deductionA resident earning wage and salary income is entitled to claim a deduction for insurance premiums paid. A resident is entitled to claim all the premiums paid to an insurer under the Medical Insurance Law or the Public Officials and Private School Teachers Insurance Law without any limitation on the deduction.
Certain limitations exist, however, for other insurance premiums paid by a resident.

Medical expense deduction

The amount of medical expenses eligible for the deduction shall be the excess amount over 3% of the resident's gross income for the year, but the deduction is not to exceed 1,000,000 Won.

Education expense deduction

A resident earning wage and salary income is entitled to claim a deduction for certain educational expenses. A resident is entitled to deduction for certain educational expenses such as entrance fees, tuition fees and any other regular school payments paid for the taxpayer to attend a school established under the Education Law (excluding graduate schools). Educational expenses paid for anyone other than the resident shall be limited to the entrance fees, tuition fees and any other regular school payments paid for lineal descendants, brothers or sisters of the resident who are students at schools established under the Education Law (excluding graduate schools).

Deductions for housing

If a resident who does not own his house deposits savings for housing or a resident who owns a specified house redeems the housing loan, the resident is entitled to claim a deduction for housing up to 720,000 Won per year.

Special exemption for contribution: Contributions made to governmental organizations or such public corporations as described by the law; up to 5% of the amount of wage and salary income. If the total amount of special deduction exceeds the total amount of wage and salary income, the excess amount will be disregarded.

TAX WITHHOLDING

Taxes are withheld when interest, dividend or wage/salary, etc., is paid to a resident individual or a non-resident individual. To a resident individual or a non-resident individual with a PE in Korea, the withholding taxes paid are regarded as prepaid taxes. In case of a non-resident individual having no PE in Korea, the withholding tax fulfills all tax obligation of the non-resident individual in Korea. Withholding rates are as follows:

Interest
Interest on non business use loans, and interest and discounts on debentures other than small sum debentures - 25%

Interest on long-term debentures specified by the ITL

Periods from issuing date to final reimburse date	Tax rate
5 - 10 years	30%
Over 10 years	25%

Interest on long-term savings specified by the ITL

Periods from initial contract date to expiring date	Tax rate
Over 10 years	30%

All other interest - 15 (20)%

If, however, the real name of the person receiving the income is not identified by the date of payment, the rate will be 40%.

Business income: 3%
Daily-base hired workers' : 10%
Other income: 20%
Class A wage/salary:
basic withholding rates prescribed by the law

CORPORATE INCOME TAX

Tax Liability

There are two important distinctions to be made for corporate tax purposes concerning a corporation in Korea. Is it a domestic or foreign corporation? Is it a profit or nonprofit corporation? Simply defined, a corporation's classification as either a domestic or foreign corporation is dependent on whether it has its head office or main office located in Korea. For a corporation's status as profit or nonprofit, the determining factor is whether the corporation has a basic objective of pursuing profits.

All income attributable to a profit domestic corporation is subject to corporate income tax regardless of the source or recurrence of the income. These corporations are liable to pay tax on liquidation income in addition to the income earned in each taxable year.

Nonprofit domestic corporations must pay corporate income tax on the income earned from profit-making business.

Profit foreign corporations are liable to pay corporate income tax only on income from Korean sources, and nonprofit foreign corporations are liable to pay corporate income tax on Korean source income earned from profit-making businesses.

TAXABLE INCOME

The taxable income of a domestic corporation during a taxable year shall be the gross income attributable or to be attributable to the year minus the deductible expenses attributable or to be attributable to the same year. Taxable income plays a basic role in determining the tax base of a corporation. The terms 'gross income' and 'deductible expenses' are defined in the following chapters.

The computation of gross income and deductible expenses under the Corporate Income Tax Law (CTL) will not always be in accordance with the Generally Accepted Accounting Principles (GAAP) in Korea. Therefore, a reconciliation procedure is required to settle the differences between tax accounting and the GAAP, resulting in the determination of taxable income for each

For additional analytical, business and investment opportunities information,
please contact Global Investment & Business Center, USA
at (202) 546-2103. Fax: (202) 546-3275. E-mail: rusric@erols.com

taxable year. The tax reconciliation is to be performed in such a manner that related items are added to or deducted from the pre-tax net income computed by the GAAP.

TAX BASE

The term 'tax base' refers to the amount or quantity of the taxable object that forms the basis for computing the tax payable. Since the taxable object of the corporate income tax is the income attributable to a corporation, the tax base for the corporate income tax is the amount of income attributable to the corporation.

Computation of tax base

The tax base for corporate income tax is the taxable income minus the deductible items listed below. The deductions must be applied in the order listed and only up to the limit of taxable income earned during the year;

The carry-over of net operating losses incurred in any of the five years prior to the taxable year and not previously deducted in computing the taxable income or tax base since the year such loss was incurred;

Nontaxable income stipulated in the CTL (e.g., income from assets of a trust organized for the public welfare) or the Tax Exemption and Reduction Control Law (TERCL); and

Income deduction under the CTL and TERCL. The term 'income deduction' refers to the tax principle where an amount of money is directly deducted from the taxable income in calculation of the tax base to grant a tax incentive to a corporation performing a certain transaction or earning a certain item of income. The following are examples of the permissible income deductions under the tax laws:

- For a corporation that has performed stipulated transactions, the corporation is entitled to an income deduction for a capital increase.

- A corporation earning income from either the transfer of a patent right, technical services, an overseas business or livestock farming is entitled to claim an income deduction.

Computation structure of the tax base

Taxable income in each taxable year	xxx
Carry-over of net operating losses	(-) xxx
Nontaxable income	(-) xxx
Income deductions	(-) xxx
Tax base	xxx

SUPPLEMENT

U.S. CONTACTS

Non-U.S. Government Contacts

Mr. Joon-Suk Jung
Commercial Counselor
Embassy of the Republic of Korea
2450 Massachusetts Ave., NW
Washington, DC 20008
Tel: 202-939-5600, Fax: 202-387-0302
Website:www.mofat.go.kr

Mr. Wang-Kyu Lee, Manager
Korea International Trade Association (KITA)
460 Park Ave., Room 2200
New York, NY 10022
Tel: 212-421-8804(Ext. 16)
Fax: 212-223-3827
Web site: www.kotis.net

Mr. Pung Park, Director
Korea Trade Center (KOTRA)
1129 20th St., NW. Suite 410
Washington, DC 20036
Tel: 202-857-7919, Fax: 202-857-7923
Web site: www.kotra.or.kr

The American Chamber of Commerce in Korea
Ms. Tami Overby, Executive Director
4501, Trade Tower, 159-1, Samsung-dong
Kangnam-ku, Seoul 135-731, Korea
Tel: 82-2-564-2040
Fax: 82-2-564-2050
Web site: www.amchamkorea.org

U.S. Government Contacts in Washington, D.C.

Market Access and Compliance Office
Desk Officer for Korea/Taiwan
U.S. Department of Commerce
14th and Constitution Avenue, NW
Washington, DC 20230
Tel: 202-482-2523
Fax: 202-482-3316
Web site: www.ita.doc.gov

Trade Information Center
U.S. Department of Commerce
14th and Constitution Avenue, NW
Washington, DC 20230
Tel: 202-482-2523
Fax: 202-482-3316
Web site: www.ita.doc.gov

Barbara Weisel
Deputy Assistant U.S. Trade Representative
for Bilateral Asian Affairs
Office of the United States Trade Representative
Executive Office of the President
600 17th Street, N.W.
Washington, DC 20506
Tel: 202-395-6813, Fax: 202-395-9515
Website: www.ustr.gov

Jonathan Mudge and Jeffrey Beller
Desk Officers for South Korea
U.S. Department of State
2201 C Street, NW
Washington, DC 20520
Tel: 202-647-7717
Fax: 202-647-7388
Website: www.state.gov

John Wingle
International Economist
Office of East Asian Nations
U.S. Department of the Treasury
1440 New York Avenue, NW, Rm 4416
Washington, DC 20220
Tel: 202-622-1960
Fax: 202-622-0349
E-mail:john.wingle@do.treas.gov
Web site: www.treas.gov

AgExport Services Division (AGX)
U.S. Department of Agriculture
Foreign Agricultural Service
Box 1052, 14th & Independence Ave., SW
Washington, DC 20250-1052
Tel: 202-720-9487/6343
Fax: 202-690-0193
Web site: www.fas.usda.gov

The Bureau of Export Administration
U.S. Department of Commerce
Export Counseling Division
Room 2705, 14th Street and Pennsylvania

Ave., N.W.
U.S. Department of Commerce
Washington, DC 20230
Tel: 202-482-4811
Fax: 202-482-3617
Web site: www.bxa.doc.gov

Jill Wilkins
Regional External Affairs - East Asia
The World Bank
1818 H Street, NW
Washington, DC 20433
Tel: 202-473-1792
Fax: 202-522-3405
E-mail:jwilkins@worldbank.org
Web site: www.worldbank.org

Tlaat Rahman
International Business Development Officer
Asian Business Development
Export-Import Bank of the United States
(Eximbank)
811 Vermont Ave., NW, Suite 929
Washington, DC 20571
Tel: 202-565-3911, Fax: 202-565-3628
Web site: www.exim.gov

Overseas Private Investment Corporation
1100 New York Avenue, N.W.
Washington, DC 20527
Tel: 202-336-8400/8799
Fax: 202-408-9859
Web site: www.opic.gov

Manisha Kothari and Paul Marin
Country Managers for Asia
Geoff Jackson
Regional Director-Asia/Pacific
U.S. Trade and Development Agency
1621 North Kent Street, Suite 200
Arlington, VA 22209-2131
Tel: 703-875-4357
Fax: 703-875-4009
Web site: www.tda.gov

Appendix F: Country Contacts

Contacts at the American Embassy in Seoul

John E. Peters, Minister-Counselor for
Commercial Affairs
US&FCS, Unit 15550

American Embassy in Seoul
APO AP 96205-0001
Tel. 82-2-397-4535, Fax. 82-2-739-1628
web site: www.cskorea-doc.gov

Frederic Maerkle, Minister-Counselor for
Economic Affairs
Economic Section, American Embassy in
Seoul
Unit 15550
APO AP 96205-0001
Tel. 82-2-397-4400, Fax. 82-2-722-1429

Edward B. Howard, Counselor for Scientific &
Technological Affairs
Science & Technology Affairs, American
Embassy in Seoul
Unit 15550
APO AP 96205-0001
Tel. 82-2-397-4159, Fax. 82-2-722-1429

Grant Pettrie, Minister-Counselor for
Agricultural Affairs
Agricultural Affairs Office (AGAFF)
American Embassy in Seoul
Unit #15550
APO AP 96205-0001
Tel. 82-2-397-4297, Fax. 82-2-738-7147

Daryl Brehm, Director
Agricultural Trade Office (ATO)
Room 303, Leema Building
146-1, Soosong-dong, Chongro-ku
Seoul, Korea
Tel. 82-2-397-4188, Fax. 82-2-720-7921

Richard C. Hermann, Consul General
American Embassy in Seoul
Unit #15550
APO AP 96206-0001
Tel. 82-2-397-4204, Fax. 82-2-725-6843

W. David Straub, Minister-Counselor for
Political Affairs
Political Section, American Embassy in Seoul
Unit 15550
APO AP 96205-0001
Tel. 82-2-397-4210, Fax. 82-2-733-4791

Stephen Rounds, Minister-Counselor for Public
Affairs
Public Affairs Section, Unit 15550
American Embassy in Seoul

For additional analytical, business and investment opportunities information,
please contact Global Investment & Business Center, USA
at (202) 546-2103. Fax: (202) 546-3275. E-mail: rusric@erols.com

APO AP 96205-0001
Tel. 82-2-397-4436, Fax. 82-2-794-2889

Celmouth Stewart Jr., Customs Attaché
U.S. Customs Service, Unit 15550
American Embassy in Seoul
APO AP 96205-0001
Tel. 82-2-397-4644, Fax. 82-2-736-6850

Col. Claude Crabtree
Joint US Military Affairs Group, Korea
(JUSMAG)
Unit 15339
APO AP 96203-0187
Tel. 82-2-7915-3292, Fax. 82-2-793-3846

Col. Thomas Riley, Defense Attaché

Unit 15550, American Embassy in Seoul
APO AP 96205-0001
Tel. 82-2-397-4254, Fax. 82-2-725-5262

Contact List of Select Korean Government Officials
(compiled by the Political Section of the U.S. Embassy; based on Official Gazettes of the Republic of Korea and Newspaper reports; edited for the purposes of this Country Commercial Guide. Names are listed according to the preferred spelling.)

Note: If calling from outside of Korea, 82 is the country code for Korea and 2 is the city code for Seoul.

GOVERNMENT OFFICIAL & TITLE		PHONE NUMBER
BLUE HOUSE (CHONG WA DAE)		770-0011
1, Sejong-ro, Chongro-ku, Seoul (110-050)		
The President		
Kim Dae-Jung		
First Lady, Lee Hee-Ho		
Presidential Secretariat	Han Gwang-Ok	770-0072
Chief of Staff to the President	Choi Jong-Il	770-0071
Protocol Secretary	Park Jie-Won	770-0577
Senior Secretary for Policy & Planning	Nam Kung-Jin	770-0005
Senior Secretary for Political Affairs	Shin Kwang-Ok	770-0027
Senior Secretary for Civil Affairs and Petition	Lee Ki-Ho	770-0090
Senior Secretary for Economic Affairs	Kim Ha-Joong	770-0037
Senior Secretary for Foreign Policy & National Security	Chung Soon-Tack	770-0209
Senior Secretary for Education & Culture	Lee Tae-Bok	770-0690
Senior Secretary for Welfare & Labor	Park Joon-Yung	770-0081
Senior Press Secretary (Spokesman)		
Presidential Security Service	Ahn Joo-Sup	770-0234
Chief		
Board of Audit & Inspection	Lee Jong-Nam	732-7228
San 25-23, Samchung-dong, Chongro-ku, Seoul (110-230)		
Chairman		
National Intelligence Service	Shin Gunn	3412-3100
Seocho P.O. Box 200, Seoul	Kwon Chin-Ho	3412-3124
	Kim Eun-Sung	3412-3116
Director General		
First Director		
Second Director		
National Security Council	Kim Ha-Joong	770-0037
Secretary General	Yoo Jin-Kyu	770-0631/3

For additional analytical, business and investment opportunities information, please contact Global Investment & Business Center, USA at (202) 546-2103. Fax: (202) 546-3275. E-mail: rusric@erols.com

Deputy Secretary General Advisory Council on Democratic & Peaceful Unification 209, Jangchoong-dong 2-ka, Choong-ku, Seoul (100-392)	Kim Min-Ha	2234-7125
Senior Vice President The Presidential Advisory Council for Science & Technology 48-25, Ineui-dong, Chongro-ku, Seoul (110-410)	Park Ik-Soo	3672-3874
Chairman Civil Service Commission Kolong Bldg., 35-34, Tongeui-dong, Chongro-ku, Seoul (110-040)	Kim Kwang-Woong	725-2700
Chairman The Presidential Commission on Women's Affairs 520-3, Banpo-dong, Seocho-ku, Seoul (137-756)	Han Myeong-Sook	2106-5000
Chairwoman The Presidential Commission on Small-Medium Industries 2, Choongang-dong, Kwacheon, Kyunggi Province (427-010)	Kim Deok-Bae	507-6640

Chairman OFFICE OF THE PRIME MINISTER 77, Sejong-ro, Chongro-ku, Seoul (110-760)	Lee Han-Dong Na Sung-Po	737-0l07 720-2003
Prime Minister	Lee Taek-Seok	737-0095
Minister, Office for Government	Kan Tae-Ryong	737-0098
Policy Coordination	Kim Jai-Chong	720-3831
Chief Secretary	Kim Duck-Bong	720-2006
Senior Secretary for Political Affairs	Huh Shin-Wook	737-0094
Senior Secretary for Petitions & Information	Lee Sam-Sun	720-2001
Senior Press Secretary	Lee Jae-Kwan	503-7701
Secretary for Administrative Affairs		
Secretary for Protocol		
Chairman, Emergency Planning Committee		
Ministry of Planning & Budget 520-3, Banpo-dong, Seocho-ku, Seoul (137-756)	Jeon Yun-Chul	3480-7990

Minister Ministry of Legislation 77, Sejong-ro, Chongro-ku, Seoul (110-760)	Cheong Soo-Boo	720-4471
Minister Government Information Agency 80, Soosong-dong, Chongro-ku, Seoul (110-140)	Oh Hong-Keun	723-0340

Minister

Ministry of Patriots & Veterans Affairs 17-23, Yoido-dong, Youngdeungpo-ku, Seoul (150-010)	Lee Jae-Dal	780-9091
Minister Fair Trade Commission 1, Choongang-dong, Kwacheon, Kyunggi Province (427-760)	Lee Nam-Kee	503-9009
Chairman Financial Supervisory Commission 27, Yoido-dong, Youngdeungpo-ku, Seoul (150-743)	Lee Keun-Yong	3771-5001
Chairman The Ombudsman of Korea 267, Mikeun-dong, Seodaemoon-ku, Seoul (110-020)	Lee Won-Hyoung	360-2600
Chairman National Commission for Youth Protection 77-6, Chongro-ku, Sejong-ro, Seoul (110-760)	Kim Soung-Yee	735-6255
Chairman MINISTRY OF FINANCE AND ECONOMY 1, Choongang-dong, Kwacheon, Kyunggi Province (427-760)	Jin Myum Kim Jin-Pyo Kwon O-Kyu Yoon Dae-Hee	503-9001 503-9006 503-9018 503-9019
Minister Vice Minister Deputy Minister Public Information Officer Planning & Management Office Tax & Customs Office National Tax Administration 108-4, Soosong-dong, Chongro-ku, Seoul (110-140)	Bae Young-Shik Kang Seong-Tae	503-9013 397-1201
Administrator Korea Customs Service 71, Nonhyun-dong, Kangnam-ku, Seoul (135-702)	Yoon Jin-Sik	512-2001
Commissioner Office of Supply 520-3, Banpo-dong, Seocho-ku, Seoul (137-040)	Kim Sung-Ho	(042) 472-2231
Commissioner National Statistical Office 920, Doonsan-dong, Seo-ku, Kwangyeok-si, Daejeon City (302-701)	Yoon Young-Dae	(042)481-2100
Commissioner MINISTRY OF UNIFICATION 77, Sejong-ro, Chongro-ku, Seoul (110-760)	Lim Dong-Won Kim Hyung-Ki Kim Hong-Jae	738-0064 738-0067 3703-2415

**For additional analytical, business and investment opportunities information,
please contact Global Investment & Business Center, USA
at (202) 546-2103. Fax: (202) 546-3275. E-mail: rusric@erols.com**

Minister		
Vice Minister		
Public Information Officer		
MINISTRY OF FOREIGN AFFAIRS AND TRADE	Han Seung-Soo	720-2301
77, Sejong-ro, Chongro-ku, Seoul (110-760)	Choi Sung-Hong	720-2305
	Yim Sung-Joon	732-2306
Minister	Park Yang-Chun	720-2314
Vice Minister	Lee Nam-Soo	720-2687
Deputy Minister for Foreign Affairs		
Deputy Minister for Planning & Management		
Spokesman		
Office of Policy Planning	Choi Young-Jin(acting)	720-3379
Deputy Minister for Policy Planning		
Office of Protocol	Son Sang-Ha	720-2403
Chief of Protocol		
Asian & Pacific Affairs Bureau	Choo Kyu-Ho	720-2316
Director General		
North American Affairs Bureau	Kim Sung-Hwan	720-2320
Director General		
Latin American & Caribbean Affairs Bureau	Chung Jin-Ho	720-3356
Director General		
European Affairs Bureau	Lee Soo-Hyuck	720-2347
Director General		
Middle East & African Affairs Bureau	Lee Joon-Hee	720-4480
Director General		
Treaties Bureau	Kim Eun-Soo	725-1015
Director General		
Cultural Affairs Bureau	(MS.)Kim Kyung-Im	725-7602
Director General		
Overseas Residents & Consular Affairs Bureau	Kim Kyung-Keun	720-2343
Director General		
Institute of Foreign Affairs & National Security (IFANS) 1376-2, Seocho 2-dong, Seocho-ku, Seoul (137-072)	Lee Seung-Kon	571-1011
Chancellor		
MINISTRY OF JUSTICE	Choi Kyung-Won	503-7001
1, Choongang-dong, Kwacheon, Kyunggi Province (427-720)	Kim Kyung-Han	503-7003
Minister		
Vice Minister		
MINISTRY OF NATIONAL DEFENSE	Mr. Kim Dong-Shin	748-6000
1, Yongsan-dong 3-ka, Yongsan-ku, Seoul (140-023)	Mr. Kwon Young-Hyo	748-6100
		748-6703
Minister	BG Hwang Ui-Don	748-6240
Vice Minister	Mr. Kim Kwang-Woo	
Spokesman		
Director, Foreign Policy Division		
ROK-US Combined Forces Command (CFC)	GEN Lee Jong-Ok	7915-6281
Deputy Commander in Chief		
MINISTRY OF GOVERNMENT ADMINISTRATION AND	Lee Keun-Sik	3703-4000

For additional analytical, business and investment opportunities information, please contact Global Investment & Business Center, USA at (202) 546-2103. Fax: (202) 546-3275. E-mail: rusric@erols.com

HOME AFFAIRS 77, Sejong-ro, Chongro-ku, Seoul (110-760)	Jeong Young-Sik Cho Myung-Soo	3703-4010 3703-4110
Minister Vice Minister Public Information Officer		
MINISTRY OF EDUCATION 77, Sejong-ro, Chongro-ku, Seoul (110-760)	Han Wan-Sang Choe-Hee-Seun Lee Sung-Moo	720-3400 739-3265 739-3345
Minister Vice Minister Public Information Officer Planning & Management Office International Cooperation Office	Lee Gi-Ho Kim Jung-Gi	720-3267 720-3044
MINISTRY OF SCIENCE AND TECHNOLOGY 1, Choongang-dong, Kwacheon, Kyunggi Province (427-760)	Kim Young-Hwan Yu Hee-Yol Park Jong-Yong Kwon Oh-Kab	503-7601 503-7662 503-7608 503-7623
Minister Vice Minister Public Information Officer Planning & Management Office Office of Science & Technology Policy Office of Planning & Coordination Director General for Research & Development Director General for Nuclear Energy Director General for Science & Technology Cooperation Director General for Basic Science & Manpower	Lee Hun-Gyu Park Yong-Il Chung Yoon Cho Chung-Won Moon Yoo-Hyun Choi Jae-Ik	503-7740 503-7637 503-6857 503-7644 503-7663 503-7616
MINISTRY OF CULTURE AND TOURISM 82, Sejong-ro 1-ka, Chongro-ku, Seoul (110-050)	Kim Han-Gill Yoon Hwung-Kyu Kwon Kyung-Sang	3704-9000 3704-9010 3704-9030
Minister Vice Minister Public Information Officer Assistant Minister Planning & Management Office	Lee Hong-Suk Oh Ji-Cheol	3704-9020 3704-9200
Cultural Properties Administration 920, Doonsan-dong, Seo-ku, Kwangyeok-si, Daejeon City (302-701)	Rho Tai-Sup	(042) 472-3400
Administrator		
MINISTRY OF AGRICULTURE AND FORESTRY 1, Choongang-dong, Kwacheon, Kyunggi Province (427-760)	Han Kap-Soo Kim Dong-Keun Youn Jang-Bae Kim Jung-Ho	503-7203 503-7205 500-2606 503-7207
Minister Vice Minister Public Information Officer Planning & Management Office Deputy Minister Agriculture Information & Statistics Agriculture Policy Office	Ahn Jong-Wun Kim Dal-Joong So Man-Ho Lee Myung-Soo Chung Seung Kim Jae-Soo Park Hae-Sang	503-7206 503-7250 503-7260 503-7290 504-9400 500-1815 503-7280

International Agriculture Bureau Rural Development Bureau Marketing Policy Bureau Agricultural Production & Horticulture Bureau Livestock Bureau	Rho Kyeong-Sang	500-1885
Rural Development Administration Seodoon-dong, Kwonseon-ku, Suwon City, Kyunggi Province	Suh Kyu-Yong	(031)292-4201/3
Administrator Forestry Administration 207, Chungryangri 2-dong, Dongdaemoon-ku, Seoul (130-012)	Shin Soon-Woo	(042) 472-3211
Administrator		
MINISTRY OF COMMERCE, INDUSTRY AND ENERGY	Chang Che-Shik	500-2301
1, Choongang-dong, Kwacheon, Kyunggi-do (427-760)	Lee Hee-Beom	500-2302
	Shin Jong-Sik	500-2305
Minister	Kim Jae-Hyun	500-2320
Vice Minister	Kim Young-Joon	500-2436
Public Information Officer	Kim Chil-Doo	500-2330
Planning & Management Office	Kim Dong-Won	500-2719
Electric Power Industry Restructuring Bureau	Kim Jong-Kap	500-2417
Trade & Investment Policy Office	Lee Hyun-Jae	500-2430
Energy & Resources Policy Office	Lee Gam-Yeol	500-2474
Industrial Policy Bureau	Jung Tae-Shin	500-2526
Technology Policy Bureau	Chung Moon-Soo	504-0103
Capital Goods Industries Bureau		
Electronics, Textile & Chemical Industries Bureau		
Korean Trade Commission		
Small-Medium Business Administration 2, Choongang-dong, Kwacheon, Kyunggi Province (427-760)	Choi Dong-Kyun	503-7900
Administrator Korea Industrial Property Office 4-dong, Government Complex, 920, Doonsan-dong, Seo-ku, Daejeon City (302-701)	Leem Lae-Guen	(042) 481-5001
Administrator		
MINISTRY OF INFORMATION AND COMMUNICATION	Yang Seung-Taik	750-2001
100, Sejong-ro, Chongro-ku, Seoul (110-777)	Kim Dong-Sun	750-2020
	Kim In-Sik	750-2800
Minister	Rho Hee-Do	750-2100
Vice Minister	Yoo Young-Hwan	750-1400
Public Information Officer	Sohn Hong	750-2300
Planning & Management Office	Byun Jae-Ill	750-1200
International Cooperation Office	Suk Ho-Ick	750-1300
Information & Communication Policy Bureau	No Jun-Hyung	750-2400
Informatization Planning Office		
Information & Communication Promotion Bureau		
Radio & Broadcasting Bureau		

MINISTRY OF HEALTH AND WELFARE 1, Choongang-dong, Kwacheon, Kyunggi Province (427-760)	Kim Won-Gil Lee Kyeong-Ho Ahn Hyo-Hwan Kang Yoon-Koo	503-7500 503-7502 503-7524 503-7519
Minister Vice Minister Public Information Officer Planning & Management Office		
Korean Food & Drug Administration 5, Nokbon-dong, Eunpyung-ku, Seoul (122-020)	Yang Kyu-Hwan	382-0184
Commissioner		
MINISTRY OF ENVIRONMENT 1, Choongang-dong, Kwacheon, Kyunggi Province (427-760)	Kim Myung-Ja Chung Dong-Soo Shin Hyun-Kook Kwak Kyul-Ho	504-9211 504-9217 504-9220 504-9230
Minister Vice Minister Public Information Officer Planning & Management Office International Cooperation Bureau Environmental Policy Bureau Nature Conservation Bureau Air Quality Management Bureau Water Quality Management Bureau Water Supply & Sewage Treatment Bureau Waste Management & Recycling Bureau	Kim Chong-Chun Lee Kyoo-Yong Chun Byung-Seong Ko Yun-Hwa Yoon Sung-Kyu Nam Kung-Eun Chung Doa-Young	504-9238 504-9236 504-9281 504-9246 504-9251 507-2451 504-9258
MINISTRY OF LABOR 1, Choongang-dong, Kwacheon, Kyunggi Province (427-760)	Kim Ho-Jin Kim Song-Ja Kong Deok-Soo Kim Won-Bae	503-9700 503-9702 503-9713 503-9704
Minister Vice Minister Public Information Officer Planning & Management Office		
MINISTRY OF CONSTRUCTION AND TRANSPORTATION 1, Choongang-dong, Kwacheon, Kyunggi Province (427-760)	Oh Jang-Seop Cho Woo-Hyun Choo Byung-Jik Han Bae-Young Choo Byung-Jik	504-9001 504-9005 504-9008 504-9030 504-9010
Minister Vice Minister Assistant Minister Public Information Officer Planning & Management Office Transport Policy Office National Development Policy Bureau Land Bureau Housing & Urban Affairs Bureau Surface Transportation Bureau Construction & Economy Bureau Technology & Safety Bureau	Kim Se-Chan Chang Dong-Kyu Kang Kyo-Sik Choi Jae-Duk Lee Chan-Jae Lee Chon-Hee Kim Chang-Se Kim Il-Joong Choi Young-Chul Jae Kwang-Shik	504-9020 504-9110 504-9120 504-9130 504-9140 504-9050 504-9021 504-9070 504-9040 504-9180

Public Roads Bureau
Water Resources Bureau
Civil Aviation Bureau

MINISTRY OF MARITIME AFFAIRS AND FISHERIES	Chung Woo-Taik	3148-6114
826-14, Yeoksam-dong, Kangnam-ku, Seoul (135-080)	Hong Seoung-Yong	3148-6200

Minister
Vice Minister

National Maritime Policy Agency	Lee Dyu-Sik	(032) 884-5506
105, Booksung-dong, Choong-ku, Incheon (400-201)		

Commissioner

MAYORS AND GOVERNORS	Koh Kun	735-6060
	Ahn Sang-Young	(051) 851-8001
Mayors	Moon Hi-Gab	(053)423-1061
Seoul	Choi Ki-Sun	(032)425-0010
Pusan	Ko Jae-Yu	(062)224-8001
Taegu	Hong Sun-Kee	(042)471-9247
Incheon	Shim Wan-Ku	(052) 229-2001
Kwangju		
Taejon		
Ulsan	Lim Chang-Yuel	(031)242-4800
	Kim Jin-Sun	(033)254-2011
Governors	Lee Won-Jong	(043)220-2001
Kyunggi	Shim Dae-Pyung	(042)251-2001
Kangwon	You Jong-Keun	(063)280-2001
North Choongchung	Huh Kyung-Man	(062)222-0690
South Choongchung	Lee Eui-Keun	(053)943-0001
North Cholla	Kim Hyuk-Kyu	(055)283-1121
South Cholla	Woo Keun-Min	(064)746-2312
North Kyungsang		
South Kyungsang		
Cheju		

LARGEST LAW FIRMS

Aram International Law Offices, 6th Floor, Daejeong Building, 51-7 Banpo-Dong, Seocho-Ku, Seoul, 137-040, Korea, Tel:(82)2-591-8100, Fax:(82)2-596-6081, Contact: Kyung-Han Sohn

Bae, Kim & Lee, Shin-A Building, 39-1 Seosomun-Dong, Chung-Ku, Seoul, 100-752, Korea, Tel:(82)2-317 4114, Fax:(82)2-757 2267, Contact: Won Il Kang

CJ International Law Offices, 9th Floor, Daejung Building, 51-7, Banpo 4-Dong, Seocho-Ku, Seoul, Korea, Tel:(82)2-3476-5599, Fax:(82)2-3476-5995, Contact: Chan Jin Kim

Central International Law Firm, 5th Floor, Korea Reinsurance Building, 80 Soosong-dong, Chongro-ku Kwangwhamoon, P.O. Box 356, Seoul, Korea, Tel:(82)2-735-5621, Fax:(82)2-733-5206, Contact: Dae Sung Kim

Choi & Kim, 4th Floor, Dongwon Building, 128-27, Dangju-Dong, Chongro-ku, Seoul, Korea, Tel:(82)2-734-6370, Fax:(82)2-735-6866, Contact: Jong Hyeon Choi

DW Partners, 51-11, Banpo 4-Dong, Seocho-Ku, Seoul, 137-044, Korea, Tel:(82)2-595-1255, Fax:(82)2-595-0020, Contact: Moon-Hyun Cho

Deryook International Law Firm, 3rd Floor, Kumhwa Building, 1572-6 Seochodong, Seocho-Ku, Seoul, 137-070, Korea, Tel:(82)2-597-8282, Fax:(82)2-523-8283, Contact: Seung-Heui Hahm

First Law Offices of Korea, Dongwon Building, 275 yangjae-Dong Seocho, P.O. Box 437 Seocho-Ku, Seoul, Korea, Tel:(82)2-589-0001, Fax:(82)2-589-0002, Contact: Young-Mo Kwon

Ha & Ha, 4F Younghwa Building, 742-20, Banpo-Dong, Seocho-Ku, Seoul, 137-040, Korea, Tel:(82)2-548-1609, Fax:(82)2-548-9555, Contact: Sang Ku Ha

Hwang, Mok, Park & Jin, 6th Floor, Peeres Building, 222, 3-ka, Chungjung-ro, Seodaemun-ku, Seoul, 120-013, Korea, Tel: (82) 2-365-6251, Fax: (82) 2-365-3370, Contact: Ju Myung Hwang

> o   Hwang, Mok, Park & Jin, formerly Kim & Hwang, founded in 1958, is the oldest and first international law firm and is also one of the largest firms in Korea. The firm is in general practice, including foreign investments, financing, maritime, insurance, admiralty, taxation, litigation, and patent and trademark. Hwang, Mok, Park & Jin is the member for Korea of Lex Mundi, a global association of 152 independent law firms.

Kim & Chang, Seyang Building, 233, Naeja-Dong, Chongro-ku, Seoul, Korea, Tel:(82)2-7374455, Fax:(82)2-737-9091/3, Contact: Young Moo Kim

Kim & Kim, Suite 1611, Kyobo Building, 1-1, Chongro-1-Ka, Chongro-Ku, Seoul, Korea, Tel:(82)2-735-2980, Fax:(82)2-732-3370, Contact: Soung Soo Kim

Kim, Chang & Lee, 9th Floor, Daeil Building, 43, Insa-dong, Chongro-ku, Seoul, Korea, Tel:(82)2-397-9800, Fax:(82)2-725-8727, Contact: Kyung-Joon Choi

Kim, Shin & Yu, 12th Floor, Leema Building, 146-1, Susong-Dong, Chongro-Ku, C.P.O. Box 3238, Seoul, Korea, Tel:(82)2-735-5822, Fax:(82)2-739-6606, Contact: Jin Ouk Kim

Lee & Ko, 17th & 18th Flrs, Marine Ctr Main Bldg, 118, 2 Ka Namdaemun-Ro, Chung-Ku, C.P.O Box 8735, Seoul, Korea, Tel:(82)2-753-2151, Fax:(82)2-753-0373/5, Contact: Tae Hee Lee

Min, Sohn & Kim, 723-2 Yoksam 2 Dong, Kangnam-Ku, Seoul, Korea, Tel:(82)2-564-3320, Fax:(82)2-564-3327, Contact: Byoung Kook Min

Myung-Shin & Partners, 12th Floor, Jindo Building, 37, Dowha-Dong, Mapo-Gu, Seoul, Korea, Tel:(82)2-714-9922, Fax:(82)2-714-9933, Contact: Myung-Shin Kim

Park & Partners, 6th and 7th Floors, Daegak Building, 1319-5 Seocho-Dong Seocho-Ku, Seoul, Korea, Tel:(82)2-580-9114, Fax:(82)2 598-4888, Contact: Jeong Woo Surh

Pusan International Law Offices, 4th & 5th Floors, Yushin Building, 7, 5-KA, Chungang-Dong, Chung-Ku, Pusan, Korea, Tel:(82)51 463-7801-3, Fax:(82)51 463-7809, Contact: Won Chul Lee

Samjong International, Korea Coal Center, 10th Floor, 80-6, Susong-Dong, Chongro-Ku, Seoul, 110-727, Korea, Tel:(82)2-725-4774, Fax:(82)2-725-4994, Contact: Hak-Se Kim

Seoul Maritime Law Office, 303, Harim Building 1699-14, Seocho 4-dong, Seocho-gu, Seoul, Korea, Tel:(82)2-595-7121, Fax:(82)2-595-9626, Contact: Hyun Kim

Shin & Kim, CPO Box 8261, Samdo Building, 4th Floor, 1-170 Soonhwa-dong, Chung-ku, Seoul, 100-130, Korea, Tel:(82)2-3164114, Fax:(82)7560900/6226, Contact: Young Moo Shin

Shin & Shin, SL. Kang Nam, Ste 1913, Champs Elysee Ctr Bldg, P.O. Box 987, #889-5 Daechi-dong, Kangnam-ku, Seoul, Korea, Tel:(82)2-565-6300, Fax:(82)2-565-7400, Contact: Chan Ju Park

Woo, Yun, Kang, Jeong & Han, Textile Center, 12th Floor, 944-31 Daechi-dong, Kangnam-ku, Seoul, 135-713, Korea, Tel:(82)2-528-5200, Fax:(82)2-528-5228, Contact: Chang Rok Woo

Yeon-Ho Kim International Law Office, Suite 3701, Korea World Trade Tower, 159-1 Samsung-Dong, Kangnam-Ku, Seoul, 135-729, Korea, Tel:(82)2-551-1256, Fax:(82)2-5515570, Contact: Yeon-Ho Kim

Yoon & Partners, Ste 831 Korea Chamber Of Comm. & Industry Bldg, C.P.O. Box 4160, 45 Namdaemoonre-4-ka, Chung-ku, Seoul, 100-743, Korea, Tel:(82)2-773-0161, Fax:(82)2-773-0161, Contact: Hoil Yoon

You Me Patent & Law Firm, Teheran Building, 825-33, Yoksam-Dong, Kangnam-Ku, Seoul, Korea, Tel:(82)2-553 5990, Fax:(82)2 553 5254, Contact: Wonho Kim

INFORMATION AND COMMUNICATIONS INDUSTRY REFORMS AND REGULATIONS

GOVERNMENT DECREES AND REGULATIONS

ACTS ON TELECOMMUNICATIONS AND BROADCASTING

Legislation	Major Provisions	Enactments & Revisions
Telecommunications Basic Act	¤·Basic guiding principles on telecommunications -Ministerial authority regarding promotion of telecommunications technology and technical standards for telecommnications facilities -Management of telecommunications networks -Organization and operation of the KCC	E : August 10, 1991 R : December 13, 1997
Telecommunications Business Act	¤·Licensing criteria and reporting procedures for telecommunications service providers ¤·Telecommunications service providers competition safeguards ¤·Rights of telecommunications service users ¤·Construction and maintenance of telecommunications facilities	E : August 10, 1991 R : August 28, 1997
Telecommunications Costruction Business Act	¤·Basic guiding principles for telecommunications construction business -Construction business classification, licensing criteria and scope -Establishment of the Association of Telecommunications Contractors	E : April 6, 1976 R : August 28, 1997
Act on Promotion of Accssibility of Computer Networks	¤·Basic guiding principles on expansion of computer networks and their utilization -Basic plan for computer networks expansion and use -Establishment and operation of the Computer Networks Coordination Committee, the National Computerization Agency, and the Korean Information Cultural Center -Promotion of the KII-G	E : May 12, 1986 R : December 30, 1996
Kora Information Society Development Institue Act	¤·Esatblishment and operation of the Institute -Objectives -Research funding	E : November 28, 1987 R : August 30, 1997
Radio Act	¤·Efficient management of radio frequency spectrum ¤·Licensing, operation, inspection, maintenance of radio stations ¤·Organization and operation of the Korea Radio Wave Regulatory Association ¤·Establishment of a basic plan for the promotion of radio	E : December 30, 1961 R : December 17, 1997

For additional analytical, business and investment opportunities information, please contact Global Investment & Business Center, USA at (202) 546-2103. Fax: (202) 546-3275. E-mail: rusric@erols.com

	communications ¤·Billing and collecting radio using fee	
Cable TV Broadcasting Management Act	¤·Licensing of CATV operators ¤·Technology standards of CATV facilities	E : December 31, 1986 R : December 13, 1997
Computer Program Protection Act	¤·Intellectual property rights(IPR) ¤·Registration of program ¤·Operation of the Program Evaluation and Coordination Committee ¤·Stipulation the scope, content, limitations and effective period of IPR protection	E : December 31, 1986 R : December 6, 1995
Software Development Promotion Act	¤·Basic guiding principles on software program development and promotion ¤·Information management ¤·Legal Framework and funding ¤·Operation of the Software Promotion Committee	E : December 6, 1995 August 28, 1997
Basic Act on Informatization promotion	¤·Basic guiding principles on building the KII and creating an information society ¤·Basic and Action plan for Informatization Promotion ¤·Establishment and operation of the Informatization Promotion Committee ¤·Operation of the Informatization Promotion Fund	E : August 4, 1995
Communications Privacy Act	¤·Regulatory matters related to communications privacy ¤·Prohibiting unauthorized access to written or voice communications and listing exceptions	E : December 27, 1993 R : December 13, 1997

For additional analytical, business and investment opportunities information,
please contact Global Investment & Business Center, USA
at (202) 546-2103. Fax: (202) 546-3275. E-mail: rusric@erols.com